NATIONALISM AND COMMUNAL POLITICS IN INDIA, 1885–1930

Nationalism and Communal Politics in India, 1885–1930

MUSHIRUL HASAN

MANOHAR
2026

First published 1991
Reprinted 2021, 2022, 2023, 2025, 2026

ISBN 978-93-88540-93-3

Published by
Ajay Kumar Jain *for*
Manohar Publishers & Distributors
4753/23 Ansari Road, Daryaganj
New Delhi 110 002

Printed at
Replika Press Pvt. Ltd.

For
Francis Robinson
and
Khalid Shamsul Hasan

Contents

List of Tables

Preface

Nationalism and Communal Politics in India was published in 1979. It was based on my Ph.D. thesis submitted at the University of Cambridge. The work was done under the supervision of Anil Seal, though I also had the opportunity of interacting with and benefiting from discussions with a number of historians then based in Cambridge. The late Eric Stokes was a source of much intellectual inspiration. I could also count on the support and friendly advice of Francis Robinson, Chris Bayly and Tom Tomlinson. Over the years they have continued to take an interest in my researches.

My book dealt with the years 1916 to 1928 and covered several important themes which were then largely unexplored. However, since the publication of my book quite a few scholarly works have offered new insights. This has necessitated a thorough revision of *Nationalism and Communal Politics in India*. I have undertaken the task, though I have discovered the hazards of rewriting one's own work after more than a decade.

The introduction, along with chapters two to six, bears little resemblance with what appeared in *Nationalism and Communal Politics in India*. For the first time I have made extensive use of Theodore Beck Papers. This rich collection, which I am editing for publication, illumines several vital facets of the Aligarh movement and sheds new light on the role of Beck and Syed Ahmad Khan, the grand old man of Aligarh.

I have modified chapter seven in the light of recent researches, though the thrust and basic structure of the argument has not been substantially altered. The following two chapters have been completely re-written, with a shift in emphasis as well as interpretation. In the discussion on the Nehru Report, I have offered a reappraisal of M.A. Jinnah's role and argued that, in the light of recent evidence, 1928 can no longer be treated as the 'Parting of Ways'. Quite clearly, Jinnah was then and for many years later still part of the nationalist mainstream. This aspect has also been discussed at length in my *A Nationalist Conscience: M.A. Ansari, the Congress and the Raj* (Manohar: Delhi, 1987).

There are several gaps in this study, though I like to imagine that at least some have been covered by me elsewhere. I have made a conscious attempt not to draw from my earlier writings. Yet, it has not always been possible to do so, for the overall theme of nationalism and communal consciousness figures in much of what I have written.

Over the years, I have received assistance, both financial and academic, from a large number of people and institutions. I am grateful to all of them. My colleagues in the Department of History, Jamia Millia Islamia, have taken a continuing interest in my work over a long period. The staff of Dr Zakir Husain Library at the university has been most helpful. I want to thank, in particular, the Librarian, Mr Shahabuddin Ansari, Mrs Nigar Nomani and Mr Nazar Burney.

A number of scholars have taken the trouble of reading and commenting on my writings. I am grateful to, among others, Ravinder Kumar, S. Gopal, Francis Robinson, Sudhir Chandra, Asim Roy, Gail Minault, Peter Robb, Rajat Ray, Asghar Ali Engineer, Anwar Jamal Kidwai, Simon Commander and Sarah Ansari. Swati Mitra read the final draft of this book and offered useful suggestions.

My principal debt is to Ravinder Kumar who has extended considerable scholarly support. He has sustained my interest in the subject and has offered invaluable advice and comments. My association with the Nehru Memorial Museum and Library, of which he is Director, proved to be fruitful and intellectually rewarding.

Shaaz and Shehzad have been wonderful. They have offered the sort of affection the value of which can hardly be expressed in words.

A final word for Zoya. She has shown much interest in this work and, as always, provided intellectual and emotional support.

I dedicate this book to the memory of my mother who is, alas, no more.

Introduction

In August 1947 a nation-state came into being amid brutal and bloody violence. Its architect, Mohammad Ali Jinnah, had joined the All-India Muslim League in 1913 on the condition that it did not imply any disloyalty to the idea and cause of a united India. Among his lieutenants were those who, not long ago, considered the Pakistan scheme 'chimerical' and 'impracticable'.

So many of those who lived through the trauma of independence and partition were unable to comprehend how a nation, built around certain common symbols and shared ideals, was so easily fragmented. So many more could scarcely understand why their dream of a united and secular India was destroyed by religious fanaticism. Urdu poets like Faiz Ahmad Faiz and Josh Malihabadi captured the mood.[1] So did Saadat Hasan Manto in *Thanda Gosht* (Cold, Like Ice), a short story which appeared soon after the gruesome riots that accompanied the emergence of free India and Pakistan. Elsewhere, he expressed the dilemma of his generation vividly. After his journey to Pakistan in January 1949, he observed:

> What my mind could not resolve was the question: what country did we belong to now, India or Pakistan? And whose blood was it that was being mercilessly shed every day? And the bones of the dead, stripped of the flesh of religion, were they being burnt or buried? . . . When I sat down to write, I found my thoughts scattered. Though I tried hard, I could not separate India from Pakistan and Pakistan from India. I

[1] Victor Kiernan, trans., *Poems by Faiz* (London, 1971). Reactions and impressions of some leading writers and poets are examined by a set of scholars in Amit Kumar Gupta (ed.), *Myth and Reality: The Struggle for Freedom in India 1945–47* (Delhi, 1987), especially the contributions of Alok Rai and S. S. Hans. For comments of *Savera*, an organ of the progressive writers, see Muhammad Umar Memon, 'Partition Literature: A Study of Intizar Husain', *Modern Asian Studies* (*MAS*), 1980, vol. 14, 3, pp. 383–86.

would repeatedly ask myself: to whom will now belong what had been written in undivided India? Will that be partitioned too?[2]

Reflecting on the events at the time of independence and partition, social scientists often reiterate the view that the colossal human tragedy in 1947 was the result of British machinations, the culmination of a separatist process initiated by a colonial government to foster its imperial interests.[3] But not all agree with this indictment. Some adhere to the view that Pakistan came into being because Muslims constituted a separate nation and their animus with Hindus started long before the British surfaced on the scene.[4] Hindu-Muslim antagonism, states a proponent of this view, 'was embedded in the historical logic of India. Britain only witnessed it; she did not create or exaggerate it'.[5] The evolution of 'Muslim nationalism', so runs the argument, was linked with an independent demand of a 'nationality' apprehensive of its own political future.[6]

This study will not support either of these polar views. Even if one were to argue that some objective similarities unified Muslims,

[2] Quoted in Khalid Hasan, 'Saadat Hasan Manto: Not of Blessed Memory', *Annual of Urdu Studies*, 1984 (4), pp. 89–90, and by the same author in *Scorecard* (Lahore, 1984), pp. 34–36.

[3] See, for example, Bipan Chandra's view that the government played 'an important role in the promotion, spread and the ultimate partial success of communalism in modern India'. *Communalism in Modern India* (Delhi, 1984), p. 242. For earlier nationalist views on the divide and rule policy, Jawaharlal Nehru, *An Autobiography* (London, 1936), p. 136; Rajendra Prasad, *India Divided* (Bombay, 1946), p. 83.

[4] The best formulation of this argument is in Ishtiaq Husain Qureshi, *The Muslim Community of the Indo-Pakistan Subcontinent, 610–1947* (The Hague, 1962), and K.K. Aziz, *The Making of Pakistan: A Study in Nationalism* (London, 1967), pp. 94–95. Their viewpoint is sometimes echoed, though in slightly different terms, in the writings of some social scientists in India. For example, Satish Saberwal has explained the rise of communalism in relation 'to the long-standing separativeness of religious networks, the acute social distancing expressing a high level of social antagonism between Hindus and Muslims. . . .' *India: The Roots of Crisis* (Delhi, 1986), p. 75.

[5] K.K. Aziz, *Britain and Muslim India: A Study of British Public Opinion vis-a-vis the Development of Muslim Nationalism in India, 1857–1947* (London, 1963), pp. 206–07.

[6] Hafeez Malik, *Sir Sayyid Ahmad Khan and Muslim Modernization in India and Pakistan* (New York, 1980), p. 252.

it would still be inaccurate to treat them as a cohesive group acting in unison and arrayed against other segments of society. The powerful bond of Islam is a fact to be reckoned with; yet, it did not prevent Muslims from pursuing separate and conflicting goals and working out their relationship outside the realm of religion and community. Religious passions were sometimes roused to a feverish pitch and appeals for restoring the unity and solidarity of the followers of Islam went out from the mosques. But such was the divide amongst them that it could not be bridged by the common symbols of Islam. This was evident time and again, when conflicting claims were advanced by men of religion, politics and education to carve out their independent spheres of influence in the bureaucratic and administrative structures created by the raj.

British historians and civil servants turned a blind eye to the wide ranging differences that set Muslim groups apart. They advanced the view, which suited imperial interests and conformed to colonial perceptions of Indian society, that the seventy million Muslims in India were a 'nation', their interests were different from and conflicted with the rest of the population,[7] and that 'the solidarity of Islam is a hard fact against which it is futile to run one's head'.[8] The lieutenant-governor of Bengal, who lived in a province where most Muslims lived, put forward the official view that

> the ethnic pageant which passes across one's vision as one travels over India is made up of many tableaux. There is one such tableau which at once arrests attention because of the many points of contrast which it provides with the rest of the procession. . . . It is the tableau in which we see represented a religion, a civilization and culture, and an outlook differing profoundly in all material respects from those of Hinduism . . . that of Islam.[9]

Not long afterwards, Jinnah and his followers echoed the same sentiments: the two-nation theory, which they put forward to

[7] T.W. Holderness, *Peoples and Problems of India* (London, 1911), p. 127.

[8] Lawrence, second Marquess of Zetland, *Essayez* (London, 1956), p. 119.

[9] Earl of Ronaldshay, *India: A Birds's-Eye View* (London, 1924), p. 214.

sustain the claim of a separate nation, derived ideological sustenance from the notion of a unified Muslim community with common concerns and shared experiences.

There is more to it than that. The ideologues of the Pakistan movement also harped on the familiar theme of perpetual Hindu-Muslim conflicts, the strength of divisive forces and the contradictions between the 'Islamic' and 'Hindu' traditions.[10] Their views, based on the writings of Henry Elliot and other colonial writers who had reasons to project a distorted image of medieval Indian society, are inconsistent with both the structures and patterns of relationships during that period. Admittedly, a fragmented form of religious consciousness existed but its essential component was hardly ever derived from the notion of a unified 'community' which formed the basis of modern day 'communalism'.[11] In general, integrative and syncretic forces were at work both at the elite and popular levels, though their progress was impeded by stray, localized and sporadic incidence of conflicts over religious symbols.[12] The dominant picture of the eighteenth

[10] According to the late Aziz Ahmad, the history of medieval and modern India 'is to a very considerable extent a history of Hindu-Muslim religio-cultural tensions... The divisive forces have proved much more dynamic than the cohesive ones'. *Islamic Culture in the Indian Environment* (Oxford, 1964), p. 74. In his subsequent writings, however, Aziz Ahmad recognized the importance of popular and syncretistic beliefs and practices. For example, *An Intellectual History of Islam* (Edinburgh, 1969), pp. 47–48.

[11] There is no standard definition of communalism. Throughout this book I have used communalism as an ideology and a movement that employs narrow religious loyalty as a basis of collective action, and, in the process, accentuates artificially contrived distinctions and heightens community-oriented consciousness. One is inclined to go along with W.C. Smith who defined communalism as an ideology 'that has emphasized as the social, political, and economic unit the group of adherents of each religion, and has emphasized the distinction, even the antagonism, between such groups; the words 'adherent' and 'religion' being taken in the most nominal sense'. *Modern Islam in India* (London, 1946), p. 157.

[12] Instances of religious conflicts are cited in C.A. Bayly, 'The Pre-History of 'Communalism'? Religious Conflict in India, 1700–1860', *MAS*, 1985, vol. 19, 2, pp. 177–203. Bayly's conclusions are tentative and based on insufficient data. Also, the view that 'by the dawn of the twentieth century, India remained a pluralistic society, fundamentally divided along religious lines'. Stanley A. Wolpert, *Morley and India 1906–1910* (Berkeley, 1967), p. 185.

century is not of the Hindus and the Muslims forming exclusive and antagonistic groups but of their co-operating in cultural life and social affairs.[13] To appreciate the significance of such trends in medieval Indian society, historians anxious to uncover the 'pre-history' of communalism may find it profitable to consider the insights provided by R.P. Tripathi, Tara Chand , K.M. Ashraf, Mohammad Habib, his brother, Mohammad Mujeeb, and son, Irfan Habib.

An effective refutation of the two-nation theory came from writers and publicists in the 1940s. Wedded to the concept of a composite Indian nationality, which was the quintessential feature of the nationalist movement, they emphasized the ongoing process of assimilation and integration throughout Indian history.[14] Some two decades later, this debate was enriched with the aid of newly-developed analytical categories, the introduction of certain unexplored themes and the shift in the focus of analysis from the national to the provincial and district arenas. Social scientists have, in this way, suggested new ways of looking at two of the most important themes in modern India—nationalism and communalism.

In his book *Language, Religion and Politics in North India*, Paul R. Brass has argued that the ideology of Muslim separateness did not flow out of the objective differences between Hindus and Muslims but out of the uses which were made of those differences through a conscious process of symbol selection. Nor was it the consequence of the objective circumstances of Muslims in the United Provinces (UP), who were better placed than Hindus in urbanization, literacy, English education, social communications and government employment.[15] Francis Robinson arrived at similar conclusions, pointing out that it was the threat of becoming backward, rather than backwardness itself, which encouraged UP Muslims to organize themselves separately. Their influence

[13] Satish Chandra, *Parties and Politics at the Mughal Court 1707–1740* (Delhi, 1972 edn.), pp. 261–62.

[14] Asoka Mehta and Achyut Patwardhan, *The Communal Triangle in India* (Allahabad, 1942).

[15] Paul R. Brass, *Language, Religion and Politics in North India* (London, 1974), p. 178 and ff.

in the province helped them to do so with much effect.[16]

More recently, Robinson has extricated himself from the historical traditions of the 'Cambridge School' in trying to establish a 'fundamental' connection between Islam and political separatism. In a lively debate with Brass, he has noted, though without conveying much conviction, the importance of Islamic traditions in the development of Muslim separatism. Siding with the primordialists as against the instrumentalists, Robinson concludes that Islamic ideas had a moulding and, on occasions, a motivating role to play amongst the elites of UP.[17] Acceptance of this bald generalization must await a detailed examination of Islamic ideas and movements. In the meantime, one must delineate the contours and content of Muslim separatism before attributing its growth to those ideas and movements which were supposedly rooted in Islam.

Brass and Robinson have traced the history of Muslim separatism in UP; others have turned to regions outside the Indo-Gangetic belt and have traversed the familiar terrain of elite politics both within and outside the formal imperial structures.[18] In recent years, however, social scientists, drawing heavily on the works of

[16] Francis Robinson, *Separatism Among Indian Muslims: The Politics of the United Provinces Muslims, 1880–1923* (Cambridge, 1975), chapter 1.

[17] Francis Robinson, 'Nation Formation: The Brass Thesis and Muslim Separatism', and Reply by Brass, *Journal of Commonwealth and Comparative Politics*, November 1977, 15, 3, pp. 215–34. Also, Francis Robinson, 'Islam and Muslim Society in South Asia', *Contributions to Indian Sociology*, July-Dec., 1983, vol. 17, 2, pp. 185–203.

[18] Stephen F. Dale, *The Mapillas of Malabar, 1498–1922: Islamic Society on the South Asian Frontier* (Oxford, 1980); K.N. Panikkar, *Against Lord and State: Religion and Peasant Uprisings in Malabar 1836–1921* (Delhi, 1989); Kenneth Mcpherson, *The Muslim Microcosm: Calcutta, 1918–1935* (Heidelberg, 1974); Rafiuddin Ahmad, *Bengal Muslims, 1871–1906: A Quest for Identity* (Delhi, 1981); Asim Roy, *The Islamic Syncretistic Tradition in Bengal* (Princeton, New Jersey, 1983); Shila Sen, *Muslim Politics in Bengal, 1937–1947* (Delhi, 1976); David Page, *Prelude to Partition: The Indian Muslims and the Imperial System of Control 1920–1932* (Delhi, 1982); Ian Talbot, *Punjab and the Raj 1849–1947* (Delhi, 1988); David Gilmartin, *Empire and Islam: Punjab and the Making of Pakistan* (London, 1988); Farzana Shaikh, *Community and Consensus in Islam: Muslim Representation in Colonial India 1860–1947* (Cambridge, 1989).

Max Weber, Louis Dumont and Clifford Geertz, have shed new light on the structure of the Muslim community, its social perceptions and cultural moorings, moulded by or independently of the colonial impact, and the extent to which these can be regarded as crucial variables in the process of identity formation and the growth of communitarian consciousness. As a result, a number of significant works have appeared on caste and social stratification among Muslims;[19] the bases of authority and codes of behaviour in South Asian Islam;[20] the patterns and strands of nineteenth century movements of reform and revivalism;[21] and the role of various groups, especially the *ulama*, in interpreting the *shariat* and preserving the Islamic way of life.[22] Thus Barbara Metcalf takes a close look at the *ulama* of Deoband, who were engaged in a self-conscious reformulation of their religious thought—a reformulation that involved new emphases and new concerns from *within* the framework of their own received tradition.[23] While work on the Barelwis is in progress, Robinson has unfolded the history of Lucknow's Firangi Mahal family, which played a large part in 'Indian Islamic life' for nearly three hundred years and came to stand for a distinctive style of Indian Islam.[24]

Some of these concerns, coupled with explorations of the nationalist movement and the communal phenomena, are of increasing relevance in a society which is traumatized by periodic outbursts of communal violence and is today engaged in narrowing down areas of conflicts and contradictions.

[19] Imtiaz Ahmad (ed.), *Caste and Social Stratification Among the Muslims* (Delhi, 1973).

[20] Barbara Daly Metcalf (ed.), *Moral Conduct and Authority: The Place of Adab in South Asian Islam* (Berkeley, 1984).

[21] Mujeeb Ashraf, *Muslim Attitudes towards British Rule and Western Culture in India* (Delhi, 1982), and the unpublished Oxford thesis of Farhan Nizami cited in Bayly, op.cit.

[22] Katherine P. Ewing (ed.), *Shariat and Ambiguity in South Asian Islam* (Delhi, 1988).

[23] Barbara Daly Metcalf, *Islamic Revival in British India: Deoband, 1860–1900* (Princeton, New Jersey, 1982).

[24] Francis Robinson, 'Problems in the History of the Firangi Mahall: Family of Learned and Holy Men', *Oxford University Papers on India*, vol. 1, part 2 (Delhi, 1987).

This study offers a reappraisal of some important themes relating to Indian nationalism and the growth of community-oriented formations, which are described in historical literature as 'communal' or 'separatist'. Its central concern, however, is to analyze how various segments among Muslims related to and defined their relationship with the nationalist forces, spearheaded by the Indian National Congress. This exercise is backed by an examination of several vital issues which reflect on the Congress movement, the structure of its support amongst Muslims and the crucial determinants that dictated its strategy towards the communal question. Also discussed is the part played by the colonial government in defining political identities in religious terms and translating them into constitutional arrangements. Some other issues, such as the role of the *ulama* in promoting an 'Islamic ideology', the content and structure of political separatism and the crystallization of communal identities, also figure in the discussion. The aim is to unfold the breakdown of inter-communal networks which had, for so long, kept intact the social fabric of Indian society, and to offer possible explanations to a larger historical question: Why did secular nationalism fail to create a united nation, drawing equally upon the participation of the major communities?

This book concentrates on the national arena, on national organizations and on political leaders who operated at the all-India level. At the same time, the provinces have not been ignored, for the high politics of premier political bodies can be meaningfully explained only by investigating their linkages with their supporters at the provincial and local levels. Besides, the ideological contours of Muslim activists cannot be easily identified without reference to their constituents and their specific regional concerns in the provinces and districts of, say, UP, Bengal and Punjab.

Bengal and Punjab were, so to speak, Muslim-majority provinces. This fact was of little importance as long as franchise was limited and only men of substance could aspire for a berth in legislative councils and local bodies. But once the Montagu-Chelmsford Reforms set in motion the process of distributing power according to the numerical strength of a community, a few Muslim groups were catapulted into prominence in Bengal and

Punjab. Their leaders, who were often castigated for playing second-fiddle to the UP-based leadership, now had the opportunity to exert their influence over the newly-enfranchised Muslim voters.

This change in the political scenario had far-reaching implications. For one, it was no longer possible for the Muslim League stalwarts of Aligarh and Lucknow to ignore, as was done when the Lucknow agreement of December 1916 was being finalized, the claims of Bengali and Punjabi Muslims. Nor could the government do so in its elaborate political arithmetic that was being worked out in Whitehall and Delhi. From the 1920s the great communal debates were, in fact, conducted in Lahore and Calcutta and not so much in UP. Eventually, of course, the political map of India had to be redrawn once Bengal and Punjab lent their fulsome support to the Muslim League campaign. Muslims of these provinces, more than any other group, made the creation of Pakistan possible.

UP Muslims, too, played a pivotal role in moulding political attitudes and in shaping the destiny of their co-religionists. The province was the arena where Syed Ahmad Khan, the genius behind the founding of the Aligarh college, conducted his educational and political activities. The Muslim Educational Conference and the Urdu Defence Associations had their headquarters in UP. The All-India Muslim League, though founded in Dacca, was run from Aligarh and Lucknow. Likewise, the most vociferous pan-Islamists belonged to UP and were at the centre of a massive mobilization campaign over the Khilafat issue. Their allies were the *ulama*, drawn mainly from famous theological centres like Deoband, Nadwa and Firangi Mahal—all located in UP.

II

More Muslims lived in the subcontinent than in any other part of the world. In 1921, they numbered 69 million, or one-fifth of British India's population. Their distribution ranged from 91 per cent in the North-West Frontier Province to less than 7 per cent in Madras. In absolute numbers they were most numerous in Bengal, where Islamic incursions took place in the eigth-ninth centuries through Arab traders and Sufi missions. What needs to be underlined is the predominantly rural character of the Muslim population in Bengal, a fact that stood in significant contrast to the general pattern of Muslim distribution in India and elsewhere. Only in the western districts of Bengal were they proportionately more numerous in urban rather than in rural areas.

In Punjab, which lies on the route by which successive armies entered India, migration and conversion created an Islamic community located predominantly in the western half of the province. Though part of the Ghaznavid Empire in the eleventh century, Punjab acquired greater commercial and strategic significance under the Ghoris. Cities like Lahore, Multan and Uch flourished, drawing large numbers of traders, administrators, soldiers, scholars and creative writers from parts of Central Asia.

Also attracted were the Sufis with their established mystical orders. Though there is evidence of some Sufi activity before 1200, the first and foremost Sufi missionary to reach India was Khwaja Hasan Muinuddin Chishti, who reached Delhi in 1193. Among his illustrious disciples were Bakhtiyar Kaki and Baba Fariduddin Ganj-i Shakar, founder of the Chishti order in Punjab. The Baba settled in Ajodhan and is said to have converted some sixteen backward Hindu tribes in that region. The Suhrawardi order, founded by Bahauddin Zakariya, gained a foothold in Multan. The Qadiris met with success in Uch. Pilgrimage to the shrines of such venerated holy men was of great symbolic value in, what Ernest Gellner describes, as the ritualistic, hierarchical popular religion of the masses as opposed to the puritanical, egalitarian, orthodox Islam of the learned.[25]

Establishment of Turkish rule influenced other parts of north Indian society, especially the area which the British constituted as the North-West Provinces and Oudh or the United Provinces of Agra and Oudh. For one, it ushered in major changes in the structure of medieval economy and gave impetus to, as was elucidated by Mohammad Habib, the growth of new towns.[26]

[25] Ernest Gellner (ed.), *Islamic Dilemmas: Reformers, Nationalists and Industrialization* (Berlin, 1985), and *Saints of the Atlas* (London, 1969).

[26] Mohammad Habib, Introduction to Elliot and Dowson's third volume of 'History of India', reprinted in K.A. Nizami (ed.), *Politics and Society during the early Medieval Period* (Delhi, 1974).

Some developed as centres of trade and industry, while others gained fame as rendezvous of the learned and resorts for artists and creative writers. Jaunpur, capital of the Sharqi Sultans (1394–1500), was the *Shiraaz-i Hind* or the *Dar al-ulum* (abode of learning). Agra, on the other hand, was a premier Mughal city for trade and commerce, with all land routes in north India radiating to and from Agra, rendering it 'the heart of the Empire' or the 'navel of the whole realm'. Lucknow, with its broad expanse of palaces, its groves and gardens, its courts and squares, and its mosques and *imambaras*, also remained a prime city at least until 1856, when Awadh was gobbled up by the British. A correspondent of the London *Times* offered a vivid description of the city. He wrote:

> Not Rome, not Athens, not Constantinople, not any city I have seen appears to me so striking and beautiful as [Lucknow]; and the more I gaze, the more its beauty grows upon me.[27]

Lucknow had a rich cultural life, with the Nawabs liberally adopting secular Hindu mores and folkways and contributing to a Hindu-Muslim cultural synthesis. They participated in Hindu festivals, on occasions even supporting the construction of temples, and freely employed Hindus as senior officers and bankers. The communal riots that shook Lucknow were those between Shias and Sunnis, not Hindus and Muslims.[28]

In the second half of the nineteenth century, the Muslim service and landed classes tried to emulate the traditions of the Nawabs, extended patronage to poets, writers, musicians and dancers, funded schools and colleges and helped to create a distinct cultural and intellectual ethos. Occasionally, they also dabbled in politics. They could be heard fulminating against the Congress,[29] discreetly

[27] W.H. Russell, *My Diary in India, in the year 1858–59* (London, 1860), p. 257. The colonial history of Lucknow is discussed in Rosie Llewellyn-Jones, *A Fatal Friendship: The Nawabs, the British and the City of Lucknow* (Delhi, 1985); Veena Talwar Oldenburg, *The Making of Colonial Lucknow 1856–1877* (Princeton, New Jersey, 1984).

[28] Thomas Metcalf, *Land, Landlords and the Raj: Northern India in the Nineteenth Century* (Berkeley, 1979), p. 37.

[29] Thus the Raja of Mahmudabad presided over an anti-Congress meeting in 1899 and criticized the 'short-sighted, ill-advised and misconceived' Congress propaganda.

lending support to the agitation against the Nagri resolution of April 1900 and preparing the groundwork for the establishment of the Muslim League.

III

It is commonplace to argue that the Indian Muslims, notwithstanding their varied historical experiences and their differentiated socio-economic structures, were united by certain common symbols of Islam. Mohammad Iqbal was the principal exponent of this view in the twentieth century. He laid stress on the egalitarian character of Islam, on congregational prayers and the rite of pilgrimage, which provides the great occasion for the meeting of Muslims from all over the world. The Kaaba, described in most vivid colours in *Rumuz-i Bekhudi*, symbolized the essential unity of the Islamic peoples.[30]

In recent years, social scientists have turned to some of the themes underlined in Iqbal's formulations. Thus Sandra B. Frietag has examined the use of Islamic symbols in Kanpur city—in 1913 and 1931—to highlight important shifts in the ways in which Muslims in north India perceived themselves and the world around them.[31] So has David Gilmartin in his analysis of the Shahidganj mosque agitation.[32] Still others have shown how the use of Islamic symbols during the Khilafat movement provided the rallying point for a massive communitarian response.[33]

Though such interpretations of local situations are useful, they tend to conceal important dimensions, including the inner ideological and socio-economic differences of both an inter and

[30] Annemarie Schimmel, *Gabriel's Wing: A Study into the Religious Ideas of Sir Muhammad Iqbal* (Leiden, 1963), pp. 195–96.

[31] Sandra B. Frietag, 'The Roots of Muslim Separatism in South Asia: Personal Practice and Public Structures in Kanpur and Bombay', Edmund Burke III and Ira M. Lapidus (eds.), *Islam Politics and Social Movements* (Berkeley, 1980), pp. 115–41.

[32] David Gilmartin, 'The Shahidganj Mosque Incident: A Prelude to Pakistan', ibid., pp. 146–68.

[33] Gail Minault, *The Khilafat Movement: Religious Symbolism and Political Mobilization in India* (Delhi, 1982), and the collection of articles in Mushirul Hasan (ed.), *Communal and Pan-Islamic Trends in Colonial India* (Delhi, 1985 edn.).

intra-regional nature. For example, adequate attention is not paid to the deep ideological divide that set Shias and Sunnis apart and to the intense rivalries between various theological schools, such as the Deobandis, the Barelwis and the Ahl-i Hadith. And it is only in recent years that scholars have begun to ask if Muslims have a monolithic perception of their faith and have reached the inescapable conclusion that they do not. Most interpret Quranic injunctions and the sayings of the Prophet in different ways—each according to their historical background and the realities encircling them.[34] Local accretions and bold theological innovations have, in some cases, even altered the basic structure of beliefs.

Doctrinal disputes and sectarian feuds have not just been a feature of Indian Islam; Muslim societies elsewhere and in most periods have never ever been free of schisms. What is perhaps unique in India is that sectarianism has hardly ever constituted the basis of political solidarity. Being a Shia or a Sunni, a Barelwi or a Deobandi, a Hanafi or a Shafai was, no doubt, a vital component of one's religious and sometimes social identity. Yet, identification with and loyalty to one or the other 'school' or 'sect' did not generally influence political decisions. Only in exceptional situations did Shias and Sunnis charter an independent political course. Again, only in rare cases did the Barelwis or the Deobandis advance separate political claims. In general, their political options were not constrained by purely sectarian considerations.

What moulded and stimulated a separate and distinct political consciousness was the placement of Muslims in the political and economic structures and their access to the levers of power, authority and influence under colonial rule. Nowhere was this fact in greater evidence than in Bengal, where more than half the population consisted of Muslims who had virtually no access to the resources of the province. And nowhere else was this fact a greater source of communal antipathy.

The impact of colonial rule, though unevenly felt in different parts of the country, affected Muslims of Bengal more than any other section of society. Here the operation of Permanent Settlement resulted in many families, mainly Muslims, losing their land

[34] See the collection of papers in Ewing (ed.), *Shariat*, op. cit.

to a new class of Hindu landlords. The Resumption Proceedings between 1828–1846 impoverished the few families which had survived the Permanent Settlement and destroyed Muslim educational institutions which were entirely run by revenue-free grants.[35] In Tippera, for example, families of Muslim zamindars, covering half the district, lost their land to Hindu landlords.[36] By the end of the nineteenth century, most of the land in Bengal, especially in the eastern districts, was owned by Hindus.

The 'reformist' initiatives of Warren Hastings and Cornwallis reversed the fortunes of those Muslims who had secured commanding positions in revenue, judicial and executive departments. Substitution of English for Persian in 1836 and the novel examination procedures added to their discomfiture. With most Muslims preferring to stay aloof from English schools and colleges, (Table 1.1) the prospects of government and professional employment were inevitably dimmed. Not surprisingly, the number of Muslim pleaders, attorneys, proctors and solicitors dwindled between 1851 and 1869.[37] And where recruitment was by test, as in the judicial and executive branches, Muslims did not have much of a chance. Consequently, when their representatives appeared before the Hunter Commission of 1882–83 and the Aitchison Commission of 1886–87 there was the familiar clamour for nomination as against competitive examinations.

Mayo and Dufferin steered a different course from the one plotted by their predecessors. Though still suspicious of Muslims and distrustful of their intentions, they were nevertheless sensitized to the need to win them over through carefully planned conciliatory gestures. Wherever Dufferin went in India, he let it be known that he was anxious to promote the education of Muslims and to appoint a great number of them in public services. After an official enquiry, the government announced in July 1885 that where Muslims did not have the 'full share of state employment' efforts would be made to 'redress this inequality'.[38] The address presented

[35] W.W. Hunter, *The Indian Mussalmans* (Calcutta, 1945 edn.), pp. 177–79.

[36] *Census*, 1921, Bengal, part I, p. 414.

[37] Hunter, *Indian Mussalmans*, p. 164.

[38] S. Gopal, *British Policy in India 1858–1905* (Cambridge, 1965), p. 158.

to Lytton by the MAO College Fund Committee on 8 January 1877 expressed gratitude to the government 'for having shown so strong a disposition to advance the cause of education amongst our community, and for issuing directions to the provincial governments to adopt special measures to supply our intellectual needs'.[39]

Outside the precincts of the Aligarh college there was little cause to feel contented, for government initiatives neither led to a significant increase in levels of literacy nor a substantial improvement in the Muslim share of government jobs. In 1911, only 12.6 per cent of the Muslim population in Bengal was literate in English. And in 1913 they held only 10.6 per cent of jobs in the executive and judicial departments.[40]

The imbalance between the relative positions of the Hindus and Muslims created the first stirrings of communal consciousness in Bengal, enabling Muslim organizations to make use of the sense of deprivation that gripped so many of their potential supporters and to conduct their mobilization along communitarian lines. Predictably, the more advanced Hindu groups combined to ward off any possible assault on their material interests.

W.W. Hunter's magisterial generalizations hardly made sense in another area of British India—UP—where the Muslim service and professional classes were not so badly off. In the first edition of *Athar al-Sanadid*, a pre-1857 archaeological study of Delhi, Syed Ahmad Khan included a chapter on the most successful and well-known of the traditional intellectual elites.[41] Their presence here and elsewhere in upper India was due, in part, to the fact that the British introduced fewer changes in the administrative machinery, and because there was much less insistence on educational attainment for securing government posts. Recruitment was not always, as Syed Ahmad's career illustrates, on the basis of college degrees but on account of family background and tried loyalty to the raj. Muslims in Punjab, for example, lagged far

[39] C.H. Philips (ed.), *The Evolution of India and Pakistan 1858–1947: Select Documents* (London, 1962), p. 183.

[40] *Census*, Bengal, part II, table VIII B; *Royal Commission on Public Services in India* (hereafter *RCPS*) (London, 1917), appendix V.

[41] Malik, *Sir Sayyid*, p. 38.

TABLE 1.1

Statement Showing the Hindu and Muslim Students who Passed the Entrance and B.A. Examinations at the University of Calcutta, 1876–86

	Entrance Examination									
Year	1876	1877	1878	1879	1880	1881	1882	1883	1884	1885–86
Hindu	1,196	980	914	905	1,421	1,170	1,216	1,338	—	1,230
Muslim	66	67	66	59	90	67	92	123	—	91
	B.A. Examinations									
Hindu	118	53	81	92	146	99	178	189	114	268
Muslim	7	3	—	4	4	1	6	15	3	8

SOURCE: *Public Service Commission, 1886–87, Report* (Calcutta, 1888), pp. 78–79.

TABLE 1.2

Employment of Muslims in the Provincial Civil Service, Punjab, 1913

	Total	Europeans and Anglo-Indians	Hindus	Muslims	Other Indians	Total Indians	Muslims per cent of Indians
Executive Branch:							
Total	136	14	52	52	18	122	42.6
Posts Rs 1,000 and over	5	1	3	—	1	4	—
Post up to Rs 1,000	131	13	49	52	17	118	44.1
Judicial Branch:							
Total	48	7	18	19	4	41	46.4
Posts Rs 1,000 and over	4	1	1	2	—	3	66.6
Posts up to Rs 1,000	44	6	17	17	4	38	44.7
Total both branches	184	21	70	71	22	163	43.5

SOURCE: *Royal Commission on the Public Services in India. Report of the Commissioners*, Command 8382 (Parliamentary Papers, 1916, VII). Appendices to Report. Appendix VIII.

behind the Hindus in western education, particularly in western districts where they constituted three-quarters of the population. There were only 57 Muslim graduates in the two decades before 1857;[42] yet in 1886–87 there were 127 Muslim officers in the uncovenanted judicial and executive branches, i.e., 41.6 per cent of all Indians.[43] By 1913, their share in the provincial service had increased appreciably: 66 per cent of the posts in the judicial sector, carrying a salary of Rs 1,000 and above, were held by Muslims. (Table 1.2)

Similarly, Muslims retained their position in the services because Urdu remained the medium of education and the language of administration.[44] The *qasbati* elites, though aware of their declining position, managed to adjust to new demands and challenges. Some sought appointment in the princely States of Rampur, Jaora, Bhopal, Arcot and Hyderabad; others like Mohsinul Mulk and Viqarul Mulk went to Aligarh to carve out their place in the expanding educational system.

Muslim landowners also survived the rigours of British rule. In spite of the trauma of 1857, so vividly described by the poet Asadullah Khan Ghalib,[45] they remained a substantial landholding interest in upper India. It is true that their fortunes remained much more stable in Punjab than in UP, where the corrosive action of commercial forces, combined with political change and the rise of monied classes, undermined the position of the traditional landholding class and placed pressures on the qasbah-based

[42] *Report of the Punjab Provincial Committee: Appendix to Education Commission* (Calcutta, 1884), p. 116; *Census*, 1901, Punjab, part II, table VIII, for Muslim literates in English.

[43] *PSC*, appendices, pp. 78–79.

[44] Anil Seal, *The Emergence of Indian Nationalism: Competition and Collaboration in the Later Nineteenth Century* (Cambridge, 1975), pp. 304–6; Robinson, *Separatism*, pp. 18–19.

[45] Ghalib was in Delhi for the entire period between the arrival of the mutineers from Meerut on 11 May 1857 and the successful British assault upon the city on 14 September. The *Dastambu* reflects his mood and that of his brethren in Delhi. 'No light burns in their (Muslims) homes at night, and no smoke rises from them by day. Ghalib, who knows this city, who had a thousand friends to speak with him and none but his shadow to bear him company'. Ralph Russell, *Ghalib: The Poet and his Age* (London, 1977).

'Islamic gentry'.[46] Yet, there was really no substantial decline in their fortunes, especially in the post-1860 period. Most zamindars and taluqdars in Awadh, extolled as the 'ancient, indigenous and cherished leaders of rural society', emerged from the 1857 upheaval with augmented, not diminished, landholdings.[47] In Muzaffarnagar and Meerut districts, a considerable portion of the Syed land, transferred between 1841 and 1861, was acquired by a few Syed families in Jansath. In Aligarh district, one of the principal regions of Muslim disaffection in 1857, a number of recently converted Muslim zamindars increased their holdings between the settlements of 1839 and 1869 from 47,822 acres to 72,218 acres.[48] W.J.D. Burkitt, settlement officer of the district, referred to 'sound business men' steadily increasing their possession.[49] Elsewhere, such men turned British rule to their profit and came to terms more easily with British revenue demands and a commercialized agriculture. Thus in parts of Agra division,

[46] Francis Robinson mentions Kanpur as an example of the rapid passage of land from the traditional to the commercial castes. Chris Bayly refers to the pressure placed on the Islamic gentry by the rise of monied men and the resurgence of Hindu landholding communities. *Rulers, Townsmen and Bazaars: North Indian Society in the Age of British Expansion, 1770–1870* (Cambridge, 1983), p. 355. Eric Stokes, however, did not agree with Robinson's larger argument about the corrosive action of commercial forces on the position of the traditional landholding classes. His conclusion was that the decisive revolution in land control had occurred before 1857, in a pre-commerical era, and was the product of institutional rather than economic change. He noted the stability of the great estates in the post-1860 period. E.T. Stokes, *The Peasant and the Raj: Studies in Agrarian Society and Peasant Rebellion in Colonial India* (Cambridge, 1978), p. 216.

[47] Ibid., p. 180. Bayly notes that the Syeds of Barha in Muzaffarnagar and Meerut districts were able to 'creep back' into some of the villages from which they had earlier been ejected. Op. cit., pp. 190, 355.

[48] Peter Hardy, *The Muslims of British India* (Cambridge, 1972), p. 78; Zoya Hasan, *Dominance and Mobilization: Rural Politics in Western Uttar Pradesh 1930–1980* (Delhi, 1989), p. 35, for land concentration of the great Pathan landlords of Atrauli and the Sherwanis of Bhikampur. Stokes noted that many of the zamindars suffered many vicissitudes and some carried a heavy load of debt and litigation, but they remained the great revenue payers of their districts. Op. cit., p. 217.

[49] Metcalf, *Land, Landlords*, p. 162.

Muslims were a major landholding group. They were dominant in Rohilkhand, owning 33.1 per cent of the land in Bareilly district. The Pathans, in particular, held considerable estates. In 1909 they held 135,289 acres or 13.38 per cent of the land, mainly in the Bareilly tahsil and in the north of the district.[50]

The foregoing survey is intended to serve as a background to the tumultuous decades, covered in this book, which witnessed the rise of nationalism and the rapid growth of unity as well as friction between sections of the Hindu and Muslim populations.

[50] *District Gazetteers of the United Provinces*, Bareilly, vol. 13, pp. 100–05.

Chapter Two

'The Muslim Breakaway'

The Indian National Congress, its development and character has been a major theme in modern Indian historical writings. In recent years, a number of regional and local studies have emphasized that the Congress did not, as had once been supposed, represent just the interests of particular class, caste or interest groups. Anil Seal's argument that the Congress was the party of English-educated and professional men, drawn mainly from the higher literate Hindu castes of the three maritime presidencies, is no longer tenable. It is becoming increasingly clear that the role of the educated in the Congress was that of publicists and spokesmen who represented a much wider range of interests and whose social composition and political aims were, in fact, much more heterogenous than either the British or some historians dominated by the official mind have argued. Moreover, since Congressmen had local roles to play and were often members of the patron-client groups in their own localities, they had a complex relationship with the elites of Indian society, both urban and rural, and with the peasants and workers whom they claimed to represent.

One of the main objectives of the founders of the Congress was to seek legitimacy as the representatives of Indian aspirations. This was necessary in order to unite the scattered and fragmented elements in Indian society and also to impress Calcutta and London that the Congress represented more than a 'microscopic minority' and was not just a 'ramshackle coalition'. Admittedly, its members were drawn from different backgrounds whose interests were not always compatible with each other; yet, pursuit of parochial goals and advancement of careers was not their sole concern. They shared a nationalist vision and were committed to the collective welfare of all Indians. They were conscious of their historic role as architects of an Indian nation; so they dwelt on the theme of 'national opinion' and 'national aspirations' with unfailing regularity. 'It is difficult to conceive', claimed the *Report of the First Indian National Congress*, 'any gathering . . . more thoroughly representative of the entire nation than the Congress'. What, in 1885, was little more than an experiment, the Madras Congress (1887) proudly announced, 'bore every appearance of becoming a national institution'.

In a divided and disparate country like India, it was no less important to proclaim the non-communal character of the Congress. Indeed, the claim of being a national body could only be sustained by transcending, even if only in theory, caste and sectarian boundaries. Besides, a non-communal posture alone could disarm the apprehensions regarding Congress policies and programmes. Thus the Congress in 1887–88 decided not to discuss any subject which either Hindus or Muslims 'unanimously or nearly unanimously' opposed.[1] In the same spirit, the Subjects Committee bowed to mounting pressure from Muslim delegates and dropped the Punjab Alienation Bill discussion from the agenda.[2] Surendranath Banerjea went on to reaffirm the unity of the Congress movement. 'Here', he declared, 'we stand upon a common platform. . . . Here we have all agreed to bury our differences.'[3]

However, such assurances were not always matched by practice: while denying religious identifications and asserting secular orientations, the Congress relied upon Hindu symbols and traditions for its legitimization. Tilak, Aurobindo Ghose and Lajpat Rai maintained that the Hindu masses could only be aroused through the use of religious predispositions, the popularization

[1] The *Tribune* observed: 'After this assurance let us hope our Mohammedan friends will no longer hesitate to join their Hindu fellow subjects. Nothing can be a stronger proof of the good faith of Congress than this resolution'. 23 January, 1889.

[2] John R. McLane, *Indian Nationalism and the Early Congress* (Princeton, New Jersey, 1977), pp. 254–56.

[3] *Speeches and Writings of Surendranath Banerjea* (Madras, n.d.), p. 265. Or, the statement of Ajudhia Nath Kunzru, a leading pleader in Allahabad during the 1880s, that the Congress 'works not for the good of this or that class, nor of this or that province, but for the benefit of the whole nation', *Tribune*, 23 January 1889.

of national historical myths, and the celebration of Hindu festivals and decided to blend Hinduism with nationalism. Tilak invoked the spirit of resurgent Hinduism to mobilize the masses, promoted the Ganapati festival to provide his followers with a recognizable identity, and rehearsed the tale of past Maratha greatness by resuscitating the memory of Shivaji. Though intended to elicit, activate and canalize dormant political energies, Tilak's mobilization strategy had a divisive impact and polarized Maharashtra's urban society around communal lines.[4] Likewise, the Swadeshi movement in Bengal, despite its contribution to the anti-colonial struggle, acquired a certain communal colouring. Worship of the elephant-headed god, Ganesh, and of Bhawani, demonstrative ablutions in the river Ganga, and fervent appeals to the 'grim goddess', Kali, all involved a religious intensity which weakened Muslim enthusiasm for the movement.[5] In fact, the coalition

[4] Bipan Chandra is of a different view. According to him, Tilak's politics, ideology and agitational methods were not communal. His campaigns were organized around political and economic issues and contained little appeal to Hinduism. This interpretation is hard to accept in the light of Tilak's own writings and the researches of a number of historians. While recognizing Tilak's vital contribution to the anti-colonial struggle, it is hard to ignore his role in heightening communal consciousness in western India. It is also no coincidence that most of his lieutenants in that region had purely Hindu concerns and were communal in their political orientation. They were in the forefront of the Mahasabha movement and the chief organizers of *sangathan* bodies. *Communalism in Modern India*, pp. 143–44.

Here it may be useful to emphasize the obvious difference between revivalism and communalism. Yet, the distinction is often blurred in some cases, a fact conveniently overlooked by historians like Bipan Chandra. The Hindu Mahasabha, for example, not only harked back to a romantic past and revelled in religious enthusiasm, but also adopted narrow, sectarian and divisive attitudes. It thus combined elements of both revivalism and communalism.

[5] Sumit Sarkar, *The Swadeshi Movement in Bengal, 1903–1908* (Delhi, 1973), p. 411; for the Hindu concept of Indian nationalism, Amales Tripathi, *The Extremist Challenge: India Between 1890 and 1910* (Delhi, 1967), p. 61; Hiren Mukherjee, 'The Role of Revivalism in the Indian National Movement', in *Essays in Honour of Professor S.C. Sarkar* (Delhi, 1976), pp. 592–93; Barbara Southhard, 'The Political Strategy of Aurobindo Ghosh: The Utilization of Religious Symbolism and the Problem of Political Mobilization in Bengal', *MAS*, 1980, vol. 14, 3, pp. 362–66, 375–76.

between religious conservatism and political extremism hindered their mobilization. A more secular-oriented political front, then and later, had a much greater chance of success in drawing diverse sections of society into the nationalist fold.

The disquieting fact was that so many Congressmen of stature were so closely identified with revivalist tendencies. The cow protectionists in Punjab were 'very generally' Congressmen.[6] The Gaurakshini Sabha in the Central Provinces was backed by Mahratta Brahmin pleaders, the same men who patronized the Congress.[7] In UP, the heartland of Aryavarta, prominent Congressmen, backed by wealthy traders, bankers and landowners, campaigned for the outlawing of cow-slaughter as well as for the recognition of Devanagri as an official script in courts and government offices.[8] Ram Charan Das, who served on three Congress reception committees, was actively involved in the cow protection movement and in all the conferences and societies which culminated in the formation of the Hindu Sabha, and ultimately in the All-India Hindu Mahasabha.[9] His mentor, Madan Mohan Malaviya, was the moving spirit behind the Hindu revitalization movement. He was connected with the Prayag Hindu Samaj, the Sanatan Dharm Mahasammelan and the Shuddhi Sabha, which enabled him to forge close links with those influential groups who shared his undaunting enthusiasm for *shuddhi, sangathan*, Hindi, the cow and the Hindu Sabha. It was on the strength of their support that this orthodox and socially conservative Brahmin wielded considerable influence in local, provincial and national politics.

The Congress mobilization campaign suffered from another serious drawback: the insistence on treating Muslims as a distinct religious community and a homogeneous political entity.[10] This implied a recognition of the government's categorization of

[6] McLane, *Indian Nationalism*, p. 305.

[7] Ibid., p. 306.

[8] C.A. Bayly, 'Patrons and Politics in Northern India', *MAS*, vol. 7, 3, July 1973.

[9] Table I in R. Gordon, 'The Hindu Mahasabha and the Indian National Congress, 1915–1926', *MAS*, vol. 9, 2, April 1975, p. 153.

[10] Addressing the Punjab Political Conference in October 1906, Lala Lajpat Rai said that the 'religious ideals' of Hindus and Muslims were so different that it was 'impossible to expect a complete union of them in the near future'.

Indian society into exclusive religious groups, who also possessed a distinct political identity. In this way the avowed goal of uniting various groups and classes around a common socio-economic programme was trimmed to suit the dictates of political expediency. It suited the early Congress leaders to strike a bargain with 'Muslim' politicians without challenging their status in the community they so boldly claimed to represent and without questioning their exaggerated claims. Even their opposition to separate electorates was feeble, because of the more pressing compulsion to keep the Congress ranks united and to sustain the image of both a popular and representative organization. There was much substance in the observation of the Lucknow writer-essayist, Abdul Halim Sharar,

> ... whether we support Congress or not, one very sad thing which we do notice about its activities is that it seems to be creating more differences between Hindus and Muslims than existed previously.[11]

However, the Congress strategy did not seem to work to its advantage. By legitimizing the role of self-appointed guardians of the faith, the Congress scuttled its own prospect of courting and nursing a potentially powerful constituency. And by accepting the notion of a politically distinct community, it lent credence to the claims advanced by the Aligarh leaders and their followers in the All-India Muslim League. By the time the Congress strategy was modified in the mid-1930s and its leaders were awakened to the reality of a communal monster, the opportunity of forging independent links with the Muslim masses was lost.

II

In explaining the 'Muslim breakaway' from the Congress—a major theme in studies on Indian nationalism—historians assume the existence of an all-India Muslim consciousness, which found

---

Panjabee, 13 October 1906, quoted in P. Nagar, *Lala Lajpat Rai: The Man and His Ideas* (Delhi, 1977), p. 252. And a more recent view of a Bengali intellectual that Indian Muslims 'constituted a society of their own with a distinct culture, and would never be absorbed in a unified nation which could be called India'. Nirad C. Chaudhuri, *Thy Hand Great Anarch! India 1921–1925* (London, 1987), p. 330.

[11] Abdul Halim Sharar, *Lucknow: The Last Phase of an Oriental Culture*, translated and edited by E.S. Harcourt and Fakhir Hussain (London, 1975), p. 23.

organized and tangible expression in the ideological orientation of Syed Ahmad Khan and his associates at Aligarh. This, however, is a questionable assumption and this section will examine why it is so. It will also try to establish that 'Muslim response' to the Congress did not crystallize at an identifiable level, and that isolated and sporadic reactions of fragmented groups must not form the basis of a highly generalized reconstruction. Bodies like the Central National Mahommedan Association and the United Patriotic Association, with their localized concerns, had no popular following and could not legitimately sustain their claim to represent Muslim interests generally.[12] Consequently, their response to the Congress, as Badruddin Tyabji perceptively pointed out, rested on 'local, special and temporary causes'.[13]

Given their different socio-economic interests there was no likelihood of a monolithic Muslim response to the Congress movement. There was none. The Congress demands affected Muslims of various classes and regions in several different ways; so, their reactions were moulded by local, regional and sometimes class-based interests as opposed to the altruistic concerns for the larger community of Indian Islam.

This section alludes to yet another contentious issue in contemporary historical writings: the part played by Syed Ahmad Khan, who is said to have orchestrated the 'Muslim viewpoint' on political matters with vigour and consistency and whipped up an anti-Congress stir among his followers. While the weight of his arguments against the Congress must be recognized, as also his influence on Muslim society, at the same time, we need to explore how a group of Muslims, imbued with the spirit of nationalism, were beginning to work out an alternative political strategy in the last decade of the nineteenth century. Admittedly, they could not match the intellectual resources of Syed

[12] There is evidence of considerable mutual antipathy between the so-called Muslim leaders. In Bengal, for example, Ameer Ali and Abdul Latif hurled mutual accusations at each other. W.S. Blunt, who was in India in 1883–84, recorded that Latif criticized Ameer Ali for having 'broken with the mass of the community by affecting English dress and ways, and posing as reformers, although they were in no way qualified in a religious sense for such a position'. W.S. Blunt, *India Under Ripon: A Private Diary* (London, 1909), p. 97.

[13] *Hindu*, 16 January 1888.

Ahmad and his disciples at Aligarh. They also did not possess the organizational strength to counter their more influential detractors. But they were not lacking in ideological conviction and consistency, a fact that enabled them to develop and pursue their nationalist aims and spearhead a pro-Congress movement in the early decade of the twentieth century. Thus, our preoccupation with Syed Ahmad's anti-Congress crusade need not lead historians to ignore alternative political currents within the Muslim community.

The mixed and diverse reactions to nationalist forces is evident from the ways in which some of the Congress demands were perceived. Most educated Muslims in Bengal and Punjab were averse to competitive examinations, because they were educationally ill-prepared to compete with the more advanced Hindus. Ameer Ali and Abdul Latif, representing two of Bengal's premier organizations, maintained that the Congress goal of a more open and competitive society, if implemented, would favour educated Hindus and accentuate existing disparities between the religious communities.[14] The same argument was echoed in upper India in order to make a case for nomination. Moreover, there was the familiar clamour for separate representation in public appointments and its extension to representative bodies, especially because many 'respected families' had been left out on account of franchise being confined to those who fulfilled property, wealth and educational qualifications.[15]

In UP, too, the Congress faced stern opposition. Here the main apprehension was of being swamped by the so-called Hindu majority in a prospective popular government—a fear reinforced

[14] *Report of the Public Service Commission, 1886–87* (Calcutta, 1888), vol. 4, pp. 196, 201, 262–68. A common grudge was that Muslims had limited chances of representation on local bodies, because franchise extended only to those who fulfilled property, wealth and educational qualifications. Thus in 1875–76, six of the 25 Indians on local bodies were Muslims. They fared still more poorly in the triennial election to the Calcutta municipality, held in 1897; there were only six Muslims as against 37 Hindus. *Administrative Report on the Municipality of the Suburbs of Calcutta 1875–76* (Calcutta, 1876), p. 6; *Statement Exibiting the Moral and Material Progress of India, 1897–98*, p. 6.

[15] Ibid., vol. 1, p. 162.

by some isolated examples in western UP. When some Muslim candidates were defeated in the municipal board elections held in 1890, the *Najmul Akhbaar* struck an alarming note: 'If the elective principle was extended to the legislative council an entire exclusion of Muslims from the council would follow.'[16] 'This is not an imaginary bugbear presented to scare away Muslims from the Congress camp', wrote a contributor to the *Aligarh Institute Gazette*, 'but a stubborn fact daily illustrated in the proceedings of the district and municipal boards scatterd all over the country.'[17] If anything, this was a reiteration of Syed Ahmad's arguments against the Congress demand for a more representative and popular government.

Though Syed Ahmad's assault on the Congress has been interpreted in several different ways,[18] most explanations are often based on later day ideological predilections. Besides, there is a tendency—more pronounced in the subcontinent than elsewhere—to try and prove or disprove that the genius behind the founding of the Aligarh college was also the progenitor of a 'Muslim nation'. This has distorted perspectives, stimulated, somewhat needlessly, acrimonious controversies, and obscured the more vital aspects of Indian polity and society during Syed Ahmad's lifetime. So far, attempts to establish him as the architect of 'Muslim nationalism' have proved to be as unrewarding as the efforts to discover in him elements of an 'Indian nationalist'.

It is, at first, hard to make sense of Syed Ahmad's fiery denunciation of the Congress. After all, he had the required credentials to be a leading light in any nationalist organization. Hindu-Muslim unity was close to his heart and a constant refrain in his public utterances.[19] Friendship between the two communities, he said, should be a matter of course, for since 'centuries we have been living on the same soil, eating the fruit of the same land . . . brea-

[16] *Najmul Akhbaar* (Etawah), 24 March 1890; *Jubilee Paper* (Lucknow) and *Azad* (Lucknow), 1 April 1890; *Mihir-i Nimroz* (Bijnor), 7 May 1890, Selections from the Native Newspaper Reports (hereafter SNNR), UP, 1890.

[17] *Aligarh Institute Gazette*, 12 September 1896.

[18] For a summary of various interpretations, C.W. Troll, *Sayyid Ahmad Khan: A Reinterpretation of Muslim Theology* (Delhi, 1978).

[19] Maulvi Mohammad Imamuddin (ed.), *Mukammal Majmuah wa Speeches* (Lahore, 1901), pp. 197–98.

thing the air of the same country'.[20] In 1873, he declared that he did not care for religion to be regarded as the badge of nationhood. He advocated separation between matters religious and political. Spiritual and religious matters, he asserted, cannot have any connection with worldly affairs. A true religion only stated cardinal principles comprising ethical values and only incidentally dealt with the problems of the world. When he was a member of the viceroy's legislative council he strove for the welfare of both Hindus and Muslims: so when he toured north India in the eighties he was feted on all sides.[21] In 1884, Syed Ahmad made clear that

> by the word qaum, I mean both Hindus and Muslims. . . . In my opinion it matters not whatever be their religious beliefs, because we cannot see anything of it; but what we see is that all of us, whether Hindus or Muslims, live on one soil, are governed by one and the same ruler, have the same sources of benefits, and equally share the hardships of a famine. . . .[22]

Common territory, in the eyes of Syed Ahmad, thus imposed upon Indians the obligation of mutual co-operation and unity in order to ensure the common good.

The Aligarh reformer was no religious bigot or Hindu baiter. He worked closely with Hindus in the Scientific Society, the Aligarh British Indian Association and the United Patriotic Association;[23] both the vice-president and the secretary of the British Indian Association were Hindus. Communal concerns did not figure in his favourite MAO college project: he sought and secured generous support from Hindu rajas and zamindars.[24]

[20] J.M.S. Baljon, *Reforms and Religious Ideas of Sir Sayyid Ahmad Khan* (Leiden, 1949), p. 36.

[21] Iqbal Ali (ed.), *Sayyid Saheb ka Safarnama-i Punjab* (Lahore, 1979), pp. 140–67.

[22] Hafeez Malik, *Sir Sayyid Ahmad Khan and Muslim Modernization*, p. 240, and Hardy, *Muslims of British India*, p. 136.

[23] S.R. Mehrotra, *The Emergence of the Indian National Congress* (Delhi, 1971), pp. 209–10; Shan Muhammad (ed.), *The Aligarh Movement—Basic Documents 1864–1898* (Meerut, 1978), vol. 2, p. 939.

[24] Among the donors was the Maharaja of Patiala. Syed Ahmad to the Maharaja of Patiala, n.d., Collection Fund, F. No. 1, Aligarh Archives, Aligarh Muslim University, Aligarh (hereafter AMUA). Blunt and Maulvi Samiullah, Syed Ahmad's close friend and colleague, had animated discus-

Hindus were well-represented in the managing committee and among the teachers, while Hindu students even outnumbered Muslims in some of the early years of the college. As a concession to their religious susceptibilities, cow-slaughter was banned on the campus.[25]

In 1888, Syed Hosain Bilgrami pontificated on Hindu-Muslim unity and its value in forging a joint anti-Congress front. 'The interest of the peoples', he wrote to the Syed, 'are one and indivisible . . . and it behoves them both to unite and make common cause against this [Congress] movement.'[26] This was a needless sermon. The Syed should have told him so. But he was too polite to tell Bilgrami that he had been echoing the same feeling well before the Congress came into being, and that it was he who compared India to a pretty bride whose two eyes were the Hindus and the Muslims.

Syed Ahmad's political concerns were no less secular and there was little in his early attitudes to suggest that he wanted separate and favoured treatment for his co-religionists. He was the first to argue that the 1857 upsurge had been caused by the monumental indifference of the East India Company to the economic plight of the masses, and the failure to grant Indians some form of advisory representation in the council. He supported local self-government, the right of Indian judges to try English defendants, wrote in defence of Indians entering the covenanted civil service and revived the British Indian Association at Aligarh to join with Surendranath Banerjea in a campaign to restore the age of entrance for the Civil Service examination from nineteen to twenty-one.[27] Banerjea had attended a meeting at Aligarh in

---

sions on a Hindu-Muslim concordat. The Maulvi explained that 'the proper conduct' for the Muslims was being debated in the college, with some people arguing the case for making common cause with the Hindus. 'All, however, were at heart vexed and angry at what had been done, and recognized in the Ilbert Bill a matter of common interest'. Blunt, *India Under Ripon*, p. 103.

[25] Rajmohan Gandhi, *Understanding the Muslim Mind* (Delhi, 1987), p. 34.

[26] To Syed Ahmad, 20 August 1888, Muhammad (ed.), *The Aligarh Movement*, vol. 3, pp. 100-02.

[27] Seal, *Emergence of Indian Nationalism*, p. 319; David Lelyveld, *Aligarh's First Generation: Muslim Solidarity in British India* (Princeton, 1978),

1877. When he returned to the city in 1884 to start a branch of a new political organization, the National Fund, with Syed Ahmad as president, he was received with 'utmost kindness'. His friendly relations with the Syed continued 'notwithstanding differences of opinion, which the Congress movement subsequently gave rise to'.[28]

With a background so remarkably similar to that of any contemporary Congress leader, Syed Ahmad's December 1887 outburst at Lucknow surprised many. He sharply criticized the application of the principles of representative and parliamentary government in so diverse, so divided and so complex a society. He also raised the spectre of Bengali dominance. 'If you accept', he said at Lucknow and repeated elsewhere, 'that the country should groan under the yoke of Bengali rule and its people lick the Bengali shoes, then, in the name of God, jump into the train, sit down, and be off to Madras.' The Congress demands, he thundered, would hurt the Muslims most. The enlarged councils would have no place for them: it would be dominated by 'Babu-so-and-so Mitter, Babu-so-and-so Ghose and Babu-so-and-so Chuckerburtty.' This was not the language one associated with a man who had once held up the Bengalis as an example to be admired and imitated, and was generally known for his balanced views on so many public issues since the publication of his celebrated *Asbaab-i Baghawat-i Hind* in 1858.

It is doubtful if Syed Ahmad worked out his arguments against the Congress on his own. Though acutely sensitive to the changing climate of opinion in India in the decades after 1857, he was only

---

p. 305. Notice the following comment by a 'Muslim: A Political Observer':

> Do not his writings and his whole political conduct of the pre-Congress days show that he had himself been an advocate of what the Congress demanded later on—the full recognition of our political rights? What was his position with regard to the Ilbert Bill?. . . Above all, had he not written the 'Causes of the Indian Revolt' in which he traced the origin of the Mutiny to the shortsighted policy (of) the British?. . . Was he not in one sense the creator of the 'spirit' that found its culmination in the Congress movement?

'The Indian Muhammadans and the National Congress', *Kayastha Samachar* (Allahabad), November 1902, vol. 6, 5 (New Series), p. 392.

[28] S. Banerjea, *A Nation in Making* (Calcutta, 1963: reprint), p. 45.

superficially familiar with the intricacies of the newly-developing institutions of representative government. In such matters he was tutored by British officials in north India, whose active backing he required for his prestigious Aligarh project. The person who influenced him most was the MAO college Principal, Theodore Beck, 'a pretty young man with pink cheeks and blue eyes.' This 24-year old Cambridge undergraduate was the political mentor and ideologue of the grand old man of Aligarh.[29]

Theodore—meaning gift to God—was educated in Quaker schools, University College, London, and Trinity College, Cambridge. He was president of the Cambridge Union in 1882 and was a key figure in the Conversazone Society, better known as the 'Apostles.'[30] In 1883, he was fortuitously chosen Principal of the Aligarh college and travelled to India to assume duties on 1 February 1884. But the college, then and later, remained peripheral to his concerns. His preoccupation with political affairs 'swallowed up' much of his time.[31] He ignored accusations of derilection of duty, took pride in having a 'finger in the political pie'[32] and boasted that there were 'very few Englishmen in the country so well up as myself in the Congress business'.[33]

Beck, says David Lelyveld, was a 'Tory' radical at Cambridge: he stood for Home Rule for Ireland, women's rights and the creation of a classless society. He denounced British rule in India for not fulfilling 'our duty, training the nation and leaving it,

[29]It has been argued that the ideological basis of Syed Ahmad's opposition to Indian nationalism had been clearly articulated well before either Beck or the Congress had appeared on the scene. This view is based on Syed Ahmad's speech on the local self-government bill of the Central Provinces, delivered in January 1833. See Lelyveld, *Aligarh's First Generation*, p. 311, and, Robinson, *Separatism*, p. 110.

[30] Other members were Walter Raleigh, Arthur Strachey and J.K. Stephens, described by Eric Stokes as the political philosopher of the Indian Civil Service. These Cambridge recruits carried to Aligarh a particular subculture of British intellectual life, one that suited the aspirations and priorities that Syed Ahmad considered appropriate to his educational efforts. Lelyveld, op. cit., p. 213.

[31] Beck to his mother, 21 July 1888, Beck Papers, India Office Library and Records (hereafter IOLR).

[32] Ibid., 7 July 1888.

[33] Ibid., 10 September 1888.

when strong enough, to itself.'[34] But Lelyveld does not tell us that the Cambridge interlude did not have a lasting impression on Beck: it was not long afterwards that he changed his views. His faith in British democracy was shaken. 'I believe', he observed on the eve of the 1892 general elections, 'it has no more wisdom in it than the oracle of Delphi had of divine inspiration'.[35] He also abandoned his undergraduate sympathy for Indian nationalism. This was not, as Lelyveld suggests, on account of 'intense indoctrination' from Syed Ahmad's son, Syed Mahmood, notorious for his drunken escapades and intellectually incapable of being anybody's mentor. In any case, Beck was too arrogant and self-righteous an individual to be guided by Syed Mahmood. By training and temperament he was a hardheaded Tory, with a deep distrust for political liberalism. He was averse to Gladstonian liberalism[36] and hostile to British politicians and civil servants who were soft towards Indian aspirations. W.S. Blunt, William Digby, Samuel Smith and John Slagg were 'cranks who unite on India'; W.W. Hunter, Richard Temple, W.C. Plowden, Richard Grath and Charles Turner were 'men of danger' and the 'dupes of every impudent journalistic liar'.[37] He reserved his harshest comments for Hunter, 'a notorious humbug . . . sacrificing both England and India for his advancement.'[38]

Though Beck described himself as one of 'England's adventurers', he reached the Indian shores with a clear sense of mission: to stamp out sedition in order to bolster imperial rule for the good of the Indian people. 'To have a great grievance shop, an anti-government cave of Adullum marching about the country will be

[34] Lelyveld, op. cit., p. 217. In India, Beck stated that he was 'a man who enjoys agitation. Fighting the authorities would be a most congenial task to me. But agitation for the backward and fanatical Muslims in upper India would be disastrous.' Beck to Badruddin Tyabji, 7 May 1888, Tyabji Papers, National Archives of India (hereafter NAI), New Delhi.

[35] Beck to his mother, 28 June 1892, Beck Papers.

[36] He regretted that the 'Gladstonians have got in' but was glad that their majority 'is so small'. To his mother, 19 July 1892, ibid.

[37] Ibid., 15 September 1888.

[38] Beck denounced the articles of Hunter in the *Times*, adding: 'I despise and loathe that man. He is a notorious humbug and all his knowledge of the people is secondhand. He is sacrificing both England and India for his own advancement'. Ibid., 21 June 1888.

bad for the peace of India,'[39] he wrote with reference to the Congress. He was constantly haunted by such apprehensions. Yet he set out to counter the 'evil' influence of the Congress with an evangelical fervour. He assiduously cultivated Muslims to create a 'strong conservative school of thought' and 'complete a breach' between them and the Bengali dominated Congress.[40] He kept his students on a tight leash. The Siddons Union Club, a Cambridge-like institution, debarred discussions on sensitive political affairs. Unlike the Cambridge prototype, the Principal had the veto power over any discussion so as to prevent the Union from becoming a forum for Bengali-style 'sedition'.[41] But Beck's eyes were set on the world beyond the Aligarh college: his aim was to establish an enduring Anglo-Muslim alliance and to stiffen Muslim feelings against the 'incendiary' Congress. 'I am more excited about this blessed Congress,' he wrote to his mother in April 1888, 'than about anything else. . . . It seems likely this Congress will create a great stir in this part of India, and I shouldn't be surprised if some jolly good rows occur. The opposition has got well on its legs. . . .'[42]

With his stature, influence and connections, Syed Ahmad was an invaluable asset to further Beck's ideals. He was, therefore, goaded into taking anti-Congress postures. Beck was dutifully present whenever his 'chief' fired his shots at the Congress. After the Meerut speech, he gleefully recorded: 'We have played off our 81 ton gun against the Congress again.'[43] He encouraged the launching of an anti-Congress newspaper,[44] herded the scattered elements of opposition to the Congress into the United Patriotic Association,[45] prompted some students to congregate at the Delhi Juma Masjid to collect signatures for an anti-Congress petition to Parliament[46] and kept on jogging up the *Pioneer* and

[39] Ibid., 3 May 1888.

[40] Ibid., 28 March and 20 September 1888.

[41] Lelyveld, op. cit., p. 220.

[42] To his mother, 24 April 1888, Beck Papers.

[43] Ibid., 28 March 1888.

[44] Ibid., 28 April 1888.

[45] Beck to Syed Ahmad, 13 February 1890, F.No. 69/10, AMUA. To his mother, 3 June 1888, Beck Papers.

[46] To his mother, 28 August 1888. He also mobilized Syed Ahmad to get

the government with little accounts of Muslim demonstrations against the Congress.[47] Beck's intentions were clear; yet, he was sometimes daunted by the outcome of his endeavours. 'It is a desperate struggle. If we relax our energies they will give us a thrashing. If we stick to it we may possibly—I say possibly, but probably—give them a desperate blow.'[48] He foresaw, thanks to his own initiatives, the emergence of a 'gigantic' Muslim organization in upper India with a distinct political creed. This would naturally suit the government, 'which will have some people to defend it. . . . We shall have a body of men bent on rooting out the fallacies of their [Congress] arguments.'[49]

Syed Ahmad could hardly match the young Principal's boundless energy and passion. Besides, after the initial spurt of activity he was reluctant to prosecute his anti-Congress campaign any further.[50] He bluntly said so to Beck in April 1888, just a few months after his well-publicized Lucknow speech. 'We have I think done enough in opposition to the Congress', he firmly stated.[51] In the same conversation, he recalled how during the turbulent days of 1857 the British employed brute force to crush the revolt—reminiscent of the atrocities perpetrated by Chingiz Khan and Timur. Beck was not pleased with the comparison. 'This little conversation', he noted despondently, 'has put a damper on my politics.'[52] But as one made of sterner stuff, he not only

a petition signed by Muslims against the Braudlaugh's Bill of Indian Councils (1889). To his father, 25 February 1890, Beck Papers.

[47] Beck referred to a meeting with UP's lieutenant-governor at which he discussed the Congress agitation. He was 'immensely flattered' at the reception he received and 'felt myself quite a big man, discussing the affairs of state with the King of the province'. Two years later, he went up to Shimla to meet Lansdowne and discussed the 'official encouragement' given to the Congress in some circles. To his mother, 3 June 1888, 16 June 1890, ibid.

[48] Ibid., 20 September 1888.

[49] Ibid., 10 April 1888.

[50] Beck was alarmed to notice that the Syed was inclined to 'take matters too calmly' and that he was not keen to prosecute the anti-Congress movement. A few month later, he complained to his mother that the Syed did not attach 'sufficient importance to educate the community in sound political thought'. 24 April and 20 September 1888, ibid.

[51] Ibid., 28 April 1888.

[52] Ibid.

kept up the tempo of his activities but also kept the Syed on a tight leash. His perseverance paid off. Constrained by his dependence on government support for the college of his dreams and ingratiated by the honour and approbation he received from the British, the ageing Syed Ahmad relented to the charms of the young Principal and lived up to his expectations of playing the anti-Congress drum loud and clear. Moreover, the rising tide of Hindu revivalism and its links with Indian nationalism reinforced his growing fears that the Congress movement was prejudicial to Muslim interests and that the 'well-being of the people of India, and especially of the Mussalmans, lies in leading a quiet life under the benign rule of the English government'.[53] Beck's aim of bringing the Aligarh reformer to the centre of the political stage was a consummate success.

There is no denying Syed Ahmad's profound impact on north Indian Muslims. He was a visible symbol of Muslim regeneration, a catalyst of social and educational reforms, a 'Notre eminent contemporain,' as Gracin de Tassy called him. His political message also carried weight: hence the Congress overtures to court his support. But his influence was by no means all-pervasive, because his anti-Congress stance did not go down well with *all* his co-religionists.[54] The United Indian Patriotic Association and the Muhammadan Anglo-Oriental Defence Association were tame affairs. They petered out, despite much fanfare, within two years of their lazy existence. Mohamed Ali, an Aligarh graduate, recalled how Syed Ahmad, his British patrons and the college trustees got together to pass a resolution against the Congress and had it published in the *Pioneer* and the *Aligarh Institute Gazette*. 'That was all that the Mussalmans would do in those days in the field of politics.'[55]

[53] *Aligarh Institute Gazette*, 18 September 1897.

[54] For criticizm of his political views in a section of the Urdu press, Prem Narain, *Press and Politics in India, 1885–1905* (Delhi, 1970), pp. 83, 92–94. Speeches of Muslim Congressmen like Maulvi Hidayat Rasul, Nawab Reza Khan, Hamid Ali Khan, Maulvi Syed-Sharfuddin and Shaikh Kadir Buksh are reproduced in A.M. Zaidi (ed.), *The Muslim School of Congress* (Delhi, 1987), pp. 345–50, 358–64.

[55] Mushirul Hasan (ed.), *Mohamed Ali in Indian Politics: Select Writings* (Delhi, 1982), vol. 1, p. 32.

Sustained and organized opposition to the Congress was generally confined to Aligarh and its neighbouring districts; elsewhere, there were enough Muslims who were unmoved by Syed Ahmad's political exhortations. In 1887, seventy Muslims from Awadh attended the Madras Congress. Of the 222 Muslims gathered at the Allahabad Congress a year later, ninety came from Allahabad and Lucknow districts.[56] In 1889, 254 Muslims turned up in Bombay, of whom 125 were from Delhi and UP. At least some of them were inspired by a *fatwa*, signed by over a hundred *ulama*, in support of the Congress and in opposition to the Patriotic Association. The signatories included Rashid Ahmad Gangohi, Mahmud Hasan and several other eminent Deobandi *ulama*.[57] The *fatwa*, published under the title *Nusrat-al Abraar*, received wide publicity. It served as a political manifesto for the succeeding generations of the *ulama* at Deoband.

Aligarh's first generation students, brought up under Syed Ahmad's benign influence and tutored incessantly on the virtues of loyalty to the raj, were not all cut out of the same cloth. His Lucknow and Meerut speeches drew no applause from several Aligarh students, including Syed Nabiullah and Rafique, soon to be a Cambridge graduate after a brief stint with the Lucknow paper, *Advocate*. The Meerut outburst, according to another Aligarh graduate, Inayatullah, 'smacked of flattery'.[58] Rafique was equally forthright in his rebuttal. 'The prospect of a united India', he observed in one of his inspired moods, 'does seem at first utopian and impracticable. But it is an object worth striving for'.[59] In a similar vein, though with greater incisiveness, Mir Mohamed Husain told Beck in April 1888:

As long as you talk to me about the interests of Muslims alone I won't

[56] J.L. Hill, 'Congress and Representative Institutions in the United Provinces 1886–1901' (Unpublished Ph.D. thesis, Duke University, 1969). Tables 1 to 3 are also drawn from this thesis.

[57] Husain Ahmad Madani, *Naqsh-i Hayaat: Khudnawisht Sawaanih* (Karachi, 1979 edn.), pp. 481–82; I.H. Qureshi, *Ulama in Politics* (Karachi, 1974), p. 227. Allan Octavian Hume boasted that in Punjab 'we are sweeping Sir Syed away. . . . The Ludhiana Maulvis have the absolute command of over 40,000 Muslims'. To Tyabji, 5 November 1888, Tyabji Papers.

[58] Beck to his mother, 3 April 1888, Beck Papers.

[59] Ibid., 10 February 1888.

listen to you. I will only look to the interests of the country. And by the country I mean these 90 per cent of poor peasants who live from hand to mouth. Every effort should be made to improve their condition. How? Not by trying to get more appointments for Muslims, but by trying to improve the material condition of the country—its industry and commerce. If you stir up ill-will between Hindus and Muslims you will ruin the country. . . . The Anglo-Indians don't like two things—union amongst us, and the improvement of our material conditions. . . . We should have joined the Congress and opposed their bad schemes. We should have directed the attention of the Congress on improving the material prosperity of the country and bettering the conditions of these poor peasants.[60]

This was 'subversive' talk by men who, in Beck's assessment, had 'gobbled up the radicalism of England and of Young Bengal.'[61] But neither he nor the sage from Aligarh could quite foresee the course of events which would slowly but steadily lead the young English-educated Muslims, especially those trained at Aligarh, to clamour for a reordering of political priorities and autonomy of political action. The anguished successors of Syed Ahmad watched helplessly as some of Aligarh's brilliant products—Mohamed Ali, Hasrat Mohani, Zafar Ali Khan, Shaukat Ali, Raja Ghulam Husain, Ghulam-us-Saqlain[62] and Wilayat Ali Bambooque[63]—moved into the political arena with a fresh disposition, a distinct style of politics and a new ideological

[60] Beck Papers, 5 March 1888.

[61] Ibid.

[62] He was at the Aligarh college from October 1889 to April 1894, where he developed a keen interest in nationalist affairs. In January 1903 he started the *Asr-i Jadeed* from Meerut, a paper with nationalist concerns. The paper ceased publication in December 1908 on account of the illness of Ghulam-us-Saqlain.

[63] Wilayat Ali was born in 1887 in Masauli village in Barabanki district. He belonged to the Kidwai clan, which traced its descent to Kidwatuddin who came to India in the wake of the Ghorid invasion of north India. He was educated at the Aligarh college and was a contemporary of Syed Mahmud, Khaliquzzaman, Shuaib Qureshi and Raja Ghulam Husain. His humorous sketches were credited with literary excellence. In July 1918, Wilayat Ali, popularly known as 'Bambooque', was stricken with cholera. Dr M.A. Ansari rushed to his bedside in Barabanki but could not save his life.

orientation. The Ali brothers—Mohamed and Shaukat—both graduates of the Aligarh college, villified Beck and his successors[64] and were at pains to establish that the radical temper of their comrades was consistent with the intentions of their mentor, Syed Ahmad. Mohamed Ali announced in an Urdu verse:

It is you who had taught the community all this 'mischief'
If we are its culmination, you are its commencement

III

Out of 1,620 individuals from UP who signed the roll as delegates to the annual Congress sessions from 1885 to 1901, 596, or slightly over one-third, were Muslims from UP (Table 2:1), the province where Syed Ahmad is supposed to have exercized the greatest of influence. Their strength increased steadily from 8 per cent in 1886 to high-points of 42 per cent in 1889 and 55 per cent in 1890.[65] The delegates included members of the dispossessed nawabi elite, newspaper editors like Munshi Sajjad Husain, editor of *Oudh Punch*, and a mixed group of teachers, lawyers, bankers and traders. Connected with secular-oriented organizations like the Rifah-i Am and the Anjuman-i Muhammadi, many of them had close cultural and professional links with Congress leaders in Lucknow and Allahabad. The Rifah-i Am was headed by Shaikh Raza Husain Khan, a close friend of Babu Ganga Prashad Varma, editor of *Hindustani* in Lucknow, and among its patrons was Pandit Ajudhia Nath Kunzru. The Anjuman-i Muhammadi elected over 150 delegates to the Congress session in 1890: its president, Nawab Ali Mohamed Khan, served on the Congress Subjects Committee in 1892 and 1899.

Six-tenths of all Muslim delegates from 1886 to 1901 came from Lucknow, the city where the composite, cross-communal traditions continued to ensure a broad secularity in public life. When the Congress met at Allahabad in 1888 and 1892, Lucknow had more Muslim delegates in attendance than the host city. There were 313 Muslims at the 1899 Congress and 288 came from

[64] Margaret H. Case, 'The Aligarh Era: Muslim Politics in North India 1860–1910' (Unpublished Ph.D. thesis, Chicago, 1970), p. 179.

[65] J.L. Hill, op. cit., p. 41, f.n. 41.

TABLE 2.1

UP Congress Delegates by Religion and Year of Attendance

Year	Jains	Christians	Muslim	Percentage of UP Delegation	Hindu	Percentage of UP Delegation
1885						
1886	..	..	6	8	68	92
1887	..	..	7	15	41	85
1888	6	18	151	26	396	68
1989	1	6	113	44	139	53
1890	..	3	82	55	62	42
1891*	—	—	—	—	—	—
1892	2	4	79	25	235	73
1893	1	1	122	9	117	89
1894	..	1	1	8	10	77
1895	1	1	1	4	21	88
1896	..	2	5	8	52	87
1897	..	1	0	0	9	90
1898	..	.	1	0	11	100
1899	2	4	304	51	288	48
1900	3	3	1	3	31	80
1901	..	3	6	7	84	90

* No delegates' lists for this year is available.

Lucknow itself (Tables 2:2–3). It was the largest Muslim attendance at any annual session before 1916.

Next to Lucknow, Allahabad, the 'city with its hoary traditions, inspiring memories, sacred associations [and] high intellectual reputation,'[66] elected one-fifth of the Muslim delegates. They included some small zamindars from Daryabad, poverty-stricken Shia dependents of the old royal house of Awadh and a group of lawyers led by Abdul Majid and Abdur Rauf who were closely tied to Ajudhia Nath Kunzru.[67] In general, however, the Shias were more numerous in the Muslim delegation. It is surprising

[66] MSS.EUR. E.251/3, Hallet Papers, IOLR.

[67] They addressed several public meetings with Kunzru who was their senior colleague at the Allahabad bar. *Tribune*, 22 February 1888.

TABLE 2.2
UP Muslim Delegates from Major Cities by Year of Attendance at the Congress

Year	Lucknow	Allahabad	Banaras	Kanpur	Agra	Aligarh
1885						
1886	3		1	. .	. .	. .
1887	1	.	. .	. .	1	2
1888	42	33	20	13	9	7
1889	32	23	2	11	7	6
1890*	—	—	—	—	—	—
1891*	—	—	—	—	—	—
1892	28	31	.	1	. .	8
1893	2	. .	. .	. .	3	5
1894	. .	. .	. .	. .	. .	1
1895	. .	. .	. .	. .	. .	1
1896	3	. .	. .	. .	. .	1
1897	. .	. .	. .	. .	. .	. .
1898	1	. .	. .	. .	. .	. .
1899	288**	1	2	1	1	3
1900	. .	. .	. .	. .	. .	1
1901	. .	2	1	1	. .	. .

*No delegates list available.
**264 of these attended in 1899 only.

that this was so. Their population was small, the level of political consciousness was low and, above all, there was no institutional or organizational structures to sustain their political concerns. Their sudden, active interest in Congress affairs can only be explained in terms of their rift with the Sunnis over the *Madhe Sahaba* issue, which gripped so many cities of UP in the last quarter of the nineteenth century.[68]

Shia leaders in Allahabad and Lucknow turned to the Congress to defend their right to take out *tazia* processions and exercize control over their endowments. They seized the initiative and, in November 1888, a Khoja Muslim from Bombay, Mohammad

[68] Mushirul Hasan, 'Sectarianism in Indian Islam: The Shia-Sunni Divide in the United Provinces', *The Indian Economic and Social History Review*, vol. 27, 2,90; J.R.I. Cole, *Roots of North Indian Shiism in Iran and Iraq: Religion and State in Awadh, 1722–1889* (Delhi, 1989).

TABLE 2.3

Total Number of Muslim Delegates from Each City of the United Provinces, 1886–1901

City	Delegates		City	Delegates	
	Number	Percentage of total Muslim Delegates		Number	Percentage of total Human An Ebyss
Dehra Dun	1	.2	Allahabad	76	13
Saharanpur	1	.2	Azamgarh	5	.8
Muzaffarnagar	2	.3	Mirzapur	6	1
Meerut	6	1	Banaras	24	1
Aligarh	19	3	Ghazipur	4	.7
Naini Tal	2	.3	Basti	1	.2
Almora	3	.5	Lucknow	355	60
Moradabad	5	.8	Barabanki	1	.2
Bareilly	5	.8	Sitapur	1	.2
Shahjahanpur	7	1	Kheri	4	.7
Agra	19	3	Fyzabad	4	.7
Farrukhabad	11	2	Gonda	2	.3
Kanpur	24	4	Rae Bareli	1	.2
Fatehpur	1	.2	Pratapgarh	5	.8
Banda	1	.2			

Ali Bhimji, was invited to address a pro-Congress Shia gathering. Sunni leaders were not to be outmanoeuvred. Maulana Mohamed Husain of the Diara Shah Hujatullah, already won over by the Syed Ahmad–Beck combine, launched a counter-attack.[69] The Congress in UP was caught up in the crossfire between the Shia zealots and the Sunni orthodox opinion. Appearing to be impartial

[69] C.A. Bayly, *The Local Roots of Indian Politics—Allahabad, 1880–1920* (Oxford, 1975), p. 130. Beck noted that the Maulvi, 'a man of great learning and piety' was drawn into the anti-Congress movement by Syed Ahmad's speeches and by the agitation against cow slaughter. Expressing satisfaction at Maulvi Mohamed Husain's presence at an anti-Congress rally in Allahabad, Beck observed: 'I think the National Congress is doing the Muslims a lot of good. These meetings are infusing spirit into the community and inducing it to shake off its fatal stagnation'. To his mother, 2 March 1888, Beck Papers.

in the deepening sectarian controversies was the only way to ensure the balance of its support. Increasingly, however, Shia-Sunni conflicts, which erupted in the years 1937 to 1939, imposed severe strains on Congress' ability to maintain an equilibrium in its relationship with the two rival sects.

The social profile of Muslim Congressmen in Bengal and Punjab[70] was no different from other regions of British India. They were urban-based and connected with various professions, such as journalism and law. Shared professional experience, besides removing mutual prejudices which often stemmed from social distancing, provided the stimulus for acting in unison on contemporary political issues. This is illustrated by the career of Abdul Rasul, a prominent Congress leader in Bengal. He went to St. John's College, Oxford, and was called to the Bar from the Middle Temple. On his return to India, he enrolled himself as a barrister of the Calcutta High Court, where he came in contact with leading lawyers like W.C. Bonnerjee and Lal Mohan Ghose and was much inspired by their political activities. Likewise, the social background of Abdul Halim Ghuznavi and Abdul Kaseem, founder of *Mussalman*, was decidedly important in the making

[70] Some of the important Congressmen in Punjab were: Muharram Ali Chishti, Syed Nadir Ali Shah, Hakim Ahmad Ali and Munshi Nabi Baksh, editors of *Rafiq-i Hind*, *Rehbar-i Hind*, *Takmilul Hikmat* and *Koh-i Noor*, respectively. Among the prominent lawyers associated with the organization were Shaikh Umar Baksh and his brother Nabi Baksh. They headed the district Congress committees of Hoshiarpur and Gurdaspur. See *Tribune*, 14 October, 25 November, and 13 December 1893. In general, however, there was not much enthusiasm for the Congress in Punjab. K.W. Jones has explained why this was so. In the case of some groups, such as the militant Arya Samajists, the Congress appeared pro-Muslim. This impression was confirmed when the Congress Subjects Committee decided to drop the discussion on the Punjab Alienation Act from the agenda as a concession to the feelings of Punjabi Muslims. Soon thereafter, plans were set afoot to organize an exclusively 'Hindu' body. According to Jones, the provincial world appeared far more real and relevant than the wider sphere of the Congress and national issues. Instead of national politics, factional struggles and communal competition commanded far greater attention. K.W. Jones, *Arya Dharm: Hindu Consciousness in 19th Century Punjab* (Berkeley, 1976); pp. 241–50, 254–55; N.G. Barrier, 'The Arya Samaj and Congress Politics in the Punjab 1894–1908', *Journal of Asian Studies*, vol. 26, May 1967.

of their ideological orientation. It helps to understand why they, along with Liakat Hossain, Hassan Jan and other Muslims, marched with the opponents of the partition of Bengal and joined heart and soul in the swadeshi *tehrik*.[71]

In western India, Badruddin Tyabji, a Sulaimani Bohra, was the prized trophy of the Congress. His father Tyab Ali was not born with a silver spoon but made a neat fortune through his matrimonial links with an affluent trading family. He did not have the benefit of studying in an English school or college but saw the advantage of educating his sons in England. That is how Badruddin became the first Muslim to qualify at the London Bar (1867) and to be enrolled as an advocate of the Bombay High Court. His brother, Camruddin, was the first Muslim to be trained as a solicitor in England and the first Muslim Indian to be admitted to the profession in that country. In this way, Tyab Ali 'triumphed in founding a family that, endowed by him with self-sufficiency, imbued with his ideals of work . . . continued to make a mark on Indian national life for over a century and a half'.[72]

Tyab Ali was a devout Muslim, though not one to harp on Hindu-Muslim differences. Badruddin Tyabji was no different. His association with the London Indian Society and the East Indian Association provide enough clues to his cosmopolitan outlook and political inclinations.[73] In 1882 he was given a place on the legislative council to represent graduates and lawyers and not simply the Muslims. And in 1885 Badruddin became one of the founders of the Bombay Presidency Association which that December played host to the first Congress. Here, as elsewhere, he worked, along with two other members of the 'trio'—Pherozeshah Mehta and K.T. Telang—'not as Hindus, Mahomedans and Parsis but as soldiers in the public cause.'[74]

Given his background and concerns, Badruddin Tyabji was the obvious person to spearhead the Congress movement. It is,

[71] Sarkar, *Swadeshi Movement*, pp. 426–35; Jayanti Maitra, *Muslim Politics in Bengal 1885-1906: Collaboration and Confrontation* (Calcutta, 1984), pp. 244–46, 249–50.

[72] Badr-ud-din Tyabji, *Memoirs of an Egoist* (Delhi, 1988), p. 7.

[73] In London, Tyabji was among those who rallied round Dadabhai Naoroji to found the London India Society.

[74] A.G. Noorani, *Badruddin Tyabji* (Delhi, 1969), p. 132.

therefore, not surprising that W.C. Bonnerjee insisted that his friend from student days in England occupy the presidential chair at the Second Congress, and the Congress Standing Committee unhesitatingly declared in November 1887 that Badruddin was 'not only the best, but the only possible man for the post.'[75] What was surprising was how quickly his election provoked a counter-reaction. Syed Ahmad was angered. He chose the occasion of Badruddin's presidency to come out publicly against the Congress.

Badruddin rebutted the views of Syed Ahmad. The Congress, he said, should be allowed to play the major role in aggregating the Muslims' articulated interests and that Muslims could by united action confine Congress to such issues as they deemed safe for discussion. On 18 February 1888 he wrote:

> My policy, therefore, would be to act from *within* rather than from *without*. . . . We should thus advance the general progress of India, and at the same time safeguard our own interests.[76]

Many Muslims, Badruddin claimed, recognized this and supported the Congress. Those who did not was because of 'certain special, local and temporary causes', which applied 'only to a particular part of India.'[77]

Syed Ahmad Khan did not think so. There was no such thing as 'the general progress of India' or 'India as one nation'. The different castes and creeds, he told Badruddin in January 1888, did not belong to a nation and their aims and aspirations were also not the same. 'You regard', he continued, 'the doings of the misnamed National Congress as beneficial to India, but I am sorry to say that I regard them as not only injurious to our own community but also to India at large.'[78] Small but significant gatherings of Muslims in Bombay endorsed Syed Ahmad's line of reasoning rather than Badruddin's plea for Muslim participation in Congress.[79] In October 1888, a dejected Badruddin suggested

[75] Hume to Tyabji, 3 December 1887, Tyabji Papers.

[76] Tyabji to Ameer Ali, 3 December 1887, ibid.

[77] *Report of the Indian National Congress*, 1887, p. 72.

[78] Syed Ahmad to Tyabji, 24 January 1888, Tyabji Papers.

[79] *Rast Goftar* and *Kaside Mumbai*, 12 August 1888; *Parsi Punch*, 19 August 1888, SNNR, Bombay.

that the Congress activities be suspended for five years because 'an overwhelming majority of Mohammedans is against the [Congress] movement'.[80] Nobody took the suggestion seriously. And nobody ever agreed with Badruddin's assessment of Muslim hostility. For once the future judge of the Bombay High Court had spoken too soon.

IV

It is worth reiterating the several different ways in which Muslims related themselves to developments around their immediate and distant surroundings. Admittedly, there was some talk of 'Muslim solidarity' and some half-hearted endeavours to steer the political discourse around religious lines, but neither Syed Ahmad nor his compatriots could translate their objectives in any tangible form. Diverse regional and local concerns, conflicting class interests and sectarian animus sharpened cleavages and impeded the growth of an all-India Muslim political consciousness. In fact, no amount of pious exhortations could bridge the wide gulf that separated, say, the East Bengal Muslim peasant from the Muslim taluqdar in Awadh. By the end of the nineteenth century, all attempts to bring about 'some degree of solidarity among the disintegrated masses of Mahomedan society' failed to achieve any measure of success.

No summing up of late-nineteenth century trends can, however, be complete without reference to the spurt in cow-protection activity and the strident demand for securing recognition of the Nagri script in government and law courts.[81] These were not isolated assertions of militant, religio-revivalist tendencies but

[80] Tyabji to Hume, 27 October 1888, Tyabji Papers.

[81] McLane, *Indian Nationalism*, pp. 271–331, for an insightful account of the cow-protection movement. See Robinson, *Separatism*, pp. 66–78, for a sensitive portrayal of Hindu revivalist tendencies, including the development of the Hindi-Urdu conflict and the campaign for Hindi. The Hindi-Urdu controversy is also discussed in: Aziz Ahmad, *Islamic Culture in the Indian Environment*, pp. 259–62, Brass, *Language, Religion and Politics*, pp. 127–138, and Jyotirindra Das Gupta, *Language Conflict and National Development: Group Politics and National Language Policy in India* (Berkeley, 1970), chapter four.

were outward manifestations of the new and burgeoning sense of Hindu consciousness. There were similar trends among Muslims. The Graeco-Turkish War of 1897 stimulated pan-Islamic feelings.[82] Islamization in Bengal and parts of upper India, inspired by the Waliullahi traditions and bolstered by the success of the Faraizi ideology, was an equally important force. Insistence on a revitalized Islamic consciousness and identity, with its corresponding denigration of Islam's local roots, was beginning to erode the syncretistic traditions and undermine inter-religious peace and understanding.[83] The massive communal rioting in the summer of 1893 was a grim reminder to the nationalists that the fabric of Hindu-Muslim unity was too fragile to withstand the onslaught of various revitalization movements. 'If the smouldering fire of religious enmity . . . is not put out', warned an observer, 'it will before long be kindled into a mighty flame and destroy the noble edifice which the Congress has built up with so much pains.'[84]

The prophecy did not come true. Though relations between Hindus and Muslims were sometimes strained, their deterioration was neither deep nor irreversible. 'Nothing strikes the intelligent traveller in India more forcibly', observed a senior police official, 'than the friendly and peaceable attitude of all castes and classes towards each other.'[85] He was right. Communal friction was not ordinarily a major source of civil disturbance in the last quarter

[82] Subscriptions were raised at Kanpur in aid of Turkey, prayers were offered at Jhansi and Agra for the success of the Khalifa, who was commonly described as the *Khalifat al-Muslimeen* in contemporary newspapers. An indication of the depth of Muslim feelings is reflected in the bitter criticizm of Syed Ahmad's views on pan-Islamism. *Zamanah* (Kanpur), 13 May 1897, *Nasim-i Agra* (Agra), 22 May 1897, *Akhbaar-i Islam* (Agra), 23 May 1897, *Azad* (Lucknow), 4 June 1897, *Shahna-i Hind*, 1 July 1897, *Riaz al-Akhbaar*, 4 July 1897, *Naiyar-i Azam* (Moradabad), 5 February 1900, *Jami al-ulum* (Moradabad), 14 February 1900, SNNR, UP.

[83] Roy, *Islamic Syncretism*, p. 251, and Ahmad, *The Bengal Muslims*, p. 184; S.M. Ikram, *Muslim Civilization in India* (London, 1964), pp. 282-86.

[84] *Al-Waqt* (Gorakhpur), 21/26 February 1894, SNNR, UP.

[85] T.C. Arthur, *Reminiscences of an Indian Police Official* (London, 1894), p. 145. English and Indian witnesses before the Public Service Commission testified to the harmonious relations between the Hindus and Muslims and took serious note of the cross-communal links. *PSC*, NWP & O Sub-Commission (Calcutta, 1888), pp. 15, 26, 23.

of the nineteenth cenutry. During the quinquennium, 1889–1894, there was no communal violence in Bengal, except one in Calcutta and its suburbs.[86] Such sporadic outbursts did not signify, as some writers are wont to suggest, the fragmentation of Indian society along communal lines. Intercommunity tensions and conflicts were counterposed to the quiet, commonplace routines in which Hindus and Muslims intermingled without notice or incident and could still be found involved in a range of 'religiously promiscuous' practices. In 1909, the *Imperial Gazetteer of India* stated that 'it was, until recently, the regular practice of low-class Muhammadans to join in the Durga Puja and other festivals'; it mentioned Muslim consultation of Hindu almanacs, worship of Sithala and Manasa, use of vermilion, and joint offerings to village deities before the sowing or transplanting of rice seedlings.[87] Another inspiring legitimation of the more mundane expressions of peaceful coexistence came daily in the sounds of Muslim *shahnai* players joining in the *arti* at Hindu temples, including the *arti* at the most sacred Vishwanath temple in Banaras.[88]

Contemporary writings took note of cordial Hindu-Muslim relations, highlighting the ongoing process of social and cultural fusion.[89] The poet Mohammad Iqbal shared the vision of a united India—one that was free of both alien domination and inner dissensions. In 'Sayyid's Tomb', he called his land of birth as a garden, and the people inhabiting it as members of a *qaum* (nation), with the two circles of Islam and *watan* intersecting and at several places coalescing into a coherent whole. *Himala*, the first poem

[86] Rajat Kanta Ray, *Social Conflict and Political Unrest in Bengal 1875–1927* (Delhi, 1984), p. 121. The Commissioner of Dacca noted the 'extraordinary fact' that in five years 'not a single riot of any description should have occurred'.

[87] *Imperial Gazetteer of India*, pp. 48–49.

[88] Judy F. Pugh, 'Divination and Ideology in the Banaras Muslim Community', Ewing (ed.), *Shariat and Ambiguity*, p. 289.

[89] For instance, Syed Ahmad Dehlavi, *Rasum-i Delhi* (Delhi, 1905), pp. 37–41, and for comments and reactions of Asadullah Khan Ghalib, see Percival Spear, 'Ghalib's Delhi', Ralph Russell (ed.), *Ghalib: The Poet and His Age* (London, 1977), p. 49. Again, for Hindu-Muslim relations in Delhi, see C.F. Andrews, *Zakaullah of Delhi* (Cambridge, n.d.), pp. 11, 15–17.

in *Bang-i Dara*, was inspired by the beauty of the land of his birth, while *Hindustani Bachhon ka Qaumi Geet* (National Anthem of Indian Children) and the *Tarana-i Hindi* (The Song of India) were refined, buoyant and non-communal expressions of patriotic sentiments.[90] In *Naya Shiwala* (New Temple), he chided both Hindus and Muslims for their narrow mental horizon,[91] and appealed to the keepers of the temple and the mosque to foster mutual goodwill and understanding.[92] Indeed, Iqbal echoed, in large measure, the ideology of secular nationalism.

Akbar Allahabadi, a merciless satirist equipped with an irrepressible sense of humour, had similar concerns. He subjected to ridicule, to scathing criticizm or damning exposure the social and political strategy of imperialism and Syed Ahmad's policy of loyal co-operation with the government.[93] And, like Iqbal, he championed Hindu-Muslim unity. Both Hindus and Muslims, he said, have to bear the blows of those who wield the rod of worldly power, but they should respond by being like water, on which the blows of a rod have only a momentary effect.[94]

Iqbal and Akbar were stating the obvious. They recognized, as indeed did others, that the direction in which patronage

[90] See the collection of essays in Hafeez Malik (ed.), *Iqbal: Poet-Philosopher of Pakistan* (Columbia University Press, 1971).

[91] I'll tell you the truth, Oh Brahmin, if I may make so bold!
Those idols in your temples—these idols have grown old;
To hate your fellow-mortals is all they teach you, while
Our God too sets his preachers to scold and revile;
Sickened, from both your temple and our shrine I have seen,
Alike our preachers' sermons and your fond myths I shun.
In every garden image you fancied God: I see
In every speck of my country's poor dust, divinity.
V.G. Kiernan, *Poems from Iqbal*, p. 8.

[92] Come, let us remove all that causes estrangement,
Let us reconcile those that have turned away from
each other, remove all signs of division.
Desolation has reigned for long in the
habitation of my heart—
Come, let us build a new temple in our land.
M. Mujeeb, *The Indian Muslims* (London, 1967), p. 485.

[93] Ibid., p. 477.

[94] I say the same to Hindus and to Muslims:

economic welfare and authority flowed in everyday life indicated the continuing importance of cross-communal networks.[95] Syed Ahmad's Aligarh project was backed by Hindus and Muslims alike.[96] He encouraged, despite his misgivings over the Nagri agitation, a Hindu-Muslim *entente* in cultural and religious matters. His contemporary, Ajudhia Nath Kunzru, owed his fortunes as much to the wealthy Muslim landholders as to his extensive banking and commission agencies.[97] In east UP and Awadh generally, the dominant factor in the politics of the towns tended to be an Urdu-speaking elite connection based on landed interests. Communal matters did not always foul the path of politics.[98]

The competing units in early municipal politics were multi-factions, not antagonistic communal groups. In the composition of early municipal factions, conflicting caste and communal considerations played a secondary role to personal rivalries and connections. A Muslim lawyer, Maulvi Serajul Islam, was elected from Chittagong to the Bengal legislative council, largely on the Hindu vote. Surendranath Banerjea, on the other hand, was backed by Muslims for a seat on the prestigious Calcutta Corporation.[99] Around the same time, a similar move was afoot in UP, where the Congress backed Hamid Ali Khan for a seat in the council.

Nor did communal divisions last long after they had been politicized. Soon after the violent eruptions in 1893, tempers began to cool everywhere and there was much display of 'mutual love and affection' in the riot-torn cities of UP.[100] Public statements

---

Be good, each as your faith would have you be.
The world's a rod? Then *you* become as water.
Clash like the waves, but still remain one wave.

Ralph Russell and Khurshidul Islam, 'The Satirical verse of Akbar Illahabadi (1846–1921)', *MAS*, 1974, vol. 8, 1, pp. 44-46.

[95] D.A. Washbrook, *The Emergence of Provincial Politics. The Madras Presidency, 1870–1920* (Cambridge, 1976), pp. 143–44, 262.

[96] For example, one Sita Narain, a barrister at Rajkot, donated Rs 45,000 to the Aligarh college and Rs 16,000 to the Central Hindu College at Banaras. *Al-Bashir*, 24 February 1901. SNNR, UP.

[97] Henry Sender, *The Kashmiri Pandits: A Study of Cultural Choice in North India* (Delhi, 1988), p. 244.

[98] Robinson, *Separatism*, p. 79.

[99] Ray, *Social Conflict*, pp. 41, 131–32.

[100] The years 1897 to 1900 may well be regarded as a period of exceptionally

and newspaper editorials on national unity and the commonality of Hindu-Muslim interests were matched by strenuous efforts of local reconciliation committees to resolve and diffuse tensions.[101] When asked how the 'upper classes' of the two communities behaved when riots occur, the Assistant Magistrate of Gorakhpur replied:

> By taking leading Hindus and Muslims into confidence, matters are satisfactorily arranged.... In Aligarh, we left the whole matter to leading Hindus and Muhammadans and everything went off without hitch.[102]

Such was the pattern everywhere, reinforcing the view that, by the end of the nineteenth century, there was no sign of Hindus and Muslims going their separate ways. If anything, the lines of cleavages in north India were more sharply drawn between the Sunnis and the Shias rather than Hindus and Muslims.[103] Though expressed in exaggerated terms, there is merit in the observations of W.S. Blunt and Henry Cotton that Hindu-Muslim animus was accentuated only after the government decided to pursue the principle of divide and rule with vigour.[104]

---

cordial Hindu-Muslim relations in most parts of the country. This was, in part, attributed to the combination of the two communities against plague measures. 'Let the people', stated the *Jami al-ulum* (Moradabad) of 21 March 1897, 'welcome the return of the plague to India a thousand times, were it for the purpose of effecting a union among them. The government was alarmed by the combination. Elgin's private secretary apprehended that 'if Hindus and Muslims were forced into active opposition (against the plague measures), the combination between them might be perpetuated and might assume a dangerous form'. Quoted in Ray, op. cit., p. 118.

[101] For example, *Riaz al-Akhbaar* (Gorakhpur), 8 January 1894; *Nagari Nirad* (Hindi weekly: Mirzapur), 8 February 1894; *Mehr-i Nimroz* (Urdu weekly: Bijnor), 7 February 1894, and *Hindustani* (Lucknow), 19 December 1894. For references to local reconciliation committees and to public meetings on Hindu-Muslim amity in UP and Punjab, see *Hindustani*, 8 June 1898, *Oudh Punch*, 9 June 1898; *Akhbaar-i Alam* (Meerut), 13 June 1898, *Riaz al-Akhbaar*, 1 November 1898, *Anis-i Hind* (Meerut), 2 November 1898, SNNR, UP.

[102] *PSC*, NWP & O, Evidence, p. 158.

[103] See Mushirul Hasan, 'Sectarianism in Indian Islam: The Shia-Sunni Divide in the United Provinces', op. cit; Cole, op. cit.

[104] Henry Cotton, *India and Home Memoirs* (London, 1911), p. 317; Blunt, *India Under Ripon*, p. 94.

Chapter Three

In Search of an Alternative

Nineteenth century orientalists sensitized western opinion to the idea of political religion, to a structure in which religion and politics combine to make Islam an aggressive, hostile and explosive force. Official opinion in India was no different. Moulded by the experience of the Faraizi movement, the 'Wahabi conspiracy' and the large Muslim presence among the 1857 'mutineers', the government began to see Muslims as a potential threat, a subversive element and a conservative force. The familiar clamour in the aftermath of the 1857 revolt was to humble them, to reduce them to nothingness and to destroy their religious and cultural symbols.

The spectre of a 'Muslim uprising' continued to haunt a section in officialdom, though less so in the 1870s when distrust of and hostility towards the Muslims was much less pronounced. Mayo's note of 26 June 1871 would have been inconceivable a generation earlier. Then, W.W. Hunter's celebrated book helped to dispel many of the impressions which had dominated official thinking. 'I cannot see any sign of disaffection (unusual) or of any belief in a struggle at hand', he wrote to contradict fears of a Muslim conspiracy. He sought sympathy and understanding for the rising generation of Muslims which would be tempered with the 'sober and genial knowledge of the West'.[1] W.S. Blunt, who toured India in the winter of 1883–84, pleaded vigorously for the advancement of Muslim education, their encouragement in commercial and industrial pursuits and protection of their religious interests outside India. 'The neglect of these things', warned Blunt, 'will secure beyond redemption their disloyalty'.[2] John Strachey played the same tune. He believed that

[1] Hunter, *Indian Mussalmans,* p. 123.
[2] Blunt, *India Under Ripon,* p. 296.

the fears that are sometimes expressed that we may see in India a general outburst of Mohammedan fanaticism, and a simultaneous rising of millions of Mohammedans against our power, seem to me....not only groundless but absurd.... The better classes of Mohammadans are already a source to us of strength and not of weakness, and a continuously wise policy might, I believe, make them strong and important supporters of our power.[3]

Mayo, Dufferin and Ripon recognized the importance of winning the confidence of the Muslims, arguing that unless conciliated they would remain the most dangerous class in the raj.

One man who chose to ignore such warnings was Anthony MacDonnell, who assumed charge as UP's lieutenant-governor in 1894. He, more than any other civil servant in UP, was uneasy with the Muslims, their interest in pan-Islamism, their position in government service and the professions,[4] and their inclination to take positions against the government. He was indifferent to the cause of Urdu, hostile to the Nadwat al-ulama which he regarded as 'an association of narrow-minded bigoted and conservative Mussalmans' and unsympathetic to the Muslim point of view over the cow-protection movement in north India. 'Taking his administration in general', wrote the ***Al-Bashir,*** an otherwise pro-government newspaper from Etawah, 'Sir Anthony MacDonnell has sowed the seeds of discord between the Hindus and Muslims...and caused general unrest and distrust in the province'.[5]

MacDonnell assumed that all Muslims were getting organized to overthrow British rule, and proceeded to clip their wings through a series of administrative and bureaucratic measures. He first fixed a communal quota for Muslims in public service: in other words, there were to be three Muslims to every five Hindus. He then placed the Devanagri script on an equal footing with Urdu, provided for its optional use in court documents and made the knowledge of both forms of writing necessary for

[3] John Strachey, *India* (London, 1888), p. 225.

[4] An instance of his hostility was when the list of candidates for tahsildarship and deputy-collectorship was rejected on the ground that the number of Muslims was too large. *Al-Bashir*, 25 December 1901, SNNR, UP.

[5] Ibid., 28 November 1901

ministerial appointments. These decisions engendered widespread disaffection amongst Muslims, undermined the basis of the Anglo-Muslim alliance, and stimulated, much to everybody's surprise, political radicalism. There were strong objections to the course adopted by MacDonnell—to the 'undoing of all that the late Syed Ahmad did...in the way of removing doubts from the minds of the authorities regarding the loyalty of Mussalmans'.[6] Altaf Husain Hali, Syed Ahmad's close friend and associate, bemoaned:

Woh din gaye ke nazaan thi qaum saltanat par
Ab qaum ko khuda ka ya apna aasraa hai

> Gone are the days when Muslims were proud of the Empire
> Now, they rely on themselves and their hopes rest with God.

Resentment centred around the April 1900 Resolution, which threatened Muslims, because unlike Hindus, they did not learn the Devanagri script in their normal course of education. Consequently, they saw the grim prospect of losing their privileged position in public service and in the liberal professions.[7] They argued in vain that material interests alone did not concern them, but that they were concerned for the effect it would have on the composite cultural ethos of the Indo-Gangetic plain. Urdu was not spoken only by Muslims; the Kayasths and the Kashmir Pandits were equally fluent in the language. It was the language of the *qasbati* elites, the language of refinement and culture, a symbol of Hindu-Muslim integration which MacDonnell was striving to destroy. Even in cases where the language of both Hindus and Muslims was entered as Urdu in the census schedule, as in Marehra in Etah district, the entries were altered at the instance of the district magistrate.[8] The language of all Hindus was shown to be Hindi and that of Muslims to be Urdu. The *Al-Bashir* regretted that this was so, for there was no real distinction between Urdu and Hindi: they were names of

[6] Maulvi Mushtaq Husain and Mohsinul Mulk in *Aligarh Institute Gazette*, 22 August and 17 October 1901.

[7] *Liberal* (Azamgarh), 10 April 1900; *Naiyar-i Azam*, 19 January 1901, SNNR, UP.

[8] *Al-Bushir*, 11 March 1901; *Shararah* (Moradabad), 21 January 1901, ibid.

one and the same language, there being slight dialectic differences between the language spoken in villages and that spoken in towns.[9] In the *mushairas* that were held in Lahore until the early decades of the twentieth century, Hindus and Muslims participated and there was no trace of the Hindi-Urdu controversy that developed in Punjab soon thereafter.[10]

The agitation against the Nagri resolution started with public meetings all over UP and the setting up of Urdu Defence Associations in Aligarh, Gorakhpur, Lucknow and Allahabad. Support from the associations came from all quarters—from Mohsinul Mulk who reorganized the Urdu Defence Association at Aligarh; from Syed Raza Ali who was present at the mammoth public gathering at Lucknow in August 1900; from Hamid Ali Khan, a Congress supporter and the moving spirit behind the Lucknow meeting; and from lawyers, pleaders and barristers in Allahabad, Moradabad, Aligarh and Gorakhpur.[11]

The protest movement, masterminded by Mohsinul Mulk, started off with great vigour but petered out within no time as MacDonnell acted tough and threatened to withdraw government support from the Aligarh college. Mohsinul Mulk was tamed. Lutf Ali Khan, president of the Urdu Defence Association, could not withstand the official wrath.[12] He, along with seven other rais of Aligarh district, ensured the decline of the Urdu movement in their area. By 1901, the lieutenant-governor had isolated the tall poppies from the Urdu agitation only to leave them discredited in the eyes of their followers. The *Azad* commented:

[9] *Al-Bashir*, 21 January 1901, SNNR, UP.

[10] Mohammad Abdullah Qureshi, 'Lahore ke mushaire aur Iqbal', *Iqbal*, October 1955, vol. 4, 2, pp. 72–77.

[11] *Rohilkhand Gazette* (Bareilly), 1 May 1900; *Azad*, 8 May 1900; *Mufid-i Aam* (Agra), 20 May 1900; *Riazul Akhbaar*, 20 May 1900; *Oudh Akhbaar*, 23 May 1900; *Jaam-i Jamshed* (Moradabad), 27 May 1900. Report of a meeting of barristers and *ulama* at Gorakhpur to found an Urdu Defence Association is mentioned in *Riazul Akhbaar*, 16 August 1900, SNNR, UP. An account of the agitation is in Syed Raza Ali, *Aamal Naama* (Delhi, 1943), pp. 88–89.

[12] *Oudh Akhbaar*, 17 September and *Riazul Akhbaar*, 24 September 1901, SNNR, UP; Rais Ahmad Jafri, *Kaarawaan-i Gumgushta* (Karachi, 1971).

By his abrupt secession from the Urdu Defence Association [Mohsinul Mulk] has shown himself to be a great coward and utterly unfit to be a leader. It was sheer cunningness, hypocrisy and deceitfulness on his part to decoy a people into a trap, and then quickly withdraw from it.[13]

The Aligarh leaders, brought up in an atmosphere of official 'billying and cooing' were at a loss as soon as they found themselves deprived of official support. 'They flinched, they faltered, and they fell, and great indeed has been their fall'.[14]

MacDonnell used the big stick to quieten senior Aligarh leaders and the first game of the match was easily won. But the next round with a group of radical Muslims turned out to be tough. Vociferous in their criticizm of government, they exposed the inadequacy of mendicant tactics[15] and expressed preference for a political forum that would be representative in its composition and democratic in its functioning.[16] The editor of *Al-Bashir* observed that the policies of the lieutenant-governor, more than anything else, led to persistent demands for an organized political association.[17] Its absence, commented the *Asr-i Jadeed,* edited by a former Aligarh graduate, was why Muslim interests were being trampled underfoot.[18]

These were muted expressions of an aggrieved group. A more strident demand—one that was destined to alter the tenor and

[13] *Azad,* 22 October 1901, SNNR, UP.

[14] By a Hindu Nationalist, 'Sir Syed as a Factor in Indian Progress', *Kayastha Samachar,* December 1902, vol. 6, 6, p. 516.

[15] *Riazul Akhbaar,* 24 September and *Oudh Akhbaar,* 17 September 1900, SNNR, UP.

[16] In October 1901, a meeting held at the home of Hamid Ali Khan resolved to launch a political organization. Lucknow and not Aligarh was chosen as the headquarter so that the college officials were not suspected of encouraging and spreading political agitation. *Hindustan,* 30 October, *Al-Bashir,* 29 October, and *Advocate,* 31 October 1901, ibid.

[17] *Al-Bashir,* 12 August 1903, ibid., Jafri, *Kaarawaan-i Gumgushta,* p. 155.

[18] *Asr-i Jadeed,* May 1903. In its issue of February 1903, the paper welcomed the initiative taken by the Lucknow meeting and reiterated its plea for an organization that would defend the political interests of Muslims. It wanted the rais and zamindars to be kept at a distance; otherwise, the new body would meet 'the same fate as the Urdu Defence Association and its President No. 1'.

content of 'Muslim politics' over the next two decades—was to make common cause with the Congress.[19] What was, after all, the difference between the 'interests' of the Muslims and the demands of the Congress? None, stated a 'Muslim Political Observer', in his contribution to the *Kayastha Samachar.* He went on to add:

> Ahmad and Abdullah have received the same education and their minds have been fed on the same strong pabulum of English literature and English History and Political Philosophy as those of Banerjea's and Bose's. Both are governed by the same laws and are suffering from the same legal and political disabilities.[20]

Quite true. The *Asr-i Jadeed* believed that it was desirable for Muslims to co-operate with the Congress on issues of common concern—the reduction of salt duty, the raising of the minimum limit of taxable income and greater employment of educated Indians in the commissioned ranks of the army.[21] Shaikh Abdullah, a vakil at Aligarh, argued that it was time for Muslims to strike out the word silence [*sukuut*] in their dictionary. He maintained that 'to refrain from public agitation simply because the Congress has adopted it, is as absurd as not to use boots for no better reason than that they are used by Christians'.[22] After all, the reasons which had led Syed Ahmad to keep his co-religionists away from the Congress did not hold good anymore.[23] In fact, his own son, the mercurial Syed Mahmood, considered presiding over the Congress session and expressed

[19] Prominent amongst those who advocated this position were: Ghulam-us-Saqlain, Hasrat and Ahmad Hasan Shaukat, editors of *Asr-i Jadeed, Urdu-i Moalla* and *Shahna-i Hind,* published from Meerut. Jamal Ahmad, 'Mussalman aur Politics', *Asr-i Jadeed,* May 1903; *Shahna-i Hind,* 24 June, 1 July 1899 and 1 November 1901; Haider Ali Qureshi, 'Muhammadans and Politics', *Hindustan Review* and *Kayastha Samachar,* October 1904, vol. 10, 4, p. 398.

[20] By a Muslim: A Political Observer, 'The Indian Muhammadans and the National Congress', *Kayastha Samachar,* November 1902, vol. 6, 5, p. 398. Similar views were expressed in *Tufrih* (Lucknow), 14 January, and *Israar-ul Alam* (Allahabad), 21 February 1907, SNNR, UP

[21] *Asr-i Jadeed,* March 1903.

[22] *Al-Bashir,* 27 June 1903, SNNR, UP.

[23] *Kayastha Samachar,* op. cit., p. 397.

sympathy for the organization.[24] In 1903, Badruddin Tyabji chaired the Muslim Educational Conference with Nawab Syed Mohamed as chairman of the reception committee. This would have been unthinkable a few years ago, for the conference had served as a platform for giving vent to anti-Congress sentiments. Tyabji was present on the occasion, because the Conference was no longer hostile to the Congress; otherwise, he would have stayed away from any forum which 'had the slightest trace of being hostile or antagonistic to the Congress'.

These were ominous pro-Congress tendencies. Senior Aligarh leaders moved quickly to counter them. Haji Musa Khan, a rais of Datauli in Aligarh district, floated the idea of a UP-based organization which would preserve Syed Ahmad's political legacy.[25] Mohsinul Mulk mooted the revival of the MAO College Defence Association,[26] but he had lost face after the collapse of the Urdu Defence Association.[27] He approached Archbold, Principal of the Aligarh college, with the idea of presenting a memorial to the viceroy.[28] The idea found favour and, on 1 October 1906, thirty-five Muslims, mainly from UP, submitted their first major political statement to the viceroy. Minto's response, its tone, as well as the promises it carried, was clearly partial to the aspirations of the memorialists.

Although Mohsinul Mulk and his club wrested the initiative from the 'young gentlemen' in organizing the Simla deputation and in founding the Muslim League at Dacca in December 1906, their glory was short-lived. They were under attack in Aligarh college, where the radical mood of some students led to a strike in February 1907.[29] A year later, news from the campus attracted

[24] S.C. Banerji, 'Syed Mahmood: Recollections and Reflections', ibid., May 1903, vol. 7, 5, p. 442.

[25] *Jami-ul-ulum,* 14 August 1900, SNNR, UP.

[26] *Aligarh Institute Gazette,* 17 October 1903.

[27] *Uruuj* (Bijnor) 14 July and *Oudh Akhbaar,* 10 December 1903; *Riazul Akhbaar,* 1 February 1905, SNNR, UP.

[28] Mohsinul Mulk to Archbold, 4 August 1906, quoted in Raza Wasti, *Lord Minto and the Indian Nationalist Movement 1905–1910* (Oxford, 1964), p. 63; Robinson, *Separatism,* pp. 143–46.

[29] Trouble was sparked off by an incident at the exhibition ground which led to the rustication of Raja Ghulam Husain. Students at the Aligarh

public notice once again. An article on 'The Educational Policy of the English in Egypt', published in Hasrat Mohani's *Urdu-i Moalla,* caused a furore. The government sentenced the editor to two years' of imprisonment while the college authorities expelled the author, a graduate student. In the ensuing controversy, which was symptomatic of the divide between the Indian and the European staff, Viqarul Mulk defended the right of the student to express his views. How could he not 'when the very atmosphere of the country seems to be surcharged with politics'. Under the circumstances, he added, it would be futile to try to keep students beyond the pale of contagion'.[30] Around the same time, a district official had prophesied that

> Aligarh is destined to be the focus of all Muhammadan intelligence and activity in India. Begun as a defensive move, it is already acquiring an offensive character.... It has already lost its reliance on Englishmen and its trust in English methods and ideals. The danger I foresee is that if it is indulged and uncontrolled it will develop rapidly on undecidedly anti-English lines.[31]

college were angered by the decision of the authorities. They chose to go on strike, the first in the history of the college. Contemporaries commented that their action was in reaction to their long-standing grouse on several issues: the predominance of the European staff on the Board of Trustees and the insensitive attitude of Archbold, the Principal, towards their problems. Some were of the opinion that Gokhale's visit to Aligarh in February 1907 stimulated political action on the campus. Newspaper articles demanded that the rustication orders be rescinded and the demands of the students considered sympathetically, 'for the nation has no love for the college building, the secretary or the Principal, but it has certainly love for students who are the ornaments not only of the college but of the nation as well'. *Israar-i Alam* (Moradabad), 7 March 1907. For reactions to and analysis of the causes of Ghulam Husain's expulsion see *Naiyar-i Azam,* 26 February 1907, *Nizam-ul-Mulk,* 28 February 1907, *Indian People,* (Allahabad), 7 March, *Shahna-i Hind,* 8 March 1907, SNNR, UP. Choudhry Khaliquzzaman, *Pathway to Pakistan* (Lahore, 1961 edn.), p. 17.

[30] *Aligarh Institute Gazette*, 29 July 1908. Viqarul Mulk's article was welcomed by, among others, the *Riazul Akhbaar*, 4 August 1908, SNNR, UP.

[31] Quoted in Irene A. Gilbert, 'Autonomy and Consensus under the Raj: Presidency (Calcutta); Muir (Allahabad); M.A.O. (Aligarh)', S.H.

The prophecy of William Marris came true a few years later when an extraordinary convergence of forces generated strong anti-government feelings and heightened nationalist consciousness.[32] There was, for example, the annulment of Bengal's partition, a decision that hurt Muslims of East Bengal most. 'Agitate and you will get what you want; remain calm and you will have your heads chopped. This is the moral we are given', observed a correspondent in the *Mussalman,* a Calcutta paper with nationalist commitments.[33] Then, the Turko-Italian War caused deep anguish, because the view gained credence that Britain acquiesced in the Italian attack on Tripoli and concluded treaties with Russia and France to partition the Ottoman Empire. 'There is a great agitation in Muslim circles', reported the viceroy, 'over the war in the Balkans, and a general feeling that the Christians are combining to thrust the Muslims out of Europe'.[34] In December 1912, Mukhtar Ahmad Ansari, an Edinburgh-trained surgeon, headed a medical mission to Constantinople.[35] In May 1913, the Anjuman-i Khuddam-i Kaaba came into being in Lucknow. Its main architect was Maulvi Abdul Bari, a renowned *alim* of Firangi Mahal. His main associates in this enterprise were Shaukat Ali, an Aligarh graduate who had quit his government post in the opium department to lend a helping hand to his younger brother, Mohamed Ali; and Mushir Husain Kidwai, a taluqdar from Gadia in Barabanki district and author of *Islam and Socialism,* a book which sought to prove that Islam was the first religion to establish a state on the principles of socialism and communism.

Both the medical mission and the Anjuman-i Khuddam-i Kaaba symbolized the growing Muslim anxiety over the future of

---

Rudolph & L.I. Rudolph (eds.), *Education and Politics in India* (Delhi, 1972), pp. 198–99.

[32] See, for example, the impressions of E.M. Forster, quoted in Mushirul Hasan, *A Nationalist Conscience: M.A. Ansari, the Congress and the Raj* (Delhi, 1987), p. 36.

[33] *Mussalman,* 12 January 1912.

[34] Hardinge to Chirol, 22 October 1912. For Bengal and Punjab, see Carmichael to Hardinge, 6 September 1914, and O'Dwyer to Hardinge 11 August 1913, Hardinge Papers (84/88), IOLR.

[35] Hasan, *A Nationalist Conscience,* pp. 42–45.

Turkey and the sanctity of the Holy Places. Nobody expressed the anguish more vividly than Shibli Nomani, a distinguished scholar of Islamic history and literature and founder of the prestigious Nadwat al-ulama. In a poem that was widely read and recited at poetry sessions [*mushairas*], Shibli, probably inspired by Hali's *Mussaddas,* lamented:

When decline has set in over political power, the
name and banner will stand—how long?
The smoke from the burnt candle of a vanished
assembly will rise—how long?
Gone is Morocco, gone is Persia. We have now to see
this helpless 'sick man of Turkey' will live—how long?
This tide of woe which is advancing from the Balkans,
the sighs of the oppressed will stem—how long?
Shibli: should you long to migrate, where can you go now?
Syria or Najd or Cyrene are sanctuaries—how long?

Likewise, the poems of Iqbal did the rounds. According to Mohamed Ali, who wrote his incomplete autobiographical account in mid-summer 1923, 'the modest, shy and retiring barrister of the Punjab' was the poet of Islam's reawakening in India and was a household word throughout the Urdu-speaking world. 'We loved Iqbal the Revolutionary', recorded Khaliquzzaman, 'calling upon his people to rise to action, the Iqbal who introduced Muslim heroes in their true glory, the Iqbal who by his own new interpretation of Quranic injunctions put life into what had been stale by philosophical ponderings'.[36] And Salim Ali, the celebrated ornithologist, recalled how Shuaib Qureshi entertained him with the 'moving, patriotic and pro Islamic verses' of Iqbal. 'One of his recitations, the beauty and sonorousness of which still rings in my ears, is the touching *shikwa* of the vicissitudes of the island of Sicily, once an important Muslim stronghold in Europe'.[37]

The belligerence of the European powers, combined with the

[36] Khaliquzzaman *Pathway to Pakistan,* p. 38; Mohamed Ali, *My Life A Fragment: An Autobiographical Sketch,* ed. Afzal Iqbal (Lahore, 1944). Also, see Abu Salman Shahjahanpuri, *Allama Iqbal aur Maulana Mohamed Ali* (Karachi, 1984).

[37] Salim Ali, *The Fall of a Sparrow* (Delhi, 1985), p. 50.

rejection of the Aligarh university scheme and the inept handling of the Kanpur mosque affair, caused uneasiness and hostility towards the government. In the words of Mohamed Ali, the key figure in organizing the protest movement on these issues, 'the Mussalmans felt themselves to be betrayed both in India and abroad'.[38] However, they were unable to give organizational expression to their resentment. The Muslim League, dominated by men who were wary of agitational methods, was a tame affair. So, when a group of lawyers, journalists and *ulama* stepped into the political space created by reckless government policies and the moderate stance of the Muslim League, there was much relief at the prospect of getting heard. Hopes were aroused to a feverish pitch as energetic and enthusiastic young leaders, mostly educated at Aligarh, went around the country imbued with a sense of mission and commitment.

People turned to the Oxford-educated Mohamed Ali, 'the centre and inspiration of the pan-Islamic movement'.[39] What he wrote was avidly read; what he spoke was listened to with rapt attention. 'Meeting the Ali Brothers was like drinking wine; it made us fresh and lively'.[40] In Punjab, Zafar Ali Khan created quite a stir. As soon as copies of *Zamindar* were brought into the bazaar, large crowds of people surrounded the news-shops and bought copies: its circulation rose from 5,000 to over 25,000 copies in less than a month.[41] Like some of his contemporaries at

[38] Mohamed Ali, *My life,* p. 35. Some years later, he wrote to the viceroy, Chelmsford:

> Muslim loyalty and support has so often been assured to government in our generation, and even Muslim contentment was so often unduly taken for granted, that other communities had with some justice made our attitude towards government almost a matter of reproach. It was strange for all this loyalty and support that, without any effective protest...blow after blow was aimed at the temporal power of Islam.

To Chelmsford, 24 April 1919, Mushirul Hasan (ed.), *Mohamed Ali in Indian Politics: Select Writings* (Delhi, 1983), vol. 2, p. 226.

[39] Mushirul Hasan, *Mohamed Ali: Ideology and Politics* (Delhi, 1981), and *A Nationalist Conscience*, pp. 37-40, for the role of Mohamed Ali in the early phase of the pan-Islamic agitation.

[40] Khaliquzzaman, *Pathway to Pakistan*, p. 33.

[41] FR (Punjab), 28 January 1915, Home Poll. A. F.No. 173, May 1916,

Aligarh, Zafar Ali Khan was moved by Shibli's poems on the evils inflicted upon Islam and inspired by his articles published in the *Muslim Gazette* in support of the Congress.[42] He was also influenced by the editor of *Al-Hilal*, Abul Kalam Azad, who denounced British imperialism in no uncertain terms and advocated communal unity and co-operation. It is no exaggeration to assert that never before did such talented men agree on so many issues of common concern. And never before did so few exercise so great an influence on so many in their community.

The second rank leadership was no less impressive. There was, for example, the fiery journalist-poet Hasrat Mohani, editor of *Urdu-i Moalla,* who was imprisoned as early as 1908 for an article on British education policy in Egypt.[43] No less important was a group of lawyers—Khaliquzzaman, Shuaib

---

NAI. Harcourt Butler, *India Insistent* (London, 1931), p. 27. Zafar Ali Khan studied at Aligarh before joining the Hyderabad Civil Service. In 1912, he visited Constantinople to present to the Grand Vizièr a part of the money raised from the sale of Turkish bond. He was in Turkey again the next year where he furthered a proposal to provide a colony in Anatolia for Muslim refugees. In January, the Punjab government forfeited the security of his paper for publishing an article entitled 'Come Over Macedonia and Help Us'. For biographical information, see Shorish Kashmiri, 'Zafar Ali Khan', *Nuqqush* [*Shakhsiaat* Number], January 1955, p. 597. In English, the only perceptive account of Zafar Ali's role is in Ravinder Kumar, *Essays in the Social History of Modern India* (Delhi, 1983), pp. 182–85. The chapter is a reprint of his contribution in *Essays on Gandhian Politics: The Rowlatt Satyagraha of 1919* (Oxford, 1971).

[42] Shibli's articles were first published in *Muslim Gazette* before being printed in volume eight of *Maqalaat-i Shibli* (Azamgarh, 1938). The editor of this Lucknow paper was Wahiduddin Salim. He had worked as Syed Ahmad's literary assistant before founding the *Maarif.* He edited the *Aligarh Institute Gazette* from April 1907 to June 1909 and the *Muslim Gazette* until August 1913. He resigned from the *Muslim Gazette* because of his criticizm of government policies and its clumsy handling of the Kanpur mosque affair. Manzar Abbas Naqvi, *Wahiduddin Salim: Hayaat aur Adabi Khidmaat* (Aligarh, 1969).

[43] Known as the *Rais al-Ahrar,* Hasrat Mohani obtained his B.A. degree from the Aligarh college in 1903. His family was attached to Shaikh Abdur Razzak of Firangi Mahal. He was himself a *murid* of Abdul Wahhab and received *Khilafat* from Maulana Abdul Bari. He was a man with varied interests and concerns. He edited the *Urdu-i Moalla* from July 1903 to

Qureshi and Syed Mahmud—all graduates of Aligarh and devoted to Mohamed Ali and Ansari. Their followers included Raja Ghulam Husain, editor of the *New Era* from Lucknow; Sajjad Husain, editor of *Oudh Punch;* writers like Sajjad Haider Yaldaram, Abdur Rahman Bijnori and Abdul Majid Daryabadi. And, of course, there was Wilayat Ali, born in 1887 in Masauli in Barabanki district. He belonged to a movement with serious intents, but while his friends and contemporaries held forth from agitational platforms or indulged in denunciatory political writings in the press, Wilayat Ali laughed at British rule and made fun of it. Writing humorous and satirical sketches under his pen name—Bambooque—this young Aligarh graduate became the centre of a lively group of wits, wags and radical intellectuals.[44]

The Bambooque house lived from one political excitement to the other. He was so thrilled by the Young Turk Revolution that he gave his young sons and nephews the names of Turkish

June 1913 [except from May 1908 to September 1909 when he was interned by the government], plunged into the swadeshi movement with a high sense of duty and identified himself with Tilak and the 'extremist' wing of the Congress. He also had considerable poetic talent and is ranked among the front rank Urdu poets. He possessed boundless energy which he used to promote the cause of swaraj; in fact, he was the first to demand complete independence in 1921 and parted with Motilal Nehru over the issue of Dominion Status.

In 1917, he gave poetic expression to his passions in a verse:

How can I instil in others a passion like my own?
I've grown weary of my fellow-travellers' lack of spirit

After 1924, however, the flames of Hasrat's poetry began to dim, though his attachment to various causes was not affected. The only biographical study of Hasrat in English is by K.H. Qadiri, *Hasrat Mohani* (Delhi, 1985). The translation of the above verse is from Saleem Ahmad, 'The Ghazal: A Muffler, and India', *Annual of Urdu Studies,* vol. 2, 1982.

[44] In the gallery of carricatures is the England-returned barrister desperately aping the Sahibs manners and speech and pretending to have forgotten his native tongue during his brief stay in England. There are, then, the specimens of the Babu culture in India from the patwari to the deputy-collector; comic both in their servility to their white superiors and their arrogance towards the common people.

generals. During the Balkan War he would recite Iqbal's *Shikwah* and *Jawaab-i Shikwah,* with tears dripping from his face. During World War I, the Bambooque circle watched the ebb and flow of German fortunes with intense anxiety, elated by German victories and depressed by German setbacks. The circle was small and consisted of young men who combined feudal graces with modern education.[45] They would meet in Masauli, eighteen kilometres from Lucknow, indulge in endless political arguments, draw up resolutions or memoranda for forthcoming Congress and Muslim League meetings, plot their future political course, and then relax in easy chairs, pulling leisurely at long hubble bubbles, filling the air with the smoke of scented tobacco, bandying Urdu or Persian verses and reciting or reading the compositions in verse or prose. Behind them hovered a short, plump, shy boy, doing the chores of the host, or running errands between the *zenana* and the men's part of the *haveli.* Little did the company suspect that he was to be their fellow traveller on the road to India's freedom and plod on to the journey's end even when some of them were to fall by the wayside or stray from the path. He was Rafi Ahmad Kidwai.

The young men of Bambooque's generation had many heroes. Their political guru was Mohamed Ali, though Azad did much to stimulate their radical consciousness. They also derived inspiration from Akbar Allahabadi, Hali and Iqbal. They admired Akbar's outspokenness in condemning western imperialism, his criticizm of government machinations in keeping Hindus and Muslims apart and his indignation at the exploitation of India's material resources.[46] They also turned to the writings of Hali, the poet-writer from Panipat, who had the distinction of being close to two outstanding intellectuals in the second-half of the nineteenth century—Syed Ahmad and Asadullah Khan Ghalib. One of Hali's earliest poems was on nationalism and pat-

[45] It included Khaliquzzaman, Shuaib Qureshi, Raja Ghulam Husain, Sajjad Husain and M.A. Ansari who was drawn to the circle through his cousin Aziz Ansari, a member of the medical mission to Turkey.

[46] See Muhammad Sadiq, 'Understanding Akbar Allahabadi', *Iqbal,* January 1968, vol. 16, 3, p. 42; Ralph Russell and Khurshidul Islam, 'The Satirical Verses of Akbar Illahabadi'.

riotism—themes that were echoed at the fourth session of the Muslim Educational Conference held at Aligarh in 1899. Such was his commitment to these causes that he told Abdul Halim Sharar in 1904 that the spread of education would make people recognize the value of national unity and 'national integration'.[47]

Nobody expressed such ideas with greater passion, eloquence and coherence than Iqbal. He was therefore the favourite poet in his days. His poems *Tarana-i Hindi* (India's Anthem), *Naya Shiwala* (The New Temple), and *Tasvir-i Dar* (Picture of Grief) swayed the imagination of young Indian Muslims. His message was simple. He stood for the repudiation of differences based on religion. He saw God 'in each speck of my country's poor dust' and wanted to build a new altar where the votaries of motherland would gather together and sing songs of love. His mission was summed up in the verse:

Let us remove once again the curtain of otherness;
bring together those divided (by religion) and wipe out
the stamp of estrangement.

Such ideas, backed by leading intellectuals and publicists, altered the course of political currents among Muslims. As the premier Muslim organization, the Muslim League was the first to feel the pinch. The influx of radical ideas overwhelmed the conservative diehards, who were lampooned in the *Oudh Punch*, *New Era*, *Comrade* and *Maloomaat*. Their world turned topsy-turvy as they helplessly witnessed the passing of an era and the decline of their prestige and authority. Everywhere, complained Haji Ishaq Khan, the 'moderate men' had lost ground with the public and were afraid of being ridiculed.[48] The Nawab of Rampur, finding the political climate in Aligarh too oppressive, resigned from the visitorship.[49] Aligarh was an inhospitable place for the protagonists of Syed Ahmad's political message of subservience to the raj. The Aga Khan, whose support for the reunification of Bengal made him a target of bitter attack,

[47] Shaikh Mohammad Ismail (ed.), *Makatib-i Hali* (Karachi, 1950), p. 54.

[48] To Meston, 21 August and 20 November 1913, Meston Papers, F.No. 136 (6), IOLR.

[49] To Ishaq Khan, 15 November 1913, ibid. (4).

suddenly bolted and relinquished the Muslim League presidential chair which he had occupied since its inception.[50] 'The time has come', wrote the Khoja leader, 'when the community must wake up and reorganize the League on a popular basis....'[51]

Change in leadership led to changes in policies. The League, having lived up to the traditions of Syed Ahmad and Nawab Salimullah, underwent a gradual transformation so as to reflect the new mood of the bulk of its supporters. The headquarter was moved from Aligarh, a decision of considerable symbolic significance. The constitution was amended at the instance of, among others, Mohammad Ali Jinnah. The League began to meet in the same city as the Congress and affirmed its goal of self-government year after year. The Congress was being increasingly seen as a national body, which was motivated to advance the interest of the country and was willing, as was evident during the debate over the Punjab Alienation Act, to accommodate sectional claims. The success in organizing the Swadeshi movement lent Congress the legitimacy it had lacked for so many years and brought home its potential as an instrument for introducing vital changes in Indian polity. Hali shared this thought.[52] So did Iqbal, already famous for his patriotic poems. In May 1906, he observed:

> If this movement [swadeshi] helps to foster unity of purpose among Muslims and Hindus and strengthens this feeling [of unity] gradually, then nothing else is needed. The fate of India will definitely change for the better and the name of my country would be written in gold letters among the countries of the world.[53]

Some years later, the Bihar lawyer, Mazharul Haq declared:

[50] The Governor of Bombay observed: 'I imagine that the Aga Khan is dead as a leader, and from what he told me I think he realizes that his power is gone. Anyhow he suddenly bolted, some weeks before he originally intended'. Sydenham to Hardinge, 18 March 1913, Hardinge Papers (85).

[51] To Wazir Hasan, 3 November 1913, Crewe Papers, I/14 (2), Cambridge University Library; To Harcourt Butler, 3 March 1913, Butler Papers, F. No. 116 (71), IOLR.

[52] *Maqalaat-i Hali* (Delhi, 1934), vol. 1, p. 308.

[53] *Zamaanah* (Kanpur), May 1906.

...there were no political questions in which the interests of both communities were not equally involved, or with regard to which they differed. As far as he himself was concerned, he would much rather be represented on the council by his friend Gokhale than by anyone else. Our interests are practically identical.[54]

Mazharul Haq was not speaking out of turn. He was stating what had become an article of faith with so many educated Muslims of his generation.[55] This was testified to by an official who was horrified to learn that most western-educated Muslims he had met in north India were in favour of combining with the 'Hindu Congress party'. The viceroy, too, grudgingly conceded that he could, alas, not count on the loyalty of Muslims, because they were inclined to make common cause with any other faction in order to express their antipathy to the government.[56] 'In mutual help and co-operation', observed Khuda Bukhsh, the well-known writer and philanthropist, 'lies our hope, in division and dissension our feebleness and death'.

II

The men who plotted this course for their community were drawn from a mixed background. They included the *ulama*, especially those based at Deoband: prominent amongst them were the Shaikh al-Hind Maulana Mahmud Hasan and his disciple, Ubaid-Allah Sindhi, two of the principal figures involved in the 'Silk Letter Conspiracy'. They played a singularly important role in heightening anti-colonial consciousness among their followers and travelled to distant lands to stir up an agitation against British rule.[57] Under their influence, institutions like the Dar

[54] *Bombay Chronicle*, 20 June 1914. His views were also quoted in *Tribune*, 21 January 1911 and *Bengalee*, 27 December 1912.

[55] WRDCI, 4 July 1912, Home Poll. B, August 1912, NAI. To Crewe, 14 August 1913, Hardinge Papers (86).

[56] *Essays on Indian and Islamic* (London, 1911), p. 267.

[57] For official versions, see P.C. Bamford, *Histories of the Non-Co-operation and Khilafat Movements* (Delhi, 1975: reprint), and the report by B. Lindsay and A. Rauf, 11 December 1918, in Hasan (ed.), *Mohamed Ali in Indian Politics*, vol. 2. Accounts sympathetic to the *mujahidin* are by: H.A. Madani, *Naqsh-i Hayaat: Khudnawisht Sawaanih* (Karachi, 1979).

al-ulum, Firangi Mahal and the Nadwat al-ulama were also politicized. Abdul Bari, once engaged only in scholarly pursuits, became the rallying point of the pan-Islamic upsurge. The Anjuman-i Khuddam-i Kaaba was his brainchild and Ansari's medical mission had his backing. In fact, many of those involved in these enterprises—the Ali Brothers, Ansari and Hasrat Mohani—were his *murids*. The influence of these men also spread to Nadwat al-ulama in Lucknow, where students went on strike in March 1914 to protest against government policies which culminated in the tragedy at Macchli Bazaar in Kanpur,[58] and later to the Dar al-Mussannifin, an institution founded in 1914 by Shibli. The Commissioner of the Gorakhpur division reported 'that the Shibli Academy is no longer what its founder intended it to be, but has become 'an extremist political institution' under the leadership of Syed Sulaiman Nadwi, Shibli's disciple and biographer.[59]

The western-educated Muslims were much more strident in criticizing government policies and much more vocal in espousing the Congress cause. They were not a monolithic group, nor did they always act in unison. Yet they shared a vision and a commitment to the welfare of all their countrymen without being indifferent to the affairs of their co-religionists. This was because of their training, their social and educational background: most belonged to petty landed families or to the service class and possessed the means and the opportunity to study in Indian or British colleges and universities. Here they came into contact with students from other communities who belonged essentially to the same economic background. Interaction at this stage and level helped to narrow down religious and cultural differences and remove mutual prejudices. Wazir Hasan, having studied in the cosmopolitan ethos of the Muir Central College in

and Jafri, *Kaarawaan-i Gumgushta,* pp. 498–536. For a recent analysis, see K.H. Ansari, 'Pan-Islam and the Making of the Early Indian Muslim Socialists', *MAS*, 1986, vol. 20, 3, pp. 509–537.

[58] Note by P. Biggane, 30 October 1914, General Administration Department (GAD), F.No. 79, 1914, UP State Archives, Lucknow (UPSA).

[59] Gracey to Lambert, 8 January 1920, GAD, F. No. 1921, UPSA.

Allahabad, could well appreciate how education on similar lines had fostered Hindu-Muslim understanding and enabled young graduates to recognize a common destiny above the 'existence of separate entities and the din of communal claims'.[60]

Notice, for example, how Saifuddin Kitchlew, the hero of the Rowlatt Satyagraha in Punjab, Syed Mahmud, Abdul Majid Khwaja, and Tassaduq Ahmad Khan Sherwani—all contemporaries of Jawaharlal Nehru at Cambridge—returned home with a broad vision and a liberal outlook. They rose to fame in the Congress movement and were rarely, if ever, moved by the communal claptrap. There are other instances too—of the Ali Brothers, of Zafar Ali Khan, Shuaib Qureshi, Khaliquzzaman, Abdur Rahman Siddiqi, Raja Ghulam Husain, Wilayat Ali and Hasrat Mohani, all products of the Aligarh college. Then, there was Mohammad Ali Jinnah, liberal and secular to the core before he spearheaded the Muslim League campaign in the 1940s. He was in London, where thanks to Dadabhai Naoroji's inspiring example, he entered politics as a liberal nationalist, joining Congress soon after he returned to India. Fazlul Haq in Bengal followed the same course. He studied Law and Mathematics at the Calcutta University, joined Ashutosh Mookerjee at the High Court in 1900, and some years later began to play a pivotal part in the Bengal Congress.

Henry Cotton, a keen sympathizer of nationalist aspirations, noted in 1914 that political co-operation between such men and their 'Hindu' counterparts was the result of a common educational background. As he explained in the *Asiatic Review*:

> 'Unity of ideas due to uniformity of training and the ideal which was present in Syed Ahmad's mind when he founded the Aligarh college—but was incapable of realization—is at last attained. Mutual trust, a desire for the achievement of common ends and objects, nationalism and self-government—these are the inspiration of the rising generation not less of Mohammedans than of Hindus.[61]

Mohamed Ali and Azad were ideal representatives of this 'rising generation', because their concerns mirrored the two

[60] *India*, 17 October 1913.

[61] 'India: Old and New', *Asiatic Review*, July 1914.

most powerful strands among Indian Muslims—pan-Islamism and sympathy for nationalist forces. Both burst on the national scene around the same time, achieved fame through journalism, and voiced, with equal vehemence, the anguish of their brethren over the Balkan issue, the Kanpur mosque and the Muslim university at Aligarh. They also spearheaded the pan-Islamic campaign, with Azad as the ideologue and Mohamed Ali its effective propagator. When the British government put them in gaol time and time again, they reflected on their role with a sense of pride, deriving comfort from the fact of occupying centre stage and influencing the course of history.[62] Azad saw himself in the same role as that of Jesus, a victim of unjust courts:

> At all events, how strange and glorious a place is this prisoner's deck where both the greatest and the best of men are made to stand! For even so great a being as He, this was no inappropriate place.[63]

Mohamed Ali wrote from the Chhindwara jail: 'Such sufferings and privations as ours have only too often been the lot of mankind in all ages and climes...'.[64] The trial, he said at Karachi on 26 October 1922, was not 'Mohamed Ali and six others *versus* the Crown', but 'God *versus* man'. And the question was: 'Should God dominate over man or shall man dominate over God?'

Mohiuddin Ahmad, better known as Azad, was not the product of the Aligarh college. He studied at Mecca and, in 1898, when the family returned to India, he was tutored by his father Maulana Khairuddin Ahmad in the Islamic Sciences. Later, he came into contact with Shibli and was exposed to the liberal, reformist writings of Egyptian scholars—Mohammad Abduh

[62] In response to a suggestion to write a historical monograph, Mohamed Ali stated: 'This is not the time for historical writing. This is the moment to create history'. The implicit suggestion in this remark is obvious. Mohamed Ali to Abdul Majid Daryabadi, 1916, quoted in I. Askari, 'Mohamed Ali: Ek Sadaa-i Shikast Saaz', *Aligarh Magazine*, 1960–61, and A.M. Daryabadi, *Mohamed Ali: Zaati Diary ke chand Auraaq* (Hyderabad, 1943), p. 14.

[63] Quoted in Ian Henderson Douglas, *Abul Kalam Azad: An Intellectual Biography* (Delhi, 1988), p. 180.

[64] To James DuBoulay, 18 February 1919, Hasan (ed.), *Mohamed Ali in Indian Politics*, vol. 2, p. 193.

and Rashid Rida. In later years, his ideological discourse was influenced by his knowledge of and his interaction with Islamic societies while his political praxis was determined by the specificity of the colonial experience in India. At the same time, he was not easily swayed by a unified stream of thought or a monolithic ideology. Though Islam was central to his worldview, his thought processes were constantly at work in a critical evaluation of established notions. 'There is no conviction in my heart', he wrote, 'which the thorns of doubt have failed to pierce: there is no faith in my soul which has not been subjected to all the conspiracies of disbelief'.[65] Moreover, allegiance to his intellectual mentors, ranging from Syed Ahmad to Shibli, also shifted from time to time as he traversed the rough terrain of religion, politics and philosophy. 'I am under no obligation', he claimed, 'for guidance to any man's hand or tongue, nor to any syllabus of education. All the guidance I have received has been from the Divine Throne'.[66] In the end, he emerged from the darkness of his inner strivings a very independent man.

The same spirit of independence was the hallmark of Azad's political career. He was nobody's follower, not even Gandhi's. Even though religion and moral fervour bound the Mahatma and the Maulana in a common quest for swaraj, their perspective on and outlook towards socio-political issues had little in common. Azad's relationship with other Congress stalwarts was ambivalent. He respected some and admired others, but rarely did he follow their dictates. This was because his political survival was never ever dependent on his paying obeisance to a Gandhi or a Nehru or his alignment with or opposition to any of the factions in the Congress. His political stature and charismatic appeal rested on his unimpeachable loyalty to the Congress, his interest in India's independence and his antipathy to communal forces in the country.

Azad's political career began in Calcutta, then in the throes of the Swadeshi agitation against the partition of Bengal. He was impressed by the revolutionaries and claimed to have joined one

[65] Cited in Kenneth Cragg, *Counsels in Contemporary Islam* (Edinburgh, 1965), pp. 132–33; Abdur Razzaq Malihabadi, *Zikr-i Azad* (Calcutta, 1960), p. 251, quoted in Douglas, op. cit., p. 29.

[66] Ibid., p. 134.

of their groups through the mediation of Shyam Sunder Chakrabarty, an associate of Aurobindo Ghose.[67] From 1910 until his imprisonment in 1921, he was closely connected with several political movements for which he was often sent to gaol. He toiled in and out of prison over a monumental *Tarjuman al-Quran*—the theological credo of Azad—and put forward the view of the transcendental oneness of all faiths and the theology of multi-religious co-operation. In the final phase of his life, he returned to the front rank of politics as the Congress' leading Muslim president from 1939 to 1946, and as the symbol of those Muslims who worked for a united India. During the last years of the freedom struggle he opposed partition heart and soul. His speeches echoed the themes of his earlier life and writings: communal harmony, religious broad-mindedness and cultural cosmopolitanism.

Mohamed Ali was born at Rampur, scion of 'a fairly prosperous and educated Indian Muslim family'. His early career followed a familiar graph—degrees obtained at Aligarh and Oxford, and an unsuccessful attempt to join the ranks of 'heaven born' in the Civil Service, followed by jobs in the princely states of Rampur and Baroda. While in service, he turned to political issues and expressed his ideas in 'Thoughts on the Present Discontent', which appeared in the *Times of India* and the *Indian Spectator* in 1907. He lectured on the contemporary political scene, took part in the foundation of the Muslim League and was *en rapport* with leading nationalists at various levels. By the time the *Comrade* was launched on 14 January 1911, Mohamed Ali—yet to acquire the prefix 'Maulana' before his name—had won many hearts and gained a substantial following in his alumni, the MAO college. Around this time, Azad was busy planning his journalistic assault in Calcutta, where the echoes of the Swadeshi movement continued to reverberate in many circles.

When the *Comrade* and *Al-Hilal* appeared, they bore the unmistakable style of their editors. Azad was a consummate

[67] For a revealing account of Azad's early political life, see Rajat K. Ray, 'Revolutionaries, Pan-Islamists and Bolsheviks: Maulana Abul Kalam Azad and the Political Underworld in Calcutta, 1905–1925', Hasan (ed.), *Communal and Pan-Islamic Trends in Colonial India*, pp. 101–24.

stylist. He wrote authoritatively. His discourse was subtle, complex and incisive. His style was often fierce and combative and was akin to the Egyptian journal *Al-Urwa al wuthqa* rather than the simple mode of expression adopted by Syed Ahmad, Shibli, Hali and Hasrat. He marshalled a wide variety of scriptural and rational arguments and assaulted the positions of his opponents generally with great effectiveness, pausing only to regret occasionally the necessity of dealing with noisome adversaries. He spoke in the language of a 'high-souled prophet', reminiscent of the pontification of Shah Waliullah of Delhi. He appealed to his community's religious passions, awakened their dormant spirits by the use of Islamic symbols and altered the language and tenor of discourse amongst the *ulama*. He envisaged leading the Muslims at the head of a 'Party of God' [*Hizbullah*], which would unite all Indians in ousting the British. He also founded the Dar al-Irshad in order to enact a radical reform in the teaching methods used in religious institutions, encourage independent thinking and make plain to the students the social applicability of what they were studying. Such activity was not only a necessary preliminary to Azad's emergence as a powerful political force, but was also a means for changing the intellectual and political attitudes moulded by Syed Ahmad and for training a whole generation of *ulama* who went forth to play a leading role in the events leading to the Khilafat movement.

Azad took educated Muslims by storm with his eloquence and fervour when he began the publication of *Al-Hilal*. 'The Muslims were set on fire by his passionate words', recalled Sulaiman Nadwi, who worked with Azad on the staff of *Al-Hilal* for a time in 1913.[68] The demand for the paper was so great that, within three months all the old issues had to be reprinted as every new subscriber wanted the entire set. At one stage the circulation exceeded 25,000.

Mohamed Ali had an equally meteoric rise in the world of

[68] Quoted in Douglas, op. cit., p. 100. And the comment of Hasrat Mohani:
From the time that I saw Abul Kalam's prose,
Even the beauty of Hasrat's poetry
faded before my eyes.

journalism. But, unlike Azad, he was neither an ideologue nor a theorist. His concern was not for historical accuracy but for the emotional effect. He was a crusader—one who sought to undo the 'wrongs' done to his community by the forces inimical to Islam. That is why he took to journalism, 'the only avenue through which I could reach a place in which I could prove of any appreciable use to it....' Though his style was verbose, pedestrian, rambling and repetitive, he moulded public opinion to an appreciable degree. The UP government thought that 'no paper has so much influence with the students as the *Comrade,* and no individual has the authority over them which is exercised by Mohamed Ali'.[69] When, at the beginning of his internment, Mohamed Ali wanted to stop the *Hamdard,* he was implored not to do so. 'I don't approve of your decision and I don't think many will', observed Wilayat Ali Bambooque, 'You can't imagine what the loss of *Hamdard* will mean to us—the Mussalmans'.[70] Wilayat Ali was not alone in recognizing the contribution of *Comrade* and *Hamdard* to a general awakening of educated Muslims. Numerous Muslims throughout the country responded with warmth and enthusiasm to the writings of Mohamed Ali.

Though Islam as expressed in Mohamed Ali's life was different from Islam as expressed in Azad's life, it was still, in both cases, a vital component in defining their identity and the main source of inspiration. The early religious training of Mohamed Ali involved but a superficial acquaintance with the rudiments of Islam and the concomitant ritual. Family influences, too, do not appear to have been such as to have either inclined him in favour of dogmatic theology, or fostered in him independence of thought and a spirit of rebellion against prevailing religious beliefs. His mother's gentle influence, to which Mohamed Ali owed so much in life, was exerted more in the direction of promoting his educational career than in creating around him a religious atmosphere.

In *My Life,* Mohamed Ali laments that he did not have the benefit of acquiring the traditional Muslim education. 'It is not

[69] Home Poll. D., F.No. 31, December 1914, NAI.

[70] Wilayat Ali to Mohamed Ali, 20 August 1915, Mohamed Ali Papers, Jamia Millia Islamia, New Delhi.

without a feeling of deep shame that I have to confess, we boys and girls born and bred in Muslim households were taught far less of our religion than most English boys and girls of our age and position'.[71] He regretted that Aligarh 'furnished' students with 'little equipment in the matter of knowledge of faith'.[72] Though he attended Shibli's lectures on the Quran, referring to the 'exquisite elation of sitting in the Principal's Hall attending [his] lectures on the Quran with all the dignity of a quasi-'Undergrad',[73] the Quran still 'practically remained a closed book to us, and the traditions of the Prophet was no more than a name'.[74]

Mohamed Ali's *Life* is a document of deep religious feeling: it serves to illuminate his inner self-awareness of Islam. He became, as he put it, intoxicated with the force and grandeur of the Quran, which he read in Maulvi Nazir Ahmad's Urdu translation. After years of ignorance of his Islamic heritage, he discovered that the Quran was a 'perennial of truth', and offered a 'complete scheme of life, a perfect code of conduct and a comprehensive social policy....'[75] *Tauhid* grew upon him as a personal reality, man in the dignity of his 'service' as viceregent of God, and himself as part of this great strength. 'This was my unique discovery in that small volume revealed some thirteen centuries ago to an Arab of the desert whose name I bore'.[76]

In this way the enforced leisure at Chhindwara, Lansdowne and Betul jails enabled Mohamed Ali to steep himself afresh in his Islamic heritage and turn to the study of his religion—charting out an unfamiliar subject, getting at its rudiments and exploring its nuances. Again, it was during those years of internment at Chhindwara and Landsowne that he read the *Sihah-i Sitah,* a compilation of the traditions [*Hadith*] of the Prophet Mohammad, and the works of Imam Ghazali, Jalaluddin Rumi and

[71] Mohamed Ali, *My Life,* p. 2.
[72] Ibid., p. 22.
[73] Ibid., p. 27.
[74] Ibid., p. 23.
[75] Ibid., p. 37 and Afzal Iqbal (ed.), *Selected Writings and Speeches of Mohamed Ali* (Lahore, 1946), p. 170.
[76] *My Life,* p. 96.

Iqbal. The reading of *Asraar-i Khudi* [Secrets of Self] was an enthralling experience. 'I experienced an exquisite thrill of delight', he wrote, 'when I found the Poet and Philosopher was, in his own inimitable fashion, giving expression to the same basic truth of Islam, which I had in a blundering sort of way discovered for myself'.[77] And on turning to the study of Islamic history, Mohamed Ali saw its great men as figures to whom he could talk, and its crises as guides to action in current affairs.[78] Studying Islam was not uncommon; in fact, people like Syed Ahmad, Shibli and Azad studied it with greater scholarship, but none with a greater personal need.[79] To Gandhi, he wrote:

> Whatever else my internment may or may not have done, it has I believe set the soul free...What I could dimly perceive before I now realize with distinctness, and it is this, that the whole aim and end of life is to serve God and obey His Commandments..I confess I had never before grasped this truth in all its fullness....Internment made us seek refuge in the Holy Quran, and for the first time, I have to confess it, I read it through and with new eyes. It was then that this truth dawned upon me and gave me coherence and a unity to a thousand vague aspirations to do good to my people, my country and women in general.[80]

The experience was, in some ways, similar to that of Azad. His three-and-a-half year internment in Ranchi kindled his Islam into warmth and fervour. He began writing the *Tarjuman al-Quran,* with his commentary on the opening *Sura, Al-Fatiha,* and its themes—Divine Providence, benevolence, justice, unity and guidance, *rububiyya, rahma, adala, tauhid* and *hidaya.*

The authors of *Tazkirah* and *My Life* asserted their faith in the transcendental truth of Islam, which offered 'a way of life, a moral code and social polity'.[81] They felt the rightness of the Islamic ideals—a complete way of life for an organized commun-

[77] Ibid., p. 127.

[78] Daryabadi, *Zaati Diary*, p. 14; to Daryabadi, 22 May and 25 July 1916, Hasan (ed.), *Mohamed Ali in Indian Politics*, vol. 1, pp. 269–76.

[79] Mohamed Ali, *My Life*, p. 18.

[80] To Gandhi, 20 February 1918, *Mohamed Ali in Indian Politics*, vol. 1, p. 240.

[81] *Al-Hilal*, 23 October 1912.

ity living out Allah's plan under the kind of government which had prevailed in the days of the Prophet. At the same time, they affirmed that the basic principles of Islam were perfectly compatible with reason or science. This was the central argument of Mohamed Ali's article, 'The Future of Islam' and of Azad's essays published in the first three issues of *Al-Hilal.* Alone among his contemporaries in the religious institutions, Azad conceived for Islam a vital socio-political role that went against the apparently triumphant secularizing tendencies of the age and conveyed first to his associates and pupils and then to Indian society at large the vibrant and comprehensive vision of Islam that had first begun to animate his being in youth.

Azad's rationalism was not only an element in his modernist, intellectual explorations, but also—and primarily—an integral part of his traditional scholastic training. Mohamed Ali, on the other hand, propounded neo-intellectual modernism. And like Azad, he was *en rapport* with Syed Ahmad and the Egyptian reformers in his appeal for cultivating scientific disciplines and rejecting *taqlid.*'I have as much right to interpret God's message as any other man', he declared in *My Life*, a personal credo from gaol. 'Formal renunciation of a 'mildewed scholasticism' will set Islam 'right with the progressive world of science' and 'right with itself'.[82] Azad echoed similar views in his inimitable scholarly manner. 'The shopkeepers of religion have given the name of 'religion' to ignorance and *taqlid*, to prejudice and indulgence', he wrote in *Al-Hilal.* Many years later, he commented:

> The greatest hindrance to human intellectual progress is unquestioning acceptance of traditional beliefs . . . the first thorn of doubt which pricked my heart was against this very *taqlid*.... The foundation of belief should be knowledge, why on *taqlid* and inheritance.[83]

The underlying rationalist strain in the thought processes of Azad and Mohamed Ali found tangible expression in their ability to reconcile their passionate attachment to Islam and pan-Islamism with the ideological underpinnings of Indian nationalism. Their Islamic heritage, combined with their Indian experiences, led

[82] Mohamed Ali, *My Life*, pp. 163–64.

[83] Cited in Douglas, op. cit., p. 76.

them to reject Syed Ahmad Khan's plea for an Anglo-Muslim alliance and to pay heed to the exhortations of Jamaluddin Afghani and Mohammad Abduh on cultivating brotherly relations with fellow-Indians in the struggle against colonial rule. In addition, they received stimulus from those groups and individuals who were beginning to clamour for concerted action in support of the rising tide of Indian nationalism and in opposition to the raj. Hasrat Mohani was among the first to say so. Known as the *Rais al-Ahrar,* he plotted, quite early in his public life, a radical course for himself and joined Tilak after the split in 1907. Shibli, agonized over the Balkan War and the Kanpur mosque incident, also came round to supporting the Congress. His essays, published in the *Muslim Gazette,* may well have motivated Azad to speak at the Congress meeting in December 1913 on Hindu-Muslim unity and in praise of Congress policies.

Mohamed Ali's first editorial was a plea for Hindu-Muslim friendship. It was his firm belief 'that if the Muslims or the Hindus attempt to achieve success in opposition to or even without the co-operation of one another, they will not only fail but fail ignonimously'.[84] In fact the *Comrade* was intended to prepare Muslims to 'contribute to territorial patriotism without abating a jot of the fervour of their extra-territorial sympathies which is the quintessence of Islam'.[85] Whatever misgivings he had about the Congress were removed in Chhindwara when he had the leisure to reflect on the role of Tilak[86] and came into contact with Gandhi, whom he had first met at Aligarh in 1915. Soon thereafter, Mohamed Ali came under the Mahatma's spell. He wrote to Saifuddin Kitchlew:

> It is Gandhi, Gandhi, Gandhi, that has got to be dinned into the people's ear, because he means Hindu-Muslim unity, non-co-operation, *swadharma* and *swaraja,* while the rest are after petty communal or local bodies, most of them tinged with personal ambition.[87]

[84] *Comrade* (Calcutta), 14 January 1911.

[85] Mohamed Ali, *My Life,* p. 46.

[86] To Tilak, 12 November 1916, *Mohamed Ali in Indian Politics,* vol. 1; p. 292.

[87] Quoted in Afzal Iqbal, *Life and Times of Mohamed Ali* (Delhi, 1978: reprint), p. 308. See, Chintamani's assessment of Mohamed Ali in 1924.

Equally noteworthy is the fact that Azad and Mohamed Ali perceived no contradiction between their nationalist concerns and their communitarian interests, such as the Khilafat issue. Asserting that pan-Islamism and nationalism were compatible ideologies, they sought to establish that their community's anguish over the future of Turkey deepened their involvement in the anti-colonial struggle and brought them closer to the Congress under Gandhi's leadership. In fact, Azad, more than Mohamed Ali, was able to draw upon the Quran and the *Hadith* to advocate Hindu-Muslim amity and to strengthen the case for non-co-operation against the British. Following closely the views of Abduh who, in answer to inquiries from India, had endorsed inter-religious co-operation, Azad reiterated, with all the religious fervour he could command, that Muslims should be up in front, fighting for freedom.

The moves towards communal unity and Congress-Muslim League co-operation were stimulated by the ideas and activities of men like Azad and Mohamed Ali. Khuda Bukhsh's comments on such developments concluded with the prayer:

The laurel, the palm and the paen to
thee, O Khwaja (Muinuddin Chishti),
for having, at least in Ajmer, effected
an enduring reconciliation between these
two communities, and united them in the
silken bonds of brotherly love and esteem.[88]

He wrote to his Liberal Party colleague, Srinivasa Sastri: ' I had seen the latter (Mohamed Ali) more than a decade ago. How completely he has been transformed. Great I believe has been the Gandhian influence over him.' Chintamani to Sastri, 6 October 1924, T.N. Jagadisan (ed.), *Letters of V.S. Srinivasa Sastri,* 2nd edn. (Asia Publishing House, 1963), pp. 139–40.

[88] Bukhsh, *Essays on Indian and Islamic,* p. 269. Also, the comment of C.F. Andrews about Maulvi Zakaullah's 'profound' and 'mystical faith' in Hindu-Muslim unity. 'That was his own ideal, and it coloured all his actions. In that faith he lived, and in that faith he died.' Andrews, *Zakaullah of Delhi,* pp. xxix–xxx.

Chapter Four

Congress-League Rapprochement: The Lucknow Pact

The setting for the Congress-Muslim League meeting in the Christmas week of 1916 was perfect. The Raja of Mahmudabad, a sympathizer of nationalist aspirations, was acting host. Qaiser Bagh, the nerve centre of political activity during the Home Rule movement, was the venue. The leaders met every morning to hammer out the details of an accord, they dispersed early when faced with contentious issues; otherwise the deliberations went on till late afternoon when it was time to enjoy the Raja's hospitality. The exercise, interspersed with *mushairas* and elaborate luncheons and dinners, continued for three days until the final details of the Lucknow Pact were made public.

The Lucknow accord took place at an opportune moment. After years of fruitless negotiations the Congress and the League leadership recognized the need to set their own house in order before embarking on a quest for constitutional concessions.[1] The League made its intention known through changes in its constitution and in its leadership. The Congress was also in an accommodating mood, seeking to lend legitimacy to nationalist elements in the Muslim League. Consequently, a series of Congress-League meetings were held between 1909 and 1915 to achieve a workable political consensus.[2] The Lucknow gathering

[1] Such initiatives were backed by contemporary writings and the speeches of leading nationalists. See, for example, *Speeches of Gokhale at Lahore* (Lahore, 1907); *Speeches of B.C. Pal* (Madras, 1907), p. 43; S.M. Mitra, *Hindu-Muslim Entente Cordiale* (London, 1909); Yatindranatha Choudhri, *Observations on the Present Situation* (Calcutta, 1907), p. 36, IOLR Tracts (1025, 1050).

[2] The first important meeting was held at Allahabad from 31 December

placed its seal of approval on all such initiatives.

There was, however, an immediate and pressing need for the sort of agreement that took place in 1916. It was occasioned by the outbreak of World War I and the expectation, aroused by official statements, that the Allies who were fighting for the cause of freedom and liberty would themselves advance the cause of self-government.[3] 'The old regime *must* change', remarked the viceroy in July 1915, 'and the people must have more to say in their administration'.[4] Reginald Craddock, his home member, submitted concrete reform proposals in recognition of India's contribution to the war efforts. The demand for political concessions, he stated, would be vigorously pressed by the political sections of the educated classes and would receive a hearing in England.[5]

Such views heightened hopes of reforms and led Indian nationalists to prepare their schedule of demands in the light of the inadequacies of the Act of 1909. Gokhale did so in February 1915, ten days before he died. Wazir Hasan, the Muslim League secretary, gave advance notice of his party's proposals and spoke of the 'shifting horizon and broadening political outlook' on Indian affairs.[6] Annie Besant and Surendranath Banerjea, hero of the Swadeshi movement, also set forth their ideas. Soon these leaders moved uneasily towards the goal of achieving unanimity

---

1910 to 1 January 1911. It was attended by, among others, Gokhale, Surendranath Banerjea, the Aga Khan, Mazharul Haq, Bhupendranath Basu, Motilal Nehru, Jinnah, Tej Bahadur Sapru, Mohamed Ali, Mohammad Shafi, Viqarul Mulk and Wazir Hasan. *Tribune* of 22 January 1912 described the meeting as 'memorable', 'historical' and 'epoch-making'.

[3] 'During the war we Indians were looking forward to a great advance in self-government at its end... Nationalism received a needed lift from talk of what was to come'. Nirad C. Chaudhuri, *The Autobiography of an Unknown Indian* (London, 1951), p. 399.

[4] Hardinge to Walter Lawrence, 29 July 1915, Hardinge Papers (94).

[5] To Hardinge, 25 March 1915, ibid. (89). Non-official opinion was more vocal on the issue. Henry Cotton was one of those who vigorously pleaded for the grant of provincial autonomy to India and its gradual admission into the Federation of the Empire. 'India: Now and After', *Contemporary Review*, February 1915, pp. 195, 200.

[6] FR (UP), Home Poll. D, F. No. 56, March 1915, NAI.

on certain basic but potentially divisive issues concerning India's constitution.

Discussions between the Congress and the League started in early October 1915. Reporting on their progress, the editor of *Leader*, C.Y. Chintamani, informed Mohamed Ali in Chhindwara jail:

> ...We are making satisfactory progress...and it is my earnest prayer that nothing may happen to bring back the old days of strife. Even on the question of representation we are most anxious to arrive at an understanding and I am hopeful that we shall succeed.[7]

Mohamed Ali was kept posted with developments, because he had pressed the Muslim League council to take a series of momentous decisions, including the holding of the League meeting in Bombay to confer with the Congress which was also going to assemble in the same city and to work

> shoulder to shoulder with the sister communities of India for securing the recognition of all the legitimate claims of India as a whole, while safeguarding at the same time all the legitimate rights and interests of the Muslim community.[8]

The much-publicized League meeting was held in Bombay in December 1915 with Jinnah as the star performer. He moved a resolution, seconded by Azad and Fazlul Haq, appointing a committee to prepare a reform scheme in consultation with the Congress. Hindu-Muslim unity was the theme of his lectures then and later. Azad, too, commended the Muslim League meeting that resulted in a 'clear and effective step...in the direction of Hindu-Muslim national unity.'[9]

The spirit of unity that Jinnah had spoken of prevailed at the joint Congress-League conclaves. To begin with, the contentious issue of separate electorates was resolved smoothly, with most Congress leaders grudgingly accepting a principle which, in their judgement, had sowed the seeds of communal dissensions. Compromise was also reached on the proportion of Muslim rep-

[7] 27 October 1915, Mohamed Ali Papers, JMI.

[8] To Wazir Hasan, 26 September 1915, cited in Hasan (ed.), *Mohamed Ali in Indian Politics*, vol. 1, pp. 225–26.

[9] Douglas, *Abul Kalam Azad*, p. 145. For a fuller analysis of Jinnah's role, see Stanley Wolpert, *Jinnah of Pakistan* (New York, 1984), chapter 4.

resentation in the councils. In some provinces, such as Bihar, Bombay, Madras and the Central Provinces, they secured seats over and above their population. In return, their seats in Punjab were reduced from 55 per cent, to which they were entitled to by their population, to just 50 per cent.

Still, the joint conference, reconvened in the last week of December 1916, was left with the daunting task of fixing the proportion of Muslim seats in UP and Bengal. After some hard and prolonged bargaining, their share was fixed at 40 per cent in Bengal. But the deadlock over UP remained. Chintamani and Malaviya agreed to only 25 per cent as against the 35 per cent seats claimed by the League representatives.[10] Bhupendranath Basu, then, suggested the figure of 30 per cent which was reluctantly accepted on both sides.

The *Tribune:* 'There must be satisfaction all over the country that the question [of Muslim representation in the councils] has set at rest any further discussion in haggling...and that the scheme of post-war reforms prepared by the joint conference can now go to government.'[11]

Discussion on all other issues went off smoothly. In the end, the Congress-League scheme postulated representative government and dominion status, with the provision that India would be an equal partner in the empire as a self-governing dominion. The councils in the provinces would consist of four-fifths elected and only one-fifth of nominated members, and the elected members, so the scheme envisaged, would be returned on as broad a franchise as possible.

How did all this come about? Why did the Congress accept separate electorates after its sanctimonious opposition for so long? Who were the architects of the Lucknow agreement? And what were its implications on future political developments?

In 1909-10, Congress leaders had denounced the Morley-Minto Reforms for introducing separate electorates. Their arguments dwelt on the identity of Hindu-Muslim interests, the danger of Muslims securing more seats than they were entitled to

[10] GAD, F.No. 140. 1917, UPSA; FR (UP), 6 January 1917, Home Poll. F.No. 5, NAI.

[11] *Tribune*, 29 December 1916.

and the grave risks involved in introducing 'unjust invidious and humiliating distinctions' between Hindus and Muslims.'[12] The climax to their opposition came in June 1911, when the secretary of UP, Richard Burn, sought the opinion of his divisional commissioners on:

1. The introduction of separate electorates in local boards.
2. The proportion of seats to be allotted to Muslims under separate electorates.
3. The laying down of special qualifications for Muslim voters and candidates.
4. Participation of Muslims in general electorates.

There was much hue and cry in the press over the infamous Burn circular. It would lead to, stated the *Advocate,* the exclusion of Hindus from the council:

> [It was] only by a majority of one vote that the municipalities and the district boards in the Bareilly division could send a Hindu to the council, under the present condition. If the proposed changes come into effect, the Bareilly division will have the privilege of being represented by Muslims both from separate and joint electorates. Such also might be the fate of six out of the eight large cities in UP. The Hindu middle class representation, meagre as it is in the council, will be reduced to nullity.[13]

Opposition to the Burn circular was followed by an agitation over the UP Municipalities Bill, which acknowledged the principle of separate representation. Based on a compromise between Motilal Nehru, Jagat Narain Mulla, Tej Bahadur Sapru and the Muslim councillors,[14] Muslims secured a large representation in

[12] *Tribune,* 4 March 1910.

[13] *Advocate,* 18 June 1911. 'If Mohamedans have more than proportional representation, Hindus will *ipso facto* have less than their proportional representation...If, in addition, Mohamedans are empowered to get into local bodies through the general electorates, will not the less than proportional representation allowed to Hindus become less? Hindus very naturally and very properly resent this differential treatment which operates entirely to their detriment and it is against this that their agitation will be principally directed.' *Leader,* 29 June 1911.

[14] Robinson, *Separatism,* p. 247; Sender, *The Kashmiri Pandits,* pp. 270–72.

areas where they were more numerous as well in areas where they were in a minority.[15] In consequence, Hindus were placed in a minority on municipal boards even in places where they outnumbered the Muslims. Malaviya, who organized the protest against the Bill, summed up his powerful indictment:

> Though the Hindus were convinced that separate communal representation on municipal boards was fraught with evil, they were willing to consent that Muslims should have separate representation. But they could not agree that they should have an excessive representation too. If there were 70 per cent of Hindus in a town and 30 per cent of Muslims it was utterly unfair that Muslims should have nearly the same representation as Hindus, and yet that was what the Act will bring about. The 30 per cent of Muslims of Allahabad would be entitled to appoint eight out of twenty-one elected representatives on the municipal boards, while the 70 per cent of Hindus would have only ten such representatives.[16]

This outcry, supported by massive protest meetings, posed a serious threat to the Congress-League negotiations which were well underway. But the Kashmiri triumvirate of Motilal, Sapru and Jagat Narain Mulla diffused the tension by securing the endorsement of the Jahangirabad amendment, introduced in the council in March 1916. Their principal interest in doing so was to keep intact the Congress-League alliance. In any case, they had come round to accepting separate electorates as a 'necessary evil', because Muslim leaders were insistent on having them. 'In order to make it possible for the Muslim community to co-operate with us', Sapru declared in the UP council, 'and in order to remove at least one of the several causes of friction, I should not grudge separate representation to the Muslims'. A satisfactory adjustment of inter-communal relations, according to Sapru, was a necessary condition for India's political evolution.[17]

Outside UP, the expediency of accepting separate electorates had been recognized much earlier. Gokhale explained in 1909

[15] Under sections 11-12 of the Act, Muslims were given 30 per cent of seats if they formed less than 25 per cent of the population; 38 per cent if their population stood between 25 to 38 per cent. Above 38 per cent, they were to receive seats in accordance with their numerical strength.

[16] *Amrita Bazar Patrika*, 21 July 1916.

[17] Quoted in Sender, op. cit., pp. 272–73.

that separate electorates would minimize friction and ensure the representation of minorities;[18] so did R.N. Mudholkar, Congress president in 1912.[19] Tilak's line of thought flowed in the same direction as Gokhale's. At the Lucknow meet in December 1916, he prevailed upon the intransigent Malaviya to reach an understanding rather than wreck the prospect of a Congress-League *entente*. He said:

> There is a feeling among Hindus that too much has been given to the Muslims. As a Hindu I have no objection to making this concession.... We cannot rise from our intolerable position without the aid of the Muslims. So in order to gain the desired end there is no objection to giving a percentage, a greater percentage, to the Muslims.[20]

Mohamed Ali, pleased with Tilak's role, wrote from Chhindwara:

> I must confess I had long been a prey to grave misgivings about the catholicity of your political and social ideals....I confess this all the more readily today because long before today I learnt to regret those misgivings and have already offered my apologies to you in spirit if not in flesh.[21]

Mohamed Ali was echoing the sentiments expressed long ago by Hasrat Mohani who wrote poems in praise of the Maharashtrian leader.[22]

II

In the opinion of the government, the main architects of the Congress-League *entente* were 'ignorant and self-seeking men', whose motives were 'love of notoriety and the lust of gain'. Thus

[18] *Tribune*, 16 July 1909.

[19] *INC.*, 1912, p. 19.

[20] D.V. Tahmankar, *Lokmanya Tilak: Father of Indian Unrest and Maker of Modern India* (London, 1956), p. 244; Stanley Wolpert, *Tilak and Gokhale: Revolution and Reform in the Making of Modern India* (Berkeley and Los Angeles, 1962), pp. 282–83.

[21] To Tilak, 12 November 1916, cited in *Mohamed Ali in Indian Politics*, vol. 1, pp. 292–93.

[22] Qadiri, *Hasrat Mohani*, pp. 156–57.

Mohamad Ali was a 'mischievous agitator' and Wazir Hasan a 'born intriguer'. Their patron, the Raja of Mahmudabad, was considered 'vain and unbalanced' by James Meston and Harcourt Butler.[23] What angered these officials was that the Raja backed the activities of young Muslims who were active in the Congress-led nationalist campaigns. They were the men of Nai Raushani' [New Light] and protagonists of 'new ideals' and 'new forces'.[24] As champions of 'democracy against oligarchy...freedom against convention...idealism against opportunism...and faith against cynicism and compromise,'[25] they were fierce in their denunciation of British colonialism and its allies. Wilayat Ali did so with candidness. So did Raja Ghulam Husain, the great crusader against the 'old race of patriots'. He summed up the ideological orientation of his group in an editorial published in *New Era* on 26 May 1917:

> A community of about 70 millions...has to work out its political destiny in close and active co-operation with the rest of the Indian people. Any other alternative...is unthinkable. Any self-respecting Muslim who knows what political freedom means for the self-realization of individuals as well as communities, can feel no enthusiasm for a political creed that does not aim at a free and united India.

Such views did not go uncontested. In Punjab, Mian Shah Din, the first Punjabi Muslim to go to England for legal studies, and his cousin, Mian [later Sir] Mohammad Shafi, were arrayed against the nationalist stream represented by Fazli Husain and Zafar Ali Khan. Of the two, Shafi was more prominent as founder of the Punjab Muslim League in 1907, member of the legislative council and patron of Anjuman-i Islamia and the Anjuman-i Himayat-i Islam, organizations where Iqbal first recited his patriotic songs. While the Morley-Minto Reforms were being formulated, the Baghabanpura Mian followed the line which the

[23] Sydenham to Hardinge, 18 March 1913, Hardinge Papers (86); FR (Delhi), 16 August 1914, Home Poll. A, September 1914, F.No. 1–3, NAI; Butler to Allan, 6 April 1913, Butler Papers (71); Meston to Chelmsford, 20 August 1917, Meston Papers (1).

[24] Mohamed Ali, *My Life*, p. 39; Mazharul Haq, quoted in *Bombay Chronicle*, 27 January 1916.

[25] *New Era*, 14 April 1917.

government was pleased to endorse. Muslims, he told Dunlop Smith, were 'the most important minority in the country' and their political importance was much more than their numerical strength. Moreover, 'they constitue a distinct community having, in part, interests of their own, which while in line with those of their rulers, are separate from and often antagonistic to those of the majority'.[26] Shafi assured Dunlop Smith that the government could safely rely on the loyalty of his community which was 'a stable element in the political atmosphere of this country'. His attachment to British rule was above reproach. As a follower of the 'Anglo-Mohammedan school of politics', he would never ever 'take part in anything calculated, in the slightest degree, to injure British interests and to weaken the stability and permanence of British rule in India.'[27]

Shafi's main political rival in Punjab was Mian Fazli Husain. Their differences first surfaced in the Anjuman-i Himayat-i Islam, though they were temporarily resolved by Nawab Fateh Ali Qizilbash, a landowner with large estates in Lahore and the Awadh district of Bahraich.[28] The final rupture took place in mid-1915, when Shafi opposed the holding of the Muslim League session in Bombay. Soon thereafter, the Punjab Muslim League, of which he was secretary, was disaffiliated by the League council and Fazli Husain was placed at the helm of affairs. Shafi had to swallow another bitter pill when his attempts to chair the Muslim Educational Conference, a prestigious forum set up by Syed Ahmad Khan, were thwarted by his detractors.[29] As his star faded, the editors of *Zamindar, New Era, Muslim Observer,* backed by Wazir Hasan and the Raja of Mahmudabad, triumphantly recorded the advance of nationalist forces in Punjab.[30]

[26] Shafi to Dunlop Smith, 18 June 1909, Dunlop Smith Papers, MSS. EUR. F. No. 166 (13), IOLR.

[27] To Dunlop Smith, 11 January, 13 April and 8 June 1909, ibid.

[28] *Tribune,* April 1910.

[29] FR (Punjab), Home Poll. Deposit, February 1917, F. No. 49, NAI. FR (UP), Home Poll. Deposit, January 1917, F. No. 42, NAI.

[30] For example, the *New Era* wrote a strongly-worded editorial against Shafi. 'He is trying', the paper wrote, 'to arrogate to himself the right to speak on behalf of the Mussalmans, and he intends in this garb to play the

In Bengal, the Nawab of Dacca and his proteges called the shots from the time the Muslim League came into being. But the annulment of Bengal's partition placed the leadership on the defensive. The death of the Nawab in 1915 was the last straw. It marked the end of an era in which the landlord-government servants combination had successfully resisted the growth of political radicalism. Reflecting on the changes ushered in by the decline of the old-style leadership, the *Mussalman,* an organ of nationalist opinion, observed:

> In every age, in every clime, and in every country there are reactionaries. Whenever any progressive movement is set on foot, they stand in the way. But they have never been able to block the way; they only place temporary difficulties in the path of progress.[31]

After the Nawab, Fazlul Haq emerged as a potential leader of a new kind. Born in 1873 in a family of Barisal lawyers, Fazlul Haq studied in Calcutta University and worked with Ashutosh Mookerjee as an articled clerk in the High Court. His involvement in politics began in 1906, when he attended the Muslim Educational Conference at Dacca and was entrusted with the task of drafting the Muslim League constitution. This was the time when he began to drift apart from his patron, the Nawab of Dacca, who had helped him secure an important position in the Rural Co-operative Societies and a seat in the legislative council. Restless with the Nawab's policy of collaboration with government and opposition to the Congress, he decided to adopt an independent course in politics. As a first step he gained control of the League in Bengal and began to marshal his resources in order to operate from a position of a strength. He was able to do so with much effect, because unlike the traditional Muslim leaders—of the Ameer Ali and Abdul Latif kind — Fazlul Haq had made his

---

traitor and bring everlasting disgrace on his community. It is the duty of every true and honest citizen in this country to expose him and take the sting out of his action by demonstrating that he represents his own views and has absolutely no right to speak on behalf of this community or country. It appears to be the old game of the separatists by trying to set the Mussalmans against the Hindus and in the end ruin both.' *New Era,* 15 and 22 September 1917.

[31] *Mussalman,* 23 January 1917.

way up the political ladder by personal ability. His education, combined with his wide professional experience, set him apart from his predecessors in the Muslim League. He excelled in organizational work and was dynamic, forward-looking and cosmopolitan in outlook.

Fazlul Haq's political views were defined by the experience of the annulment of Bengal's partition. He realized, as did so many young Muslim leaders of his generation, that the government could no longer be relied upon for the redressal of Muslim grievances. It was not even willing to consider their submissions. Such was, after all, the experience of Mohamed Ali and Wazir Hasan, who undertook a journey to England in September 1913 to explain the 'Indian Muslims' point of view' to the British government.[32] But they were snubbed: Montagu did not grant them an interview. The secretary of state did not want to meet them, because it would be misunderstood by 'those of your co-religionists with whom you are not in accord, who claim equally with you to represent the political attitude and temper of the Mussalman community'.[33] The secretary of state should have known better, for nobody represented the political temper of his co-religionists more than Mohamed Ali and his associates. Mohamed Ali returned home with the conviction that an agitational course was the only option that remained with his aggrieved community. As he reported to Shaukat Ali:

> It may be that government organs here may give us *darwaza band* [but] we cannot be effectively gagged. Besides, if we are gagged here, we would not be gagged in India and I appealed to Sir James Dunlop Smith to consider the likely effect of our going back to India and telling our people, whether in a loud voice from the public platform or in whispers to our closets, that if the smallest official is unjust to you in this country there is no house of redress except by our taking the law into our hands.[34]

Mohamed Ali and his comrades chose the public platform,

[32] *Mohamed Ali in Indian Politics*, vol. 1, pp. 164–65.

[33] Holderness to Wazir Hasan and Mohamed Ali, 11 November 1913, Crewe Papers, F. No. 1/14 (2).

[34] To Shaukat Ali, 24 October 1913, *Mohamed Ali in Indian Politics*, vol 1, p. 167.

which they often shared with the Congress leaders, to mount a sustained agitation against the government.

III

The Lucknow Pact enhanced the value of India's constitutional demands and bridged the gulf that separated the Congress and the League. It was masterminded by Jinnah whose nationalist credentials were beyond reproach. 'Young India ought to be proud', observed a correspondent, 'that in the Hon'ble Mr. Jinnah it has found a leader who labours under no illusions as to what United India ought to have.'[35]

But not all agreed with the fairness of the accord. Hindu Sabhas, forerunners of the All-Hindu Mahasabha, were most vocal in denouncing separate electorates and communal representation. The feeling was strongest in UP, where Muslims were allowed 30 per cent of seats in the council though their population did not exceed 14 per cent. Hindus and Sikhs in Punjab, on the other hand, were allowed only a small amount of weightage. In places like Lucknow, Allahabad, Banaras and Kanpur there were loud and angry protests over the arbitrary distribution of seats proposed by the Congress-League scheme.[36]

Among Muslims there were cranks like an *alim* from Madras who told Montagu, the secretary of state, that there was no sanction in the Quran for an alliance with non-Muslims.[37] There were others who were alarmed at the growing nationalist tide among Muslims and were dismayed by their Congress leanings. 'The stereotyped Congress slogans', observed Syed Hosain Bilgrami, once member of the Imperial Legislative Council and tied to the court in Hyderabad, 'are a threat to our very existence'.[38]

[35] *Amrita Bazar Patrika,* 6 December 1916; *Bengalee,* 4 January 1917; *Young India,* 3 January 1917.

[36] FR (UP), 1 January 1917, Home Poll. Deposit, F.No. 26, February 1917, NAI; *Leader,* 30 December 1916.

[37] Quoted in H.F. Owen, 'Negotiating the Lucknow Pact', *Journal of Asian Studies,* vol. 31, May 1972, p. 581.

[38] To Mohamed Ali, 12 June 1915, Mohamed Ali Papers. Bilgrami told

Nobody perceived the threat more seriously than the rajas, zamindars and taluqdars, who were brought up in the traditions of sturdy loyalty to the raj whose 'salt they had eaten' and were nursed through successive legislations, such as the Taluqdari Succession Law (1869) and the Encumbered Estates Act (1870). 'We must preserve and develop', stated Harcourt Butler, 'a landed aristocracy, and work through it if we wish to keep an absolute foot in India . . . I do not see how we can carry on without it'.[39]

Encouraged by their patrons, the landed classes and their allies launched a well-orchestrated campaign against the Congress-League alliance. As early as 1913, Fateh Ali Khan, acting at the behest of James Meston, UP's lieutenant-governor, condemned the resolution on self-government adopted by the League and made an abortive bid to have it rescinded.[40] A year later, he floated the scheme of a Shia College in Lucknow, a move intended to divide the Aligarh university movement.[41] This project also had Meston's backing. But it failed to take off because the Raja of Mahmudabad, himself a staunch Shia, did not extend his patronage to a scheme which, he feared, would estrange Shia-Sunni relations.

Another abortive move came in the form of an attempt to prevent the League from holding its meeting in 1915 at Bombay, also the venue of the Congress session.[42] A group of traders, merchants and government servants, having first agreed to host the session, developed cold feet and aired their opposition to the Jinnah-Wazir Hasan combine. Urdu newspapers began an acrimonious vilification campaign. Prominent amongst them were the *Al-Bashir*, the *Aligarh Institute Gazette*, *Al-Mizan*,

---

Meston that he did not want to be 'ruled by men like Mr. Jinnah, Mr. Malaviya, or even the Raja of Mahmudabad.' He described Jinnah as a man of very low birth'. To Meston, 14 November 1917, Meston Papers (4).

[39] To H.E. Richards, 16 September 1906, Butler Papers (65).

[40] To Meston, 21 August 1913, Meston Papers (6).

[41] The aim was 'to produce an educated class with which will be associated every kind of healthy progress and which will produce members who will readily constitute a pious community of loyal subjects.'

[42] For details, see Owen, op.cit., pp. 571–72; Robinson, *Separatism*, pp. 242–45.

Mashriq and *Zul Qarnain.*[43] Jinnah offered a powerful rebuttal to the charges levelled against him. In a rejoinder to an editorial comment in the *Times of India,* he stated:

> Surely the Mahomedans who have shown the greatest self-restraint and control throughout these grave and momentous crisis may be trusted to formulate their demands along with their Hindu leaders. Can there be a better opportunity than this that the Congress and the League should meet in one place and confer together as to the future of India?...May I say that it is not the energies of the few members of the League that has put the Mahomedan community in rather an awkward position but it is the 'wire-pullers' and 'Jo-hukams' who are responsible for all this. I still venture to say that all the thinking Mahomedans all over India are in favour of holding the next session of the League in Bombay.[44]

The League session was eventually held amid much fanfare, with Jinnah, Mazharul Haq, Wazir Hasan and Fazlul Haq as the main performers.[45] Those who stayed away felt humbled and isolated. Suleman Cassim Mitha, Fazulbhoy Currimbhoy and Maulvi Rafiuddin, chief detractors of Jinnah, lost face with the government whose interests they were trying to promote. Meston took note of their sliding fortunes and insisted on devising a new political strategy in the light of the waning influence of the 'conservative' Muslims. In a note to the viceroy, he sorrowfully reflected :

> In deciding either on the strategy of its post-bellum policy or to handle the Home Rule agitation, the Government of India will no doubt have

[43] *Al-Bashir,* 8 June 1915; *Al-Mizan,* 12 June 1915; *Medina,* 22 October 1916; *Mashriq,* 19 December 1916, SNNR, UP.

[44] Syed Sharifuddin Pirzada (ed.), *The Collected Works of Quaid-e-Azam Mohammad Ali Jinnah* (Karachi, 1984), vol. 1, p. 135.

[45] The Governor of Bombay played a key role in uniting the different factions and made it easier for the League session to be held in the city. But Meston was unhappy with his role. He believed that Willingdon had given the 'Lucknow gang an inflated sense of their own importance'. He was of the opinion that 'the small clique, which Wazir Hasan organizes and Mahmudabad feeds, are in no sense representative of the Muslims of north India', but that a 'triumph of this coterie will be taken as a triumph for Mohamed Ali and his followers'. To Hardinge, 23 December 1915, Hardinge Papers (90).

regard to the strength of the Nationalist feeling in India at the present moment. It is unquestionably greater than it has ever been in our time. The Christmas meetings at Lucknow caught up and consolidated popular sentiment as few political events have done. Extremists and Moderates have united after years of misunderstanding; and, greatest marvel of all, the Mahomedans also had come into the fold. A few Moderates may grumble here and there; and a few conservative Mahomedans may urge that the League does not represent their community. But they do nothing. They are voiceless in public; they do not hold meetings; they have completely lost command of the Press. For all practical purposes they have, for the time at least, disappeared as a separate party. The resultant union of all voices has filled educated India with a pride and a feeling of nationality which it is impossible to ignore.[46]

Meston was making this observation just when a powerful agitation was being mounted against the Lucknow Pact in Bengal and Punjab.[47] While Muslims of UP and Bihar were jubilant that their representatives had extracted both separate electorates and weightages, reactions in Bengal and Punjab were much less subdued. Fazlul Haq and Fazli Husain, having backed the Congress-League *entente cordiale,* were now bitter that the claims of their constituents were sacrificed in the course of the hard bargaining that preceded the Lucknow Congress. In late November 1916, Fazlul Haq had sounded a warning. In a letter to Mohamed Ali, he had written:

To me it seems that that there is no hope for the Muslim community in Bengal and it would indeed be a miracle if, at some future date, the Bengali Muslims can be so fortunate as to attain a position on account of which they might be recognized as any living community in India.... May God have mercy upon us to see better days.[48]

Placed on the defensive by mounting criticizm, the principal negotiators of the Lucknow Pact, including Fazlul Haq, tried to retrieve their position by insisting on having 50 per cent of seats

[46] 7 February 1917, Meston Papers (17).

[47] *Paisa Akhbaar,* 17 and 19 July 1917, 22 December 1918, SNNR, Punjab; *Moslem Hitaishi,* 5 January 1917, SNNR, Bengal; *Searchlight,* 1 September 1918.

[48] To Mohamed Ali, 23 November 1916, Hasan (ed.), *Mohamed Ali in Indian Politics,* vol. 1, p. 307.

in the council and half the positions in public services. But they were still not able to win over their lost following. Accused of a sellout, they remained the target of attack in the press. The Lucknow Pact, stated the *Resalat,* would place Muslims under the 'thumb of the Hindus'. Communal riots in Bihar in September 1917 hardened attitudes. The *Resalat's* warning to 'learn a lesson from the universal ruin of their brethren in Bihar' struck a sympathetic chord in many circles.

> Those who apprehend that the Muslims will suffer political death if they do not unite with the Hindus are greatly mistaken. We have already stood alone for 1300 years. What is wanted is that we should firmly abide by our religious laws and not become faint-hearted.[49]

This was the *Moslem Hitaishi* giving vent to its anger against the Lucknow Pact.

Taking advantage of such feelings, the Central National Mohammadan Association and the Indian Muslim Association staked their respective claims to represent their community in Bengal. They demanded 52 per cent of seats as against the 40 per cent allotted by the Lucknow Pact. In a memorial submitted to Montagu and Chelmsford, they argued that as the trend of government policy was towards granting autonomous administration to various provinces and towards reduction of the British element, it was essential 'to have the rights of Muslims...placed upon a firm...basis'. The spirit of the address was characterized by the concluding section:

> For England now to place the Indian Muslims, without proper, definite and ample safeguards, under the heels of a hostile non-Muslim majority, would, your humble memorialists venture respectfully to submit, be a cruel act of breach of faith and violation of trust.[50]

W.H. Vincent, a member of the governor-general's executive council, endorsed the demands of the various associations. But the Southborough Committee (Franchise) was willing to recommend only 54 per cent of the territorial seats. The Bengal

[49] *Resalat,* 2, 7 and 17 December 1917, *Mohammadi,* 14 December 1917, *Moslem Hitaishi,* 10 August 1917, SNNR, Bengal.

[50] Addresses presented at Calcutta, Montagu Papers (34).

government was willing to go only this far.[51] In the end, the efforts of the Bengal Muslim leaders to nullify the effects of the Congress-League scheme and to secure major concessions from Montagu and Chelmsford proved unsuccessful. Nawab Ali Chaudhuri, the main architect of the Indian Muslim Association, failed to impress and belied all hopes that had been aroused by his activities. The Montagu-Chelmsford Report, much to the dismay of educated Muslims in Bengal, recognized the Congress-League compact as 'the most complete and authoritative settlement between the claims of the majority and the minority' and as an 'accomplished fact and a landmark in Indian politics'. Moreover, the image of Nawab Ali and his associates was tarnished because of their complicity in the September riots in 1918.[52] Having lost face with the public, the Nawab withdrew into the safety of the council chamber.

In UP and Punjab, opposition to the Lucknow Pact was initiated and sustained by the landlords. In 1917, they were advised to advance their claims before Montagu and Chelmsford so that the Congress-League scheme was undermined and the professional groups were prevented from dominating the councils. Michael O'Dwyer made his intentions known. He was committed to defending the interests of the landed gentry in Punjab, who 'were in close touch with the rural masses...the recognized leaders and an invaluable support to the administration'. This was the class to which the Punjab government 'has looked and never looked in vain in times of stress and difficulty'.[53] Meston followed a similar course in UP, urging the Nawab of Rampur to throw his weight behind the UP Muslim Defence Association, organized at his instance by Nawab Fateh Ali Khan, Nawab Muzammilullah Khan, a zamindar with large estates in Aligarh and Etah districts, Syed Abdur Rauf, member of UP legislative council from 1913 to 1916, and Ibni Ahmed, a petty zamindar of Budaun and a practising lawyer at the Allahabad High Court. His advice to the Nawab was:

[51] J.H. Broomfield, *Elite Conflict in a Plural Society: Twentieth Century Bengal* (Berkeley and Los Angeles, 1968), pp. 126–29.

[52] Broomfield, op. cit., pp. 192–93.

[53] *The Political Situation in India* (Calcutta, 1917), p. 47.

It is assuredly time to stop a great deal of the nonsense that is preached by the leaders. You will remember my parting prayer to you the other day, and my earnest entreaty that you should come forward and take your right position at the head of your community. I never give advice which is likely to be embarrassing, and even if I give it, I never resent it being rejected. But I do ask Your Highness to think over this opportunity of taking a brilliant and dominant part in organizing wise and moderate and orthodox Moslem opinion in India.[54]

The Defence Association got into the act of presenting an address to the secretary of state and the viceroy. Quite familiar views were orchestrated. For example, any 'large measure of self-government which might curtail the moderating and adjusting influence of the British government would be nothing short of cataclysm'. A number of demands flowed from this formulation, but they were completely out of tune with the realities of contemporary political life. With British influence gradually being curtailed in legislative bodies, there was no chance of the demands of the Association being accepted. And with the agitation against the Montagu-Chelmsford proposals gathering momentum, the Defence Association was left with no *raison d'etre:* it petered out after a brief and lazy existence.

IV

The Lucknow accord ushered in an era of Congress-League co-operation on vital political and constitutional issues. In August 1918, the League followed the Congress line in rejecting the Montagu-Chelmsford reforms. Both protested against the insinuation contained therein that the Indian people were unfit for responsible government, reaffirmed their ideas on self-government [adopted at their annual sessions in Lucknow and Calcutta], and emphasized that self-government within the Empire alone would satisfy Indian aspirations.[55] On several other issues, such as the Rowlatt Bills and the ghastly happenings at Jallianwala Bagh, the Congress and the League spoke and acted in unison.[56]

[54] To Hamid Ali Khan, 12 November 1917, Meston Papers (4).

[55] *Tribune*, 5 September 1918.

[56] 'It is impossible to go through the proceedings of the session (Muslim League) without being struck by the fact that the national inspiration is as

The distinction between the two organizations was blurred, at least for the time being. The concurrent sessions of the Congress and the League became a convention over the next five years and provided Gandhi and his Khilafat allies with an enlarged arena for mounting their campaigns.[57]

Unity between the Congress and the League created a climate for inter-community fraternization. It was common for leaders of different religious persuasions to visit temples and mosques and to exhort on the virtues of communal unity. Such sentiments were echoed at the Nakhoda mosque in Calcutta, the Juma Masjid in Delhi and the Sonepur mosque in Bombay. Elsewhere, there were dramatic scenes of Hindus and Muslims joining in each other's festival and removing the irritants in their otherwise harmonious relationship. Allahabad, Agra, Azamgarh, scenes of communal rioting in earlier years, were, in 1917-18, examples of Hindu-Muslim amity.[58] At some of these places, local Congress committees and Home Rule Leagues organized and conducted religious processions which, in the past, were sources of discord. In Bengal, Hindus and Muslims of Patnakhali joined each others prayer meetings and resolved to attain Home Rule. Such instances, recorded in official reports, can be cited from other areas as well. In sum, they held out hopes of a stable and durable resolution of communal disputes which were occasioned by local feuds over processions, cow-slaughter and music before mosques. Gandhi was able to capitalize on the existing goodwill to cement the bonds of Hindu-Muslim friendship during the Rowlatt

---

strong, as deep and as universal in the League as in the Congress and the country.' Ibid., 13 January 1918.

[57] See essays in Ravinder Kumar (ed.), *Essays on Gandhian Politics,* and J.M. Brown, *Gandhi's Rise to Power: Indian Politics 1915–1922* (Cambridge, 1974).

[58] *Leader,* 18 September, 4 and 15 November 1917; *Tribune,* 21 and 30 November 1917. J.C. Smith, the Collector and magistrate of Azamgarh, issued the following statement on 2 November: 'The district of Azamgarh is to be congratulated on the fact that the Dasehra and Muharram ceremonies passed off without disturbances of any kind. For more three years past the government have been anxious regarding this matter and it is highly creditable to the people that at so critical a period there has been no sign of hostility between the different communities'. *Leader,* 15 November 1917.

satyagraha and the Khilafat movement. The editor of *Amrita Bazar Patrika* wrote : 'Though the Rowlatt Act sits like a dread nightmare on our breasts, it has united both Hindus and Mussalmans in a way which has never been witnessed.'[59]

In the years following the Lucknow Pact, a number of younger Muslims were drawn into the Congress movement and played a leading part in the Home Rule movement and the Rowlatt satyagraha. The Bihar Congress, for example, was dominated by Mazharul Haq, Hasan Imam, Mohammad Shafi and Sarfaraz Husain Khan. In UP and Delhi nationalist feeling was in full flow with Ansari, Ajmal Khan, Hasrat Mohani, Wazir Hasan, Shuaib Qureshi and the Ali Brothers in the forefront of the Congress and Home Rule movements. They had a large following of young Muslims, graduates from British and Indian universities, trained in the professions of journalism and law. They included Asaf Ali, who rose to prominence in Delhi during the Rowlatt satyagraha; Abdul Majid Khwaja, Jawaharlal's contemporary at Cambridge and founder of the Home Rule League in Aligarh; Zahur Ahmad, Kamaluddin Jafri, Manzar Ali Sokhta and Wahid Yar Khan, all connected with the Nehru household in Allahabad; Shuaib Qureshi, Khaliquzzaman, Raja Ghulam Husain and Abdur Rahman Siddiqi—Aligarh graduates bound to Ansari and Mohamed Ali by personal and political loyalty.[60] According to Meston, this 'clique of noisy and aggressive Muslims', patronized by the Raja of Mahmudabad, 'make the Raja's house their headquarters and live and agitate at his expense.'[61] He was alarmed that both the 'extremists' and the 'moderates' in his province had combined in the Home Rule agitation; and, the 'greatest marvel of all, the Muhammadans had also come into the fold'.[62] The same process was underway in other areas, such as in Bombay where Jinnah, Omar Sobhani and Syed Abdullah Brelvi were involved in nationalist agitations. M.C. Chagla recalled: 'When I left India in 1919, Jinnah was the uncrowned King of Bombay. He was the idol of the youth. His personality

[59] Motilal Ghose to Mohamed Ali, 14 April 1919, Mohamed Ali Papers, JMI.

[60] For a fuller discussion, see Hasan, *A Nationalist Conscience*, pp. 25–30.

[61] To Chelmsford, 20 August 1917, Meston Papers (1).

[62] Home Poll. Deposit, May 1917, File No. 3, NAI.

and his sturdy independence appealed to the best elements in the city. He was the President of the Home Rule League, and had made stirring speeches in Shantaram Chawl, which was then the venue of political meetings.'[63]

A few general conclusions flow out of our analysis of the Lucknow Pact. The first relates to the different ways in which Muslims reacted to its provisions and the several different ways in which they sought to promote their interests in the power structures envisaged by Montagu and Chelmsford. Political activists in UP were mainly interested in securing separate electorates and weightages in order to retain their advantages in the council and local bodies. Their counterparts in Bengal, on the other hand, were much more concerned with representation on the basis of population rather than separate electorates.

Religious associations, small and large, had their own ideas. Sometimes they reflected local concerns, as did the Anjuman-i Islam of Bombay which approved the Congress-League scheme but demanded a larger share for Muslims in the legislative council. Often, their concerns were limited to religious affairs. The *ulama* of Deoband, for example, wanted a berth for an *alim* in the councils. They wanted *auqafs* and mosques to be placed under the charge of a Shaikhul Islam and called for a strict application of the Islamic Personal Law, which was divine and immutuable.[64]

Religious groups were not always united in putting forward their views. One group of Ahmadiyas, 'a body of about 50 persons' was sympathetic to the Lucknow accord but the other was not.[65] Similarly, the Barelwis were averse to extending any support to the demands of the Deobandis. The Anjuman-i Islam in Saharanpur decided to strike a somewhat different chord. It regarded the political implications of the Lucknow agreement 'ruinous' and announced:

[63] M.C. Chagla, *Roses in December: An Autobiography* (Bombay. 1973), p. 78.

[64] Maulvi Mohammad Ahmad to Sheweth, 30 October 1917, Meston Papers (19).

[65] Memorial submitted by the Anjuman-i Ahmadiya Ishaat-i Islam, Lahore, Montagu Papers (35).

our instinct of self-preservation compels us to always keep at a safe distance from them [Hindus] in politics.... We are fully convinced that without *equal* strength, we are not for one minute safe with them in the political arena, because their interests happen to be so diametrically opposed to ours and their angle of vision so irreconcilably different.[66]

This manifesto was not consistent with the political mood of the *ulama,* especially those based at Firangi Mahal, Nadwa and Deoband. It also did not reflect the radical temper of large sections of Muslims who, for a variety of reasons, hitched their fortunes with the nationalist struggles.

With such glaring differences it was not surprising that Montagu and Chelmsford received not one but forty-four representations from 'Muslim' bodies—each one of them purporting to represent the community. And each one posed as the defender of the faith and the custodian of 'Muslim interests'. These were dubious claims. No organization, not even the Muslim League, had acquired the status of a truly national and representative body in the first quarter of the twentieth century. Moreover, given the multiplicity of interests at different levels it was not easy for anyone to identify the so-called Muslim interests and to then formulate a set of coherent and unified demands. Montagu knew it. He recognized that the communal categories imposed by the raj made no sense and that it was not right to treat Muslims as a distinct political interest. But he could not reverse a process initiated long ago. Likewise, he was averse to communal representation, regarding their introduction as 'a great mistake in the history of India and as more harmful perhaps in its consequences than the permanent settlement of Bengal or the partition of that province'.[67] Yet, for all the nobility of principles displayed by such

[66] Meston Papers (19).

[67] E. Montagu, *An Indian Diary,* vol. 2, p. 62, Montagu Papers (39). The *Report* observed that 'division by creeds and classes means the creation of political camps organized against each other, and teaches men to think as partisans and not as citizens; and it is difficult to see how the change from this system to national representation is ever to occur. The British Government is often accused of dividing men in order to govern them. But if it unnecessarily divides them at the very moment when it proposes to start them on the road to governing themselves, it will find it difficult to meet the charge of being hypocritical or shortsighted.' *Report on Indian Constitutional Reforms* (London, 1918), Cd. 9109, p. 187.

statements, no attempt was made in 1919 to abolish the system. On the contrary, it was expanded to include Sikhs in the Punjab and Eurasians elsewhere. The reasons in 1919 were the 'settled facts' of Minto's promise of 1906, the Act of 1909 and the belief that Muslim regarded separate representation and communal electorates as their only adequate safeguards.

One final point. By negotiating the Lucknow Pact on the questionable terms of communal representation, the Congress legitimized what were later derided as 'separatist' and 'communal' demands. By allowing itself to be dictated by narrow regional and sectarian causes, the Congress created a space within which such concerns had to be accommodated even at the risk of destroying the democratic and secular structures it was striving to build. Instead of curbing divisive tendencies through a concerted ideological campaign, the Congress settled for hastily concluded agreements for immediate political benefits. Consequently, it lost the moral authority and the political conviction to challenge the assumptions that went into the making of the Montagu-Chelmsford Reforms. The British translated their assumptions into concrete legislative proposals and, in the process, created a separate and distinct political identity for the Muslims. The Congress, caught up in its own contradictions, woke up to this painful reality only after the Khilafat and Non-Co-operation movements had petered out. By then, the contours of Indian politics had changed. So had the terms of discourse.

Chapter Five

Islam, Khilafat and Nationalism-I

Sambhlo ke wo zindaan goonj utha, jhapto ke wo qaidi choot gaye
Utho ke wo baitheen deewaren, dauro ke wo tooti zanjeeren

(Josh Malihabadi)

Take heed,
the prison-house reverberates
Spring forward,
the prisoners are free;
Arise,
the walls are collapsing
Surge ahead, the chains
have snapped asunder

Between 1919 and 1921 India experienced an unprecedented political upheaval, 'a magnificent struggle', characterized by mass involvement and by messianic ambitions on the part of some of its leaders.[1] In scholarly literature, however, the Khilafat upsurge is often treated as an artifact, a compound of material fears topped up by a dash of ideological whipped cream by the 'Young Party' Muslims,[2] as a movement 'devoid of

[1] Shahid Amin, 'Gandhi as Mahatma: Gorakhpur District, Eastern UP, 1921–2', Ranajit Guha (ed.), *Subaltern Studies III: Writings on South Asian History and Society* (Delhi, 1984).

[2] For example, Robinson argued that the professional politicians had 'continually to manufacture issues and to whip up agitations to keep their newspapers going, their organizations active and their coffers full....The issues were religious, usually pan-Islamic: these were the only sure sources of the money they needed.' *Separatism,* p. 354. This interpretation is not shared by, among others, Gail Minault. She has tried to analyze the different meanings of the Khilafat symbol in the Indian context and examine how certain leaders attempted to create a self-conscious and unified Indian Muslim

constructive thought...purely negative in its aims, methods and policy'.[3] Its disintegration is attributed to an ideology that was romantic and out of touch with actualities,[4] to the religious fervour heightened by reactionary political forces,[5] to the apocalyptic spirit in which the movement was conducted, and to its being out of tune with the political realities in West Asia.

I propose to read existing historical accounts 'against the grain' so as to bring ideology to the centre of my analysis. I will argue that there was always a significant group of Muslims who could find in their tradition the ideological resources which would enable them to bridge their sense of 'difference' and the nationalist movement, which would enable them to be both good Muslims and ardent supporters of India's plural nationhood. In short, the object of this chapter and the one to follow is to describe and analyze both the Islamic and nationalist components of the Khilafat movement.

II

It is not commonly recognized that the Muslim intelligentsia in India has taken much pride in fostering its fraternal links with fellow-Muslims in other societies. It has followed the history of the lands from the *huertas* [irrigated lands] of Andalusia, to the oasis of the Maghrib, to the valley of the Nile, the Sawad of Iraq, and all the way to Farghana.[6] Iqbal explained why this was so.

---

constituency. This quest, according to Minault, grew out of Islamic cultural and educational reform movements of the nineteenth century. *The Khilafat Movement*, p. 208.

[3] Hardy, *Muslims of British India*, p. 196.

[4] Smith, *Modern Islam in India*, p. 240.

[5] Bipan Chandra, *Communalism in Modern India*, p. 172.

[6] One of the most eloquent instances of this nostalgia for the departed glory of Muslims is in Hali's famous poem 'The Flow and Ebb of Islam', composed in 1879. So great was its influence that Syed Ahmad Khan is reported to have said that if he was asked about his good deeds on the Day of Judgement, he would say: 'I got Hali to write his *Mussadas*'. See Table 5:1 as illustrative of the interest in the political, social and cultural history of Muslim countries. Of course, the list of publications is by no means exhaustive.

The record of the past, he observed in *Rumuz-i Bekhudi,* 'illuminates the conscience of a People, memory of the past achievements makes it self-aware;...the present thrusts its head up from the past, and from thy present shall thy future stem'.[7]

When Islam fell on evil days in the nineteenth and twentieth centuries, the heritage of the past stood forth as a symbol of community pride and distinction. [Table 5:1] Some eloquent instances of nostalgia for the departed glory was expressed in Hali's 'The Ebb and Flow of Islam,[8] in Shibli's pan-Islamic anguish and in Iqbal's ode to once-Arab Sicily.[9] Iqbal also wrote *Bilaad-i Islamia* (Muslim Cities) to express his deep emotional loyalty to the world of Islam——to Delhi, Baghdad, Cordova—'the light of Muslim's eye,' Constantinople and Medina—the *watan* of all Muslims, their centre and refuge. All these places had fine, grand and sublime achievements to their credit. Mohamed Ali told his readers that

[7] A.J. Arberry, *The Mystery of Selflessness* (London, 1953), p. 97.

[8] For example,

Would anyone see humiliation transgressing her limits?
Let him look at Islam, not lifting her head after falling.
That high tide follows low tide, he would never admit,
Who would watch the ebbing wave of this ocean of ours.

G.E. Ward and C.S. Tute, *The Quatrains of Hali* (Oxford University Press, 1932), p. 65.

[9] The poem read:

Once thou wast the cradle of the civilization of this race
The fire of whose glance was world captivating beauty
The nightingales of Shiraz wailed over Baghdad;
And Dagh wept tears of blood over Delhi

To sing the dirge of ruin was to fall to my lot;
This torture—yea, self-torture was reserved for me,
Tell me of thy anguish; I am too full of pain;
I am the dust raised by that caravan which once broke its journey here.
Paint me that picture of the old,
Rouse me by telling the tale of bygone days;
And I shall carry thy gift to India,
And make others weep as I weep now.
S.A. Latif, *The Influence of English Literature on Urdu Literature* (London, 1924), pp. 111–13.

the Indian Mussalman's heart throbs in unison with the Moor of Fez, who sees his country passing into alien hands, with the Persian of Tehran who feels the grip of the Russian Cossack on his throat, and with the Turk of Stamboul who has to watch an act of shameless brigandage with impotent rage.[10]

There was more to it than just that. Muslims were asked to seek inspiration from their own *Islamic* heritage and turn to the Quranic and *Sunna* ideal paradigm as a blueprint to confront colonial aggression and exploitation. Syed Ahmad in India and Mohammad Abduh in Egypt sought a reformed, revitalized Islam that would neither be beholden to western trends nor weighed down by age-old accretions. They insisted that a reformed Islam, with its supportive values of brotherhood, community and union and its proven ability to express the poetry of collective life, could co-exist with western ideas, accept their challenges and replace the imitation, either of Europe or of antiquated tradition, with a dynamic and innovative culture such as distinguished Islam at the time of first generation of *salaf*. Thus the *salafiya* doctrine in Egypt came to be associated with attacks on mysticism, saint-veneration, and specifically the sufi doctrines, just as it was embedded in programmes for modern education that emphasized reason and rational sciences.

As the modernist-reformist ideas of Abduh and Jamaluddin Afghani gained adherents in countries under colonial domination, Islam became an ever more frequent symbol of and channel for nationalists protests. In fact, pan-Islamism—a multifaceted, often opaque search for an Islamic meaning in the modern world—was the vehicle through which radical and nationalist ideas were conveyed. Thus Tan Malaka, representing Indonesia at the fourth Congress of the Comintern in 1922, maintained that pan-Islamism meant 'the national struggle for freedom'.[11] Transposed into Islamic terms, it signified the unity and solidarity of all Muslims against the common threat of western empires which had penetrated into the heartlands of the Muslim world. A

[10] *Comrade*, 14 October 1911.

[11] R.V. Niel, 'From Netherlands East Indies to Republic of Indonesia 1900–1945', Harry Eveling (ed.), *The Development of Indonesian Society* (Queensland, 1979), pp. 112, 120.

TABLE 5.1
Published writings on some Muslim countries

Author	Title	Year/Place of Publication
Maulvi Mohammad Inshaullah	*Saltanat-i Usmania ke Maujooda Halaat* (Amritsar, 1897).	
Sirajuddin	*Hayaat-i Salauddin* (Amritsar, 1897).	
Author not known	*Musafir-i Damishqi* (Lucknow, 1899).	
Author not known	*Ayyam-i Arab* (Lucknow, 1899).	
Syed Shah Kabir	*Tazkirat al-Ikraam: Tarikh-i Arab wa Islam* (Kanpur, 1900).	
Author not known	*Tarikh-i Turkaan-i Rum* (Moradabad, 1889), vol. 1.	
Mirza Hairat	*Khilafat-i Usmania* (Delhi, 1901).	
Mohammad Farhatullah	*Tarikh-i Ref* (Bijnor, 1901). History of Morocco.	
Aghlab Mohani (Mohammad Husain)	*Nairang-i Afghan: Qaumi aur Mulki Tarikh Afghanistan* (Lucknow, 1904).	
Hakim Abdullah Rashid	*Mauritius aur Islam* (Bombay, 1906).	
Mau na Shibli Nomani	*Safar Nama-i Rum wa Misr-o-Shaam* (Azamgarh, 1340 A.H.) and his multi-volume history of Persian literature.	
Mohammd Abdullah	*Damishq* (Amritsar, 1911).	
Sajjad Hyder Yaldaram	*Lehra: Ek Turkish novel ka tarjuma* (Aligarh, n.d.).	
Abdul Halim Sharar	*Shaheed-i Wafa* (Lahore, 1920). Account of the social and cultural life of the Muslims in Spain.	
Wajahat Husain	*Anwar Pasha* (Lahore, 1921).	
A.R. Bulandshahari	*Seerat-i Ghazi Mustafa Kamal Pasha* (Bijnor, 1921).	
Ameer Ali	*Short History of the Saracens* (London, 1921).	
Abdul Wahid Ibn-i Ali	*Khilafat-i Muwahidda* (Madras, 1922). Translated from the Arabic—a history of Morocco and Spain.	
Asghar Ali Nizami	*Shaan-i Islam aur Turki Talwaar* (Lahore, 1923).	
S. Khuda Bukhsh	*Contributions to the History of Islamic Civilization* (Calcutta, 1929). 2 vols.	

Abdul Rab	*Sair-i Undalus* (Allahabad, 1934). Historical novel on the Muslims in Spain.
Abdur Rahman Shauq	*Hayaat-i Khalid bin Walid* (Lahore, 1936).
Mohammad Aslam Jairajpuri	*Tarikh-i Millat* (Delhi, in 10 vols.)
Qazi Abdul Ghaffar	*Aasaar-i Jamaluddin* (Delhi, 1940).
Maulana Saeed Ahmad	*Mussalmanon ka Urooj-o-Zawaal* (Delhi, 1942).

renewed commitment to faith and action, individual or collective, private or public, was understood by the ideologues of the pan-Islamic idea not only as an act of defense against the intellectual and cultural imperialism of the West, but as the pre-condition for the building of a strong, united Islam as the only road of salvation for the world.

India was not the only country swept by the pan-Islamic tide. Abdul Hamid II, who reigned from 1876 to 1908, attracted allegiance from many African Muslims who acknowledged Turkey as the only remaining Islamic power in a world of aggressive Christian States. Thus the Sultan had been addressed by and replied to the Muslims in Lagos in 1894 on the importance of western education. From the 1870s there were close contacts between Istanbul and Cape Town Muslims. The Sultan of Zanzibar was entertained by Abdul Hamid, and as late as 1910 Friday prayers in the capital were still being said in the name of the Ottoman Sultan. At the outbreak of World War I, the Ottoman call for a *jehad* against the Allied powers was widely distributed in North Africa. It surfaced also in East and Central Africa, where, in 1915, the British arrest in Nyasaland of a Muslim from Mozambique uncovered Swahili tracts bearing Istanbul's call for holy war against the English. Likewise, pan-Islamic sympathies came to the fore in Sudan. That it did not develop greatly was on account of special efforts to counteract the pan-Islamic propaganda and on account of the fact that the Mahdi's revolt had been directed against the Turko-Egyptian regime. One of its aims was to reject the Khalifa at Istanbul as the representative of the Muslim world. The position had not changed when World War I broke out and there was no reason for the Mahdists to co-operate with the Turks in the name of Islam.[12]

In Indonesia, pan-Islamism constituted a danger to the political *status quo*. So also the modernist Islamic ideas being taught in Cairo, in particular those stemming from the teachings of Abduh.[13] Snouck Hugronje, the Dutch authority on Islam,

[12] C.C. Stewart, 'Islam', A.D. Roberts (ed.), *The Cambridge History of Africa* (Cambridge, 1986), pp. 199–200.

[13] See Daniel Noer, *The Modernist Muslim Movement in Indonesia 1900–1942* (Oxford, 1973).

observed that Indonesians then studying in the international Islamic milieu of Mecca were absorbing pan-Islamic notions 'which can make their disposition towards the European administration of their fatherland unfavourable'. But he altered the government policy of restricting pilgrimage to Mecca on the grounds that as a religious doctrine Islam should be free of interference, although as a political force it should be destroyed.[14] During the 1880s, some 2,000 pilgrims were counted annually as leaving the Dutch provinces for Mecca. After the opening of the Suez Canal in 1869, the number grew steadily each year until, by the late 1890s, the figure was fluctuating from more than 11,000 in 1895 (a 'Great Pilgrimage' year) to 7,000 in 1900.[15]

C. Poenson, a nineteenth century missionary in Central Java, noted the profound influence of *Haj* in heightening anti-imperialist consciousness.[16] More recently, William R. Roff has described the impact of even brief exposure to a wholly Muslim environment in which the universality of the faith was demonstrated by a congregation of pilgrims of all races, all levels of society. Returning to the Indies, to the towns and villages, the mosques and religious schools, they took with them not only a renewed zeal for purification of action and belief but a certain readiness to reject the colonial *status quo* if the occasion should present itself.[17]

[14] George McTurnan Kahin, *Nationalism and Revolution in Indonesia* (Cornell, 1952), pp. 44–48.

[15] William R. Roff, 'South-East Asian Islam in the Nineteenth Century', in P.M. Holt, Ann K.S. Lambton, Bernard Lewis (eds.), *Cambridge History of Islam* (Cambridge, 1970), vol. 2, pp. 180–81. In India, too, an average of just over 12,000 pilgrims sailed from Bombay from 1882 to 1893. The numbers increased as the government initiated several measures, including the formation of *Haj* committees, to make the journey less painful. See UP Government (GAD), Poll. F.No. 89, 1894 and F.No. 142, 1913, UPSA. Also, see J.A. Rahim, *Report of the Special Haj Enquiry,* in Public and Judicial Department, F.No. 8/758, IOLR.

[16] He noted that Arabia was not just the 'uniting centre' for devoted pilgrims, but that the *Haj* provided both the occasion and an opportunity for political leaders to devise future plans. Quoted in Noer, op. cit., pp. 25–26. Like many of his contemporaries, Poenson was haunted by the spectre of a pan-Islamic conspiracy being hatched annually at Mecca.

[17] Roff, op.cit., p. 172. Again, this was also the point made by Iqbal and

III

Among Sunni Muslims, who formed the overwhelming majority of the Muslim population, Turkey's Sultan was the *Amir al-Mumineen* (Commander of the Faithful) or the *Khilafat al-Muslimeen.*[18] The Khilafat was the viceroyalty of the Prophet of Islam, ordained by Divine Law for the perpetuation of Islam and the continued observance of the *Shariat.* In addition, the Khalifa was the defender of the Holy Places of Islam *(Jazirat al-Arab),* which at one time extended—from Aden to the Mountains of Syria—and the sea coast to the agricultural lowlands of Iraq.[19] The *Jazirat al-Arab* included Constantinople,[20]

several other writers in India. For Iqbal, see Schimmel, *Gabriel's Wing,* pp. 195–96. Also, Meer Hasan Ali, *Observations on the Mussulmans of India* (Reprint of 1834 edn., Oxford, 1974), pp. 112–13; Mushir Hosain Kidwai, *Pan-Islamism and Bolshevism* (London, 1937), pp. 224–26.

[18] The *Sadiq al-Akhbaar* of Lahore commented on 24 February 1904 that whenever the Turkish Sultan is in danger, the Muslims in India offer prayers and observe fast for his well being. Quoted in I.A. Malik, *Punjab Muslim Press and the Muslim World 1885–1911* (Lahore, 1974). Likewise, the secretary of state for India was surprised to learn that Muslims 'pray weekly for the Sultan.' Austen Chamberlain to Chelmsford, 29 August 1916, Home Poll. Deposit, December 1916, F.No. 20, NAI.

[19] Mohamed Ali reiterated time and again that the mandate of *Jazirat al-Arab* 'has been given to us by the Prophet'. Mazharul Haq stated that the areas located therein 'touched the deepest religious sentiment of the followers of Islam' and that it 'must remain under the suzerainty of the Muslim Khalifa'. *Motherland,* 19 January 1922, quoted in Qeyamuddin Ahmad and J.S. Jha, *Mazharul Haque* (Delhi, 1976), p. 91. Obviously, the prospect of the areas in *Jazirat al-Arab* falling under non-Muslim control caused much consternation. So also the widely circulated rumours of the sacred precincts being desecrated. Circulated through vernacular pamphlets, such rumours were clearly intended to rouse religious passions. See, for example, S. Ghafoor Shah, *Khoon-i Khirman aur sada-i intiqaam;* Munshi Wali Mohammad, *Islam ki Faryaad* (Delhi, 1971); Majid Ahmad, *Dard-i Khilafat* (Aligarh, n.d.). Proscribed Publications (8, 44, 142), IOLR. Notice the following verse:

Ae barq aaj shola-fishaan kyon nahin hai tu
Ae abr aaj girya kunaan kyon nahin hai tu
Darya-i qahr aaj rawaan kyon nahin hai tu
Islam aaj kufr ke narghe men aa gaya
Baadal siyah rang ka Kaaba pe chaa gaya

Jerusalem, Medina, and, above all, Mecca with its *Baitullah,* the focal point of daily prayers and the annual *Haj.*[21] Mohamed Ali announced in London :

We, who consider ourselves to be the spiritual heirs of Abraham, Moses and Jesus, consider that this is a land apart and consecrated in a peculiar degree and reserved for us. We are charged with the duty of maintaining its sanctity inviolate, of keeping it peaceful and tranquil, a sanctuary for the faithful, and safe for theocracy. In order to preserve that sanctity and peace and tranquillity which we desire, it is necessary that it should remain with us. It would be a sad day indeed for us when any part of it goes out of the hands of the Muslims, for then we would have betrayed a divine trust. Muslims will never acquiesce in any arrangement that permitted any form of control being exercized by a non-Muslim power over any part of the *Jazirat al-Arab.*[22]

O the thunderbolt why dost not thou scatter flames?
O the lightning why thou wailest not?
O the clouds why weepest not thou?
Why is the river of curse a frozen puddle and flows not?
Islam has been swamped and overwhelmed by the Unbelief
And the Kaaba has been engulfed by darkness.
Proscribed Publications (8), IOLR.

[20] Constantinople was one of the holy cities, ranked next only to Mecca, Medina and Jerusalem. It was identified with the past glories of Islam and regarded as a 'relic of a great national and religious value by the whole Muslim world'. Yaqub Hasan to Lloyd George, 1 July 1919, Foreign and Political Dept., External B, F.No. 361–68, October 1920, NAI; Home Poll. A, F.No. 363–68, May 1919, NAI.

[21] The number of Muslims who undertook the arduous journey, so vividly described by Meer Hasan Ali, an English woman married to a Shia official in Lucknow, was quite considerable. The numbers increased in the first decade of the twentieth century (Table 5.2) for the reasons indicated above.

TABLE 5.2

Number of Pilgrims from British India, 1907–8 to 1913–14

1907–8	1908–9	1909–10	1910–11	1911–12	1912–13	1913–14
21,648	15,947	20,901	17,884	22,995	15,555	15,186

Source : *Statistical Abstract for British India, 1916–17* (Calcutta, 1919), vol. 4, p. 129.

[22] See Hasan (ed.), *Mohamed Ali in Indian Politics*, vol. 2, pp. 231–32, vol. 3, pp. 65, 79, 125–26.

For these reasons, interest in Turkey's welfare continued: each time it was involved in hostilities, like the Russo-Turkish war of 1877–78 or the Greco-Turkish war of 1897, Indian Muslims took up the cudgels for Turkey and reaffirmed their attachment to and prayed for the well-being of its Sultan. 'If the Muhammadans of the world were compared to the human body', commented the *Akhbaar-i Am,* 'the Sultan would be the heart and brain'.[23] Anthony MacDonnell, lieutenant-governor of UP, quoted to the viceroy a leaflet describing the Ottoman Sultan as *Amir al-Mumineen* and *Padshah-i Mussalmanan* and reported the 'great sympathy' for him 'partly due to incitement from outside India and partly spontaneous'. Many more people, he was told, had taken to wearing the Turkish *fez.* This, he concluded, 'is perhaps the straw indicating how the wind is beginning to blow'.[24]

The incitement from outside came from two distinct sources. In the first place, the British government exploited pro-Turkish sensibilities in order to secure Indian Muslim loyalty, as in 1857, and to protect their imperial interests from Russian encroachments by bolstering 'the sick man of Europe', as they did from the Crimean war of 1853-56 onwards. Then, the Sultan of Turkey, Abdul Hamid II, sent his agents to India, as to other lands, to rally support and enthusiasm for his feeble regime which was threatened by external aggression and internal strife, caused by nationalist movements sprung up among his Christian Balkan subjects [American, Greek, Romanian and Bulgarian] in southeast Europe.

Syed Ahmad was the only prominent Muslim to dispute Abdul Hamid's pretensions. The pan-Islamic surge threatened to wreck his effort to prop up the Anglo-Muslim alliance in India; so he wanted to cut the silver cord which tied

[23] *Akhbar-i Am,* 14 March 1895, SNNR, Punjab.

[24] Hardy, *Muslims of British India,* p. 177. Blunt was told on the eve of his visit to India that he should not say anything against the Sultan of Turkey, because his name 'was now venerated in India as it has not formerly been'. Blunt, *India Under Ripon,* p. 13. Also, see Yusuf Husain Khan, 'Indian Muslims and the Caliphate', S.T. Lokhandwalla (ed.), *India and Contemporary Islam* (Indian Institute for Advanced Study: Shimla, 1971), pp. 168–174.

Muslims to the international fraternity of 'all believers', personified in the Khilafat. He spoke against the Turcophilia among his co-religionists, arguing that they were legally bound to obey the writ not of an external Muslim Khalifa but of the British Indian government. In 1900, one of Syed Ahmad's associates suggested that Muslims should refrain from printing the Crescent on their book on the ground that it may be mistaken as a sign of their leaning towards the Turkish government. But such endeavours to sever the Muslim attachment to the Turkish Khilafat were greeted with suspicion and distrust. Nawab Mohsinul Mulk, one of Syed Ahmad's most distinguished successors at the Aligarh college, learnt his lesson the hard way. When he expressed unhappiness over the ever-increasing pan-Islamic meetings on campus, he was castigated as a 'downright sycophant'.[25]

The most bitter criticizm of Syed Ahmad's views came from that celebrated roving reformer., teacher and political agitator, Jamaluddin al-Asadabadi 'al-Afghani'. He regarded the Aligarh reformer's religious views and his educational programme as ancillaries to his political servitude to the British and chided him for relying on them instead of joining hands with the Indian nationalists. Afghani considered Syed Ahmad as his main adversary in India, opposed to pan-Islamism, isolating Indian Muslims from the rest of *Dar al-Islam,* especially from the Turks, and hostile to the conception of a universal Muslim Khilafat. According to him, the reassertion of Muslim identity and solidarity were prerequisites for restoring political and cultural independence, and unity and solidarity were essential at both levels.[26]

[25] *Jasus* (Agra), 14 July 1906; *Al-Aziz* (Agra), 28 July 1906, SNNR, UP.

[26] Afghani was in India between 1857 and 1865. He came again in 1879 and spent three years travelling to places like Bombay, Hyderabad, Bhopal and Calcutta. The purpose of his visit was to

> meet with all the *navvabs* and princes and *ulama* and grandees of that land and to explain to them one by one the results that are manifested from unity and solidarity in the whole world and the injuries that have appeared from division and disunity; and to caress their ears with the mystery of the *hadith;* ...and to express inspiring and prudent words and to attract the friendship and co-operation of the learned and the eloquent; and to breathe into them the new spirit of love of nationality and to rend the curtain of their neglect

The Muslims were to be united as the Germans and Italians were united, and Afghani passed his life in search for a Muslim monarch to whom he could be a Bismarck or a Cavour. The enemy from which Islam needed to be saved was Europe, and especially Britain, the imperial power in India and Egypt. Afghani therefore spent the greater part of his life travelling from one country to the other as the chief exponent of pan-Islamism. His efforts did not go unrewarded: his pan-Islamic vision inspired various activist groups in different lands and lives on patiently, if amorphously, in the aspirations of many Muslims.[27] It is also curious and relevant that the only instance where his political programme of combined radicalism, modernism, nationalism and pan-Islamism ever became a serious political agenda of a vibrant and spirited opposition was in the Khilafat agitation in India, years after his death.[28]

---

to explain to them the place of the luminous Sultanate in the world of Islam; and to reveal and make manifest to this group the fact that the perpetuation of religion depends on the perpetuation of this government. And in all the mosques of the famous cities I shall light a flame in their inner hearth by means of appealing sermons and *hadith* of the Best of the Prophets, and I shall together burn out their patience and long-suffering.

Quoted in Nikkie R. Keddie, *Sayyid Jamal ad-Din "al-Afghani": A Political Biography* (Los Angeles, 1972), p. 130.

[27] See Keddie, op.cit., p. 167; Fazlur Rahman, *Islam* (London, 1966, p.277; Albert Hourani, *Arabic Thought in the Liberal Age 1798–1939* (Oxford, 1970), pp. 118–19; Anwar Moazzam, *Jâmal al-Din al-Afghani: A Muslim Intellectual* (Delhi, 1983), p. xiii, points out that Afghani's main contribution was to provide a 'broad intellectual framework for redefining the relationship between Islam and the changing world'.

[28] It is often argued that Afghani's reputation and influence was to a large extent posthumous and the work of disciples, or else of academic writers and publicists 'eager to discover trends and precursors' to magnify the importance of their subject. Elie Kedourie, *Afghani and Abduh: An Essay on Religious Unbelief and Political Activism in Modern Islam* (London, 1966), p. 3, and Keddie, op. cit., p. 26. Apart from the fact that contemporarary writers like Blunt point to Afghani's influence on a section of Muslims, it must also be borne in mind that Afghani's ideas gave moral support to the 'instinctive and natural tendency' among many Muslims to see western military and political domination, as enemy number one. It has been rightly suggested that 'even if this was only the initial phase of the various

The power of Afghani's appeal was felt generally in the first decade of the twentieth century, when he became a symbol of the pan-Islamic enterprise. Among those who came under his spell was Shibli who visited Istanbul in 1893, received a medal from Abdul Hamid, and parleyed with Afghani's co-worker and disciple, Mohammad Abduh.[29] His pan-Islamic ideas were echoed in Hali's *Musaddas*. His strong advocacy of the co-existence of diverse religious faiths was in accord with Mohamed Ali's idea, expressed in 1923, of the 'Federation of Faiths'. And his view of a natural solidarity beyond the nation: that which binds together all the peoples of the East threatened by the West, was developed by Ansari, who led the medical mission to Constantinople and was a key figure in the Khilafat agitation. At the All-India Khilafat Conference, the Edinburgh-trained physician-surgeon spoke of an Asiatic Federation that would promote solidarity among the peoples and countries of Asia and rescue them from the political and economic bondage of Europe.[30] Such suggestions were, to an appreciable degree, inspired by the anti-colonial concerns of Afghani.

Afghani also influenced Iqbal and Azad. The future *Shaair-i Mashriq* acknowledged that 'the man whose deep insights into the inner meaning of the history of Muslim thought and life, combined with a broad vision engendered by his wide experience of man and manners, would have made him a link between the past and the future, was Jamal-ud-Din Afghani'.[31] He was

national independence movements which later, for the most part, almost ceased to appeal to Islam, this form of 'Islamic protest' had a direct and more lasting effect in the spheres of culture and religion'. Jacques Waardenburg, 'Islam as a Vehicle of Protest', Ernest Gellner (ed.), *Islamic Dilemmas: Reformers, Nationalists and Industrialization* (Berlin, 1985) p. 28.

[29] Shibli Nomani, *Safarnama-i Rum wa Misr-o-Shaam* (Azamgarh, 1921); Ahmad, *Islamic Modernism*, p. 129.

[30] *The Indian Annual Register*, 1923, vol 1, p.921.

[31] Mohammad Iqbal, *The Reconstruction of Religious Thought in Islam* (Delhi, 1974: reprint), p. 97. In fact, Iqbal admired Afghani who 'never claimed to be a prophet; yet no other man in our time has stirred the soul of Islam more deeply than he'. He was of the view that 'if somebody deserves to be called renewer after Abdul Wahab—the founder of the Wahabi movement—it is Jamaluddin Afghani'. Quoted in Schimmel, *Gabriel's*

interested most of all in Afghani's endeavour to find in Islam a means of unification in resisting the domination of the West, and shared his desire to express unity on the religious basis of Muslims as a supra class and a supra-national entity. Iqbal, who was still composing and reciting his patriotic songs on the eve of and during World War I, tied his hopes for liberation from colonial dependency to pan-Islamic solidarity. This was reflected in the poem *Shama Aur Shaair* (The Candle and the Poet), written in 1912. In his reply to the *Shikwa* (Complaint of God), he struck the same note :

The trouble that is raging in the Balkans
Is a message of awakening to the forgetful
Thou may'st think it the means of vexing thy heart
But in reality it is a test of thy self-sacrifice and self-reliance[32]

It is not sufficiently recognized that Azad's leadership of the Khilafat movement, far from being a sudden or accidental phenomenon, was the outcome of several years of diligent political, ideological and organizational work. Nor is it adequately appreciated that when he began his public career in 1911–12, he had behind him nearly a decade of close and dedicated involvement in the affairs of the nation and the community, of study, writing and reflection, and—not least—of concerned observation of the state of Islamic societies.

Afghani's influence on Azad can be seen from the time of his stay in Constantinople and Cairo, when he first developed close relations with the *Al-Manar* [The Lighthouse] group of Syrian and Egyptain scholars.[33] This is when the young Azad may have

---

Wing, p. 21, and L.R. Gorden-Polonskya, 'Ideology of Muslim Nationalism,' in Hafeez Malik (ed.), *Iqbal: Poet Philosopher of Pakistan,* pp. 115-16.

[32] Latif, *The Influence of English Literature on Urdu Literature,* pp. 111-12.

[33] Aziz Ahmad, *Islamic Culture,* p. 67. For Afghani's influence on one of Azad's devoted followers, see Abdul Ghaffar, *Aasar-i Jamaluddin* (Delhi, 1940). Ghaffar claimed that he was inspired by Ajmal Khan and Ansari to undertake the work. Also, see Amin Afghani, *Syed Jamaluddin Afghani* (Amritsar, 1940). For a different version, see Douglas, *Abul Kalam Azad,* pp. 82-83.

evolved a distinctive vision of Islam, embracing its spiritual, intellectual, social and political dimensions, to which he held fast for more than half a century. He developed, sometime around 1909–10, the nationalist and anti-imperialist thrust of Afghani's ideas in the *Al-Hilal,* inspired by the *Al-Urwa al-wuthqa* [The Indissoluble Link], an anti-imperialist journal published by Afghani in collaboration with Abduh. He also tried to galvanize Muslims into strong pan-Islamic fervour and action. Political fidelity, according to Azad, was due to the Ottoman Khalifa and compliance with his wishes was binding on the faithful.[34] He went on to argue, as did Jamaluddin Afghani, that *jehad* was imperative against those who had occupied even a part of the *Dar al-Islam.*[35]

Azad provided greater ideological coherence to the concerns of fellow-Muslims who had come to terms with Indian nationalism and its ideal of a unified anti-colonial struggle. In addition to his symbolic use of Islam in heightening anti-colonial consciousness, he emphasized the need for a powerful inter-communal union; in fact he cited the Hudaybiyya Treaty of 628 as a valid historical precedent for a Hindu-Muslim alliance. He asserted that uniting with one category of non-Muslims, the Hindus, against another category of non-Muslims, the British, was obligatory.[36] In a similar vein, Ansari, in December 1920, quoted the *Sura-i Mumtahanah* [60:8–9] to argue that Muslims should behave 'righteously, affectionately and in a friendly manner towards all those non-Muslims who are neither at war with Muslims nor are they assailants intending to invade or occupy their territories.[37] Earlier, both Azad and Ansari had commended the Muslim League meeting at Bombay in 1915 that resulted in 'a clear and effective step...in the direction of Hindu-Muslim

[34] Azad tried to legitimize the institution of Khilafat on the ground that the Ottoman Empire provided the 'political centre' (*Siyaasi Markaz),* so essential for the survival of a community and a nation.

[35] He wrote that so long as the world of Islam did not come together in an 'international and universal alliance' the future of Muslims everywhere would be in jeopardy. Quoted in S.M. Ikram, *Modern Muslim India and the Birth of Pakistan* (London, 1965), p. 146.

[36] Hardy, *Partners in Freedom,* pp. 22, 28-29.

[37] Quoted in Hasan, *A Nationalist Conscience,* p. 82.

national unity', and lent their approval to the Lucknow Pact a year later.[38]

This emphasis on a peaceful *modus vivendi* with the Hindus reflected the viewpoint of Afghani and Abduh who, in answer to inquiries from India, had endorsed inter-religious co-operation.[39] Afghani, in particular, advocated inter-communal oneness and defied any breach in the anti-British front. In his articles published in the Hyderabad journal, *Muallim-i Shafiq,* he evoked not only the universal Islamic but also national aspirations with special emphasis on the affinity of Hindu-Muslim interests. And just as he helped awaken Egyptian nationalism by alluding to the ancient glories of the past, so in India, even when talking to a primarily Muslim audience, he harped on the glory of ancient India.[40] His appeal to take pride in that epoch of India's past was no different from his earlier exhortation to Egyptian Muslims to seek inspiration from pre-Islamic Egyptian greatness. In both cases Afghani appealed to an effective basis for solidarity against the foreigner.[41] His message inspired, among others, Azad. He was one of those Muslims who pioneered the pan-Islamic movement in the first decade of the twentieth century and later piloted the Khilafat campaign in all its tumultuous phases.

Azad never ever wavered in his conviction that Indian Muslims should be up in front fighting for freedom.[42] Nor was his commitment to Hindu-Muslim unity ever in question. 'Not only is our national freedom impossible without it', he declared as Congress president in 1923, 'we cannot create without it principles of humanity within ourselves'. He continued:

If today an angel descending from the clouds were to declare from the top of the Qutb Minar in Delhi, 'Discard Hindu-Muslim unity and

[38] Douglas, op.cit.

[39] Hourani, op.cit., p. 118.

[40] Keddie, op.cit., pp. 155, 159–60.

[41] Ibid., p. 160, and by the same author, *Islamic Response to Imperialism: Political and Religious Writings of Sayyid Jamal al-Din "Al-Afghani"* (California University Press, 1968), p. 59.

[42] Azad proclaimed that it was God's wish that Muslims should stand up for the freedom of India and it was His Pleasure *(marzi-i Khudawandi)* that they should give new life to the forgotten duty of *jehad (farz-i Jehad)* Hardy, *Partners in Freedom*, p. 22.

within twenty-four hours swaraj is yours', I would prefer to sacrifice swaraj rather than Hindu-Muslim unity. For delay in the attainment of swaraj will be a loss to India alone, but if our unity disappears, it will be lost to the whole world of humanity.[43]

The influence of Afghani is also evident in the exercise—one that has scarcely received scholarly attention—to reconcile pan-Islamic sentiments with nationalistic aims and to remove the widespread conception that the essence of pan-Islamism implied a break with territorial nationalism. The ideologues of the Khilafat movement insisted that the sum and substance of pan-Islamism was to remove foreign domination; so their activities, bound with the concept of an emerging Indian nation, had an obvious nationalist dimension. They also pointed out that, in spite of their pan-Islamic ambition, or fantasy as some preferred to call it, they had their own Indian community clearly in mind and were not oblivious to its trials and tribulations. The emblem used on the Khilafat delegation stationery, which was made up of twin circles of equal size and overlapping, with the word 'Khilafat' on one and the word 'India' on the other, was symbolic of their loyalties and their vision of a free India and the liberation of Muslim countries from the yoke of colonial rule. Ansari linked colonial policies in India with the larger interests of the West in exploiting the weaker nations of the East and in perpetuating 'the bondage and slavery of Asiatic people'. To him it was not only a question of India's honour and freedom, but of a great struggle for emancipating all the enslaved people from the thraldom of the West.[44]

It has been argued that such notions of independence from foreign rule were advanced to restore a single Islamic state under a revived Khilafat, that the call for *jehad* had a strong traditional basis, and that the anti-colonial rhetoric was merely eyewash, a clever device for achieving sectarian ends. It is also pointed out that the Muslim alliance with nationalist forces was of an 'ephemeral and opportunistic' nature, because they were moved only by loyalty to the invisible theocracy of which God was the

[43] Douglas, op.cit., pp. 193–94.

[44] Quoted in Hasan, *A Nationalist Conscience*, p. 83.

ruler, and that they had developed a nationalism of their own which was Islamic in tone and content.

I have tried to question some of these formulations by arguing that the Khilafat agitation, in fact, served an objective need of mobilizing large segments of Indian society against colonial authority, and, in the process, made them more conscious than even before of forging and strengthening inter-communal links. Muslims, in particular, were at the head of this mobilization. This was a singularly important feat. It was also an unprecedented one. What deserves equal consideration is that the Khilafat movement, despite its pan-Islamic bias, merged into a general political struggle far outstripping its original limitations.

The relationship between the Indians and the Turks was in the nature of a compact, because both Turkey and India were subjected to colonial rule. Azad observed that the agitation in India had, at first, been directed towards the salvation of the Khalifa and the Ottoman Empire, but later it became an integral part of the issue of British imperialism. Khilafat workers must win India's liberty by means of non-co-operation; only then would they be able to save the Khalifa. In the presidential addresses delivered before the Khilafat Committee from 1921 to 1925, Azad was very careful not to let his audience divert its attention from the Indian scene and used pan-Islamic sentiments to generate enthusiasm for India's swaraj. Mohamed Ali's advice was the same: Muslims must fight for swaraj with their non-Muslim brethren, for only in this way would it be possible to achieve the Khilafat aim. He also tried to show the consistency between pan-Islamism and nationalism and to establish that his community's reactions to events in Turkey deepened their involvement in the anti-colonial struggle in India and brought them closer to the Congress under Gandhi's leadership.[45] That, according to him, was the reason why Muslims were able to easily swing back and forth between pan-Islamic and local nationalist appeals; depending upon which was a more appropriate anti-imperialist weapon in a specific Indian situation.

It is a lesser known fact of modern Indian history that the

[45] See chapter three above, and Mohamed Ali to the Sultan of Turkey, 28 May 1920, Hasan (ed.), *Mohamed Ali in Indian Politics*, vol. 3, p. 88.

Khilafat committees were often indistinguishable from local Congress bodies, volunteer groups, Kisan Sabhas and Home Rule Leagues in their composition and political objectives. 'There is nothing to choose locally', commented an official, 'between a gathering under the auspices of the Kisan Sabha or of the Khilafat Committee. Both movements appear to have been completely captured by the non-co-operation party...'[46]. This was not just a joyful demonstration of the newly-found sense of solidarity, but an awareness of the 'extraordinary stiffening-up' of a demoralized, backward, and broken-up people taking part in disciplined, joint action on a countrywide scale.[47]

In several areas of UP peasant unrest was not just tacked on to the Khilafat and non-co-operation programme, but Khilafat committees and Kisan Sabhas provided a tangible sign of acting in unison in attacking their common identifiable enemy, the landlord, who was perceived as an ally of the government. Here lay the danger in governments' assessment, a fact referred to when the secretary of the Rae Bareli Khilafat Committee spoke at a Kisan Sabha meeting on 6 February. 'What might have been in its way a harmless and beneficent movement', observed an official, 'is in danger of being rapidly perverted into a vehicle for virulent abuse of and violent agitation against the Government'.[48] Evidence of the potentially dangerous alliance came from other areas as well. A Kisan Sabha rally at Fyzabad, held on 20-21 December 1920, was probably organized by Khilafat workers.[49] Local Khilafat leaders, Lal Mohammad and Maulvi Riasat Husain, addressed a similar gathering at village Salethu in Maharajganj on 2 February 1921; the meeting at village Balla in the same police station area a week earlier was organized by Amid Syed, a local Khilafat agitator.

A notable feature of such meetings was the attempt to establish

[46] S.R. Mayers to A.G. Shireff, deputy-commissioner, 25 February 1921, UP Government (GAD), F.No. 50, 1921, Box No. 135, UPSA. All subsequent references are drawn from the same file.

[47] Nehru, *An Autobiography*, p. 76.

[48] Note on Rae Bareli disturbances, op.cit.

[49] M.H. Siddiqi, *Agrarian Unrest in North India: The United Provinces 1918–22* (Delhi, 1978), p. 149; Kapil Kumar, *Peasants in Revolt: Tenants, Landlords, Congress and the Raj in Oudh* (Delhi, 1984), pp. 146, 165.

a definite link between the demands of the Kisans and the Khilafatists, on the one hand, and the attainment of swaraj, on the other; in fact, words like 'Khilafat', 'kisan ekta', 'swaraj', 'Gandhi' were all intended to conjure up in the minds of the people a picture of bringing about a better world under the direction of better leaders.[50] Peasants in many places believed that the promised swaraj was coming soon and their economic salvation lay in the preservation of their faith, the Khilafat and the interests of the Muslim world outside India.[51] Thus Maulvi Salamatullah, associated with Abdul Bari, assured a Kisan Sabha gathering that the peasant interests would be protected only after the dignity and prestige of the Khalifa was restored. Kamaluddin Jafri, the Allahabad-based lawyer, linked the redressal of their grievances with the attainment of swaraj under the Congress directives. This view, expressed at a Kisan Sabha meeting at Akbarpur in Fyzabad district on 27 January 1921, was endorsed by Hafiz Alam and Mohammad Nabi of Tanda, important Khilafatists in eastern UP.[52] Jawaharlal Nehru was among those present at the conference.

The collaboration between the Khilafatists and groups of

[50] The idea was summed up in the following verses of Mohammad Haider, a school teacher in Pilibhit:
Jamaa do Qaum ka sikka bajaa do deen ka danka
Mohamed, Shaukat-o-Gandhi ke pairokar ho jao
Swadeshi se karo raghbat bidesi se karo nafrat
Ki jis se muflisee ho door aur zardaar ho jaao
Let the respect for the nation be restored
And the trumpet of the faith heralded
Follow Mohamed (Ali), Shaukat and Gandhi
Adopt swadeshism and shun all that is from outside
So that poverty is removed and self-reliance is achieved.
Proscribed Publications (43), IOLR.

[51] Jawaharlal Nehru noted that 'even in remote bazaars the common folk talked of the Congress and Swaraj, and what had happened in the Panjab, and the Khilafat—but the word 'Khilafat' bore a strange meaning in most of the rural areas. People thought it came from *khilaf,* an Urdu word meaning 'against' or 'opposed to', and so they took it to mean: opposed to Government!'. *An Autobiography,* p. 69.

[52] UP Government (Police Dept.), F.No. 51–N, 1921, UPSA. Note by Lakhte Husain and Jagannath, 28 February 1921, op.cit.

peasants and workers was equally pronounced in Bengal, where the joint Hindu-Muslim command under C.R. Das, Maulana Akram Khan, Ashrafuddin Choudhury, J.M. Sengupta and other leaders of the province emphasized the economic and political rather than the religious aspects of the Khilafat protest, and where the agitation, according to some government sources, 'was entirely Muhammadan but not religious'.[53] Facilitated by the failure of harvests between 1918 and 1922, the rise in prices, the fall in the price of jute and the influenza and cholera epidemics, the common slogans centred around the attainment of swaraj rather than the restoration of the Khilafat.

In Punjab the North Western Railway strike, initially called at the end of April 1920 for the improvement of the workers' material conditions, subsequently coalesced with the Khilafat agitation as the strikers began to perceive it as a movement against a 'tyrannical and exploitative' government.[54]

In assessing such strands in the Khilafat agitation, it is also worth taking note of the Congress-Khilafat-League *entente*. These organizations met in the same city and around the same time; often, Khilafat Committees and the Muslim League took their political cue from the Congress and endorsed its decisions. The 1918 League session did so, and, as in the Congress, so in the League, wrote an intelligence officer, 'the moderate have lost all control'. The same spirit prevailed a year later, though speeches made at the League platform 'were more violent in their language and defiant in their general attitude than the extremist Hindus at the meetings of the Congress'. Anti-British spirit 'reigned supreme'.[55] In July 1920, the League insisted that the Congress

[53] Tajul Hashmi, 'Peasants and Politics in East Bengal 1920–1974' (Unpublished Ph.D. thesis, University of Western Australia, 1986), p. 72.

[54] Khizar Humayun Ansari, 'The Emergence of Muslim Socialists and their Ideas in India between 1917–1974' (Unpublished Ph.D. thesis, University of London, 1985), pp. 83–85.

[55] Home Poll. B, F.No. 160–3, January 1919, NAI, WRDCI (January 1920), Home Poll. Deposit, F.No. 52, February 1920, NAI. Notice the comment of Jawaharlal Nehru that 'the political and the Khilafat movements developed side by side during the year 1920, both going in the same direction...'. *An Autobiography*, p. 46.

meet first so that it could recommend and decide the course of action for the Muslims.[56]

Such demonstrations of political unity were matched by spontaneous expressions of communal harmony. When O.M. Martin visited Noakhali in December 1921, he was struck by the 'curious spectacle of Muslims and Hindus spinning cotton thread as enjoined by Mahatma Gandhi, as a symbolic act indicating Hindu-Muslim unity in the attempt to drive the British from India'.[57] It is not without significance that communal violence was a rare occurrence, and that frictions over cow-slaughter and music before mosques were settled amicably. Such was the role of Prem Sabhas and Anjuman-i Islam in Delhi and Punjab.[58] The spirit of the time was captured by Zafar Ali Khan in the verse:

Aaee hain Aasman se chal kar woh quwaten
Jo Muslim-o-Hunood ko Sheer-o-shakar karen

Heavenly forces have helped to forge the bonds of friendship between the Hindus and the Muslims.
Or, by Agha Hashr:

Ho gaeen bikhri huee eenten baham tameer ki
Mil gaee har ek kari tooti huee zanjeer ki
But-shikan wahdat-parast ek jism ek jaan ho gaye
Ghul hua duniya me phir kafir Musalman ho gaye

The disjointed pieces have been put in order again
The links of the broken chain have been discerned
The idol-worshippers and the iconoclast have joined hands
There is a dinning clamour that the kafirs have again embraced Islam.

Short-lived as this unity was, the fact that it was accomplished

[56] Zahur Ahmad to G.N. Misra, 26 July 1920, All India Congress Committee [AICC] Papers, Supplementary, NMML. In distant Malabar every mosque became a centre of Congress-Khilafat activity. Taluqa and district level leaders toured the Muslim centres with Muslim colleagues, organizations and Khilafat volunteers. E.M.S. Namboodiripad, *How I became a Communist* (Trivandrum, 1976), p. 35.

[57] 'Memoirs of O.M. Martin', p. 113, O.M. Martin Papers, Centre for South Asian Studies, Cambridge.

[58] *Tribune,* 13 October 1919; *Fateh* (Delhi), 1 July 1920; Swami Shraddhanand, *Inside Congress* (Bombay, 1946), p. 37.

was a sufficient indication of the strength and fervour of the nationalistic spirit of which it was the outward expression. The secretary of the Bengal Khilafat Committee recalled:

> The scenes that were enacted before my eyes made me feel that the artificial barriers that had long been preventing the two major communities of the country to come together, had been miraculously swept away by the onrush of the all-embracing non-co-operation movement.[59]

IV

Shaikhji tum ko mubarak Rum-o-Reh
Hum to kehte hai ke Gandhiji ki jai

The Shaikh is welcome to think of Constantinople and Persia
I prefer to say, victory to Gandhism

(Akbar Allahabadi)

The architect of Hindu-Muslim unity during the Khilafat and non-co-operation days was no other than Mohandas Karamchand Gandhi. The cause was dear to him in South Africa, where he was convinced that his doctrine of Ahimsa would be put to its severest test on the issue of Hindu-Muslim unity.[60] The conviction was still there after his return to India in 1915. He sought and secured the friendship of leading Muslims in the Congress and the Muslim League, because he was eager to understand the 'Mussalman mind'.[61] He prized his contact with, among others,

[59] Abul Hayat, *Mussalmans of Bengal* (Calcutta, 1966), p. 37.

[60] Nanda, *Gandhi, Pan-Islamism, Imperialism and Nationalism*, pp. 198–9; Judith M. Brown, *Gandhi's Rise to Power: Indian Politics 1915–1922* (Cambridge, 1972), pp. 151–154.

[61] In his autobiography, Gandhi noted: 'I was seeking the friendship of good Mussalmans, and was eager to understand the Mussalman mind through contact with their purest and most patriotic representatives'. *An Autobiography or the Story of My Experiments with Truth* (Ahmedabad, 1958: reprint), p. 325. On another occasion he told a Khilafat meeting that his desire of meeting 'good' Muslim leaders was satisfied after meeting the Ali Brothers. 'It was a question of love at first sight between us', he said. His circle of friends widened after he had met Ansari and Abdul Bari. Speech on Khilafat, Bombay, 9 May 1919, *CWMG*, vol. 15, p. 295.

the Ali Brothers and mounted a campaign for their release. He assured Mohamed Ali: 'I need hardly say that you are never out of my mind, although we may not for some time come to meet face to face'.[62] He added that his interest in Mohamed Ali's release was quite selfish—to utilize his services to achieve a 'common goal'. In the proper solution of the 'Mohammeden question lies the realization of Swaraj'.[63]

The 'Mohammedan question' that concerned the Mahatma was the future of Khilafat, an issue that was, in his judgement, more important than the repeal of the Rowlatt Act.[64] It was so as it affected the religious susceptibilities of some of his countrymen. Moreover, in helping Muslims in 'the hour of their peril', he hoped to cement the bonds of communal unity'—a thousand times more valuable than...our connection with the British', and secure their much needed support for the nationalist struggle. He made it clear in *Young India:*

> It goes without saying that it is the bounden duty of the Hindus...to associate themselves with their Mohammedan brethren. It is the surest and simplest method of bringing about the Hindu-Mohammedan unity. It is the privilege of friendship to extend the hand of fellowship, and adversity is the crucible in which friendship is tested. Let millions of Hindus show to the Mohammedans that they are one with them in sorrow.[65]

Again, he observed in May 1920:

> If I kept aloof from the Khilafat question I would consider myself as having lost all my worth. That work is my dharma par excellence. It is through the Khilafat that I am doing the triple duty of showing to the world what ahimsa means, of uniting Hindus and Muslims, and of coming in contact with one and all...[66]

From May 1919 onwards, Gandhi was busy exhorting the *ulama* to mobilize their constituency and urged his co-religionists to join Muslims in fasting, prayer and hartal and thus 'put a sacred seal on the Hindu-Mohammedan bond'.[67] 'It is impossible', he

[62] 29 June 1919, ibid., p. 404.

[63] 18 November 1918, ibid., p. 64.

[64] Speech on Khilafat, Bombay, 9 May 1919, ibid., p. 297.

[65] To Mangalbhai, 3 May 1920, Mahadev Desai (ed.), *Day-To-Day with Gandhi* (Varanasi, 1968), vol. 2, pp. 154.

[66] Ibid.

noted in *Navajivan*, 'that one of the four limbs of the nation be wounded and the rest of the nation remains unconcerned. We cannot be called one nation, we cannot be a single body, if such a wound has no effect on us'.[68] At the same time, he assured his Muslim audience: 'You are my neighbours and my countrymen. It is my duty to share your sorrows. I cannot talk about Hindu-Muslim unity and fail in giving effect to the idea when the test comes'.[69] This assurance was a proclamation of Gandhi's intent and an appeal to Congressmen to follow his lead.

The All-India Muslim Conference in September and the All-India Khilafat Conference in September 1919 confirmed Gandhi's overall dominance of the Khilafat agitation. He settled its tone and tenor. At the Khilafat Conference, for example, he firmly opposed the resolution on the boycott of British goods.[70] So, consensus was reached only on the boycott of Peace Celebrations. The extent of Gandhi's influence is further apparent from the Muslim League session in December 1919. In deference to his wishes, the League resolved to prohibit cow-slaughter on *Bakr Id*, a concession never ever offered by any Muslim organization. Moreover, gratitude was expressed to the King for the spirit in which the Royal Proclamation was issued. In this resolution, too, the Mahatma's influence is noticeable, for he was at the same time carrying a similar motion through the Congress amidst strong opposition.[71]

[67] Letter to the Press, 10 October 1919, *CWMG*. vol. 16, p. 227.

[68] Ibid., p. 104. And his speech at the Khilafat Conference on 24 November 1919, p. 308.

[69] Speech on Khilafat, 9 May 1919, ibid., p. 297.

[70] Speech at Khilafat Conference, 23 November 1919, ibid., p. 307. While opposing Hasrat's resolution on boycott of foreign goods, Gandhi stated on 24 November that 'there is a world of difference between withdrawal of co-operation and boycott. It is a man's privilege to withhold co-operation when he likes, but we must have regard for the opinion of the world before adopting any political step. What we intend to do cannot be effected through boycott'. Ibid., p. 310. Gandhi's speech was in response to Hasrat's insistence that 'we want something that will produce an immediate effect on the British. Let your boycott of foreign cloth stand, we do not mind it, but give us something quicker, and speedier in addition'. Quoted in D.G. Tendulkar, *Mahatma: Life of Mohandas Karamchand Gandhi* (Publications Division: Delhi, 1969: Reprint), vol. 1, p. 274.

[71] Brown, op.cit., p. 188.

The Khilafat protest reached a new level of intensity in early 1920 on account of Gandhi's involvement, and also because of vigorous campaigning by Azad, the Ali Brothers and Zafar Ali Khan, all of whom were released from prison at the end of 1919.[72] Inspired by Gandhi's initiatives, they set out to secure wider support for the Khilafat agitation, particularly in Sind and the North-West Frontier Province which had, for the most part, remained politically inert. The Aligarh students were mobilized for the purpose: they addressed meetings in Kohat and Peshawar and raised Rs. 23,000 for the Khilafat Fund. In February the renowned *alim* of Firangi Mahal, Abdul Bari, Azad and Shaukat Ali were busy in Sind, where they spoke at largely attended Khilafat meetings.[73] This was followed by a tour of eastern Bengal. In addition, several missions were active in UP and Punjab. The campaign was in full swing and was well orchestrated through mosques and madrasas.

In most parts of the country the *ulama*, with some exceptions, were the most vehement advocates of non-co-operation. Inspired by the militant stance of Azad and Abdul Bari, they made fiery speeches, as at Hyderabad on 4/5 January 1920, and clamoured for *jehad* against the enemies of Islam. At the Bengal Khilafat Conference on 28 February, they decided to boycott British goods in spite of Gandhi's reservations, expressed just a few months earlier. On this occasion, however, Gandhi went along with Abdul Bari and his more militant followers, including the Ali Brothers, Hasrat Mohani and Azad Sobhani. In view of the popular excitement which had been mounting steadily since the observance of the first 'Khilafat Day' on 17 October,[74] Gandhi tailored his strategy to suit the mood of his more vocal Khilafat

[72] Hasan, *A Nationalist Conscience*, pp. 95–96; Minault, *Khilafat Movement*, pp. 84–86.

[73] *Amrita Bazar Patrika*, 18 February, 15 March 1920.

[74] The decision to observe Khilafat Day was taken at the All-India Muslim Conference on 21 September. Held at the Aminabad Park in Lucknow, the Conference was attended by over 5,000 delegates, including a large number of *ulama*. *Tribune*, 27 September 1919, and Robinson, *Separatism.*, pp. 295–96. For details on the success of the first Khilafat Day, see the first edition of my *Nationalism and Communal Politics in India*, pp. 152–55, and Minault, *Khilafat Movement*, pp. 76–78.

friends. In fact, a week after the Bengal Conference, his own mainfestô advocated non-co-operation with the British more vigorously than ever before. The intention was to keep up his alliance with the 'extremists' who, since the Muslim League session in December 1919, were demanding action instead of words.

The decisions of the Bengal Conference, backed by Gandhi, were adopted by, among others, the UP Ulama Association. In the Subjects Committee, with Abdul Bari in chair, it was planned to depute students to preach *jehad* in mofussil towns. In March 1920, the Punjab Khilafat Committee recognized the need to boycott British goods. This was enthusiastically backed by nearly ten thousand *ulama* present at the meeting.[75] Never before did so many of them gather at one place, on one platform and for a single cause. It was a striking demonstration of how religion had roused the *ulama* from their slumber and an indication of their gaining control of Khilafat committees and their policy decisions.

The second Khilafat Day on 19 March 1920 was quite a success. Its effect, as in October 1919, was felt throughout the country. Hartal was widely observed in Bombay presidency and there was a 'complete cessation' of business in Bombay city, particularly in Mahim, Dadar and Bandra areas.[76] In Sind, four honorary magistrates resigned in protest against the government's anti-Islamic policies. There were a spate of meetings, with the Pirs occupying centre-stage.[77] In Bengal, the Khilafat Committees sustained their agitation with meticulous care. In Calcutta there was much enthusiasm, with the famous Hogg market, which had remained open even during the Swadeshi movement, 'barred, padlocked and guarded'. In Dacca, Mymensingh and Chittagong public meetings endorsed the decisions of the Bengal Khilafat Conference.[78]

Hartal, fasting and prayer were the general features of Khilafat day in Punjab, while public meetings at Amritsar, Lahore. Multan, Sialkot and Peshawar demanded the settlement

[75] *Amrita Bazar Patrika,* 5 March 1920.

[76] *Bombay Chronicle,* 20 March 1920.

[77] *Mahratta,* 21 March 1920.

[78] *Amrita Bazar Patrika,* 20 and 22 March 1920.

of the Turkish question in consonance with Muslim sentiments and ideals.[79] In neighbouring Delhi, there was an impressive religious service at the Juma Masjid, and the suspension of all business. 'A very complete hartal was observed', reported an intelligence officer, 'with Muslim League and other volunteers posted in most of the bazaars and were insistent and almost aggressive in discouraging the collection of even the smallest crowd'.[80] In UP, prayers were widely offered for the Khalifa. A meeting at Allahabad was attended, among a great many others, by Zahur Ahmad, Hyder Mehdi, Kamaluddin Jafri, Maulvi Wilayat Husain, Jawaharlal Nehru and Purshotamdas Tandon.[81] In Mainpuri, a resolution was carried sentencing to religious ostracism any one who did not observe the rules of Khilafat day. A government report noted :

> By means of violent declarations that the Powers meant to obliterate Islam, emissaries from the big cities worked on the feelings of their brethren in outlying places and on the actual day it became apparent that an increased number of small towns had been affected. Hartal was carried out as generally as on the 6th April 1919.[82]

The publication of Turkish peace terms on 14 May heightened Muslim resentment and lent depth to their relentless campaign against the government.[83] Gandhi was quick to sense their anger and disappointment and offered a powerful indictment of the peace terms. He declared non-co-operation as the 'only effective remedy...for healing the wounds inflicted on Mohammedan opinion',[84] and informed the Viceroy: 'I consider that as a

[79] *Tribune*, 21 March 1920.

[80] Home Poll. Deposit, F. No. 4, April 1920, NAI.

[81] *Leader*, 21 March 1920.

[82] 'The Khilafat Movement in the United Provinces 1919–1924' [Printed], UPSA.

[83] The terms were described by the *Moslem Outlook* [20 May 1920], a weekly newspaper published by the London-based Islamic Information Bureau, 'as a monument of hypocrisy and the blackest breach of faith'. The *Mohammadi* declared that Muslims 'vow in God's name never to accept these terms'. 2 April 1920, SNNR, Bengal.

[84] Press Statement on Turkish Peace Terms, *CWMG*, vol. 17, pp. 426–27. Incidentally, Gandhi had already committed himself to non-co-operation on 7 March 1920 as 'the only remedy left to us' and the

staunch Hindu wishing to live on terms of the closest friendship with my Mussalman countrymen, I should be an unworthy son of India if I did not stand by them in their hour of trial'.[85]

But not everybody shared Gandhi's enthusiasm. The Liberal leader, Srinivasa Sastri, was alarmed at the prospect of Muslims 'breaking out here and there in futile demonstrations'.[86] Others were wary of Muslim influence in Congress affairs[87] and the possible outbreak of widespread violence.[88] Such apprehensions were echoed in May 1920, when Gandhi first explained his non-co-operation programme to the All India Congress Committee, and also on 1–3 June at the Central Khilafat Committee meeting in Allahabad.[89] Tej Bahadur Sapru, Annie Besant and Jamnadas Dwarkadas voiced their dissent.[90] So did Motilal Nehru, Madan Mohan Malaviya and Lajpat Rai. But Gandhi ignored their defiance and hastily appointed a sub-committee to

---

Central Khilafat Committee had endorsed his decision at its meeting held on 14 March. This was reaffirmed in early June when a committee was formed, with Gandhi as chairman, to give practical effect to the non-co-operation programme. On 22 June, Muslims informed Reading that they would withdraw co-operation from the government from 1 August 1920 if their demands were not fulfilled. Gandhi wrote to the viceroy separately, informing him that he was advising Muslims to adopt non-co-operation, because the peace terms violated ministerial pledges and disregarded Muslim sentiments.

[85] To viceroy, 22 June 1920, *CWMG*, vol. 17, p. 503.

[86] To Sivaswamy Aiyer, 13 April 1920, quoted in Kanji Dwarkadas, *India's Fight for Freedom* (Bombay, 1966), p. 146.

[87] For example, it was observed that the adoption of non-co-operation would mean that the Congress would gradually become 'a part and parcel' of the Muslim League and the Khilafat Committee and 'its predominant Hindu influence would be lost'. *Nayak,* 8 September 1920, SNNR, Bengal.

[88] Ibid., 8 March 1920. The *New India* had announced on the eve of the first Khilafat Day: 'Madras does not want Hartal ... and Mahatma Gandhi's name must not be used to ask Madras to do that which it is unwise for it to do, and which might disturb rather than cement the good relations hitherto subsisting between the two communities'. *New India,* 15 October 1919.

[89] Home Poll. B, F.No. 109, 1920, NAI.

[90] Dwarkadas described Gandhi's programme 'as an unnecessarily circuitous method of dislocating the functions of the State and paralyzing Government to the detriment of public safety and peace'. *Bombay Chronicle,* 7 June 1920.

give practical effect to non-co-operation. And when the work of the committee was hampered by certain elements in the Congress, he adopted a course unforeseen in Congress history—launching of the non-co-operation movement a month before the special session of the Congress was to meet in Calcutta.[91] This extraordinary step was calculated to take the sting out of the mounting campaign against non-co-operation and give himself and his allies enough time to garner support well before the Calcutta Congress, where he expected stiff opposition.

By December 1920, Gandhi had outmanoeuvred his opponents, with most leading politicians marshalled on the side of non-co-operation. In September his plan had already been approved in the Subjects Committee and at the open Congress session in Calcutta. Lajpat Rai, who held different ideas at the All India Congress Committee meeting in May 1920, was converted to the Mahatma's credo.[92] Motilal Nehru, once in search of a constituency for the UP legislative council, tailored his political stance to suit the mood in Calcutta.[93] The picture was no different in Nagpur, where the opponents of Gandhi were humbled one by one.[94] The Chief Commissioner of Central Povinces wrote :

[91] Gandhi defended his decision of not consulting colleagues in the following words: 'In my humble opinion it is no Congressman's duty to consult the Congress before taking an action in a matter in which he has no doubts...'. *Young India*, 4 August 1920, *GWMG*, vol. 18, p. 112.

[92] Robinson, *Separatism*, p. 318, f.n. 1.

[93] Nehru, *An Autobiography*, pp. 64-65. On Motilal's conversion to non-co-operation, see Ravinder Kumar, *The Making of a Nation: Essays in Indian History and Politics* (Delhi, 1989), pp. 108–10.

[94] C.R. Das, for example, made the dramatic announcement that he would move the main resolution in support of non-co-operation. He is said to have changed his earlier stance, because the boycott of legislatures, to which he was chiefly opposed, was no longer an issue as the elections had already taken place. S.C. Bose, *The Indian Struggle 1920–1942* (London, 1964), p. 44. For the view that it was Das's programme which won at Nagpur, not Gandhi's, see Rajat Ray, *Social Conflict and Political Unrest in Bengal*, pp. 262–63. Of course, the man who was clearly humbled at Nagpur was Jinnah. His opposition to the non-co-operation resolution was howled down with cries of 'shame, shame'. For details, see Wolpert, *Jinnah*, pp. 71-72.

The outstanding feature of the Congress has been the personal domination of Gandhi over all political leaders and followers alike. He has carried through the policy that he had decided for this Congress without any material modification...The moderates of Nagpur were not heard; the extremist opponents under Khaparde and Moonje were brushed aside; Pandit Madan Mohan Malaviya's efforts were negatory; Jinnah carried no influence; Lajpat Rai wobbled and then became silent.[95]

The Chief Commissioner should have added that Gandhi's triumph at Nagpur was largely due to the overwhelming Muslim support of those who had flocked to the Congress session in large numbers. As in Calcutta where Muslim delegates 'swamped the rest',[96] the Congress pandal in Nagpur was packed with Muslims; they constituted nearly 72 per cent of the total number of delegates.[97]

V

Idhar taaid bari hai udhar taaleem Gandhi hai
Dar-i Uumeed ko khole khuda himmat to baandhi hai

With divine assistance, on the one hand, and the teachings of Gandhi, on the other
May God open the promised door, we have now gird up our loins
(Akbar Allahabadi)

With non-co-operation gaining such overwhelming support.

[95] F. Sly to Chelmsford, 1 January 1921, Chelmsford Papers (26).

[96] Willingdon to Montagu, 15 September 1920, Montagu Papers (20); *Bombay Chronicle* and *Amrita Bazar Patrika,* 10 September 1920. Of the 217 Bombay-based delegates who voted for Gandhi's resolution on 9 September , 43 were Muslims. Of the 161 delegates from Madras 125 voted for non-co-operation. *Bombay Chronicle,* 9 and 10 September 1920; *Hindu,* 16 September 1920. Out of the 57 persons from the Central Provinces who attended the Calcutta Conference and voted for the non-co-operation resolution, 16 were Muslims, including Samiullah Khan, a leading Khilafatist in the province. 'History of the Khilafat Movement in the Central Provinces and Berar' (Printed), p. 2. This report was made available to me by Dr D.E.U. Baker of St. Stephen's College, Delhi.

[97] See Gopal Krishna, 'The Development of the Indian National Congres as a Mass Organization', *Journal of Asian Studies,* May 1966, vol. 25, p. 418.

the Khilafatists, especially the *ulama,* pursued their concerns with renewed zeal and vigour. The Shaikh al-Hind, Maulana Mahmud Hasan, now returned to India after his wartime imprisonment in Malta, called for a total boycott of government-administered educational institutions.[98] So did other Deobandi *ulama* like Maulvi Mohammad Idris Kandholwi and Maulana Shabbir Ahmad Usmani.[99] The sweet-tongued Maulana Abdul Majid of Budaun extolled the virtues of those who surrendered titles and honours,[100] while Abdul Bari issued a *fatwa,* which was endorsed by five hundred *ulama*, in support of non-co-operation.[101] A *fatwa* on similar lines emanated from the *Pirs* of Almohar in Sialkot district and from Sail Sharif in Hoshiarpur.[102] The *Pirs* of Sind were also swept by the pan-Islamic tide. It was reported that they had joined hands with the *ulama* in spreading the 'infection of religious enthusiasm among many classes of the inhabitants of Sind', and that the excitement caused by non-co-operation was 'growing in intensity among all classes of educated Muhammadans'.[103]

No less touching were reports of Muslims resigning from government, surrendering titles and suspending their legal

[98] Address read out at the foundation laying ceremony of the National Muslim University, Aligarh (Jamia Millia Islamia), 29 October 1920, and Bashir Ahmad, *Tark-i Mavalaat* (Deoband, 1920), Proscribed Publications (53–54), IOLR.

[99] In *Al Ahkaam al-Quraniya Mavalaat al-Burtaniya* (Delhi, 1920) the author cited the *fatawa* of Shah Abdul Aziz and Maulvi Abdul Haye to establish the validity of non-co-operation. Assisting the enemies of Islam *(Ahl-i Harb)* through trade or employment was unlawful while an alliance with the *Ahl-i Sulah,* i.e., the Hindus, was lawful. Shabbir Ahmad Usmani made a similar plea at the Jamiyat al-ulama conference in Delhi, though he cautioned Muslims against the tendency to place Gandhi on a spiritual pedestal. See *Tark-i Mavalaat par zabardast taqreer* (Delhi, 1920), pp. 17, 22, 24–25

[100] See *Fazle-al Khitaab* (Delhi, n.d.), and 'Khilafat ka Paighaam Mussalmanon ke naam', pp. 17–18.

[101] For a collection of the most important *fatawa* on the Khilafat issue, see Rais Ahmad Jafri (ed.), *Auraaq-i Gumgushta* (Lahore, 1968).

[102] Home Poll. F.No. 459, 1922, NAI.

[103] WR (Sind), 12 and 26 November 1921, J.C. Curry Papers, Centre for South Asian Studies, Cambridge.

practice. In November 1920, twenty-two out of the forty-four lawyers who gave up practice were Muslims.[104] By November 1921, the number of Muslim policemen who had resigned was thirty-one, forty and seventeen in UP, Bengal and Bombay.[105] Among those who renounced their titles were Hakim Ajmal Khan, Syed Ali Nabi and Maulana Badruddin of Phulwari.[106]

The legislative council elections, which took place on the eve of the Nagpur Congress, were also boycotted, particularly in the Muslim constituencies. Similarly, in Madras only six of the provincial council seats were contested by Muslims, and only a small number of enfranchised Muslims voted—6.6 per cent of those eligible.[107] In C.P. 'the boycott of the Councils was more successful...than was thought to be probable'.[108] In UP, only 7 per cent votes were polled in the Muslim urban constituencies as compared to 14 per cent in the non-Muslim urban constituencies, and in many areas groups of *ulama* and students prevented voters from going to the polling booths.[109] In eastern and northern parts of Bengal, there was a dearth of candidates and little polling was reported from most areas. In Rajshahi and Dinajpur the

[104] F.No. 5, 1920, AICC Papers.

[105] Brown, op.cit., p. 309. For the Central Provinces and Berar, see D.E.U. Baker, 'The Muslim Concern for Security: The Central Provinces and Berar, 1919–1947', in Hasan (ed.), *Communal and Pan-Islamic Trends*, pp. 221–2+3.

[106] *Mussalman*, 6 August 1920. While renouncing his government titles, Hakim Ajmal Khan stated: 'As a humble Muslim, I have decided to relieve myself of all honours conferred upon me by the Government and I return herewith the gold medal of Kaiser-i-Hind together with the two silver medals of the Coronation Darbar of England and India, and, henceforward, I give up the title of Haziq-ul-Mulk'. Quoted in Tendulkar, *Mahatma*, vol. 1, p. 287.

[107] Kenneth Mcpherson, 'The Political Development of the Urdu and Tamil-speaking Muslims of the Madras Presidency 1901–1937' (Unpublished M.A. thesis, University of Western Australia, 1968), p. 127.

[108] 'History of the Khilafat Movement in the Central Provinces and Berar', p. 3.

[109] Valentine Chirol happened to be in Allahabad on the election day and made round of the polling booths. At one rural polling station, about fifteen miles from Allahabad city, he found that not a single voter had appeared. Nehru, *An Autobiography*, p. 67.

bulk of educated men, including pleaders, refrained from voting Almost all Muslims from Rangpur town abstained, as did large numbers of Muslims in Gaibandha sub-division of Rangpur district. In Bakarganj, very few Muslims voted and, in Mania, not a single voter, Hindu or Muslim, appeared.[110]

Among those who resigned their seats from the councils or withdrew their candidature from Muslim constituencies were Nur Mohammad, Kader Baksh, Kazi Azimuddin, Sheriff Deoji Kanji, Mohammad Arif Mulla and Salembhoy Karamji from Bombay; M.A. Wasim, Maulvi Wahid Husain, Mandud Rahman, Mazharul Haq, Mahbubul Haq, Maulvi Nadir Ali, Mazharul Anwar, Hasan Suhrawardy, Abdul Karim, Fazlul Haq, Syed Sultan Ali, Azizul Haque, Maulvi Shamsuddin, Maulvi Tamizuddin Ahmad, Maulvi Mohammad Daud, Maulvi Saidullah, Maulvi Ikramul Haque, Nuruddin Ahmad, Fazlur Rahman Adil, Abdur Rashid Khan, Abdul Halim, Abdul Jabbar and Maulvi Abdul Halim from Bihar and Bengal; and Kamaluddin Jafri, Sheikh Zahur Ahmad, Hafiz Alam, Zahuruddin, Syed Zahur Ahmad, Syed Hyder Mehdi and Aziz Ahmad Khan from UP. These names give a clue to the varied background of at least some non-co-operators. They included rich merchants from Bombay, petty landowners like Abdul Jabbar from Bengal and successful lawyers like Kamaluddin Jafri and Syed Zahur Ahmad from Allahabad. Most non-co-operators were Sunnis but there were some notable Shias as well. They shared the view that non-co-operation was the only way to defend the Holy Places.[111]

[110] Rajat K. Ray, 'Masses in Politics: The Non-co-operation Movement in Bengal 1920–22', *The Indian Economic and Social History Review*, December 1974, vol. 2, 4, p. 362; Hashmi, 'Peasants and Politics', p. 80.

[111] The Shias consider the first three Khalifas, recognized by the Sunnis, as 'usurpers' of the rights of Ali since, according to them, the Prophet of Islam acting under divine guidance designated Ali, his son-in-law and cousin, and his descendants to a continuing authority. Yet, the Shias were closely associated with the Khilafat movement in India. According to a report from Sind, they were sympathetic to the Angora government 'in spite of their different religious standpoint as regards the Khilafat'. WR (Sind), 11 June and 26 November 1921, Curry Papers. For more details, see *Comrade*, 7 October 1911, *Paisa Akhbaar*, 22 June 1920, SNNR, Punjab,

Students and teachers responded to the non-co-operation call with equal enthusiasm.[112] This is best illustrated by the turn of events at the Aligarh Muslim University, where pan-Islamic sentiments coalesced with patriotic and nationalist feelings in good measure and generated a powerful anti-colonial movement.[113]

The M.A.O. college of Syed Ahmad Khan's days followed an ardent and sustained pro-British policy and steered clear of political movements. It was hard to be otherwise. The founder considered education as the sole means for the regeneration of his community and regarded Anglo-Muslim rapprochement as a necessary condition for its upliftment. The *raison d'etre* of the college was, thus, to make Muslims 'worthy and useful subjects of the Crown', to groom students to go on to British universities, and to train them for government employment. These expectations were fulfilled during Syed Ahmad Khan's lifetime. Students cultivated English habits and tastes, expressed loyalty to the Crown by decorating their rooms with portraits of Queen Victoria and the Prince of Wales, and paid heed to repeated admonitions to avoid political discussions. The campaign against the Congress, launched by Syed Ahmad Khan, struck a favourable chord in Aligarh circles.

In the early years of the twentieth century this most 'benighted' and conservative of institutions suddenly exploded into political

---

Bombay Chronicle, 7 May 1921, and Minault, *Khilafat Movement,* pp. 129–30.

[112] Minault, op. cit., pp. 118–19. There were reports of strikes at the Calcutta Madrasa and the Government College, Lahore. In Amritsar the Anjuman-i Islam refused to accept a government grant. The overall situation in various educational centres was summed up by H. Sharp, secretary to the government of India. According to him, 'within the last few weeks, strikes of students have occurred upon a considerable scale in Bengal and it appears that in other provinces, where the trouble seemed to have been scotched, it has now attained a new lease of life'. Home Poll. B, F.No. 259, 1921, NAI.

[113] The account on Aligarh is based on my *A Nationalist Conscience,* pp. 98–108, *Mohamed Ali: Ideology and Politics,* pp. 17–20, and 'Nationalist and Separatist Trends in Aligarh 1915–1947', in Gupta (ed.), *Myth and Reality: The Struggle for Freedom in India 1945–47* (Delhi, 1987), pp. 116–151.

activity confronting the British with the most serious Muslim movement of dissidence they had faced since the 1857 revolt. The agitation against the Nagri resolution of 18 April 1900, followed by the students' strike of February 1907, represented a new trend in Aligarh politics—a trend to steer the Muslim community on a course different from that plotted by Syed Ahmad Khan. Though this strain in Aligarh politics reflected the changes taking place at other levels of Muslim society, contemporaries were never tired of pointing out how, just a few years before the new trend appeared, there was not the slightest sign of its imminence. This earlier quiescence, attributed to Syed Ahmad Khan's influence and to the predominance of landed interests on the Board of Trustees, was gradually replaced by a position in favour of the Congress and in opposition to the government. In so doing, the Aligarh students threw to the winds all the caution that had been enjoined upon them by Syed Ahmad Khan.

Inspired by the poems of Shibli Nomani, Hasrat Mohani, and Hashmi Faridabadi and the exalted prose of Mohamed Ali, Azad, and Zafar Ali Khan, political activity on the campus was sustained during the course of World War I. Students raised funds for beleagured Turkey, offered prayers for the success of Turkish armies, and took a deep interest in the Anjuman-i Khuddam-i Kaaba. Four Aligarh graduates joined Ansari's medical mission to Constantinople and at least one Aligarh Old Boy—Mahendra Pratap—was part of the 'Silk Letter Conspiracy,' and headed the Provisional Government in Kabul. This was not all. The themes of capitalist exploitation, class conflicts, of revolt against imperialism, of nationalism, and of socialism figured in the works of important writers and poets at Aligarh, including Hasrat Mohani, Sajjad Hyder Yaldaram, Wilayat Ali Bambooque, Qazi Abdul Ghaffar and Abdur Rahman Bijnori. The Progressive Writers' Association, formed in the mid-1930s, represented the continuation and development of the literary and political trends set by writers who were either in or closely connected with Aligarh. Its activities gave Urdu literature a vital stimulus, a new vigour and a liberating consciousness.

Encouraged by reports of nationalist activity on the campus, Gandhi and his Khilafatist allies turned to Aligarh to muster support for the non-co-operation programme, adopted by the

Congress in September 1920. Gandhi fired the first shot. He reached Aligarh on 11 October in the company of Ansari, Azad, Ajmal Khan and the Ali Brothers, and addressed a students' meeting the same evening. According to an eye-witness account, he spoke haltingly in Hindustani, trying to find the right words but his accent seemed droll to his 'pseudo-sophisticated' audience who did not agree with him because their political and economic background and affiliations did not predispose them to accept his radically new doctrines of non-co-operation. The first shot had clearly misfired. He then appealed to the trustees

> to decline any further Government grant, disaffiliate the great institution of which you are the trustees and reject the charter of the Moslem University. The least that the Aligarh boys can do, if you fail to respond to the call of Islam and India, is to wash their hands clean of an institution acknowledging the aegis of Government that has forfeited all the title to the allegiance of Islam and India and to bring into being, a larger, nobler and purer Aligarh that would carry out the inmost wishes of its great founder.

The trustees were not impressed. They had unanimously decided, much before Gandhi's letter of 24 October reached them, to run the institution on 'old established lines' and reiterated that the college aimed to make Indian Muslims 'worthy and useful subjects of the British Crown'. Sir Akbar Hydari, a trustee, commented:

> After my personal experience of the doings and sayings of Mr. Mohamed Ali and his student-following in Aligarh, I am firmly convinced that it is in the highest degree necessary...to get them not only outside the precincts of the college, but to absolutely prevented (sic) them from establishing what they are pleased to call a National Muslim University in Aligarh, but what is really...an instrument for seducing students from collegiate study and working them up to a pitch of religious frenzy and hatred.[114]

After repeated failures to counter Mohamed Ali's influence, who meddled in Aligarh affairs brazenly, the trustees at last had

[114] Akbar Hydari to Muhammad Ali, 17 November 1920. Also M. Habibur Rahman Khan and S.R. Masood to Muhammad Ali, 17, 18 November 1920, UP Government (Education Dept.), F.No. 40, 1918, UPSA.

their taste of revenge. The doyen of agitational politics was able to muster the support of only 10 members; the rest rallied round the loyalist Principal, Ziauddin Ahmad, who consistently warned students against being swept away by forces outside the college and had introduced an official ban on their joining the Anjuman-i Khuddam-i Kaaba.

Undeterred by this rebuff, Ansari, Azad Sobhani, Azad and the Ali Brothers returned to Aligarh on 23 October and addressed numerous meetings with a small group of students led by Zakir Huşain, a graduate in economics, and Kunwar Mohammad Ashraf, a Meo Muslim from Alwar State who rose to political prominence in the 1930s. On this occasion there was a change of heart. A graduate student wrote defiantly that he had his

> doubts removed within the last four or five days, and I am now a strong supporter of non-co-operation. I can and will read in your college only in the case it is nationalized [sic], otherwise I am ready to face the doom awaiting my non-co-operating brothers. I consider it my duty to intimate you of these views, so that I may not be considered a double game player.

One Nurul Hasan of Azamgarh, impressed by Azad and Azad Sobhani, gave up his studies to join the growing band of non-co-operators. Amidst fiery and passionate speeches, resolutions, promises and assurances, many more students responded—estimates range from 200 to 700—to the call of non-co-operation and enrolled themselves with the newly founded Jamia Millia Islamia. Mohamed Ali thus scored a major victory; the college authorities were humbled. The pan-Islamic fervour, combined with the nationalist upsurge, swept the campus and Syed Ahmad Khan's vision of sustaining the Anglo-Muslim rapprochement through the M.A.O. college was all but shattered.

In the late 1920s, Aligarh remained an advanced centre of political activity. K.G. Saiyadain, who joined the Teachers' Training College on his return from the University of Leeds in 1925, recalled his participation in the Jubilee Debate in 1926, when his fellow-students endorsed a policy of united nationalism. He argued, in the presence of luminaries like the Aga Khan, Jinnah and Ali Imam, that Indian Muslims should not organize themselves on communal lines but must work, together with nationalist forces, for the freedom and progress of the country. The message was well taken. A few years later the vice-president of the Students' Union spoke of Aligarh's role in the freedom struggle and exhorted his audience to

> turn ourselves into the biggest, the most disciplined, the most educated and the most united army that India possesses, to fight against the evils that have made India the laughing stock of the world and let nobody say that Aligarh lagged behind anybody in India's battle of freedom ...To be indifferent towards anything that happens in a depressed country like India is criminal. To be ignorant of one's own political status is far worse than death. And not to think of and dream of a brilliant future for one's own country is a state which will reduce one to a lifeless mass of flesh.

Such pronounced nationalist sentiments were echoed because political activity on the campus was not inspired by communal concerns. In 1931 Tofail Ahmad Manglori, one of Aligarh's distinguished Old Boys, wrote a powerful critique of the Muslim demand for separate electorates, arguing that the real cause for the communal tangle was the recognition of special interests 'which appears to have dimmed the national outlook.' His view was an article of faith with many comrades in Aligarh who spurned leaders with communal proclivities and followed instead, T.A.K. Sherwani, Khaliquzzaman, Shuaib Qureshi, and A.M. Khwaja—all graduates of Aligarh and closely associated with Jawaharlal Nehru and the Congress movement in UP. All of them were members of the most powerful university body—the University Court. Likewise, most office-bearers of the influential Students' Union belonged to the radical *alumni* circles, anti-British and pro-Congress; the widely circulated *Aligarh Magazine* retained its pro-Congress bias, and the theme of national unity and communal harmony evoked a ready response.

Equally important was the influence of socialism and communism which, though feeble in the early 1920s, was more pronounced in the 1930s. Syed Mohammad Tonki, who was actively involved in the non-co-operation movement and who later turned to 'Islamic Socialism' under the influence of Hasrat Mohani, recalled receiving M.N. Roy's writings 'which discussed the Russian revolution, the reality of the socialist system, and the weakening of the big empires as a result of capitalist and imperialist exploitation.' He and Kunwar Mohammad Ashraf often discussed 'what a socialist system might achieve in India'.

It is noteworthy that Muslims like Ashraf were initiated into the political mainstream during the Khilafat excitement and imbibed the nationalistic spirit and fervour which gripped large segments of Indian society during the years 1919 to 1922. Even thereafter,their interest in and association with nationalist forces continued, though regional and local compulsions sometimes distorted their perspective. What is equally important is the degree to which the top brass of the Khilafat leadership, tutored in the virtues of patriotism and anti-colonialism, eventually moved away from the Khilafat cause either in response to the spurt in communal activity or simply in search of new solutions to new problems.

The strength of the Khilafat movement lay in its proven ability to express the poetry of collective life: not the frenzy stirred by modern-style demagogues, but the intensity of earnest moments. Caught up in their millenium-seeking exhilaration, its leaders lived in a kind of intoxication during the years 1919–22—full of excitement, optimism and buoyant optimism. Even after their hopes were shattered and the bottled-up energy of their followers found an outlet in communal clashes, the principal Khilafat leaders remained convinced that, not long before, an immense event had taken place, that there had been a moment of power in the history of their country, a moment so close that it was almost within their grasp.

Chapter Six

Islam, Khilafat and Nationalism-II

The *ulama** were at the heart of the Muslim concern over Turkey and the Holy Places. They galvanized their followers in dedication to the Khilafat idea, foisted the flag of 'pure Islam' to carry it into battle against external and internal enemies and deployed the cultural and intellectual resources of Islam in an attempt to mobilize and legitimize anti-colonial aspirations. Their passionate commitment and fervour helps us to see more clearly the roles Islam has played in politics, as well as sensitizing us to the many

*The role of the *ulama* in modern Indian politics has received considerable scholarly interest. Some well known writings on the subject are: W.C. Smith, 'The Ulama in Indian Politics', C.H. Philips (ed.), *Politics and Society in India* (London, 1963), pp. 39–51 and his *Modern Islam in India;* Ishtiaq Husain Qureshi, *Ulema in Politics: A Study Relating to the Political Activities of the Ulema in the South-Asian Subcontinent from 1556 to 1947* (Karachi, 1974 edn); Hardy, *Partners in Freedom,* and his *Muslims of British India.* The history and role of the Dar al-Ulum, Deoband, is covered in the works of: Sayyid Mahboob Rizvi, *History of the Dar al-Ulum Deoband* (Deoband, 1980); Metcalf, *Islamic Revival;* Z.H. Faruqi, *The Deoband School and the Demand for Pakistan* (Bombay, 1963); Mushirul Haq, *Muslim Politics in Modern India 1857–1947* (Delhi, 1970). For the role of the Deobandi *Ulama* and the Jamiyat al-ulama during the Khilafat and non-co-operation movements, see Minault, *The Khilafat Movement,* pp. 103–07, 121–22, and her 'Islam and Mass Politics: The Indian Ulama and the Khilafat Movement', Donald E. Smith (ed.), *Religion and Political Modernization* (Yale University Press, 1974), pp. 168–82; Robinson, *Separatism,* chapter seven; M. Naeem Qureshi, 'The Ulama of British India and the Hijrat', *MAS,* 1979, vol. 13, i, pp. 41–59. Aseer Adrdai, *Tarikh-i Jamiyat al-ulama-i Hind* (Deoband, 1960) and Parween Rozeena (ed.), *Jamiyat al-ulama-i Hind: Dastaaveez 1919–1945* (Islamabad), in two volumes; Mohammad Miyan, *Ulama-i Haq aur unke kaarname* (Deoband, 1972 edn.).

ways the cultural norms and social precepts of Islam were invoked in the early twenties.

It is well known that Islam did not provide for a priesthood or a comparable religious institution. Gradually, however, a body of men developed to perform specialized religious functions—chiefly readers and reciters of the Quran and experts in recording and interpreting the sayings and doings of the Prophet of Islam. These were the *ulama,* literally those who possessed knowledge (*ilm*). They formed an 'unnumbered aggregate of academicians of all degrees of learning and intelligence'. Still, the hallmark of an *alim* was his learning in subjects like *Ilm-i Hadith* (science of Prophetic Tradition), *Tafsir* (Quranic exegesis), *Fiqh* (Jurisprudence) and *Ilm-i Kalaam* (Theology).[1] According to Fakhr-i Mudabbir, a fourteenth century chronicler at the Delhi court, the *ulama* owed their special status to their knowledge. He observed:

> All people know that after the apostles and prophets rank the truthful persons, martyrs and scholars. The scholars are included in the category of siddiqis and have preference over the martyrs. The Prophet has said: 'The ulama are the heirs of the prophets'. The world exists on account of the piety of the learned. The laws of shariat...are enforced by them... and things illegal and not sanctioned by the shariat are suppressed by them.[2]

Again, the *ulama* are described as those

> who will stand higher than the martyrs on the Day of Judgement. It is because of their learning, probity and piety that the world is

[1] Hardy, *Partners in Freedom,* p. 11. The following observation of Mohamed Ali is useful:

> Had I belonged to one of the families that specialize in religious training, I would, no doubt, have spent half a lifetime in the study of the Quran and its *tafsir* or exegesis, or *Hadith*.... or *Fiqh*.... and *Aqaid* and *Kalaam* or dogmatics and dialectics, which form the scholastic philosophy of the Musalmans regarding their creed....As a necessary preliminary to these religious studies, I would have had to receive instruction for a number of years in Arabic grammar and along with it in some secular Arabic literature. Mohamed Ali, *My Life,* pp. 2–3.

[2] K.A. Nizami, *Some Aspects of Religion and Politics in India during the Thirteenth Century* (Bombay, 1961), p. 150.

replenished. It is up to them to see that the commands of the Shariat are observed and good work is performed. Under their spiritual influence vices diminish and recede into lurking places....[3]

Such a glorified image was not entirely a product of Fakhr-i Mudabbir's fantasy but was, indeed, grounded in Muslim ethics; it helps to explain why the *ulama* occupied such a privileged position in Muslim societies.

The *ulama* were a powerful group in medieval India. They dominated the upper echelons of religious hierarchy, manned the judicial and ecclesiastical services, and wherever there was a mosque—and every Muslim locality had one—the *imam,* the *khatib,* the *muhtasib* and the *muftis* represented an interest which received State recognition. Some simply acquiesced in the *status quo,* repeated the utterances of the State and gave the deeds of rulers religious sanction and cover. But their functions were not restricted to legitimizing authority. They also performed regulatory functions in social and economic life, and the more prominent amongst them derived, not only social prestige, but also wealth from the performance of these functions. As a result, the *ulama* prospered: they acquired property, accumulated respectable fortunes, established matrimonial alliances with ruling houses, and emulated the *umara* in lavish expenditure. Criticizm and denunciation of their life-style and involvement in the politics and revolutions of the palace came only from the sufis and other men of religion, who led an abstemious life of pious devotion to religious learning and often eschewed entanglement in materialistic pursuits and political affairs.[4]

The medieval rulers needed the intellectual, administrative and educational services of the *ulama.* They also secured the one important element of authority which force alone could not command—legitimacy.[5] As quasi-officials of the State, they upheld the dominant political viewpoint, capitulated before the whims of even the 'impious' rulers, quoted scriptures and used it

[3] *Tarikh-i Fakhruddin Mubarak Shahi,* quoted in Agha Mahdi Husain, *Tughlaq Dynasty* (Allahabad, 1960), p. 361

[4] Nizami, op. cit., p. 152.

[5] See K.M. Ashraf, *Life and Conditions of the People of Hindustan* (Delhi, 1970 edn: reprint), p. 44.

against their 'enemies', and, above all, taught the faithful a dull stagnation in matters of belief and the acceptance of political autocracy, knowing all the time that almost everything the Sultans did as persons and as rulers was repugnant to the *shariat*.[6] They did all this in order to retain their control over the religious structure which was almost entirely dependent on State patronage. But opportunism does not explain everything, for the ideology of the *ulama* was also at work: the fear of chaos, disunity, and fragmentation of the ordered practice of religious duties. This attitude is illuminated by a writer from a different culture in a passage that applies here very well:

> Better that thousands should suffer than that a people should become a disintegrated mass, helpless like dust in the wind. Obscurantism is better than the light of incendiary torches. The seed germinates in the night. Out of the dark soil springs the perfect plant. But a volcanic eruption is sterile, the ruin of the fertile ground![7]

The establishment of British supremacy, however, led in the long run to the undermining of the position of the *ulama* in society. They were apprehensive of and opposed to clear breaches of Islamic traditions in education, the removal of important sections of law from under the jurisdiction of the *qazis*, the growth of local governments and the gradual secularization of some sections of Indian society. In his address to the first Congress of Nadwat al-ulama in April 1894, Shibli lamented:

> Gentlemen: In the days of the Muslim rule the worldly as well as the religious affairs of the Muslims were in the hands of the ulama...the reins of the affairs of the community relating to both this and the next world were in the hands of the ulama. Now that things have changed, and worldly affairs have come under the authority of [the British] government, we have to see what relationship the ulama have with the community.[8]

[6] In the nineteenth century, the traditional idea of a partnership between the rulers and the *ulama* was brought up to date by, among others, Rafi Al-Tahtawi (1801–73) of Egypt. See Hourani, *Arabic Thought in the Liberal Age*, p. 76.

[7] This is drawn from a secondary source, but I am unable to locate the reference.

[8] Quoted in Robinson, *Separatism*, p. 275; Shaikh Mohammad Ikram, *Mauj-i Kausar* (Lahore, 1970), p. 233.

The *ulama* instinctively distrusted government's trespassing on their turf and reinterpreting their age-old doctrines. Asserting the pre-eminent position of the *shariat*, they advanced their sole right to interpret its meaning for all groups and classes,[9] initiated steps to prevent the influx of subversive ideas from the religiously alien and 'morally inferior' British, and, as behind-the-scenes propagandists, discouraged unorthodox thought and learning, which was calculated to undermine their position amongst Muslims. Thus Shibli declared that the purpose of Nadwa was to defend Islam against contemporary times.[10] He held the view that through such institutions the *ulama* would be able to determine what was true or desirable in the light of the Quran and *Hadith* and thus maintain uniformity in belief and practice. Likewise, the objectives of the Dar al-Ulum at Deoband, as envisaged by Mohammad Qasim Nanotawi and Rashid Ahmad Gangohi, were to renew and establish contact between the *alim* and the average Muslims and to reorientate the community to its 'original' cultural and religious identity.[11]

Traditionally, madrasas formed the basis of Muslim education.[12]

[9] Thus Shibli insisted that the Muslim community could not develop unless the *ulama* had undisputed control over its secular and religious life: *Mauj-i Kausar*, p. 233. Shibli also organized a memorial against the Privy Council decision of 1894, which had set aside the law of *waqf-ul alal-aulaad*. Some decades later, the *ulama* of Firangi Mahal demanded special treatment in judicial matters, such as the establishment of special courts presided over by Muslim judges. Note by W.S. Marris, 17 November 1918, Meston Papers (34).

[10] *Makaatib-i Shibli* (Azamgarh, 1928), vol. 1, p. 329. Also, see *Rudaad-i Nadwat al-ulama*, 22–24 April 1894 (Kanpur, n.d.), vol. 1, pp. 22–24.

[11] The Dar al-Ulum, stated the 'official' historian of the institution, 'is not only a religious teaching institution but is also... an effective and active movement. This movement, cleansing the Muslims' beliefs and action of all the rubbish and trashery, acquainted them with pure and unalloyed Islam, liberated them from polytheism and superstitions...' See Rizvi, *History of the Dar al-Ulum Deoband*, p. 107, and pp. 108–10 for its aims and objectives. Also, Ahmad, *Islamic Modernism*, p. 104; Faruqi, *Deoband School*, p. 27.

[12] The earliest known madrasas were established by Iltutmish (1211–1236) and Balban (1266–1286) in the thirteenth century. Under Mohammad bin Tughlaq (1325–1351), Delhi alone had over a thousand madrasas. Jaunpur had at least thirty. A sixteenth century English traveller

Their curriculum, which remained largely unchanged over the centuries, included the study of Arabic and Persian language and literature, logic, philosophy, *Shariat, Hadith* and commentaries on the Quran. Aurangzeb, the last of the great Mughal emperors, reprimanded his former teacher for having taught him Arabic, grammar and philosophy, rather than subjects more practical for a future ruler of an empire.[13] But his pungent criticizm was of no avail. In the eighteenth century, Mulla Nizamuddin Sihalawi introduced the Dars-i Nizamia, which was regarded as the most comprehensive form of education and was therefore adopted as the basis for instruction in several institutions.[14] In this system, the curriculum was largely confined to purely religious sciences (*maqulaat*), with a bit of grammar and literature thrown in. The core areas of study included *Hadith, Fiqh, Kalaam* and *Tafsir,* with the Quran being at the heart of the curriculum and its memorization the highest scholastic attainment.

Maktabs were usually of two kinds: the first, of a purely religious character in which the rituals and tenets of Islam were taught, and the second, of a more secular type in which a good measure of Persian literature was also taught.[15] The most important of the

---

visiting Thata—now a picturesque ruin near Karachi (Pakistan)—reported 400 large and small madrasas. See Rizvi, op. cit., pp. 52–64.

[13] Shaikh Mohammad Ikram, *Ruud-i Kausar* (Karachi, 1958), pp. 424–26. Syed Ahmad Khan held that the Muslim schools of the old sort were 'altogether useless', because their syllabus and books 'deceive and teach men to veil their meaning...to describe things wrongly...and in irrelevant terms....and to relate facts like tales and stories. All these things are quite unsuited to the present age and to the spirit of the time, and thus instead of doing good they do much harm to the Muhammadans'. Quoted in Philips (ed.), *The Evolution of India and Pakistan,* p. 174. And Syed Ahmad to Mohsinul Mulk, 11 February 1872, quoted in Shan Muhammad, *Sir Syed Ahmad Khan: A Political Biography* (Meerut, 1969), p. 59.

[14] Details of the *Dars-i Nizamia* are outlined in Mujeeb, *Indian Muslims,* pp. 407–8. Some of the famous madrasas in UP were: Madrasa-i Kalaan in Sandila, Madrasa-i Chashma-i Rahmat in Ghazipur and the madrasa of Haji Imam Bukhsh in Jaunpur. In Bengal, such madrasas flourished in Murshidabad, Birbhum and Burdwan. The famous Jalaliya Madrasa was established by Munshi Sadruddin at Burdwan. Maulana Khairuddin Ahmad, *Tazkirat al-ulama* (Calcutta, 1934), pp. 13–14.

[15] In Punjab, besides the Quran and the *Kanzul-i Mussali,* a book of

first type, which later developed into a Dar al-Ulum [institution of high learning], was founded in a sleepy village of Deoband in 1867. As a protagonist of the Hanafi doctrines, the Dar al-Ulum achieved much fame and distinction as a theological seminary. Its goal was clear: to train well-educated *ulama* who, as prayer-leaders, writers, preachers and teachers, would tenaciously maintain the religious identity of the believers. A traditionalist course of studies was planned to the exclusion of modern sciences, because it was believed that the 'perfection' of the community lay in conserving its traditional heritage and in preventing the unprecedented and precipitous decline of Muslim traditional sciences (*manqulat*).[16] There was actual opposition, led by Gangohi, to the teaching of logic, philosophy and jurisprudence.[17]

The Nadwa, founded in 1894 as a middle of the road institution between the extremes of Aligarh's 'secularism' and Deoband's 'rigid conservatism', failed to combine both religious and secular types of education because of the attachment to the narrow curriculum of Nizamuddin.[18] The institution developed conservative contours and there was not much to choose between their theological and intellectual outlook and that of Deoband.[19]

---

prayers in verse, several works on rituals and the Islamic tenets were prescribed. These included the *Rah-i Najaat, Risaala- Namaazaan, Masaail-i Hindi, Nasihat Nama, Subha ka Sitara,* and *Masaail-i Subhaani.* H.S. Reid, *Report on Indigenous Education and Vernacular Schools* (Agra, 1852); R. Nathan, *Progress of Education in India 1896–77 to 1901–2* (Calcutta, 1904), vol 1, p. 375. In 1916–17, the enrolment to government-aided maktabs in UP was nearly nine thousand. By 1926–27, the figure rose to 43,973. This was a fair indication of the popularity of maktabs. *Report,* UP, 1921–28, vol. 2, p. 140.

[16] Ahmad, *Islamic Modernism,* p. 104. Nanotawi is reported to have said in 1874 that it was proper and desirable to pay attention to only traditional sciences and 'harmful beyond the capacity of students to be trained simultaneously in too diversified and too many a discipline'. Quoted in Faruqi, *Deoband School,* p. 30.

[17] Metcalf, *Islamic Revival,* p. 101.

[18] This was the time when scholars like Rafi al-Tahtawi in Egypt and Khayr al-Din (1810–1889) in Tunis urged the *ulama* to come to terms with the new learning and be in touch with the spirit of the times. See Hourani, op. cit., pp. 92–93.

[19] Ahmad, *Islamic Modernism,* p. 112.

Shibli's attempt to work out a new theology, a new *Ilmul Kalaam,* was widely attacked as heretical.[20] A government report noted:

> Generally, it would appear that Shibli's ideal in the early days of his connection with Nadwa was the adoption of a system of education not markedly progressive like that of Aligarh, but possessing (*sic*) as a medium of correction to the old maktab system a measure of western education. [But] he failed to influence the maktabs, and though the Nadwa can point to logic, history, mathematics and geography classes, the internal dissensions which have been such a marked feature of its history in recent years...would appear to militate against efficiency.[21]

Both the Dar al-ulum and Nadwa were attempts to make Muslims aware of their Islamic identity, to maintain the charismatic or divinely-instituted nature of the community and to warn the government that the *ulama* would brook no intrusion in their special field of religious interpretation and instruction. There were shared paradigms of religious renewal, rooted in the Quran. The basic concern of the *ulama* was to eliminate 'false accretions' derived from the Sufis or the Shias—on a detailed Islamization of every aspect of religious and everyday life. Their visions were meant to be a challenge to the world in general—and the West in particular—and as such had become powerful beacons for large numbers of backward and impoverished Muslims living in a cruel and uncertain world.

But not everybody was enthused by their role. This was because the *ulama,* in general, clung to the vestiges of their religious identity with a desperate vigour, zealously guarded their theological strongholds, treated the scriptures as if they were fossilized, scholastic parchments rather than inspirations for a dynamic world outlook, and presented an Islam that was static and lacking the dimension of internal evolution.[22] Their turbans and flowing gowns made them stand out as symbols of conservatism, especially at a time when the modernists or reformists proclaimed Islam to be a flexible, dynamic system that was and should

[20] Police Dept., F.No. 79, 1908, UPSA.

[21] Metcalf, *Islamic Revival*, p. 339.

[22] For a powerful criticizm of the role of the *ulama* on these lines, see *Asr-i Jadeed*, December 1908, p. 460.

always be interpreted and moulded from within to accommodate the social and political changes of the times.

Hali in his *Musaddas* and Akbar Allahabadi in his numerous poems lamented that most *ulama* concerned themselves with minutiae of ritual and in fruitless disputes, excelled in denouncing each other, and dubbing the adherents of other schools of thought as ignorant, irreligious and atheistic.[23] A religion which was once the fountainhead of ethics had become a rigid jumble of ritual and prayer in the hands of those who regarded their own traditional interpretations more as authoritative than the simple word of God or of His Prophet.[24] Azad, too, spoke out against the *ulama* demanding *taqlid* from their congregations, retaining a monopoly over religious texts, and preventing the believers from gaining access to true Islam.[25] Iqbal, on the other hand, attacked them for their conservatism, clumsy bookish wisdom and lifeless traditionalism. *Mulla* is for him the representative of the traditional way of those who learnt by heart texts which they themselves did not understand and who imposed upon people innumerable religious and ritual prescriptions without knowing their inner meaning. The theological hair-splitting in which they indulged was nothing but a welcome opportunity for the devil to blindfold the power of Islam.[26]

Such criticizm did not, however, undermine the position of the *ulama.* Though some failed to rise to any heights and performed a variety of roles without attracting notice, others, whose

[23] See, for example, M. Manzar and R.A. Khan, *Deoband aur Bareilly ikhtilaaf par Nazaa aur faislakun Munaazara* (Sambhal, 1966). For debates between the Ahl-i Hadith and the Hanafis, see *Rafi al-Akhbaar,* 8 July 1901, SNNR, UP. The Ahl-i Hadith have been the target of sharp criticizm from the same quarter. They were charged with 'betraying' Muslims in the 1857 revolt and supporting the British. Maulvi Nazir Husain of Delhi, Nawab Siddiq Husain Khan (1832–1890), a leading exponent of Ahl-i Hadith thought, and Maulana Mohammad Husain Butalwi were derided and accused of collusion with the British. Bashir Ahmad Qadiri, *Ahl-i Hadith aur Angrez* (Abu Hanifa Academy: Karachi, 1979), pp. 28–29, 55, 71–72, 104–5.

[24] Ahmad, *Islamic Modernism,* p. 99.

[25] Douglas, *Abul Kalam Azad,* pp. 76, 166–67, 273.

[26] Schimmel, *Gabriel's Wing,* pp. 75–76.

authority became more firmly held and more generally conceded by the public opinion, represented the Muslim community in matters relating to faith and law. They not only continued to make their presence felt through mosques and shrines, maktab and madrasas, but also endeared themselves for their ceaseless efforts to preserve, maintain and renew the unity, continuity and the divine guidance of the *Ummat an-Nabi,* the community of the Prophet. Above all, they played a variety of roles as guardians, transmitters and authorized interpreters of the *shariat,* which comprehends Muslim beliefs, rituals, public and personal law. They clarified controversial points of the doctrine and expressed views on subjects as wide-ranging as divorce, inheritance and disputes over property. That is how the Deobandi *ulama* issued 1,47,851 *fatawa* from 1911 to 1951, with Rashid Ahmad Gangohi, giving rulings that it was lawful to learn English if there was no danger to religion, that it was unlawful to take interest from a Christian, to use money-orders and bills of exchange in which the element of interest enters, and to wear a cross or a *topi.*[27] Such rulings were rarely flouted, at least not openly. The *ulama* were becoming, in the Gramscian sense, traditional intellectuals, enunciating an ideology that was powerful and favoured by the majority.

How did the *ulama* fit into an individual's daily life? One can begin to answer by imagining what kind of contact an average Muslim had with them. As a young boy he would attend a maktab, where he would be taught to recite some portions of the Quran from memory and to read and write. He may then go on for higher education at the madrasa which, like the maktab, was staffed by the *ulama.* In this way they exercized a near-monopoly over learning, sanctity and, consequently, moral authority.

The *ulama* had the greatest influence in regulating religious life. On Friday, the average Muslim would perform the *namaaz* and listen to the weekly sermon by the *khatib,* who was usually the prayer leader (*imam*). Here the *ulama* would come into contact with all classes and groups of people. Likewise, an *alim* or two would be drawn to conduct the marriage ceremony as well as the

[27] Hardy, *Muslims of British India,* p. 171; Ahmad, *Islamic Modernism,* p. 105.

funeral service. There were numerous other occasions when the *ulama* entered the 'private' domain and the 'public' sphere of individuals and groups to lend their name and legitimacy to religious rituals and social obligations.

Thus the *ulama* served as an important link between various Muslim groups, commanded considerable resources and the loyalties of diverse groups of people. It is, therefore, not surprising that, in small towns and villages, where the Muslim population was more susceptible to religious exhortations through local mosques and madrasas, the men of religion provided the inspiration behind a burst of Khilafat activity. They were successful in doing so because of their dominant religious hegemony which transcended class and caste divisions, enabling them to develop an extensive network of social connections which ranged from the Oudh taluqdar to the impoverished Muslim peasant in East Bengal.

It is true that in the realm of earthly politics the men of religion were frequently attacked for their conservatism and, as often, blamed for the backwardness of the Muslim people. Yet, even in a world turned upside down, their support was continually sought by, for example, the promoters of the Aligarh Muslim University. A conciliatory attitude towards the Muslim divines was intended to allay their fears about the future character of the institution and convince the government that the university movement was backed by influential Muslim groups. Likewise, the Muslim League leaders needed powerful allies to rally public opinion around their brand of agitational politics;[28] so they wooed the *ulama* and tried to remove their fears about the *la-dini* (religionless) character of the League. For the time being, the dividing line between the Western-educated and the orthodox

[28] The *Nai Roshni* of Allahabad, edited by Wahid Yar Khan, stressed the need to draw the *ulama* into the struggle against the repressive policies of the government. Likewise, the *Mohammadi* of Calcutta thought that the *ulama* should be encouraged to take the lead in making the masses conscious of the impending danger to the world of Islam. 'Let the alim', stated the paper, 'betake themselves to work. Let the first steps in this great national work be begun in the mofussil and let it be explained from each village mosque'. *Nai Roshni,* 23 December 1917, *Intikhab* (Gujranwala), 10 January 1920, SNNR, Punjab; *Mohammadi,* 23 April 1920, SNNR, Bengal.

was gradually blurred, almost obliterated, and with it were buried their bitter doctrinal feuds. The younger Muslims, observed the lieutenant-governor of UP, 'try to work with the priests, hoping through them to influence the mob. For the time being, however, it would be idle to deny that they have attained success'.[29]

In March 1915, Meston tried to explain why this was so. According to him, young educated Muslims were 'restless', 'dissatisfied' with the world around them and in search of a 'cause', a call, something that they could be proud of. 'This he finds in his religion. It gives him a link with great traditions'. Meston concluded:

> At this point he comes into touch with the priest of the arrogant domineering type, whose ambition lies in swaying the passions of the tolerant masses. Hence arises Pan-Islamism, the idea of the Muslim 'nation' and many of the fantasies generated from.[30]

Meston missed out a crucial aspect in his analysis—the ways in which the revocation of Bengal's partition, the Turko-Italian War, the furore over the Kanpur mosque affair, and the rejection of the Muslim University scheme added thrust to the converging courses in politics of the modern and the traditionally-educated.

The *ulama* responded favourably to these overtures, mainly because they were politically unorganized and indeed unaccustomed to political life. Moreover, their bitter doctrinal disputes and mutual rivalries created fissures in the apparent solid phalanx of orthodoxy and prevented them from moving in unison.[31] By 1911, however, they were rudely awakened by the growing threat to Islam—an awakening which coincided with, and was also to a certain extent caused by, the political upheaval in Turkey. They were conscious that they must now be active in addressing themselves to the current anxieties—political, social and religious—of Indian Muslims, or else see true Islam as they understood it, and their own claims to guide the community go by default. Such a realization led some *ulama* to cultivate the

[29] Meston to Hardinge, 25 March 1915, Hardinge Papers (89).
[30] Ibid.
[31] Robinson, *Separatism*, pp. 268–71.

modern-educated Muslims who had some experience of conducting constitutional politics and, in the words of Mohamed Ali, 'to pocket their pride and in a way even accept the lead of men whom they had but a generation ago finally consigned to perdition'.[32] An early move in this direction was initiated by Maulana Mahmud Hasan, who was convinced of the need to further greater fraternity between the alumni of Deoband and Aligarh.[33] The Jalsa i-Dastarbandi, convened in 1910 and attended by a delegation from Aligarh led by Aftab Ahmad Khan and the Jamiyat al-Ansar, founded by Ubaid-Allah Sindhi, was the fruition of such endeavours.

These initiatives were followed by the establishment of the Anjuman-i Khuddam-i Kaaba in May 1912. This was the beginning of the formal participation of the *ulama* in Indian politics in their capacity as religious leaders. Above all, the Anjuman provided the basis for an alliance between leading *ulama* of all shades of opinion and the modern-educated. This was of great significance because it illustrated that, on purely religious issues, the *alim* and the modernized Muslim could strive together for common ends. The orthodox and the anglicized 'were drawn together and as in a flash of lightning, saw that after all they were not so unlike each other as they had imagined'. Mohamed Ali wrote optimistically:

> Once more Muslim society in India presented a level of uniformity and the bitterest opponents of a generation ago stood shoulder to shoulder.... If even a decade previously anyone had ventured to foretell such a result, he would have been laughed at for such a fantastic prophesy.[34]

Having gained the trust and confidence of some leading *deendars,* the men of 'New Light' or 'Nai Raushani' began to use the existing networks of religious organizations and institutions to propagate pan-Islamism. In March 1914, Mohamed Ali, Ajmal Khan and Ghulam-us-Saqlain, editor of *Asr-i Jadeed,* were asked to enquire into the affairs of Nadwa. Mukhtar Ahmad Ansari was elected president of the Anjuman-i Islamia, Ghazipur, a position which had always been occupied by the local maulvis. In December 1918, Ansari and Shuaib Qureshi.

[32] Mohamed Ali, *My Life,* p. 43.
[33] Faruqi, *The Deoband School,* pp. 56–57.
[34] Mohamed Ali, op. cit., p. 43.

son-in-law of Mohamed Ali, addressed a meeting at Juma Masjid, Delhi, where they spoke in support of the Muslim League. In return for such concessions, the *ulama* expected the League leadership to orchestrate their specific religious demands.[35] For the same reason, leading *alim* like Abdul Bari rallied round Gandhi, submitted to his leadership because he was the only guarantor of Congress support, and accepted non-violence with all its implications. It was not easy for the *ulama* to grasp the idea of non-violence. But they accepted it, making it clear that they did so as a policy only and not as a creed, for their religion did not prohibit the use of violence in a righteous cause.[36] Writing to Gandhi in November 1920, Abdul Bari observed: 'I have accepted his [Gandhi] support in getting our aims fulfilled and for that purpose I think it is necessary to follow his advice.... I know that the strength of Islam lies in association with him.[37]

The same sentiment was echoed by his *murid,* Mohamed Ali. In July 1921 he wrote:

> When the Congress was adopting for the first time the Khilafat programme of non-violent non-co-operation, the essential thing was the unity of Hindus and Muslims and even if Muslims had been ready for violence, which they were not, they couldn't have succeeded without Hindu goodwill.... Long before we were free we had made up our minds to bring about a complete entente between Hindus and Muslims...and the best man among the Hindus to deal with was Mahatma Gandhi, a peace-loving and non-violent patriot who was intensely religious without a fury of a theologian and whose honesty all could rely upon. He found us to be equally religious and equally without a fury of a theologian, and as Muslims we could not pledge ourselves to remain non-violent in all circumstances, he found that we too regarded force at present to be futile, and above all he could trust our word as much as we trusted him. Even if we ourselves wished to use force immediately, which we did not and could not, we would have lost his support and thus have lost the chance of bringing about the Hindu-Muslim entente and of bringing the government to its senses.[38]

[35] See, for instance, Maulvi Mohammad Ahmad to Sheweth, 30 October 1917, Meston Papers (19).

[36] Nehru, *An Autobiography,* pp. 45–46.

[37] Home Poll. Deposit, F.No. 4, 1921, NAI; WRDCI, March 1919, Home Poll. B, F.No. 148–52, 1919, NAI.

[38] Quoted in Brown, *Gandhi's Rise to Power,* pp. 330–31; Also.

Such a subservient posture was distasteful to, among others, Syed Ahmad Raza Khan of Bareilly who was hostile to non-co-operation and to Gandhi's domination of the Khilafat movement.[39] But such men were few and wielded limited influence during the popular pan-Islamic upsurge. Most *ulama* favoured accommodation with Congress and political co-operation with Hindus because of the vital necessity of enlisting their support for the Khilafat campaign. For this reason alone they found Gandhi's leadership very welcome.

II

The principal shibboleth of the 'fundamentalists' in both Sunni and Shia Islam is that Islam is an all-encompassing way of life in which there can be no distinction between religion and politics. During the first decade of the twentieth century, Shibli and Azad insisted that 'a very large part of the national life is in the *ulama* right of ownership (*haqq-i-malkiat*) and they alone have or can have absolute sway (*mutlaq-al anaan*) over it'.[40] In his address to the first Congress of Nadwat al-ulama, Shibli berated the *ulama* for being lackadaisical and urged them to combine and organize themselves to offer an enlightened interpretation of religion, to reorganize Arabic and Persian studies, to exert pressure on the government for a revision of its legal policy, and to control and efficiently administer *waqfs*.[41] All this entailed, so he argued, active and vigorous involvement in politics. In 1912, his distinguished disciple, Azad, summed up his political ideology in an attempt to provide guidance to the *ulama*.

> The question whether political discussion should be separated from religious education is very important. But you must know that this is the foundation on which we intend to build the whole edifice of Al-Hilal. If

Mohamed Ali to Chelmsford, 24 April 1919, quoted in my *A Nationalist Conscience*, p. 70.

[39] Syed Jamaluddin, 'The Barelwis and the Khilafat Movement', in Hasan (ed.), *Communal and Pan-Islamic Trends*, pp. 400–13.

[40] *Khutbaat-i Shibli*, pp. 29–33, quoted in Shaikh Mohammad Ikram, *Modern Muslim India and the Birth of Pakistan, 1858–1951* (Lahore, 1965 edn.).

[41] Ahmad, *Islamic Modernism*, pp. 109–10; Smith, *Modern Islam*, p. 39.

you say that the arch is not beautiful we may try to alter its shape, but if you wish that the key-stone should be removed, then we cannot accede to your wishes. There will be nothing left with us if we separate politics from religion.[42]

This was common talk in the early 1920s, when the theological weight of Indian Islam was fully behind the Khilafat movement. Maulana Abul Muhsin Mohammad Sajjad, *Naib Amir-i Shariat* and *Nazim* of Jamiyat al-ulama, suggested to Abdul Bari that the *ulama* should 'take the reins of politics in their own hands and cross their voices with those in authority' in order to establish their religious supremacy and to fulfil their higher aim of protecting Islam from Western imperialism.[43] Maulvi Kifayatullah of Madrasa-i Aminia in Delhi, founder of the Jamiyat and its president from 1920 to 1939, echoed similar sentiments at the Muslim League meeting in December 1918. He declared:

In Islam religion and politics are not two separate things. For a long time they were together, but probably those who have received modern education think that they are separate from one another. This, however, is a wrong concept: they think that they should monopolize politics and leave religion for the *ulama*.[44]

Words were soon translated into deeds. The *ulama* thronged to the Muslim League session to determine the temper of the meeting, assert the voice of orthodoxy, assume leadership of the Khilafat agitation and contribute to its radical development. Soon after, they called upon the believers to wage *jehad* against the government, boycott foreign goods, and migrate (*hijrat*) to the *dar al-Islam*. They exercized their right to issue *fatawa* freely, using the Quran and the *Hadith* as powerful weapons to gain the adherence of the masses who accepted them as infallible. Abdul Bari, the chief ideologue of the *ulama,* did so on many occasions. He was among the signatories to the famous *fatwa* on non-co-operation. So was Azad. He was also the author of the *fatwa* on

[42] *Al-Hilal,* 8 September 1912, quoted in Mushirul Haq, *Muslim Politics in Modern India,* p. 72.

[43] A.M.M. Sajjad to Abdul Bari, 4 December 1918, *Nuqqush* (Lahore), 1918, p. 91.

[44] Cited in Qazi Abdul Ghaffar, *Hayaat-i Ajmal,* P. 185.

hijrat.[45] The lesser known *ulama* did not lag behind. The maulvis of Sukkur in Sind, inspired by Abdul Bari's *istifta* [questionnaire] of January 1919, issued a *fatwa* declaring the Jazirat al-Arab as a sacred place 'wherein non-Muslims cannot rule or remain in possession'.[46] Twenty-six *ulama* issued a *fatwa* in Bengal forbidding Muslim participation in the Peace Celebrations.[47] In legitimizing the local leaders and exhorting the hesitant to take up arms for *jehad,* Abdul Bari and Azad bestowed unity—however temporarily—on fragile alliances, because they used religion as a language with its own potent meanings and universal symbols.

There were strong objections to such outbursts from some quarters. The *istifta* was opposed, among others, by the *ulama* of Deoband. The *Muttaffiqa fatwa,* which made non-co-operation mandatory on all Muslims, was rejected by Maulana Ashraf Ali Thanwi, Ahmad Raza Khan and the Bahr al-ulum Party of Firangi Mahal.[48] Others like Maulvi Mohammad Ikramullah of Nadwa supported non-co-operation but not the boycott of educational institutions.[49] The *Pirs* of Sind were equally divided. The *Pir* of Kingri, for instance, not only opposed non-co-operation but also advised his followers to rally round the government. Rashidullah, another influential *Pir,* held aloof from the non-co-operation campaign as it was 'initiated and controlled by Hindus'.[50]

However, such opposition, often inspired by cynical government officials, failed to stem the pan-Islamic tide. As Ishtiaq Husain Qureshi observed:

> The stand taken up by the supporters of Non-co-operation found overwhelming support. Hardly any one examined the reasoning behind

[45] Azad declared that for the Indian Muslims there was no *shariat* alternative to *hijrat*. 'Before the Great War *hijrat* was commendable but now it was mandatory.' The exact date of this *fatwa* is not known, though it is said to have been issued in April or early May 1920. Qureshi, 'The Ulama of British India', op.cit., p. 51

[46] *Tribune*, 21 March 1919.

[47] *Mohammadi*, 12 December 1919, SNNR, Bengal.

[48] Qureshi, *Ulema in Politics*, p. 270.

[49] Maulvi Mohammad Ikramullah, *Maslr -i Taaleem aur Tark-i Mavalaat* (Aligarh, 1920), pp. 34, 36.

[50] WR (Sind), 9 April 1921, Curry Papers.

> the pro-Non-co-operation *fatwa*. The general feeling was that the British and their allies were out to destroy Islam as a force in international affairs, hence they were the enemies of Islam, therefore, non-co-operation against them must be right.... The Muslims supported the movement with rare abandon.[51]

The *ulama* were not content with sheafs of *fatwa*, but wandered from rural areas to cities and other rural areas in order to mobilize their followers through a well-modulated campaign. The governor of Bengal nervously reported that they were busy travelling all over eastern Bengal enjoining the faithful to perform *jehad*.[52] The Ahl-i Hadith group was particularly active in Dinajpur, western Rangpur, northern Rajshahi and north-western Bogra. So strong was its impact in parts of Rangpur district that a swaraj *thana* was established by one Ghyasuddin Ahmad, popularly known as 'Gandhi-darogha'. In some areas 'free villages' were organized under the aegis of local Anjuman-i Islamia's.[53] This was not all. The Majlis-i Ulama of Madras toured the presidency to incite Muslim emotions on the Khilafat issue, and, in May 1920, the United Provinces' Ulama Association sent students to preach *jehad* in the mofussil. A few months earlier, Abdul Bari and Shaukat Ali toured Gujarat together, preaching the sanctity of the Khilafat and Hindu-Muslim unity; later, they were joined by Azad for a tour of Sind.[54]

The *ulama* quickened the tempo of their agitation, establishing *shariat* tribunals in a few places and national schools in parts of the North West Frontier Province.[55] In Bengal, the *ulama* 'who had formerly held aloof from politics' were drawn into the boycott movement.[56] In UP, the homeland of most vociferous pan-Islamists, educational centres like the Nadwat al-ulama and the Dar al-Musaniffin became the main foci of agitations.[57] The

[51] Qureshi, *Ulema in Politics*, pp. 271–72.

[52] 16 May 1919, Diary of Ronaldshay, Ronaldshay Papers, MSS.EUR. F. No. D 609 (1), IOLR.

[53] Tajul Islam Hashmi, 'Peasants and Politics in East Bengal', pp. 74–75.

[54] For details, see Brown, *Gandhi's Rise to Power*, pp. 224–25.

[55] Bamford, *Histories*, p. 151.

[56] FR (Bengal), November 1921, Home Poll. Deposit, December 1921, F. No. 18, NAI.

[57] After leaving Nadwa in 1913, Shibli went to Azamgarh where he

pan-Islamic ferment at Nadwa, generated by Shibli's poems on the Balkan,[58] the Indian Medical Mission to Constantinople, and the Kanpur mosque incident, culminated in the effective students' demand in November 1920 to refuse the grant, sanctioned by J.P. Hewett in 1908.[59] At the Dar al-Musaniffin, Syed Sulaiman, one of Shibli's favourite pupils at Nadwa and member of the 1920 Khilafat delegation to Europe, urged Muslims to sacrifice their lives in defence of the Holy Places and insisted that the political emancipation of India was a 'religious duty'. If Muslims wanted to liberate Kaaba, he told Abdul Bari, they would have to liberate India first.[60]

Masud Ali, founder of a Khilafat Committee (in April 1920) and its branch committees in the Azamgarh district, was a leading non-co-operator. According to the Commissioner of Gorakhpur,

---

collected a small band of followers to carry on his literary activities and especially to assist him in the compilation of the life of the Prophet. In this way the Dar al-Musaniffin came into being. After the death of Shibli in November 1914, the society was registered in Lucknow on 4 July 1915 and secured grants from Hyderabad and Bhopal. Though formed as a literary society, the Dar al-Musaniffin, or the Shibli Academy, soon became 'the centre of the political activities in Azamgarh district'. Its press printed and distributed pamphlets on the Khilafat issue. A government report added : 'There is no doubt that the Shibli Academy is no longer what its founder intended it to be, but has become an extremist political institution of a class with which I feel sure that neither...the Nizam nor...the Begum of Bhopal would wish to support'. H.R. Gracey to G.B. Lambert, 8 January 1921, Police Dept., 1921, F.No. 1, UPSA.

[58] The Nadwa came under suspicion for its pan-Islamic leanings due to Anthony MacDonnell who regarded its founder, Shibli, as disloyal to the government. However, Hewett did not share this view. At Shibli's request, he sanctioned an initial grant of Rs 6000 and laid the foundation of the Nadwa building on 28 November 1908. Education Dept., 1908, F.No. 79, UPSA. In 1911–12, Shibli's involvement in the pan-Islamic movement was again discussed when the question of giving him an award was considered by the government officials. The matter was deferred on the grounds that he was already a *Shams al-ulama*, 'which seems a sufficient distinction for a gentlemen whose most praise-worthy quality is that he is a good writer of Urdu prose'. L. Porter to DuBoulay, 25 July 1911, Hardinge Papers (50).

[59] The strike was called off following the intervention of Aftab Ahmad Khan, Ajmal Khan and Nawab Mohammad Ishaq Khan. C.F. De La Fosse to O'Donnell, 8 February 1914, 1908, F.No. 79, UPSA.

[60] Gracey to Lambert, 8 January 1926, GAD, 1921, F.No. 1074, UPSA.

his activities turned the Dar al-Musaniffin into 'an extremist political institution' and a centre of radical politics in Azamgarh. His influence extended to small towns in the region, such as Mau, Sarai Mir and Pharuja. In Mau, which was predominantly inhabited by Muslim *julahas,* Abdul Aziz, a barber, Maulvis Mohammad Sabir, Abdullah and Zamir pushed the honorary magistrates into resigning and persuaded the local Islamia College to renounce its government aid. 'Mau, in short', noted an official, 'is the danger point in the district and wants watching'. In Sarai Mir, Khilafat activities were centred around the Arabic school. The manager, M. Hamiduddin, the staff and students were found busy explaining the significance of the *fatawa* issued by Abdul Bari and Azad. 'These mullahs', observed an alarmed official, 'are ignorant and fanatical and will believe anything if they believe their religion to be in danger. They get worked up to the boiling point by itinerant, professional agitators, who are in my opinion the most dangerous class now'.[61]

Such organized activity, supported by the rapid circulation of a variety of opinions and images, was a priceless asset and the key to the extraordinary vigour of the Khilafat agitation. Jawaharlal Nehru aptly summed up the position of the *ulama* during this period.

> Owing to the prominence given to the Khilafat movement in 1921, a large number of Moulvis and Muslim religious leaders took a prominent part in the political struggle. They gave a definite religious tinge to the movement, and Muslims generally were influenced by it. Many a Westernized Muslim, who was not of a particularly religious turn of mind, began to grow a beard and otherwise conform to the tenets of orthodoxy. The influence and prestige of the Moulvis, which had been gradually declining owing to new ideas and a progressive Westernization, began to grow again and dominate the Muslim community.[62]

III

'Take great care', the *Independent* of Allahabad warned its readers on 3 June 1920, 'that the control of the Khilafat movement does not fall entirely within the hands of theologians and

[61] Note by Bigg Wither, 7 December 1921, Police Dept., 1921, F.No. 1074, UPSA.

[62] Nehru, *An Autobiography*, pp. 71–72.

divines'.[63] But nobody paid heed to the warnings of those who stressed the necessity, or at least the desirability, of minimizing the intrusion of religion in political life. By early 1921, however, it was clear that the *ulama* were no longer an asset but a liability. This was indicated at the Meerut Khilafat Conference in April 1921, when some hot-headed elements objected to the Hindu involvement in the Khilafat movement and demanded its scope to be defined according to the *shariat.*[64] This was followed by Abdul Bari's warning that Muslims were ready to adopt violent methods to redress their grievances. Words were soon translated into deeds.[65] In May 1921, *Darul Qaza* courts (House of Justice) were set up in parts of Bihar and the North-West Frontier Provinces, and talk of *jehad* filled the air in the countryside.[66] The Jamiyat al-ulama, founded in November 1919 mainly on Abdul Bari's initiative, took a momentous decision in March 1921: it was declared *haraam* [sinful] for a Muslim soldier to serve in the army.[67] The Karachi Khilafat Conference in July 1921 simply endorsed this resolution which was introduced by Maulana Husain Ahmad Madani and supported by the Ali Brothers, Pir Ghulam Mujadid, a Sindhi follower of Abdul Bari, and Maulana Nisar Ahmad of Deoband.

Gandhi supported the Karachi resolution. But he was nervous about the growing militant posture which threatened to destroy

[63] A number of writers, mostly in Pakistan, have argued that involving the *ulama* in the political agitations of the day was a mistake. For example, Abdul Hamid, *Muslim Separatism in India : A Brief Survey 1858–1947* (Lahore, 1971 : reprint), pp. 151–52; Mohammad Noman, *Rise and Growth of the All-India Muslim League* (Allahabad, 1942), pp. 213–14.

[64] WRDCI, 11 April 1921, Home Poll. Deposit, June 1921, F.No. 54, NAI.

[65] Abdul Bari said in June 1921 that Muslims held non-violent non-co-operation as 'a useful weapon to get our grievances redressed' but that they were not committed to 'always adhere to this principle'. Home Poll. 1921, F.No. 45, NAI. Reporting the deliberations of the Provincial Conference held sometime in November 1921, Jawaharlal Nehru reported to Gandhi that its president, Hasrat Mohani, expressed dissatisfaction with the creed of non-violence. 'Several other speakers used violent language and apparently looked forward to a time when violence would have full play. All this took place on the Karachi Resolution. S. Gopal (ed.), *Selected Works of Jawaharlal Nehru* (Delhi, 1972), vol. 1, p. 201.

[66] Bamford, op.cit., pp. 168–69.

[67] *Dastaaveez*, op. cit., vol. 1, pp. 129–30.

the credibility of his non-violent non-co-operation technique. He was aware of the discontent amongst some of his Congress comrades, particularly after the Moplah riots in August 1921, and was anxious that they should not be alienated any further. But the hard-liners were not easy to tame. They flocked to various national gatherings in December 1921 and demanded the immediate adoption of civil disobedience. Their enthusiasm was temporarily curbed by Ansari, Azad and Ajmal Khan.

The showdown came soon thereafter, when the poet-politician, Hasrat Mohani, representing the more militant *ulama,* proposed that the Congress and Muslim League should strive to attain 'complete independence' and declared that if martial law was imposed Muslims would either have to abandon non-co-operation or face the bullets and bayonets. In the latter event, violence was the natural course to adopt in self-defence. This was symptomatic of the tensions between Gandhi's ideal of satyagraha and the Khilafat leaders' adoption of it as a political technique, a fact which remained a constant feature of the Khilafat movement. Gandhi himself created this tension, despite his laments about Muslim motives, by making non-violence the pre-condition of his support. His hopes of transmuting the pan-Islamic sentiments of the Muslims into a nationalist movement seem to have failed, because some Khilafatists, notably the *ulama,* were not willing to go along with him in the realization of his ideals. They merely extended grudging support to the non-violent non-co-operation programme as a price for securing Gandhi's adherence to the Khilafat cause.

Gandhi threw his weight against Hasrat's resolution, arguing that complete independence could not be incorporated in the Congress creed unless and until Hindu-Muslim unity was completely accomplished.[68] This was another way of saying that

[68] He said : 'Let us understand our limitation. Let Hindus and Muslims have absolute, indissoluble unity. Who is here who can say with confidence : Yes, Hindu-Muslim unity has become an indissoluble factor of Indian Nationalism?' *Young India,* 19 January 1922, *CWMG,* vol. 22, p. 108. Writing to Montagu within a few days of the close of the Ahmedabad meeting, Reading observed that the discussion...must be regarded as very serious, not only because of the language used but also because the defeat of Hazrat (*sic*) Mohani's motion was really on grounds of inexpediency'. The Marquess

the idea of complete independence was premature, as it was unlikely to find favour with a section in the Congress. Congress finally backed Gandhi rather than Hasrat Mohani, as did the Subjects Committee of the Muslim League on 30 December. Hasrat's resolution, opposed by Ajmal Khan, Ansari and Syed Raza Ali, was rejected by thirty-six votes to twenty-three.

The *ulama* were enraged. Having first mooted the idea of complete independence in March 1921, the Jamiyat al-ulama felt cheated by these attempts to curb the militant instincts of its followers. Consequently, some harsh words were exchanged, which reflected the rift between the Mahatma and the Muslim priests. Hopes of a reconciliation were dimmed in the absence of the Ali Brothers who, having acted as mediators between Gandhi and the *ulama,* were languishing in British jails. By the end of 1921, the Khilafat movement was beginning to slip out of Gandhi's control. The viceroy had rightly assessed in 1921 that Mohamed Ali was a 'real factor in the situation' and a 'link' between the Congress and the Muslims. His view, vindicated by later day events, was that any strains in Gandhi-Mohamed Ali relations would lead to 'the collapse of the bridge over the gulf' that separated Hindus and Muslims.[69]

There was some distancing between the Khilafatists and a group of Hindu politicians as well. It started from Mohamed Ali's statement in April 1921 that, in the event of an Afghan invasion of India, India's Muslims would stand by them against the British.[70] This unrestrained commitment to anti-colonialism was widely misunderstood and raised quite a few eyebrows. There was talk of Islamic hegemony being established in India and of Hindus 'raising their heads' to thwart all such attempts.[71]

of Reading, *Rufus Isaccs First Marquess of Reading, By his son,* (London, 1945) pp. 242–245.

[69] The Marquess of Reading, ibid., p. 199.

[70] P. Parasram to the Ali Brothers, 8 July 1921, Mohamed Ali Papers, JMI; Brij Narain Chakbast to Sapru, Sapru Papers, National Library Calcutta, and the comments of Lajpat Rai in V.C. Joshi (ed.), *Lala Lajpat Rai : Writings and Speeches* (Delhi, 1966), vol. 1, p. 203.

[71] Moonje to Shankaracharya of Puri, n.d. (Report), Moonje Papers (35).

This distrust and imaginary fears were reinforced by the Moplah riots along the Malabar coast of South India.

Stirred by the pan-Islamic euphoria, the Moplahs directed their long suppressed anger against the Hindus, desecrated temples and resorted to forcible conversions. Reports of such happenings, often distorted and exaggerated, widened the breach in the Hindu-Muslim front. Congress leaders, in general, adopted a partisan attitude, accusing each other of instigating violence and speaking for and on behalf of their respective communities in Malabar. Some argued that oppression and exactions on the part of 'Hindu' landlords were at the root of the trouble denying that fanaticism entered into the picture at all. Hasrat Mohani said to the Congress Subjects Committee that the Moplahs suspected Hindus of collusion with government and were, therefore, justified in 'presenting the Quran to the Hindus. And if the Hindus became Mussalmans to save themselves from death, it was a voluntary change of faith and not forcible conversion'.[72] Syed Mahmud told Gandhi that there were no forced conversions; Abdul Bari accused government of circulating false rumours in order to drive a wedge between Hindus and Muslims. But Malaviya, Lajpat Rai, Moonje and Shraddhanand were not satisfied with these explanations, arguing that fanaticism was used as an instrument by pan-Islamists to excite Muslims against the Hindus. They demanded that the Hindus should be united, integrated and consolidated in defence against any such future occurrence. Moonje, the aggressively anti-Muslim leader from Nagpur, mooted the idea of providing the settlement of 'our warlike races, such as the Marathas, Rajputs, Sikhs etc., in Malabar which alone, I think, can solve the problem of Moplah terrorism over the meek and helpless Hindus'.[73] This was in preparation of launching the *sangathan* movement, which greatly embittered Hindu-Muslim relations throughout the country.

Amid such heated controversies, Gandhi dropped a bombshell by suspending civil disobedience. 'The whole conception of

[72] Quoted in Ram Gopal, *Indian Muslims : A Political History 1858–1947* (Bombay, 1959), p. 157.

[73] Moonje Papers (13).

civil disobedience', Gandhi informed the Congress Working Committee, 'is based upon the assumption that it works in and through its non-violent character... I personally can never be a party to a movement half violent and half non-violent'.[74] Two other reasons might have also influenced Gandhi's decision. First, its patchy success in some areas,[75] and secondly, the growing strains in his alliance with the Khilafatists and his inability to curb their militant activities. The Karachi resolutions of July 1921 were intemperate enough to alarm Gandhi and the violent and xenophobic speeches of the *ulama* confirmed fears of an outbreak of violence. He was also aware of the effects of the Moplah riots on Hindus. He tried to soothe their feelings, but reached the inescapable conclusion that Hindus were becoming increasingly apathetic to the Khilafat cause and were anxious to extricate themselves from the travail of non-co-operation. Having read the danger signal, Gandhi recognized the political necessity of withdrawing civil disobedience.

For Muslims, however, the future of Khilafat and the Holy Places was still very much a live issue. As a consequence, Gandhi's arbitrary call in the summer of 1922 was received with anger, dismay and disappointment. 'Abandon Mr Gandhi's remedy of non-co-operation', stated Maulvi Mohammad Kazim Ali at the Bengal Provincial Conference in April, 'and find another path and follow it'. 'It is proper', added another speaker, 'that there should be assaults and bloodshed', and that 'he who is your enemy should be met with the sword'.[76] Hasrat Mohani rejected the Bardoli programme.[77] So did his political mentor, Abdul Bari, when he attacked Gandhi and the Bardoli resolution at the Jamiyat al-ulama conference held in Ajmer.[78]

After the suspension of civil disobedience, Muslims had

[74] To members of the Congress Working Committee, 8 February 1922, *CWMG*, vol. 22, pp. 350–51.

[75] Brown, *Gandhi's Rise to Power*, chapter 9.

[76] 'History of the Khilafat Movement in Bengal', p. 4, *Tarikh-i Jamiyat*, op.cit., pp. 61–62. And the later day verdict of A.B. Rajput and Ziauddin Suleri, quoted in Sayeed, *Pakistan : The Formative Phase*, p. 60.

[77] Home Poll. February 1922, F.No. 18, NAI.

[78] According to a report, his speech was 'wild, impolitic and full of destructive programme'. Home Poll. February 1922, F.No. 501, NAI.

another surprise in store. On 21 November, 1922, the Turkish National Assembly at Ankara decided to separate the Khilafat from the sultanate. And since the maintenance of the temporal power of the Khalifa was one of the main objects of the Khilafat movement, this action by a purely Muslim body completely took the wind out of its sails. In March 1924, the final blow was struck by Mustafa Kamal Pasha who burst the bubble of the Khilafat. Its immediate result was the disruption of the Khilafat Party. From 1918 to 1922, religious zeal and the overwhelming anti-British bias had united various groups amongst Indian Muslims. But once the initial euphoria had worn thin, the inherent contradictions in the alliance destroyed the appearance of unity and brought to surface the division among the ranks of the *ulama*, as among Muslims in general. The Jamiyat al-ulama was divided with Nisar Ahmad of Kanpur and Abdul Majid Budauni joining the *tanzim* movement and also founding a parallel ogranization in Kanpur.[79] The rapprochement between the political and religious wings of the Khilafat movement was also unable to sustain itself because international developments had undermined its *raison d'etre* and because there was no sound basis for permanent adjustments of diversified and, in some cases, conflicting interests.

One of the immediate consequences of such developments was the disappearance of Muslim divines from the national scene. They had gained in confidence from the time of the Muslim League session in 1918, but the unexpected setback shattered many of their plans and reduced their growing influence in national politics. The result was bewilderment, confusion, and even inactivity. Having once mobilized new groups, roused their religious fervour and articulated their grievances, the *ulama* were now like a contrary jack-in-box refusing to retire, out to seek new outlets for their energy, and to build something positive out of the Khilafat experience. Some doggedly kept the Khilafat movement gasping, some capitulated to the communalist camp, and some, including the *ulama* of Deoband, entered the arena of religious controversies and organized the *tabligh* and *tanzim* societies as a counterpart to *shuddhi* and *sangathan*.

[79] Qureshi, *Ulema in Politics*, p. 302.

The Khilafat agitation provided the *ulama* with a distinct enemy and goals; when the enemy and goals proved elusive other whipping boys and solutions had to be found. Much of their interests, geared to religious goals, remained, because they seemed to be the hope for the Muslim community. In consequence, many of the *ulama* who participated in the Khilafat movement reverted to their former religious preoccupations. For the time being, the Jamiyat al-ulama, despite its nationalist sympathies, moved along a course parallel to that of the nationalist Muslim political leadership. It was mainly concerned to secure safeguards against interference with the *shariat* and guarantees for its preparation and implementation. At Calcutta in March 1926, the Jamiyat directed its members to educate in the proper requirements of the *shariat* those Muslims who were following customary laws of inheritance. The Jamiyat also demanded the setting up of qazi courts for the settlement of disputes over marriages, divorce, inheritance and *auqaf*.[80]

The *ulama* of Firangi Mahal, too, were marginalized. Abdul Bari, the chief architect of the alliance between the *ulama* and the Congress, felt despondent, isolated and alienated from the Congress. In August 1923, he complained: 'The position of the Muslims has been rendered very awkward. Those who pretended to be our friends at one time and made a catspaw of the *ulama* now seem anxious to get rid of them'.[81] Abdul Bari was right. The *ulama* had been brought into political life because of their influence in the countryside and their ability to gather various groups under their own banner. But in the aftermath of civil disobedience and the Khilafat fiasco, their services were no longer required. They were bluntly told not to dabble in politics. Men like Abdul Bari were remembered merely as 'interesting' and 'esteemable representatives of the good old days' and as a 'distinguished figure out of the fast disappearing galaxy of that ancient culture which is still dear to us'.[82]

The widespread confusion in the ranks of various influential

[80] Hardy, *Partners in Freedom*, p. 35.

[81] Statement to the Press, Abdul Bari Papers.

[82] Maulvi Mohammad Yaqub, UP Provincial Muslim League, Annual Session, 24 April 1926 (Moradabad, n.d.).

Muslim groups, including the *ulama*, was best summed up by Khaliquzzaman:

> The history of the next sixteen years of Muslim India is a mass of confusion and a chapter of political benightedness. The disruption of the Khilafat organization was like a breach in the embankment of the flowing stream of Muslim mass emotion, which diverted it into several petty streams, some leading to desert lands there to dry up, some flowing by zig-zag routes to meet the original bed in their headlong march and some others rushing towards the mighty ocean to drown themselves. To try to find any consistency, sound reasoning or logical method in Muslim politics during that period would be utterly futile. We were divided between ourselves.[83]

IV

Events following the Khilafat and Non-Co-operation movements have been a subject of much historical research. Yet, it may still be useful, before we cover them in some detail in subsequent chapters, to offer a corrective to certain established notions on the state of communal relations.

There can be no doubt that Hindu-Muslim relations worsened during 1922-1926 and the edifice of inter-communal unity began to crumble in a way that was unforeseen by the architects of the Khilafat and Non-co-operation agitations. Still, it would be misleading to draw the conclusion, tempting though it is, that the two communities were arrayed against each other or that Indian society came to be hopelessly polarized along communal lines. Notwithstanding mounting religious and communal tensions, most people continued to lead, as they had always done, a life of harmonious co-existence. In fact, bonds of socio-economic interests and centuries of common historical experiences were strong enough to withstand the communal onslaught. The pan-Islamic euphoria, which had caused so much excitement in the subcontinent, did not take much time to disappear as the Turkish nationalists began to rewrite their political agenda without a Khalifa/Sultan. Faced with this reality, unpleasant though it was to the more committed pan-Islamists, there was an unmistakable reordering of priorities. From now on, Islam was once more firmly rooted in the Indian soil and

[83] Khaliquzzaman, *Pathway to Pakistan*, p. 76.

the interests of its followers were seen to be more closely linked with the people they lived with and the society they were born in. It is sheer romanticism to suggest that 'the ideal of the Islamic community shaped and shapes their [Muslim] apprehensions of what is legitimate, desirable and satisfactory political action'.[84]

The *ulama* based at Deoband and those connected with the Jamiyat al-ulama were vocal champions of composite nationalism and firmly attached to the nationalist forces. It is fair to uncover their motives but it is no less important to assess their objective role in heightening anti-colonial consciousness. After all, their track record was enviable, for time and time again they rallied round the Congress-led agitations. In 1928-29, they sided with the Congress in boycotting the Simon Commission and adopted complete independence as their political creed. And in 1930-31, they took a prominent part in the civil disobedience campaigns.[85] The meeting at Amroha where some of these vital decisions were taken echoed their unmistakable commitment to the political radicalization of the nationalist struggle.[86] Some like Maulana Anwar Shah declared that the country's liberation from foreign domination was consistent with the Hanafi code.[87] Others like Maulana Shah Muhiuddin Ahmad of Phulwari insisted that Muslims should join Gandhi's Dandi March and defy government laws.[88] There were still others—Hafiz Mohammad Said, Mufti Kifayatullah and Ataullah Shah Bukhari—who languished in jails for organizing local civil disobedience campaigns.[89]

[84] Francis Robinson, 'Islam and Muslim Separatism', in Hasan (ed.), *Communal and Pan-Islamic Trends in Colonial India*, p. 373.

[85] Hasan, *A Nationalist Conscience*, pp. 182–83. A number of leading *ulama* appealed to Muslims in the name of Islam to join civil disobedience. The occasion for the appeal was the unfurling of the national flag on New Year's day. *Bombay Chronicle*, 31 March 1930.

[86] See Hasan, *Mohamed Ali: Ideology and Politics*, p. 105.

[87] *Medina*, for the week ending 5 April 1930, SNNR, UP.

[88] *Hamdam*, for the week ending 26 April 1930. Syed Shah Muhiuddin issued a manifesto, which was endorsed by the Bihar branch of the Jamiyat al-ulama, endorsing the decisions of the Amroha conference. *Rozana Akhbaar* and *Medina*, for the week ending 12 and 19 July 1930, SNNR, UP.

[89] *Amir-i Shariat* Ataullah Shah Bukhari made a vigorous plea at the

It was by no means easy for such men to maintain this degree of consistency, especially in periods of intense communal conflicts, and to face the wrath of some *ulama* from among their own ranks.[90] Though Husain Ahmad Madani and his band of followers were condemned and villified in the press and at public platforms,[91] they remained true to their ideals. In 1938 the Jamiyat al-ulama president, Madani, delineated the broad contours of his theory of composite nationalism in his letters to Iqbal. He pointed out that regardless of religion, common habitat or race the word *qaum* (community) was applicable to any collective group and that it did not have the same meaning as *millat*, which refers to a collectivity with a *shariat* or *din*. Indian Muslims, though separate from others in religion, were fellow-nationals with other communities and groups in India. They were therefore advised to join in a collective endeavour to achieve freedom and independence.[92] In independence thus gained Muslims and non-Muslims would be co-partners in creating a society and an administration which, though not modelled entirely on the

---

Amroha meeting for adopting civil disobedience and was a key figure in promoting the movement in Punjab. For details of his role, see Jaanbaaz Mirza, *Hayaat-i Amir Shariat* (Lahore, 1970). Bukhari was also involved in organizing meetings in support of Bhagat Singh. One such meeting—attended by over 1,500 Muslims and addressed by Zafar Ali Khan—was held in Delhi on 19 March 1931. Tegart Papers, Centre for South Asian Studies, Cambridge.

[90] Prominent amongst them were Shabbir Ahmad Usmani and Ashraf Ali Thanwi. See Munshi Abdur Rahman, *Maimaaraan-i Pakistan* (Lahore, 1976), and Mohammad Sadiq Qasuri, *Akaabir Tehrik-i Pakistan* (Lahore, 1979 edn.).

[91] Maulana Razi, *Mutahidda Qaumiyat aur Islam* (Lahore, 1967 edn.) was a powerful rebuttal of Madani's ideas on composite Indian nationalism. Asrarul Haq Siddiqi, *Congressi Ulama Ki Siyasi Karwaten* (Delhi, n.d.), was a sharp criticizm of Madani's presidential address at the Saharanpur session of the Jamiyat al-ulama. While such pamphlets were being written, the *Inqilab* of Lahore was carrying on a vicious campaign against the leaders of the Jamiyat. See its editorial comments on 11 September 1937, 19 May 1938, 6 January 1939, 5 March 1939, 15 March 1939. Also, see Choudhry Habib Ahmad, *Tehrik-i Pakistan aur Nationalist Ulama* (Lahore, 1966).

[92] Ahmad, *Islamic Modernism*, pp. 192–93; Hardy, *Muslims of British India*, pp. 227–28. For Madani's presidential address at the June 1940 Jamiyat al-ulama conference, see Faruqi, *The Deoband School*, pp. 103–4.

conception of an Islamic State, would comprise effective and influential Muslim elements in it.[93]

Inspired by this elucidation in *Mutahhidah Qaumiyat aur Islam* (Composite Nationalism and Islam), the Jamiyat al-ulama joined the Congress in a common endeavour to rid the subcontinent of its British masters rather than set a course for the partition of the region.[94] The creation of an 'Islamic State' was therefore not the work of the *ulama* but rather the determined effort by informed, western-educated Muslims who developed the capacity to whip up a massive agitation in support of their claim for a separate nation.[95]

Some of these aspects must await a detailed examination. But two general conclusions flow from the literature available to us. First, the *ulama* can no longer be regarded merely as standard-bearers of orthodoxy whose concerns, according to popular understanding, were limited to regulating the religious and educational life of the Muslims. They were not, as Ishtiaq Husain Qureshi once suggested, ignorant of politics or of the forces working in the world of today'.[96] Such a view ignores their wide range of interests and their involvement in organizing, conducting and leading several political campaigns.

The ideological basis of the politics of the *ulama* also needs to be re-examined as a corrective to the oft-repeated notion that their concerns were mainly communitarian and their anti-colonial stance, grounded in Islamic theology, was not consistent with the secular thrust of Indian nationalism.

It is true that the future of Muslims and of Islam were central to the concerns of the *ulama*. Given their position and their role in Muslim society, it could not have been otherwise. In fact, at

[93] Ibid., p. 191.

[94] See Faruqi, op. cit., pp. 96–101.

[95] Lawrence Ziring, *Pakistan The Enigma of Political Development* (Dawson : Westview, 1980), p. 24.

[96] In *The Future Development of Islamic Polity* (Pakistan Literature Series No. 8 : Lahore, 1946), Qureshi opined that the *ulama* 'have neither the training nor the vision to be of any use' and that 'the work of the reconstruction of political thought in Islam cannot be left in the hands of the *ulama*, because they have no knowledge either of politics or of the forces working in the world of today'. pp. 11–12.

the dawn of the twentieth century and with the beginning of organized politics, the concerns of the *ulama* were restricted to the religious domain and to issues which impinged on the *shariat*. Their political intervention, on the other hand, was of a varied and complex nature. Yet, it must be said that an important section of the *ulama* did not always see their role solely in relation to their community. They developed, as was the case with Maulana Mahmud Hasan, Ubaid-Allah Sindhi, Azad, Mufti Kifayatullah and Husain Ahmad Madani, a theory of composite Indian nationalism and intervened in political affairs to effect an integrated alliance with other groups and communities. The Prophet's covenant with the people of Medina, including Jews and pagans, still retained, in Azad's view, validity as a precedent for other situations and in other lands in the subsequent history of Islam, and was especially pertinent in India.[97] The use of such religious idioms and Islamic symbols served the secular objective of rallying the Muslims around the nationalist struggle.

[97] Ahmad, *Islamic Modernism*, p. 189; Douglas, *Abul Kalam Azad*, pp. 249–250.

Chapter Seven

The Communal Breach

The 37th Annual Session of the National Congress at Gaya marked the close of an historic period in our struggle for liberation.... Non-Co-operation as a political force is dead, that is, that orthodox brand of Non-Co-operation which makes religion out of politics and has turned the traditional organ of national struggle into a prayer-hall and conclave of theologians.*

M.N. Roy, 15 February 1923.

In short conditions in India have never ever been worse. The reaction of the N.C.O. movement which set in in 1922–23 has since been slowly but surely undermining all public activity. There is not much of it left now but the rot is still proceeding—at a quicker pace now than before. The only education the masses are getting is in communal hatred .... The older people among the nationalists have given way to despair. The younger men are taking greater interest in their own advancement by whatever means and however reprehensible in their opinion of 2 years ago. Imagine Congressmen in the Assembly & the Councils tumbling over each other to shake hands with officials, stealthily attending functions after taking care that their names are not reported to the press, actually applying for invitations to such functions....**

Motilal Nehru to Jawaharlal Nehru, 30 March 1927.

By 1922–23 the edifice of communal unity, so assiduously built by the Mahatma, lay in a state of fragile vulnerability, the Non-Co-operation campaign was brought to a halt by Gandhi, the struggle for establishing swaraj was thrown into the

*'Open Letter to C.R. Das', 3 February 1923, Sibnarayan Ray (ed.), *Selected Works of M.N. Roy* (Delhi, 1988), vol. 1, p. 77.

**Jawaharlal Nehru Papers, part 1, vol. 1, p. xix.

background and the nationalist fervour, which had been aroused to a high pitch against Pax Brittanica, petered out. India's secretary of state sensed the mood when he observed:

> The greatest thing is to have got the co-operation of the people without whose co-operation government would after all be bound sooner or later to break down; the advanced thinkers, the suspects of 1910 are the co-operators of today; some of them active and strenous participators in the work of government.[1]

The changed political scenario is most commonly attributed to Gandhi's abrupt decision to suspend civil disobedience.[2] The argument of the early communist ideologues was that the bottled-up energy of the people, unleashed during the non-co-operation days, found an outlet in communal clashes. Jawaharlal Nehru agreed. Reflecting on the events of the period, he observed:

> The drift to sporadic and futile violence in the political struggle was

[1] Montagu to Ronaldshay, 23 February 1922, Ronaldshay Papers, MSS.EUR. D. 609 (5–A), 1, IOLR. Only a few years later, Surendranath Banerjea, the most persistent and outspoken among living Indian agitators, recorded the change. 'Our angle of vision', he wrote, 'has changed with closer contact [with the European community] and with better knowledge. In public work and in helping the Reforms, we have become colleagues, and the feeling between European and Indian leaders is being gradually transformed into one of mutual esteem and respect'. Banerjea, *A Nation in Making*, p. 311.

[2] R.P. Dutt and other left-wing writers regarded Gandhi's decision as a 'betrayal' and a concession to the capitalists, landlords and other propertied classes who felt threatened by the ever-increasing militancy and radicalization of the Non-Co-operation movement. The question, observed Dutt, was not that of violence or non-violence, but of 'class interest in opposition to the mass movement, which was the breaking point of the national struggle in 1922'. *India Today* (Bombay, 1947), p. 353. This interpretation is no longer accepted as an authoritative Marxist formulation. See, for example, Sumit Sarkar, *Modern India* (Delhi, 1983), pp. 225–26, and Bipan Chandra, Mridula Mukherjee, Aditya Mukherjee, Sucheta Mahajan, K.N. Panikkar, *India's Struggle for Independence 1857–1947* (Delhi, 1987), pp. 192–95. The Gandhian motive for calling off civil disobedience is also discussed by Ravinder Kumar in his introduction to *A Centenary History of the Indian National Congress* (Delhi, 1985), vol. 2, pp. 18–20, and by Nanda, *Gandhi, Pan-Islamism, Imperialism and Nationalism*, pp. 350–56.

stopped, but the suppressed violence had to find a way out, and in the following years this perhaps aggravated the communal trouble. The communalists of various denominations, mostly political reactionaries, had been forced to lie low because of the overwhelming mass support for non-co-operation and civil disobedience movement. They emerged now from their retirement.... *It is just possible that if civil resistance had not been stopped and the movement had been crushed by Government, there would have been less communal bitterness and less superfluous energy left for the subsequent communal riots* [emphasis added].[3]

Gandhi was also held guilty for introducing religion into politics through his support of the Khilafat movement,[4] which was the precursor of the 'worst form of denationalizing [*sic*]...movement of communalism, pure and simple'.[5] His alliance with the pan-Islamists, so runs the argument, was 'built on the unreliable foundations of religious sentimentalism'[6] and encouraged 'the most retrogade form of Islamic group consciousness'.[7] In fact, M.R. Jayakar, member of the Bombay legislative council and a leading light in the Hindu Mahasabha movement, attributed the rise of communalism to

Gandhi's policy during the last four years, which aimed at a most artificial and unreal unity between Hindus and Muslims, awakening sentiments and impulses in the latter community which, like the Frankenstein, it is now very difficult to allay. It makes me very sad to think that so great a patriot should have on this issue bungled so easily.[8]

Recent historical writings have hinted at some additional reasons which served to heighten communal consciousness, such as the 'methods' adopted by the Congress leaders during the Non-Co-

[3] Nehru, *An Autobiography,* pp. 86–87.

[4] This view was widely shared, though it was forcefully expressed in the writings of M.N. Roy. See, G. Adhikari (ed.), *Documents of the History of the Communist Party of India, 1923–1925* (Delhi, 1974), vol. 2, p. 210.

[5] *Mahratta,* 4 July 1927; *Leader,* 2 January 1927.

[6] G. Adhikari (ed.), op.cit., p. 211. Nehru spoke—some thirty years after the event—about 'the artificial unity Gandhi had forged out of diverse discontents'. Quoted in A.C. Niemeijer, *The Khilafat Movement in India 1919–1924* (The Hague, 1972), p. 93.

[7] N.C. Chaudhuri, *Thy Hand Great Anarch! India 1921–1952* (London, 1987), p. 39.

[8] To Lajpat Rai, 8 September 1925, F.No. 405, Jayakar Papers, NAI.

operation movement and in subsequent electoral and agitational campaigns.[9] There is, then, the baldly stated view of Bipan Chandra that communalism in the twenties or thereafter had no objective reality; if anything, it symbolized 'a distorted or perverse reflection of reality.' In the absence of a 'real conflict' between communities, the use of religion as a vehicle of political organization and mobilization was an aspect of 'false consciousness.'[10]

These explanations have no doubt enriched scholarly discourse, but they fail to come to grips with the intense and complex nature of communal antipathies at the regional and local levels. This is in large measure due to the inadequate attention paid to the impact of the Montagu-Chelmsford Reforms, more so in the provinces of British India.[11] It will not do to minimize this vital aspect, for the operation of the Act of 1919 quite perceptibly altered the tenor of relationships between dominant classes, especially in the Muslim-majority provinces, stimulated sectional concerns all around, and sharpened mutual rivalries in areas with scarce resources.

II

It is not uncommon to trace the roots of conflicts to the Act of 1909 which, for the first time, provided institutional legitimation to the notion of a distinct, separate Muslim political identity. Introducing separate electorates was a clever and novel British device to create a sense of communitarian solidarity and to then watch the spectacle of alignments being forged on the basis of religious affiliations. The measure of success in achieving such goals is, in part, reflected in the arguments marshalled to advance and sustain sectional claims. Muslim groups, in particular, not only

[9] Gyanendra Pandey, *The Ascendancy of the Congress in Uttar Pradesh 1926–34: A Study in Imperfect Mobilization* (Delhi, 1978), p. 115.

[10] Bipan Chandra, *Communalism in Modern India,* p. 23.

[11] This does not apply to the works of J.H. Broomfield, *Elite Conflict in a Plural Society: Twentieth Century Bengal* (Berkeley: Los Angeles, 1968); R.J. Moore, *The Crisis of Indian Unity 1917–1940* (Delhi, 1974); David Page, *Prelude to Partition.*

discovered a new vocabulary to articulate their aspirations but also insisted on being heard as representatives of their community. Their claims were dubious, for they were, in effect, pleading on behalf of dominant classes, both in urban and rural areas, for a share in the new power structures created first by the Act of 1909 and, a decade later, by the Montagu-Chelmsford Reforms.

Such claims went uncontested in official circles, for it suited the British, more than any other group, to turn a blind eye to the limited following and concerns of the so-called 'Muslim' organizations. Time and again they were propped up, rescued from oblivion and used to counterbalance the nationalist forces.

The Act of 1919 enlarged the scope of communal politics. The franchise was extended,[12] the elected and non-official members were represented in much greater strength in enlarged legislatures (Table 7:1), and, above all, they received some degree of authority, at least in the 'transferred' departments. Moreover, local bodies experienced vital structural changes as a result of wide ranging reforms, including the extension of the principle of election.[13] In 1920–21, the elective system was in force in all but five of the 116 municipalities in Bengal.[14] In Punjab, at least 75 per cent of elected members were, by 1922–23, directly returned from a much broader franchise.[15] Likewise, the UP District

[12] The number of electors to the pre-reform legislative council was only 2,774, of whom 2,306 were Muslims and landholders, who returned six members by direct election, and the remaining 468 were members of district and municipal boards who returned thirteen members. According to the first electoral roll drawn up in 1920, the number of voters stood at 1,347,922. By the time of the second election in 1923, the 'disqualification' clause that was applied to women was dropped. So the size of the electorate rose to 1,509,127, of whom 49,067 were women. *Report on the Working of the System of Government: United Provinces of Agra and Oudh* (henceforth *Report*, UP) (Allahabad, 1928), p. 175.

[13] A private bill introduced in the UP legislative council, which was adopted in 1922, reduced certain categories of municipal qualifications to the level of those required of electors to the legislative council. Ibid., p. 190.

[14] *Resolution Reviewing the Reports on the Working of Municipalities in Bengal* (Calcutta, 1922), p. 1.

[15] *Report on the Working of the Municipalities in the Punjab, 1922–23* (Lahore, 1923), p. 1.

Boards Act of 1922 incorporated important provisions: the official element disappeared, franchise was extended and the number of elected members went up.[16] 'Real local self-government in the rural areas of the United Provinces may with some justice be claimed to have been born in 1923', wrote the governor of the province.[17]

These changes meant that, for the first time, Indian ministers began to exercize some degree of control over education, local self-government, public works, public health and sanitation. It also meant that they could provide jobs, give out contracts for public works undertakings and grant permission to organize and regulate bazaars, melas and religious processions. As chairman of the Allahabad municipal board, Jawaharlal Nehru was 'pestered with the applicants for appointments...chits and recommendations have been brought to me from friends and attempts have been made to influence me in favour of various applications.'[18] With the scope and functions of local institutions enlarged, there was a corresponding increase in their power and sphere of influence.[19] This was an added incentive for influential groups to contend for a seat on local bodies and for their allies to take a keen interest in the electoral process.[20]

[16] *Report,* UP, vol. 2, p. 230.

[17] *Indian Statutory Commission: Memorandum submitted by the Government of the United Provinces to the Indian Statutory Commission* (London, 1930), vol. ix, p. 481.

[18] S. Gopal (ed.), *Selected Works of Jawaharlal Nehru,* vol. 2, p. 7.

[19] This was, of course, related to increases in both the income and expenditure of local bodies. Municipal incomes in Bombay, for example, rose by 40 per cent between 1918 and 1922. The increase there and elsewhere was a reflection of the post-war boom following the rise in property taxes and increases in octroi and other levies on trade. One of the areas which benefited most from these increases was education. There was a consequent expansion of schools and an increase in expenditure from 12.48 lakhs in 1920 to 17.60 lakhs in 1922. Hugh Tinker, *The Foundations of Local Self-Government in India, Pakistan and Burma* (London, 1968), pp. 121–24.

[20] In the 1925–26 elections in Bengal, 61.3 per cent of the electorate voted in Dacca, over 70 per cent in the seven wards of Rajshahi division and about 75 per cent in the four wards of Commilla division. *Bengal Municipalities 1925–26,* appendix B, pp. 73–76. For Bombay municipal elections, see Tinker, op.cit., p. 132.

TABLE 7.1

Composition of the Provincial Legislative Councils Established under the Montagu-Chelmsford Reforms

Province	Total (*ex-officio*, nominated and elected).	Nominated				Elected														
						By special electorates				By communcal electorates							By general electorates			
		Total (nominated and *ex officio*).	Officials (nominated and *ex-officio*).	Non-officials.	Total (elected).	Total	University.	Landholders.	Commerce and Industry including mining and planting.	Total	Urban Muslims.	Rural Muslims.	Europeans.	Anglo-Indians.	Indian Christians.	Sikhs.	Total.	Rural. Non-Muslims.	Urban. Non-Muslims.
1. Madras	127	29	23	6	98	13	1	6	6	20	11	2	1	1	5	..	65	56	9
2. Bombay	111	25	20	5	86	11	1	3	7	29	22	5	2	..	..	..	46	35	11
3. Bengal	139	26	20	6	113	21	1	5	15	46	33	6	5	2	..	..	46	35	11
4. United Provinces	123	23	18	5	100	10	1	6	3	30	25	4	1	..	..	..	60	52	8
5. Punjab	93	22	16	6	71	7	1	4	2	44	27	5	..	..	..	12	20	13	7
6. Bihar and Orissa	103	27	20	7	76	9	1	5	3	19	15	3	1	..	..	..	48	42	6
7. Central Provinces	70	16	10	6	54	7	1	3	3	7	6	1	..	..	..	..	40	31	9
8. Assam	53	14	9	5	39	6	..	..	6	12	12	..	..	...	..	..	21	20	1

SOURCE : *Statement Exhibiting the Moral and Material Progress and Condition of India* (London, 1921), Cmd. 202, p. 249.

The implications of the Reforms were not felt at the height of the Non-Co-operation movement, when provincial elections in 1920 were generally boycotted. But once that phase was over, the writing on the wall was clear. In 1922, a powerful lobby of Punjab-based traders, merchants and moneylenders resorted to the boycott of municipalities to protest against the provision of separate representation for the Muslims.[21] In another region, the Calcutta-based Hindu commercial and professional men were up in arms when Surendranath Banerjea, the first minister for local self-government in Bengal, conceded separate electorates in the 1923 Calcutta Municipal Bill.[22] 'How can he [Banerjea] face a non-Muslim constituency with this fatal record of pro-Muslim activities?', wrote the *Amrita Bazar Patrika* in its campaign against Banerjea's election to the council.[23] Its outcry was reminiscent of the furore over the Jahangirabad Amendment Act of March 1916, when a spate of loud and angry protests led to the boycott of and resignation from the municipal boards in UP.

The divisive effects of devolution of power were mostly felt in Bengal where Muslims were economically and politically weak and were therefore less well represented within the councils and, for that reason, less capable of utilizing the Reforms to their advantage.[24] This was why the more vocal educated Bengali

[21] For background studies, see N.G. Barrier, 'The Punjab Government and Communal Politics', *JAS*, vol. 27, May 1968, P. 529; Jones, *Arya Dharm*, p. 286; *Reports on the Working of Municipalities in the Punjab, 1896–97*.

[22] In November 1921, Banerjea proposed the abolition of separate electorate in a bill introduced in the council. But such was the intensity of Muslim opposition in Bengal that Banerjea accepted a compromise: provision for separate electorates was made for the first ten years, after which Muslims were to have reserved seats in general electorates. Leonard A. Gordon, *Bengal: The Nationalist Movement 1876–1940* (Delhi, 1979), p. 204. Banerjea did not mention this fact in his account. While chiding the swarajists for extending the 'communal system', he self-righteously proclaimed: 'In the meantime I remain unconvinced and prefer to tread the old path of obstinate opposition to the communal system in the constitution of our local bodies'. Banerjea, *A Nation in Making*, p. 340.

[23] *Amrita Bazar Patrika*, 1 December 1923.

[24] In 1921, Muslims were nearly 54.6 per cent of the population in the

Muslims, already aggrieved by the terms of the Lucknow Pact, insisted on securing the benefit of their majority position. Maulvi Abdul Karim observed:

Theoretically it is all very well to say that communal representation stands in the way of the building up of a national state. But in India, which is a land of many communities, many creeds, many cultures and many traditions, it is not possible to have a thorough national fusion, completely separating the religious and socio-religious concerns of life from the economic and political interests. For the present the interests and aspirations of different communities must be separately considered and satisfied....[25]

Karim was stating what was then and later an article of faith with educated Muslims in Bengal and elsewhere. At the same time, they were wary of the fact that those who controlled the levers of power in urban and rural areas would resist sharing it with others on an equitable basis. A keen and bitter contest was therefore unavoidable, especially in Bengal and Punjab. We focus on these provinces of British India because of the intense communal competition, and because nowhere else was the interplay of religion and politics as stark and as ominous.

The exclusion of UP from the discussion is because the standard political explanation for the growth of communalism in Bengal and Punjab will not fit the facts in the province. In UP, the landholders constituted the largest single group in the council and held their position not as representatives of Hindus or Muslims but as spokemen of landed interests.[26] The Zamindar Party, founded by the Nawab of Chattari in 1921, was only marginally involved in communal controversies. Its primary function was to consolidate the gains that accrued to the landlords in the 1919

---

electoral area but were allowed only 39 seats. Hindus, on the other hand, had 46 seats against their population of nearly 45 per cent.

[25] Maulvi Abdul Karim, *Letters on Hindu-Muslim Pact* (Calcutta, 1924), p. 21.

[26] Though communal issues figured in the council, Hindu and Muslim landlords spoke with one voice and acted in unison on most issues that concerned their class. Thus the resolution to increase the representation of the zamindars of the Agra province was introduced by the Nawab of Chattari and supported by Thakur Jagannath Bakhsh Singh and D.R. Ranjit Singh. *Proceedings of the UP Legislative Council*, March 1923, vol. xii, pp. 160–69.

Act and to maintain their rural dominance, which was threatened by the spurt in peasant activity in several parts of UP. Shaikh Habibullah of Barabanki conveyed this concern to Harcourt Butler, an ardent champion of the UP landed aristocracy. He stated: 'Formerly it was the tenants who were in need of protection, now it is the landlords who need the protection of government'.[27]

The Oudh Rent Act [1921] and the District Boards Bill, introduced the same year, heightened the feeling of insecurity. Both pieces of legislation were stoutly resisted by the landlords, even though Harcourt Butler was able to secure their passage. But they sensed the impending threat to their prestige and power. 'The landless agitator is out for the destruction of the landholders', warned the Raja of Jahangirabad. He criticized the 'self constituted champions of the oppressed' for inciting the peasantry and pleaded with his audience at the UP Landholders' Conference to play a greater part in 'moulding public opinion'. Raja Durga Narain Singh of Tirwa [Farrukhabad district] harped on the same theme.[28]

Such pleas gave a semblance of unity to the Zamindar Party. Winning as many as 58 of the 77 rural seats, the landholders emerged as the largest single group in the 1923 council. Yet, they could not consolidate their gains. Divided and disorganized, they were unwilling to subordinate their personal interests or beliefs to those of the Zamindar Party. 'It is very distressing to me', wrote Harcourt Butler, 'to feel that the landowners are so divided among themselves and allow personal feelings to come before personal interests.'[29] Clumsy, naive and self-seeking, the Zamindar Party remained fragmented and out of touch with the realities of Indian politics.

27 Habibullah to Butler, 6 March 1921, Butler Papers (80).

28 Speech on 14 July 1922, ibid.

29 Butler to the Nawab of Chattari, 20 December 1923, Chattari Papers, NMML. Earlier, Butler's predecessor, James Meston, had expressed his deep anguish over the disunity that plagued the group of landlords. On the eve of Montagu's mission to India, he made strenuous efforts to organize them and to 'stir them up to realize the magnitude of the occasion'. To Willingdon, 22 August 1917, Meston Papers (17).

III

By the end of 1922, the Civil Disobedience Enquiry Committee found the country unprepared for civil disobedience. But this judgement did not settle the controversy between those who favoured the continued boycott of the new councils and those who urged the reversal of Gandhi's ban on council entry. When the 'No-Changers' turned down the plea for council entry at the Gaya Congress in December 1922, the dissidents constituted themselves into the Congress-Khilafat-Swaraj Party, headed by C.R. Das and Motilal Nehru. Throughout the summer of 1923, the swarajists steadily gained ground. The tide finally turned in their favour in September of that year, when the Congress approved the modification of the boycott in favour of council entry and made it possible for them to breach the 'citadel of bureaucracy' both from inside and outside the councils. In the elections, the swarajists did quite well except in Punjab, Bihar, Orissa and Madras. They won a clear majority in the Central Provinces. In Bengal, they represented the strongest individual group. In UP and Bombay, they did not secure the majority of votes but were returned in considerable numbers.

The only way to bring the bureaucracy to its knees was to command the weight of united public opinion, to count upon the undivided support of the legislative council members. Nowhere was this need greater than in Bengal, where one-third of the members happened to be Muslims. Hence the suggestion of a pact—the condition precedent to concerted action within and outside the council walls.[30] The terms, worked out by Das with a section of the Khilafat leadership, were:

[30] Khuda Bukhsh referred to a meeting at his residence—5 Elliot Road—where the details of the proposed Bengal pact were hammered out. He noted that throughout the discussion Das showed a 'spirit of charity and compromise' and was willing to give any undertaking that would satisfy Muslims of his good faith. *Studies: Indian and Islamic,* p. 259. Maulvi Abdul Karim mentioned that a draft of the proposed pact, drawn up in consultation with Azad, Maulvis Nasim Ali and Waheed Husain, was discussed with Das on 9 December 1923. It was approved by the swarajist members of the council on 16 December. *Letters on Hindu-Muslim Pact,* p. 3.

1 For the provincial council—representation on a population basis with separate electorates for Muslims.

2 For the local bodies—representation in district boards and municipalities in the proportion of 60 to 40 in every district : 60 to the majority community and 40 to the minority. The question of separate electorates was kept open.

3 For government appointments—55 per cent seats were fixed for Muslims and the remaining 45 per cent were for other communities.

4 To ensure religious tolerance and communal harmony, music was to be prohibited before the mosques and Muslims were to enjoy the freedom to perform cow-killing for religious purposes *[Qurbani]*.

Das held out an olive branch, pleaded for reconciliation and an end to religious feuds. The Muslim leadership in Bengal reciprocated warmly. They swelled the ranks of the swarajists and helped turn the party into an effective political force. 'Mr Das', announced a Muslim councillor, 'was the only man in Bengal who was trying to bring about the unity of the communities', while Bose was 'the second man in Bengal who was trying to improve the position of the Muslim community'.[31] He was, in the words of Khuda Bukhsh, a principal negotiator of the pact, 'the healer of many festering wounds, the composer of the many apparently unadjustable differences, the man of the occasion'.[32]

The detractors of the pact, on the other hand, had no reason to eulogize its author. According to them, he betrayed the 'Hindu' cause[33] by entering into an 'unholy', 'unauthorized' alliance with Muslims.[34] Though they used nationalistic arguments and voiced patriotic sentiments to denounce the pact, it was apparent that

[31] For appreciation of Das's role and his contribution to the cause of communal amity, see Sisir K. Bose (ed.), *Subhash Chandra Bose Netaji: Collected Works* (Calcutta, 1981), vol. 2, p. 129; Kenneth Mcpherson, *The Muslim Microcosm,* p. 77; Gordon, *Bengal: The Nationalist Movement,* pp. 219, 220; Rajat Ray, *Social Conflict and Political Unrest in Bengal,* pp. 135–16, 322.

[32] *Studies: Indian and Islamic,* p. 269.

[33] *Amrita Bazar Patrika,* 17, 19, 22 December 1923.

[34] 'It seems strange', wrote the *Amrita Bazar Patrika,* 'that these gentlemen should meet in a secret enclave and enter into a contract with one another in matters affecting the rights and liberties of more than four million of the people'. 23 December 1923.

they were alarmed by the prospect of losing their political and economic hegemony to a relatively new class of Muslim professional men and up-country merchants. From all sides rang stridently vocal shouts—'Down with the pact; down, down with it'.

To begin with, the hue and cry was on account of the Muslim seats raised in the council from 40 per cent, as provided by the Lucknow agreement of 1916, to 55 per cent. In local bodies, too, the principle of 60:40 representation upset the balance of power in favour of Muslims, more so in areas where they were numerically strong [Table 7:2]. This was so in places like Dacca where a substantial increase in Muslim representation led to a corresponding fall in the share of Hindus—from 72 per cent to only 40 per cent. The most obvious fall out of such an arrangement was that some Muslims in certain areas had the opportunity, denied to them by the Lucknow concord and the Act of 1919, to wrest control of local bodies and of local patronage from Hindu zamindars and their clients.[35]

Das was not unduly perturbed by these implications of the pact, for he insisted that Muslims had not received more than their share. But the fairness of the arrangement was hardly an issue at stake. The detractors of Das, notably Surendranath Banrerjea and his group who were smarting under the crushing defeat they suffered at the polls, were eager to pick up any stick with which to beat the swarajists.[36] Their assault was reinforced by Lajpat Rai, Malaviya, Jayakar, Moonje and N.C. Kelkar, some of whom exerted pressure on the 1923 Kakinada Congress to scuttle the pact. Das was furious:

You may delete the Bengal National Pact from the resolution, but I

[35] John Gallagher, 'Congress in Decline: Bengal 1930 to 1939,' in John Gallagher, Gordon Johnson and Anil Seal (eds.), *Locality, Province and Nation: Essays on Indian Politics 1870 to 1940* (Cambridge, 1973). Notice the Swaraj party campaign in 1925 against the extension of Union Boards in Noakhali. It was feared that the Village Self-Government Act would give more power to the Muslim peasant and relax the hold of the urban Hindu lawyer class over the villages, on which the party relied for mobilizing support. Rajat Ray, *Social Conflict*, p. 337.

[36] *Amrita Bazar Patrika*, 25, 29 December 1923 and 23 December 1925. For general criticizm of the pact, see Mcpherson, *The Muslim Microcosm*, pp. 78–79.

TABLE 7.2:
Representation of Hindus and Muslims on local and district boards in Bengal districts (excluding Darjeeling), 1923 [Percentages]

Name of Districts	Population		Local Boards		District Boards	
	Hindus	Muslims	Hindus	Muslims	Hindus	Muslims
Burdwan	78.0	18.5	88.1	11.11	79.5	19.05
Birbhum	68.1	25.1	81.3	18.7	75.0	25.0
Bankura	86.3	4.6	91.7	8.3	86.7	13.3
Midnapur	88.2	6.8	91.7	8.3	94.1	5.9
Hooghly	81.9	16.4	84.7	15.3	81.3	15.38
Howrah	79.3	20.3	94.4	5.5	87.5	12.5
24 Parganas	64.2	34.6	76.7	23.3	63.5	36.5
Nadia	39.1	60.2	80.0	20.0	71.3	28.7
Murshidabad	45.1	53.6	55.6	44.4	50.8	49.2
Jessore	38.1	61.8	83.4	.16.6	66.7	33.3
Khulna	50.0	49.8	81.3	18.7	62.1	37.9
Dacca	34.2	55.4	72.8	27.2	70.2	29.8
Mymensingh	24.3	74.9	54.2	45.8	39.0	61.0
Faridpur	26.3	63.5	58.4	41.6	54.6	45.4
Bakargunj	28.8	70.6	50.0	50.0	43.6	56.4
Chittagong	22.6	72.8	50.0	50.0	43.3	56.4
Tippera	25.8	74.1	46.7	53.3	34.0	65.6
Noakhali	22.4	76.6	29.2	70.8	31.2	68.8
Rajshahi	21.4	76.5	45.5	54.5	33.4	66.6
Dinajpur	44.1	49.1	66.7	33.3	60.0	40.0
Jalpaiguri	55.0	24.8	85.7	14.3	88.9	11.0
Rangpur	31.6	68.0	55.6	44.4	46.3	53.7
Bogra	16.6	82.5	50.0	50.0	40.7	59.3
Pabna	24.1	75.8	58.4	41.6	52.8	47.2
Malda	40.6	51.5	66.7	33.3	—	—
(Province)	43.7	53.6	67.0	33.0	60.8	29.2

SOURCE: *Census*, 1921, *Resolution Reviewing the Reports on the Working of the District Boards in Bengal, 1923–24* (Calcutta, 1925).

assure you, you cannot delete Bengal from the Indian National Congress or from the history of India. Bengal demands the right of having her suggestions considered.... She is an integral part of the constitution of the Indian National Congress. And she is intimately associated with the history of all political agitations from the commencement of this Congress down to the present day.[37]

Das warded off the attack against him by prevailing upon the Bengal Provincial Conference to ratify the pact in May 1924. His successor, J.M. Sengupta, kept it alive in order to retain Muslim votes in the November 1926 elections. But the 'Big Five' were not prepared to let go.[38] They were of the view that if the Congress, already bedeviled by factionalism, was to maintain its ascendancy in Bengal it was necessary to correct the popular image of being favourably disposed towards Muslims. Otherwise, the new mass of Hindu electorate would seek refuge in communal organizations, such as the Hindu Mahasabha, and other militant expressions of Hindu resurgence, including the Cow Preservation League, presided over by the vice-chancellor of the Calcutta university, Ashutosh Mukherjee, and patronized by rich Marwaris.[39]

Given the political climate in Bengal, it was not surprising that the pact, pushed too hard and too fast by its author, was thrown to the winds at the earliest. In this way, 'an immense funeral pyre was set up at Krishnanagar town and preparations were made to burn up the movement of swaraj...on that pyre'.[40] 'Two-fold is our debt to Mr Das', commented Khuda Bukhsh. 'We are beholden to him for his liberal-mindedness and we are beholden to him, far more, for opening our eyes to the true Hindu feeling and attitude towards us'. He added:

The pact is at an end, but this little episode is not without a lesson and a warning. What Swaraj would be like, who can say? But one thing is

[37] Quoted in Gordon, *Bengal*, p. 197.

[38] See *Forward*, 25 June 1926.

[39] Rajat Ray, op. cit., pp. 333–34. In June 1926, Madan Mohan Burman and Jatindra Mohan Das Gupta of the Bengal Hindu Sabha convened a conference to safeguard 'Hindu interests'. *Forward*, 8 June 1926.

[40] *Mohammadi*, 28 May 1926. For reactions to the rejection of the pact, see *Asr-i Jadeed* and *Hanafi*, 23 May 1926, SNNR, Bengal.

beyond doubt—it would be a paradise where the followers of the Prophet would have no milk or honey. It is idle, then, to look to Swaraj for the cure of our present ills. And equally idle is to look to it for a reign of right or righteousness.[41]

These fears, though expressed in exaggerated terms, reflected the strong sense of anger and disappointment at the drift of events in Bengal politics. Most educated Muslims wanted to know what went wrong. After all, they had stood by the Congress through thick and thin, even though the rank and file of the party firmly resisted the few concessions and constitutional safeguards given to them.[42] But the repudiation of the pact was too bitter a pill to swallow. The view gained wide credence that 'neither in terms of the Muslim interest nor of the *proja* interest, was it possible to rely any longer on the Congress.'[43]

This perception was reinforced by instances, cited daily in the 'Muslim press', of discrimination against Muslims in the employment market and their exploitation by Hindu zamindars and mahajans. The 'Hindu' swarajists, most of whom were zamindars, were taken to task for their pro-landlord position in the council. Abdur Rahim lambasted them for obstructing the Tenancy Bill beneficial to the 'dumb millions of cultivators of whom the majority are Muslims.'[44] Kazi Nazrul Islam, the revolutionary

[41] *Studies: Indian and Islamic*, pp. 269–70. And the following comment in the *Moslem Chronicle* of 18 June 1926:

We confess we were never enamoured by the artificial alliance which Das's instinct of self-preservation prompted him to conclude with the Muslim community.....We know that the Hindu politicians were playing a foul game, and when the pact was put to test within a few months of its birth, the astuteness of Hindu politics was quite apparent.

[42] Mcpherson, op. cit., pp. 84–86. Also, resistance to concessions was echoed by *Dainik Basumati*, 3 January 1926 and *Desher Vani* (Noakhali), 29 December 1925.

[43] Quoted in Partha Chatterjee, 'Agrarian Relations and Communalism in Bengal, 1926–1935', Ranajit Guha (ed.), *Subaltern Studies I: Writings on South Asian History and Society* (Delhi, 1982), p. 10.

[44] Sharifuddin Pirzada (ed.), *Foundations of Pakistan*, vol. 2, pp. 56–57; Broomfield, *Elite Conflict*, p. 274.

poet, denounced the vested interests in the council which had conspired to betray the people's cause.[45]

Once the political honeymoon with the swarajists ended, a number of Muslim groups, including Congressmen of long-standing, changed their political course.[46] In the 1926 elections, of the 39 Muslims elected, only one was a swarajist. The remaining thirty-eight members searched for a role in other political groupings.

Not long ago the swarajist movement seemed to hold the Bengali Muslims in thrall. Now, they hoped against hope that some spark would relight the flame that was snuffed out by short-sighted and hot-headed swarajists. The hope lay, according to some, in carrying on

> C.R. Das's work to its consummation. Let us hush our differences. Let us prove ourselves worthy of the torch handed over to us by him—a torch which he held with heroic steadfastness.[47]

IV

Writing in the context of the bloody Calcutta riots, M.N. Roy referred to the 'office-hunting intelligentsia' as the spokemen of communal interests.[48] In this apt description, two individuals fit in quite well—the Barisal lawyer, Fazlul Haq, and the Madras High Court judge, Abdur Rahim. They stand out as champions of interests, which were defined, elaborated and articulated within a strictly communal framework.

Fazlul Haq was the most prominent Muslim in the Bengal Congress during the all too brief honeymoon of Hindu-Muslim

[45] Rajat Ray, op. cit., p. 338. Even the *Ananda Bazar Patrika* complained that the Congress was apathetic towards the cultivators and that many of its pious resolutions were not put into action. 'There is no wonder then that this sham-campaign of swaraj will come to nothing like a bewildered traveller in the desert'. 29 April 1927, SNNR, Bengal.

[46] *Mussalman*, 10 September 1926.

[47] Khuda Bukhsh, op. cit., p. 260.

[48] 'The Calcutta Riot', Sibnarayan Ray (ed.), *Selected Works of M.N. Roy*, vol. 2, p. 436.

relations. He was one of the principal negotiators of the Lucknow Pact, leaving behind the political legacy of his one-time mentor, the Nawab of Dacca. But he split from the Congress over the non-co-operation programme. 'You know very well', he stated in response to an invitation to join a Congress meeting, 'that between me on one side and those representing the present-day politics of the Congress, there is a gulf of difference which no worldly diplomacy can possibly bridge over. Your ideals and mine are different. You have adopted an ideal in the Congress to which I cannot subscribe.'[49]

Fazlul Haq's defection was a blow to the Congress in Bengal, for he was a leader with considerable mass appeal and organizational flair. In losing his support the Congress lost an important spokeman of its cause among Muslims.

The offer of a ministerial berth in 1924 marked the fulfilment of Fazlul Haq's political ambitions. But his luck ran out—the ministry was overthrown by the swarajists within six months of its being in office. During this period of heady confrontation, Fazlul Haq and his colleagues gave up all scruples to stay in office. The cat was let out of the bag when word spread that a greedy council member had agreed to abstain from voting for the swarajists after accepting a bribe of Rs 3000.[50] It was also known that Fazlul Haq worked behind the scenes trying to convince the governor to induct Rai Bahadur Pyarelal into the ministry, because he commanded the votes of Bhusan Roy and Allabux.[51]

Along with these efforts, Fazlul Haq raised the cry that the Hindus, as it were, hatched a conspiracy to overthrow a 'Muslim Ministry'. This was the trump card. But this was not all. Khan Bahadur Musharraf Husain was pressed into service to demand the recruitment of a certain percentage of Muslims in government service. The motive was to embarrass the swarajists, create communal schisms in their rank, and weaken their opposition to the ministry. But the move led to no immediate gains. When the

[49] To S.C. Bose, 22 February 1921, quoted in A. Rab, *A.K. Fazlul Haq*, p. 56.

[50] To Lytton, 9 July 1924, Lytton Papers, MSS. EUR. F. No. 16 (46), IOLR.

[51] 4 August 1924, ibid.

demand for ministerial salaries was rejected for the second time on 26 August, the ministers resigned and the governor promptly suspended the constitution. Fazlul Haq, who had masterminded the communal strategy, was crestfallen. With his political ambitions thwarted, he now bitterly complained of 'having fallen a victim to the vilest conspiracy' of the Hindus.[52] The accusation was false, for the ministry was overthrown by the combined opposition of the swarajists. Out of thirty-seven elected Muslims voting in the council, the majority—nineteen—voted against the ministers. The significance of this fact was not lost on Mujibur Rahman, always mature and sober in his judgements. He rejected Fazlul Haq's claim to stand for the so-called Muslim interests. To say that the Muslim ministers held on to their posts to serve the cause of Islam and to protect Muslim interests was to palm off a gigantic fraud upon the entire community.[53]

By the end of 1925, Fazlul Haq's image in Bengal politics was tarnished. The Swaraj party made great play of the fact that he offered bribes to several councillors to buy their votes. In his own words, it 'had the effect of weaning away the sympathy of some of my best friends and supporters'.[54] His credibility with the government was also low; his claims were ignored when a new ministry was constituted in 1926. Bitter and sullen, he told Lytton:

> I sacrificed a position of assured success at the Bar to take to politics [more with a view to serve my community than anything else], and politics has given me but a poor return.[55]

Though shaken by his fluctuating political fortunes, Fazlul Haq was aware of his charismatic appeal in the Bengal countryside, especially among the Muslim peasantry, and was conscious of his organizational skills. Determined to regain the position he had once occupied in Bengal, he chose the easiest political course available to him—to merge with the swelling ranks of Muslim political formations in Bengal and emerge as their sole spokesman. His aim was to create a strong and unified Muslim party which

[52] 2 September 1924, (18).
[53] Rajat Ray, op.cit., p. 323.
[54] To Lytton, 11 March 1925, Lytton Papers.
[55] 25 November 1925, ibid.

would provide him with a strong base to negotiate with the Bengal Congress and the provincial government.

Fazlul Haq launched himself in this new role on the eve of the provincial elections in November 1926. As a first step, he founded the Bengal Council Party with the help of Husain Suhrawardy, former deputy mayor of the Calcutta Corporation, Mujibur Rahman, editor of *Mussalman,* Haji Abdur Rashid Khan, Calcutta Corporation's deputy executive officer and Maulana Akram Khan, lawyer and defector from the Non-Co-operation movement. The organ of the new party wrote:

> We have, after all, realized that the Congress is a Hindu organization and Muslims have no chance of holding its leading strings. They are welcome within the ranks of Congress as long as they prefer to remain as the henchmen of Hindu leaders and slaves to their cunningly planned intrigues to keep Muslims out of real power.[56]

This was the voice of aggrieved politicians. Having failed to make much profit out of the so-called Hindu-dominated council, they were now busy fanning communal passions. They were playing with fire.

Abdur Rahim, a zamindar of Midnapur and a former judge of the Madras High Court, moved into the political arena after the expiry of his term on the executive council. His first act was to address the Muslim League session in December 1925 at Aligarh, where he spoke against the Congress to create a constituency among the Urdu-speaking Muslims of Bengal. By mid-April 1926, he had garnered enough sympathy for his newly-formed Bengal Muslim Party. Its manifesto stated:.

> The experience of the last three years has shown how time after time the Muslim members of the council belonging to the swaraj or nationalist parties, which are organizations controlled by astute Hindu politicians who supply the brains and the funds of the parties, had to sacrifice, at their behest, the clear interests of the Muslim electorate and the Muslim community.[57]

[56] See *Moslem Chronicle,* 20 August and 24 September 1926.

[57] *Indian Quarterly Register,* January-June 1926, vol. 1, p. 67.

The Bengal Muslim Party promised to remove the 'considerable disabilities and difficulties' faced by Muslims. It proposed to achieve this by ensuring their representation—56 per cent in the council, local bodies, public services, universities and other professions. In other words, everything was to be organized along communal lines and Muslims *per se* were to have power and influence in proportion to their population.

With this distinctly communal platform, Rahim plunged into the election fray in November 1926. Everything worked in his favour. He exploited to the full the bitter legacy of the Calcutta riots in April 1926 and went to the electors with a simple religious appeal: 'Mussalman! who are you going to vote for? For the servants of Rahim or for the slaves of Rama?'[58] Most Bengali Muslim voters fell in behind Rahim, giving his party a majority of seats in the council. Rahim's own popularity reached commanding heights: he secured 641 of the 648 votes in the North Calcutta seat.

Rahim was invited to form a ministry in January 1927 but was unable to recommend a Hindu member willing to co-operate with him.[59] He tried to win over the Muslim MLCs by representing the intransigence of Hindus as a gross insult to the Muslim community. He said:

> There can be no doubt that this [the willingness of the Hindus to cooperate with him] is the result of a combination among B. Chakravarti and P.C. Mitter and some other Hindu gentlemen of their ways of thinking to prevent me from forming a ministry. For some time past politicians of this class have been carrying on a ceaseless campaign against me simply because I sought to unite the representative men of my community in order to protect and safeguard its just interests.[60]

Suhrawardy and A.K. Ghuznavi, who were themselves

[58] Quoted in Broomfield, op. cit., p. 280.

[59] He was described as the 'high priest of communalism'. The *Amrita Bazar Patrika*, an arch critic of Abdur Rahim, was of the view that Abdur Rahim's association with the ministry plunged Bengal 'into the vortex of communal strife'. *Amrita Bazar Patrika*, 23 January 1927. Page, *Prelude to Partition*, p. 45, and Mcpherson, op.cit., p. 98 discuss the role of Abdur Rahim.

[60] Ibid., 27 January 1927.

jockeying for a position in the ministry, refused to oblige. The governor approached Ghuznavi, who formed a ministry by weaning away some of Rahim's own supporters. Ghuznavi also won over a few dissident swarajists, led by Byomkesh Chakravarti. In this way the political initiative in Bengal still rested with communally-oriented leaders.

Bengal, after all, provided an ideal setting for them to exploit communal tendencies. With most Muslims, especially in the eastern region, nursing a long-standing grievance against the landlord-moneylender combination and the 4,22,000 enfranchised rural voters being susceptible to religious and communal exhortations, men like Rahim, Ghuznavi and Suhrawardy found an excellent target for attack in the dominant Hindu community to which belonged the landholders and their agents, the moneylenders, the lawyers, the tax collectors, and other government officials with whom every Bengali Muslim, rural and urban, was obliged to have dealings. To charge this group with tyranny and to call for united backing to break its stranglehold was one way of arousing popular enthusiasm. What lent weight to this appeal was that the symbols of Islam—mosques, shrines and religious festivals—often cut across the dividing lines of caste and class and simplified the task of mass communication.[61]

V

The balance of forces in Punjab was strikingly different from that of Bengal where educated Muslims had to settle their claims only with Hindus. In upper India, the Sikhs, too, demanded their due share in the distribution of seats. Although their population was less than 14 per cent, they claimed a far higher proportion of

[61] Broomfield, op. cit., p. 328. Some folk writings in Bengal were full of venomous remarks against the usurious mahajans and the exacting Hindu zamindars. Villifying them and their agents, a Muslim bard wrote:

I think....of the great zamindar, who does not recite the name of Allah. even once in a month.

The raja, the zamindar and all their *amla* (staff) suck the *proja* like jackals and dogs.

Quoted in Tajul Islam Hashmi, 'Peasants and Politics in East Bengal', p. 125.

seats—about 30 per cent—on the grounds that they were the former rulers of the province and formed a large proportion of the army. Added to this was their belief that Sikhs possessed a 'separate identity as a community given to us by our Gurus' and their insistence that 'we will not be prepared to merge it into any other community'.[62]

Certain Muslim groups in Punjab were relatively better placed than their co-religionists in Bengal. This was so in government services.[63] Moreover, Punjab had a well-entrenched Muslim aristocracy which was nursed over the decades by the British government and was, consequently, a strong pillar of the imperial edifice. It owned vast tracts of land in Gujrat, Jhang, Jhelum and Attock, and also in eastern districts where the Hindu and Sikh landowning position was much stronger.[64] To the west of Lahore, Muslims were the main landholding group: in the districts opened up by irrigation projects, notably Gujranwala, Lyallpur and Montgomery, they shared this dominance with the Sikhs, but further west, in the districts where Muslims constituted more than 80 per cent of the population, their pre-eminence was unqualified.[65]

The fortunes of the landed aristocrats in Punjab were indissolubly linked with the raj. Both had equal stakes in maintaining the *status quo*. The British bolstered their interests and accommodated their claims in constitutional arrangements, because they were the chief source of recruitment to the army, made substantial financial contributions to the imperial coffers, and served as the

[62] R.M. Sahni, 'Communal Representation,' *Tribune*, 19 September 1924; Rajiv Kapur, *Sikh Separatism: The Politics of Faith* (London, 1986), chapter six.

[63] While Muslims were not employed in the higher echelons of government in numbers proportionate to their share of the population, their proportion was much higher than the level of literacy. In the Police department, for example, they held 25 per cent of appointments and held nearly 50 per cent of the posts in the scale of Rs 200 to Rs 300. The Sikhs and the Hindus, on the other hand, jointly held just over 16 per cent of the positions. *PSC* 1913, vol. 12, appendix 15, pp. 156–158.

[64] See Talbot, *Punjab and the Raj*, p. 20.

[65] Page, *Prelude to Partition*, p. 48.

instrument through which the *sarkar* exercized its authority in far-flung areas.

Thus the chief beneficiaries of the 1919 Reforms were members of the Punjab Muslim Association and the Punjab Central Association, the latter representing the Sikhs and Jats. Influential Muslims who dominated the council were the Nuns and Tiwanas who exercized social authority in the north-western parts of the canal colonies and whose services had proved to be of special value for the supply of recruits and other contributions to the war effort.[66] Umar Hayat Khan Tiwana served first in the council of state from 1920 to 1929 and then on the secretary of state's council during the crucial period when the Act of 1935 was being framed. Feroz Khan Nun, who represented Shahpur West from 1920 to 1923 and Shahpur East from 1926 to 1936, was minister for local self-government in 1927 and minister for education in 1931.[67] The Daulatanas, too, figured as a major force in Punjab politics. Ahmad Yar Khan Daulatana had an estate of 45,000 acres and was elected to the council from east Multan in 1920 and 1926 and from the Muslim landholders constituency in 1930. In the mid-twenties, they added to their already vast riches when their private canal, the Daulatwah, was amalgamated into the Sutlej valley project. The government gave them handsome compensation in the form of further grants of canal colony land.[68]

The first Punjab Council comprised, besides 23 nominated officials and non-officials, 71 elected members. Out of them 35 were Muslims, 15 Sikhs and the rest were Hindus. As in UP, these members were neither loyal to any communal formation nor were they obsessively concerned with the claims of their community. Generally, their formation, as Fazli Husain suggested:

> has taken the line of the 'have-gots', and 'have-nots', with the result that there is a party existing of most of the Muslims and some of the landholding Hindus and Sikhs, because these are the communities which have been more or less excluded by the 'have gots' who had

[66] Imran Ali, *The Punjab under Imperialism 1885–1947* (Princeton, 1988), p. 82.

[67] For details, see Page, op. cit., pp. 61–63.

[68] Imran Ali, op. cit., p. 83.

enjoyed the monopoly of the public services under the pre-reform administration.[69]

Landlords belonging to all religious denominations, including the emerging class of rich Jat farmers like Lal Chand and Chhotu Ram, formed the core group in what is commonly designated as the agriculturist party. The aim of the Punjab Unionist Party, outlined in its 1923 election manifesto, was to advance the interests of the backward classes and communities, irrespective of their caste or creed.[70] Thus the move to repeal the Punjab Alienation Act of 1901 was stoutly resisted, for it was seen as an assault on the rural dominance of the Unionist Party members.[71] The response to the increasing criticizm of the Act was to stiffen the resolve of the 'agricultural class' to stand by 'the Magna Carta of their political and economic life'.[72] They also pinned their hopes on other legislative enactments, such as the Moneylenders Registration Bill, The Punjab Courts Fees [Amendment] Bill and the Punjab [Urban Property] Rent Regulation Bill.

These measures evoked sharp criticizm from moneylenders, traders, merchants and the Lahore-based professional groups. But they were most strident in denouncing the policies of Fazli Husain who, as minister of education, doled out patronage to Muslim educational institutions, offered grants, where none had been available, to existing schools and colleges,[73] and aided the

[69] Azim Husain, *Fazli Husain*, p. 152.

[70] The programme of the Unionists was to attain dominion status within the British Commonwealth of Nations, secure a fair distribution of taxes on rural and urban areas, prevent the exploitation of economically backward classes and support the Punjab Alienation Act.

Serious research on the Unionist Party has been undertaken only in recent years. In addition to Azim Husain's biography of his father and Ashiq Husain Butalvi's *Iqbal ke aakhri do Saal* (Karachi, 1961) which covers the early history of the Unionist Party, there are now quite a few scholarly works. Notable amongst them are the writings of David Page, Imran Ali, Ian Talbot and David Gilmartin. Prem Chowdhry, *Punjab Politics: The Role of Sir Chhotu Ram* (Delhi, 1984) highlights the role of a key figure in Punjab politics.

[71] *Punjab Administration Report 1922–1923* (Lahore, 1924), p. 17.

[72] Gilmartin, *Empire and Islam*, p. 38.

[73] By the close of the nineteenth century, Punjab had a large number of

setting up of new ones.[74] He founded three intermediate colleges in Gujrat and Campbellpur for the large Muslim population in western Punjab,[75] and distributed seats at the Lahore Government and Medical Colleges amongst Hindus, Muslims and Sikhs in the ratio of 40:20:20. He introduced separate electorates in municipalities and district boards and apportioned elected seats in proportion to the population of communities. Between 1917 and 1920, the Punjab government increased the number of municipalities with communal electorates; so the percentage of Muslim seats rose from 40 to 44 per cent. Fazli Husain's new formula bolstered their position all around,[76] with Muslims controlling over 53 per cent of district boards. (Table 7:3)

Such concessions impinged on the socio-economic position of

---

special Muslim schools which were mostly under private management. In places like Lahore, Multan and Sialkot there were local *anjumans* whose main function was to further the cause of education in local community, and they maintained a college as well as a number of high, middle or primary schools. The Anjuman-i-Himayat-i Islam, for example, was entirely supported by private subscriptions and donations, and it maintained a college, a high school and a primary school for boys and girls. Other institutions were the M.A.O. High School, Amritsar, and Mamuje High School, Rawalpindi.

[74] In justification of his policy of giving financial aid to Muslim schools and colleges, Fazli Husain argued that there was an unequal distribution of grants to government-aided institutions. He provided the following figures for 1921–22 to illustrate his point. These figures set out the amount of grants sanctioned [in Rupees] to government-aided schools in five districts.

	Hindus	Muslims	Sikhs	Christians	Total
Ambala	55,245	15,800	8,698	20.887	.100,430
Jullundur	52,396	13,741	30,943	27,287	123,367
Lahore	97,413	61,954	88,189	117,224	364,780
Rawalpindi	46,220	37,015	60,039	40,253	183,527
Multan	35,287	30,249	17,073	250	83,333
Total	286,561	158,929	204,942	205,901	856,333

SOURCE: *Punjab Legislative Council Debates,* 5 March 1924 (Lahore, 1924), vol. 6, no. 8, p. 315.

[75] Ibid., 18 November 1924, vol. 7, no. 7, p. 470.

[76] Muslims formed 53 per cent of the municipal population; from 1920 to 1923 the proportion of Muslims was increased from 44 to 49 per cent.

TABLE 7:3

Composition of the District Boards, 1925

	Population			Number of Members Elected or Nominated		
District Boards	Muslims	Sikhs	Hindus and Others	Muslims	Sikhs	Hindus
Hissar	18,571	42,956	487,620	11	—	27
Rohtak	91,854	432	604,291	5	—	34
Gurgaon	189,119	846	420,933	16	—	24
Karnal	235,618	12,280	580,828	11	3	26
Ambala	157,388	95,155	311,122	9	—	27
Kangra	38,197	1,830	722,600	1	—	37
Hoshiarpur	279,450	132,250	495,326	13	12	18
Jullundur	303,427	199,923	202,347	15	21	3
Ludhiana	147,336	230,777	111,519	10	24	1
Ferozepur	437,462	291,788	251,580	14	22	7
Lahore	227,198	90,684	88,599	20	17	4
Amritsar	343,073	262,067	144,887	12	22	2
Gurdaspur	385,661	133,892	269,259	15	15	12
Sialkot	580,532	74,939	282,352	20	12	5
Gujranwala	387,152	45,027	99,782	21	10	4
Sheikhupura	357,797	85,253	110,023	19	7	4
Jhelum	422,979	18,626	35,463	25	3	2
Rawalpindi	214,070	10,819	11,254	24	4	2
Attock	436,418	14,631	15,840	32	2	2
Mianwali	288,451	2,242	33,281	25	—	5
Montgomery	497,945	93,297	91,827	17	5	6
Lyallpur	515,122	145,063	177,868	27	11	3
Jhang	475,388	9,376	85,795	24	1	5
Multan	671,307	16,342	105,432	29	3	4
Muzaffargarh	482,134	4,530	57,697	24	1	5
Dera Ghazi Khan	385,104	670	39,577	29	3	4
Shahpur	552,014	24,490	65,692	32	3	1
Gujrat	670,340	47,105	50,609	35	2	2

Source: *Punjab Legislative Council Debates,* 30 November, 1925, vol.8, no. 26, p. 1319.

the Punjabi Hindu elite. Hence the hue and cry. Fazli Husain was maligned as the apostle of communalism and the high priest of separatism. The minister rebutted the charge in the council: 'If there is any one man who can claim to have brought Hindu-Muslim unity, I claim, Sir, that I am that man'. But he was not heard. Amar Nath Chopra, a High Court vakil in Lahore, lamented that Fazli Husain was 'out to relegate Hindus to an insignificant position in the Punjab'.[77] The Municipal Amendment Bill evoked a similar reaction. Lala Duni Chand, member of the legislative assembly, and Lala Ganga Ram, member of the Punjab legislative council, persuaded Hindu voters and candidates to withdraw from the municipal elections (held on 17 December 1923) in protest against increased Muslim representation on municipal boards.[78] In Lahore, Rawalpindi and Ferozepur, where Muslims gained control of the municipalities, Hindu members resigned.[79] They did not do so in places like Gojra, Hissar and Rohtak, where their dominance was intact. The Sikhs also joined in the boycott to press for separate representation instead of representation by election jointly with the Hindus.[80]

Communal controversies further deepened in the council chamber. The Moneylenders Registration Bill,[81] a progressive piece of legislation, was given a communal colour simply

Tinker, *Foundations of Local Self-Government,* p. 135. See, Page, *Prelude to Partition,* p. 71.

[77] *Tribune,* 28 December 1923.

[78] The municipality of Ambala had an equal number of Hindus and Muslims. But, in pursuance of Fazli Husain's reforms, the number of Muslims increased from six to eight. The number of Hindus remained at six. *Punjab Legislative-Council Debates,* 29 February 1924, vol. 7, no. 1, p. 89.

[79] FR (Punjab), 1 July 1923, Home Poll. F.No 125, 1923, NAI.

[80] *Legislative Council Debates,* 29 February 1924, vol. 6, no. 5, p. 205.

[81] Most moneylenders in Punjab, especially in the western districts, belonged to the Agarwal, Khatri and Arora castes. The debtors, on the other hand, happened to be Muslims. The extent to which indebtedness had grown amongst them is illustrated by the case of western Dera Ismail Khan district where approximately 86,000 [8 per cent] of cultivable land was transferred from 1880 to 1885. S.S. Thorburn and M.L. Darling were alarmed by the growing indebtedness of Muslim cultivators and the transfer of landed property by mortgage and sale to the urban moneylenders. The

because it was to benefit the Muslim peasantry more than any other group.[82] Pandit Nanak Chand, representing the non-Muslim rural constituency of Hoshiarpur and with extensive trading and banking connections, declared it as 'a Muhammadan measure because in the Quran people are asked not to lend money on interest'.[83] Ram Singh of Kangra was equally vehement in his denunciation.[84] A legislative measure, wrote M.N. Roy in 1924, 'checking the flagrant abuse of the Hindu usurers is not taken on its merit, but made a butt of communal antagonism'.[85]

Irrespective of the nature of issues, the dominant Hindu groups arrayed themselves against Fazli Husain in a bid to oust him.[86] In March 1923, Raja Narendranath, president of the Punjab Hindu Sabha, introduced a vote of censure against Fazli Husain. He charged that the Hindus had received insufficient weightage in the Panchayat Act, the Municipal Act and the District Board Act, and that communal representation in the services had led to 'competent' Hindus being replaced by 'incompetent' Muslims.[87] Chhotu Ram, Fazli Husain's chief ally in the Unionist

---

government intervened to pass the Punjab Land Alienation Act which prevented a professional moneylender from dispossessing an agriculturist who had cultivated his land for more than twenty years. Besides, the peasant could neither be evicted nor arrested for debt; his plough, cattle, implements and seeds could not be attached for the redemption of his debt. The Moneylenders Registration Bill was intended to remove some of the loopholes in the Punjab Alienation Act. Moneylenders were, for example, required to register themselves with the government so that their accounts could be checked and monitored.

[82] *Tribune*, 25 October 1924, M.N. Roy in Ray (ed.), *Selected Works*, vol. 2, pp. 439, 441–42.

[83] *Punjab Legislative Council Debates*, 18 November 1924, vol. 7, p. 514.

[84] Ibid., p. 523.

[85] Ray (ed.), *Selected Works of M.N. Roy*, vol. 2, pp. 442–443.

[86] See speech of Lala Sevak Ram, *Punjab Legislative Council Debates*, 14 March 1925, vol. 8, no. 2, p. 559.

[87] For the role of Raja Narendranath, see Bruce Cleghorn, 'Religion and Politics: The Leadership of the All-India Hindu Mahasabha in Punjab and Saurashtra,' B.N. Pandey (ed.), *Leadership in South Asia* (Delhi, 1977). In June 1926, the Raja told C.Y. Chintamani that he could not join any party that did not protect the 'just' and 'legitimate' rights of the Punjab Hindus. His ideal was to attain swaraj with justice to the Hindu minority in the province. 7 June 1926, Chintamani Papers, NMML.

Party, echoed the same view while endorsing the censure motion.[88]

Significantly enough, the motion against Fazli Husain was backed by elected Hindu and Sikh members: the only non-Muslims who opposed it were L.K. Rallia Ram, a nominated Christian, and Harkishen Lal and Sunder Singh Majithia, both of whom held official posts. The minister was able to save his skin on account of the timely support of Muslims and British officials. In this way, a beleagured Fazli Husain, deserted even by his Jat allies, not only relied more and more on the Muslim bloc but became their chief spokesman, especially after his appointment to the viceroy's executive council in 1930. From this position, he played a critical behind-the-scenes role in the early 1930s 'as informal strategist and director of Muslim policy during the great constitutional reappraisals of these years'.[89] Fazli Husain's major goal was to protect Muslim interests—interests he identified with those of Punjab's Muslims.[90]

The mud-slinging that accompanied the introduction of Narendranath's censure motion was not just a setback to Fazli Husain's political career in Punjab but also a bad omen for communal relations in the province. A sober politician, with years of close association with the Congress and a firm commitment to Hindu-Muslim unity, was needlessly pushed into the All-India Muslim Conference, a body consisting of political reactionaries and obscurantists. Fazli Husain was not spared even after he was moved to the viceroy's council in the summer of 1925. The *Tribune* gleefully recorded:

> The disappearance of Sir Fazli Husain from the stage of Punjab politics, even though temporary, will undoubtedly make many people heave a sigh of relief.... The tide of communalism among the educated and politically-minded Muslims of Punjab, thanks largely to Fazli Husain's policy, has been so high during the last four years, that it is no easy thing for any individual or group...to go against the tide.[91]

[88] Chowdhry, *Punjab Politics*, p. 171.

[89] Ayesha Jalal and Anil Seal, 'Alternative to Partition: Muslim Politics Between the Wars', *Modern Asian Studies*, vol. 15, no. 3, 1981, p. 433.

[90] See Gilmartin, *Empire and Islam*, p. 111

[91] *Tribune*, 26 August 1925.

VI

When a group of leading Congressmen visited Punjab in March 1923, they were appalled to discover that 'each community had practically arrayed itself in an armed camp against each other'. They found that almost the whole of the province was divided along communal lines, though not always for the same reasons. 'The reasons which apply to the so-called educated classes are entirely different from those which apply to the masses and we feel constrained to say that the latter have to no small extent been exploited by interested parties among the former for their own selfish purposes'.[92] In such a fragmented and communally-polarized society, it was easy for revivalist tendencies to gain a firm foothold and for communal bodies to secure recruits. The revival and resurgence of the Hindu Sabha and the Arya Samaj can be seen in this light.

The Hindu Sabha was not new to Punjab.[93] It was founded in 1907, almost immediately after the Muslim League came into being in December 1906, and attracted notice in 1909 by its condemnation of the Punjab Alienation Act and the 'extravagant and unwarranted', Muslim demands for representation in the councils.[94] 'The Hindus', stated the *Indian Patriot*, 'have organized themselves into a separate body in the belief that by such separate organizations alone can they safeguard the interests of their community'.[95] The issues raised by the Sabha provided topics for excited discussions as its followers hoped for a better future—one in which they could maintain their status and prevent further governmental action against their interests.[96]

On the eve of and during the Khilafat and non-co-operation agitations, the Punjab Hindu Sabha maintained a low profile. Thereafter, a vigorous ideological crusade was set afoot, drawing upon the sympathy of those who were anxious to thwart Fazli

[92] F.No. 3, All-India Congress Committee (AICC) Papers, NMML.
[93] See Jones, *Arya Dharm*, pp. 288–290, 294–299.
[94] *Tribune*, 6 April and 3 November 1909.
[95] Quoted in ibid., 3 November 1909.
[96] Jones, op. cit., p. 291.

Husain's belligerence. There was the familiar cry of 'A Dying Race', of the imminent disintegration of the Hindu community through conversion and more rapid growth rates among Muslims, and of discrimination against Hindus in government service.

'Many a Congressman', stated the younger Nehru in his autobiography, 'was a communalist under his nationalist cloak'.[97] One person he must have had in mind was the rustic, narrow-minded and bigoted Lala Lajpat Rai. In Jawaharlal's judgement, he did not have a good enough 'intellectual or cultural background'; hence his 'peculiar behaviour' in public life'.[98] He was conservative in political matters with pronounced communal proclivities.[99] Such a person spearheaded the Hindu Sabha movement in Punjab.

There is no denying Lajpat Rai's influence in his home province.[100] He had the image of a relentless crusader, a tough bargainer and a symbol of Punjabi Hindu identity. He was active in cow-protection societies and the Arya Samaj, which, in his own words, taught the 'true and genuine Hinduism of the Vedas', worked to serve the Hindus and defended them from the 'onslaught of alien religions'.[101] *Shuddhi*[102] and *sangathan* were

[97] Nehru, *An Autobiography*, p. 136.

[98] Gopal (ed.), *Selected Works of Jawaharlal Nehru*, vol. 2, p. 255.

[99] Nehru, *An Autobiography*, p. 158.

[100] According to the *Tribune* [7 December 1923]: 'In the Punjab and at the present time the Congress and Lala Lajpat Rai are inseparable terms. His influence, authority and prestige are the influence and authority of the Congress itself'. Although this is an exaggerated assessment, it gives some idea of Lajpat Rai's influence in Punjab.

[101] Lajpat Rai, *A History of the Arya Samaj* (Bombay, 1967), p. 183.

[102] *Shuddhi* means purification. In religious terminology it was applied to (1) conversion to Hinduism of persons belonging to 'foreign religions'; (2) reconversion of those who adopted one of the 'foreign religions', (3) reclamation, i.e., raising the status of the depressed classes. The *shuddhi* movement received direct inspiration from the Arya Samaj movement, launched by Dayanand Saraswati in 1875. The proselytizing work of the Samaj was effected largely by a branch of the Arya Pratinidhi Sabha which was established in 1909. Later, other organizations, such as the Hindu Ashrams, the Hindu Sabhas, the Rajput Shuddhi Sabha and the All-India Khatri Sabha, also joined in.

his other passions. 'The principle of *shuddhi*',[103] he observed, 'has now been accepted by the Hindu Sabha, and I am free to confess that the idea at the back of this decision is partly political, partly communal, and partly humanitarian'.[104]

Acting as a spokesman of Punjabi Hindus, Lajpat Rai's aim was to unite Hindus against communal representation and, in co-operation with their brethren in other provinces, to 'arrange for a permanent machinery to clarify and crystallize Hindu public opinion on all political questions'.[105] For this reason, he pleaded with his community to set aside differences and unite under the flag of the Hindu Mahasabha, which would shape the destiny of the 'Hindu Nation' in all its social, political and cultural aspects.[106]

The Punjab Hindu Sabha served as a rallying point for a multitude of revivalist groups: the Shuddhi Sabha, the Arya Samaj and the Sanathan Dharma Sabhas. A prominent leader of the Shuddhi Sabha was Mahatma Munshi Ram, known as Swami Shraddhanand, who came under the influence of the Arya Samaj leader, Dayanand Saraswati, early in his life. In the 1890s, he was associated with the Antaranga Sabha, a branch of the Shuddhi Sabha, before renouncing his legal career to conduct a *gurukul,* an educational institution, with the aim of reviving ancient Indian philosophy, history and literature.[107] During the Rowlatt Satyagraha, he followed in the footsteps of the Mahatma to

[103] The *sangathan* movement aimed at consolidating and uniting the Hindus. Moreover, it sought to efface the image of a Hindu as a *dhoti*-wearing coward and to replace it with the image of a militant Hindu willing to maintain his honour and that of his community. G.R. Thursby, *Hindu-Muslim Relations in British India* (Leiden, 1975), p. 159.

[104] Lajpat Rai, 'Hindu-Muslim Problem', *Tribune,* 13 December 1924.

[105] Lajpat Rai to Purshotamdas Thakurdas, 13 December 1924, Thakurdas Papers, NMML.

[106] *India Quarterly Register,* January-June 1925, vol. 1, pp. 378–80. From April to December 1925, the Lala was busy enlisting support for the Hindu Sabhas and the *sangathan* movement. He presided over the Calcutta session of the All-India Hindu Mahasabha, visited Assam, Burma and Sind to organize *sangathan* and local Hindu Sabhas, and chaired a meeting of the Bombay Hindu Conference in Bombay.

[107] See M.R. Jambunathan (ed.), *Swami Shraddhanand* (Bombay, 1961).

emerge, along with M.A. Ansari, as a front-rank satyagrahi in Delhi. He was a symbol of communal amity when invited to preach to the Friday congregation at the Juma Masjid, and was part of the Khilafat deputation to the viceroy. But the Swami's fascination for Gandhi faded and his enthusiasm for the Khilafat cause dampened. He developed a dislike for the militancy of the Khilafatists and lost faith in the efficacy of the Gandhian methods. His interests lay elsewhere: in the *shuddhi* movement, which was conceived by him as an essential part of a broader movement for Hindu solidarity, or *sangathan*. He was present at the first ceremony of reclamation of Malkanas to Hinduism at Raibana, near Agra.[108] Within the first months five thousand Malkanas were reclaimed, and by the end of the year the total had risen to about thirty thousand. Shraddhanand and his Arya Samaj collaborators were the acknowledged leaders of this initial push. But, in the process, they strained the already fragile communal equations in north India. Iqbal expressed his fears in 1923:

> It is a pity that in the Punjab the jealousy, no, rather enmity of Hindus and Muslims is growing. If it remains like that, then life will become difficult for both the communities during the next 30 years.[109]

The fears of the poet proved prophetic.

[108] The Malkana Rajputs were converted under the Afghans and settled as military colonies in the Jumna tract in the neighbourhood of Agra and Delhi. Their origin, however, is not clear. Malkanas—a title and not a clan name—were probably Jadon Rajputs formerly, some were Jats and others were Agarwal *banias*, Many Malkana Rajputs in the Mathura district were descendants of Tarkar Brahmans.

[109] Schimmel, *Gabriel's Wing*, p. 13[illegible].

Chapter Eight

Competing Symbols, Revivalism and Mobilization

Interested persons who were disappointed during the balmy days of non-co-operation, now that it has lost the charm of novelty, have found their opportunity and are trading upon the religious bigotry or the selfishness of both the communities. The result is written in the history of the feuds of the past two years. Religion has been traversed. Trifles have been dignified by the name of religious tenets. ... Economic and political causes have been brought into play for the sake of fomenting trouble.*

M.K. Gandhi, 26 December 1924.

It is always difficult to calculate the dynamics of rioting; one observes all the signs and the portents, but it is not easy to determine the exact temperature at which feelings will boil over. The atmosphere may continue surcharged for prolonged periods without an outburst, unless some chance spark produces a sudden blaze.**

Malcolm Hailey, 7 May 1927

The record of Hindu-Muslim riots dates back to 1800, but in no other period were they so bloody, so gruesome and so widespread as in the mid-twenties.[1] In 1923–24, most parts of UP and Punjab were thoroughly inflamed. The fire of communal hatred even engulfed Delhi and Kohat which had an impressive record of communal amity. Gandhi was shaken by the happenings. He

* *CWMG,* vol. 25, p. 477.

** To Alexander Muddiman, 7 May 1927, F. No. 10 (B), Hailey Papers.

[1] See table 7 in Page, *Prelude to Partition,* p. 74, and for UP table 5:1 in Pandey, *The Ascendancy of the Congress in Uttar Pradesh,* p. 116.

began a fast——'the final plunge'—to do 'penance...for sins unwittingly committed'.[2] A Unity Conference ensued.[3] But platitudinous resolutions could not stem the tide of violence. Gandhi himself expressed his disappointment. The resolutions, he said, were 'inadequate; those attending it were imperfect; hence the beginning too has been deficient'.[4]

The Mahatma was agonized and started to despair. The Hindu-Muslim problem, he announced in March 1925, was an 'insoluble puzzle' and so he would keep out of it.[5] At public meetings in Madras and Calcutta he talked of a 'hopeless tangle' being 'put away in my cupboard'. He felt that in the prevailing 'surcharged atmosphere' and 'mutual distrust' he would not be able to persuade either the Hindus or the Muslims to accept his solution.[6]

In the following year—1926—the *Young India* dwelt on the Hindu-Muslim problem only twice: when Shraddhanand was assassinated by a Muslim fanatic[7] and when Syed Mahmud pleaded with Gandhi to resolve the communal tangle by bringing to an end his self-imposed political exile.[8] But the Mahatma was not convinced. He told the Bihar lawyer that 'my meddling at this juncture, I am convinced, can only do harm'.[9] Like the War of Roses in England, in India, too, 'order must come out of present chaos'. Unity, he emphasized in an unprophetic statement, will not precede but will succeed freedom.[10]

Gandhi's refusal to be drawn into the communal controversies of the day made no sense. His admission of 'defeat' also came a bit too soon. It is true that his political credibility among Muslims was low, but he alone could still command their allegiance. Muslim Congressmen, in particular, still gathered around him and turned to him for guidance and leadership. But they were

2 'All About the Fast', 22 September 1924, *CWMG*, vol. 24, pp. 199-200.
3 See *Indian Quarterly Register*, vol. 2, pp. 149-160.
4 *CWMG*, vol. 24, p. 263.
5 Interview to the Press, 5 March 1925, ibid., vol. 26, p. 233.
6 Speech at public meeting, Madras, 7 March 1925, ibid., p. 244.
7 *Young India*, 30 December 1926, ibid., p. 473.
8 9 September 1926, ibid., vol. 38, p. 316.
9 Ibid.
10 Ibid.

disappointed by his intransigence and his reluctance to thwart the mounting pressure of Hindu communalists in the Congress and to censure their chief spokesmen—Malaviya and Lajpat Rai. It was commonly felt then and later that a sulking Mahatma, with his studious silence and self-imposed inactivity, could not have boosted the morale of those engaged in fighting the demon of communalism. He pursued his other 'hobbies'—charkha, removal of untouchability and cow-protection—while the country experienced communal riots all around.

Neither Gandhi nor his Congress colleagues made a serious attempt to analyze the factors behind the sudden eruption of Hindu-Muslim violence. There were generalized contemporary assessments, most notably by Jawaharlal Nehru and his Marxist comrades, who saw riots as a 'special product of British rule' [11] and as the end result of British economic policies which created arenas of conflict and competition.[12] There was, then, the favourite official view with its emphasis on the long-standing antagonism between the followers of Hinduism and Islam which were intensified by social segregation, separate religious rituals and practices.[13] But this interpretation did not answer why communal disturbances occurred more frequently and with greater intensity in the mid-twenties and not earlier.[14]

In the end, one will have to explore both the immediate causes

[11] See, for example, Nehru's presidential address at the Bundelkhand conference, 13 June 1921, Gopal (ed.), *Selected Works of Jawaharlal Nehru*, p. 185. And the comments of M.N. Roy, quoted in Ray (ed.), *Selected Works of M.N. Roy*, vol. 2, pp. 537-38.

[12] Palme Dutt, *India Today*, p. 445.

[13] *Report of the Indian Statutory Commission: Survey*, Cmd. 3568 (London, 1930), vol. 1, p. 27. Zetland, governor of Bengal and later secretary of state for India, detailed the differences. According to him, the Hindu-Muslim divisions were not only due to religious belief and practice 'but to a profoundly different outlook on life resulting in social systems which are the very antithesis of one another'. This being so, it was, in Zetland's judgement, 'inevitable that an artificial...system such as that of communal electorates should encourage the fissiparous tendencies already existing'. Lawrence. Second Marquess of Zetland, *Essayez* (London, 1956), pp. 119-120.

[14] There were 88 recorded riots during the years 1923 to 1927. The casualty list was high—400 dead and 5,000 injured.

of Hindu-Muslim friction as well as the subtle institutional and socio-economic processes, set in motion by the colonial government, which engendered various forms of caste, communal and regional conflicts.

II

In general, the communal pot was kept boiling by disputes over music before mosques, cow-protection and routes of religious processions. There were a few more irritants—the process of conversion and reconversion, conducted under the aegis of *tabligh* and *shuddhi* societies, and the constant flow of polemical literature designed to heighten and offend religious sensibilities.[15]

Routes of religious processions and the playing of music before mosques were among the principal reasons of discord. This was not so in earlier decades when Hindus and Muslims took part in each others festivals and religious processions. Rajendra Prasad recalled how in the Zaradei village of Bihar there was mutual celebration of Holi and how the *tazias* of prosperous Hindus were bigger and brighter than those of Muslims.[16] This was no longer the case in the mid-twenties. Even places like Delhi and Lucknow, which had an excellent record of communal cordiality and were regarded as symbols of India's rich, composite life, were overwhelmed by the communal tide.[17] Given the prominence accorded to religion and religiosity in public life, it was common for religio-cultural formations to stake claims which came in conflict with the beliefs or practices of others. Thus the Hindus refused to entertain any suggestion of

[15] G.R. Thursby, *Hindu-Muslim Relations in British India*, chapter one.

[16] Rajendra Prasad, *Autobiography* (Delhi, 1957), pp. 13-14. Also see Blunt, *India Under Ripon*, p. 72 and W. Crooke, *The North-Western Provinces of India: Their History, Ethnology and Administration* (London, 1897), p. 263, for Shia-Sunni and Hindu-Muslim participation in Muharram observances. And for examples drawn from Bombay, see Jim Masselos, 'Change and Custom in the Format of the Bombay Muharram during the Nineteenth and Twentieth Centuries', *South Asia*, December 1982, pp. 54, 57.

[17] Home Poll. F.No. 249/x, 1924, NAI.

banning music before the mosques, arguing that both rituals and social customs required processions, accompanied with music, to pass thoroughfares.[18]

It was quite common in the past for religious processions to go through crowded streets and for music to be played around mosques. The only notable difference then was that wherever disagreements arose, one could hope for their resolution through existing local mechanisms, which were evolved in almost every locality through centuries of corporate living. It was possible to turn to mohalla committees, voluntary associations and civic bodies for sane advice and sober judgement. But with the rise in communal temperature and the consequent hardening of attitudes the local command structures collapsed and there was hardly an initiative to take recourse to traditional institutions for resolving localized differences. Militant groups could now be seen to take pride in flouting the few general rules or norms that regulated religious processions. Having tasted 'victory' in one area they could stridently move elsewhere to test their muscle power. This was the pattern everywhere—at Lucknow and Allahabad in September 1924, at Dehradun in 1925, at Rawalpindi in 1926 and at Bettiah in August 1927.[19]

By far the worst incident, caused by a drummer in an Arya Samaj procession passing by a mosque, took place at Calcutta on 2 April 1926. The casualty list was high and the damage to property considerable.[20] The rioters were drawn from many sections of society, though the 'goonda' elements, brought to Calcutta by rich Marwari traders and merchants to guard their homes and property, were principally involved in looting and arson. They

[18] See Home Poll. F.No. 166, 1927, NAI.

[19] Thursby, *Hindu-Muslim Relations*, pp. 90-94.

[20] From April 2 to 12, 44 persons were killed with 584 injured. During the first four days 151 cases of fire were reported. Besides, 8 temples, 3 gurudwaras and 10 mosques were destroyed. The areas worst affected were Harrison Road, College Street and Raja Bazaar near the Sealdah Railway Station. For official accounts, see The Earl of Lytton, *Pundits and Elephants: Being the Experiences of Five Years as Governor of an Indian Province* (London, 1942), pp. 167-73. And *Report of the Calcutta Riots of April 1926*, Lytton Papers, F.No. 160 (46).

were doing more than protecting their employees; they were committing assaults as well.[21]

Cow-slaughter was another issue that undermined the traditional fabric of corporate social life. As is well-known, Islam enjoins upon the faithful to offer animal sacrifices at the *Id al-Zuha* or, as it is called in India, the *Bakr Id.* It also lays down that, while the minimum obligatory offering for a Muslim is a sheep or a goat, the offering of a camel, cow or buffalo is equivalent to seven sheeps or goats, and by such a single offering seven persons can participate in the sacrifice. And because horned cattle were numerous and cheap in India it was economical to use one of them for *qurbani* (sacrifice) rather than to provide the equivalent number of sheeps or goats. These were the reasons, stated the two *fatawa* issued by the Anjuman-i Zahirin Ala Haq, Jabalpur, and the Anjuman-i Islamia, Panipat, why Muslims preferred the sacrifice of cows. The timing of these religious decrees was significant: they were issued and circulated in the aftermath of bloody riots during *Bakr Id*.[22]

The sanctity of the cow was recognized in pre-British days; in fact a number of medieval Sultans, including Zainul Abidin of Kashmir and Zahiruddin Babur, founder of the Mughal Empire, imposed a ban on cow-slaughter. But the first recorded society for the protection of the cow was formed in 1882 by Dayanand Saraswati before its branches spread to Bengal, Maharashtra, Punjab and UP. In 1893 and in September-October 1917, the cow issue was the spark which ignited widespread riots in eastern UP[23] and in the Shahbad district of Bihar—at Piro Bazaar, 25 miles from Arrah on the Sassaram road, Bhagalpur, Milki and Ibrahimpur. A mob of nearly ten thousand went on a rampage killing Muslims and burning and looting their property. Those

[21] Memoirs of O.M. Martin, p. 149, Centre for South Asian Studies, Cambridge.

[22] See *Adaalat Gaushala Parasthan* (Jabalpur, 1922). *Mussalmanan-i Panipat ki Bipta aur Afsaana* (Delhi, 1926). Also, see A. Raoof, *Submission About the Qurbani Question* (Calcutta, 1911), IOLR Tracts (1084).

[23] McLane, *Indian Nationalism*, pp. 273, 326-27; Thursby, *Hindu-Muslim Relations*, pp. 76-88; Gyan Pandey, 'Rallying Round the Cow: Sectarian Strife in the Bhojpur Region, c. 1888-1917', Ranajit Guha (ed.), *Subaltern Studies II: Writings on South Asian History and Society* (Delhi, 1983).

found guilty were high-caste Hindus, supported by Ahirs, Kurmis and Telis. Among the 37 charged with offences of dacoity and rioting were 8 Brahmans, 5 Rajputs, 9 Bhumihars and 3 Kayasths. In Katar, situated east of the Sassaram-Arrah Road, high-caste Hindus were the principal offenders. Among the 105 accused were 40 Rajputs and a leading zamindar family from the neighbouring district. So also in Mauna village, located in the Nasirganj police station. The assault, led by the Brahmin-Rajput-Bhumihar combination, 'is a grim and moving story, the isolated position of this Muslim village surrounded by big Hindu villages,...the determination of the Muslims to resist, the erection of barricades, the five hour battle in the course of which thousands of Hindus were more than once repulsed by the defenders, with fatal results'.[24]

In his judgement, H.L.L. Allanson commented that such events 'went far beyond a riot to stop *qurbani*' and opined that they were the result of a deliberately engineered conspiracy to stir up religious passions against the Muslims. He went on to add:

> The thousands of rioters did not content themselves with merely preventing the *qurbani* taking place on that day [i.e., 28 September] but looted and damaged the property of the Muslims in those three villages, forced the women to give up their ornaments and outraged their religious feeling by entering and damaging the mosque and destroying the Quran.[25]

Disputes over land, indebtedness and non-payment of dues lent a local specificity to such organized assaults.[26] At the same time, Bihar and its neighbouring districts in UP had a long and consistent record of violence over the cow question. The Gaurakshini Sabhas, financed by the Rajas of Banaras and Darbhanga, had been active in the region. And for nearly two decades the cow symbol remained an integral part of nationalist mobilization and was linked with militant assertions of 'Hindu identity'. In the creation and articulation of this identity,

[24] 'In the Court of Commissioner of the Special Tribunal of Arrah', 18 January 1918, p. 5, H.L.L. Allanson Papers, Centre for South Asian Studies, Cambridge.

[25] 20 November 1917, p. 6, ibid.

[26] 18 January 1918, p. 7, ibid.

high-caste Hindus discovered in the cow a powerful symbol of common identification. Its utility in defining the broad contours of 'Hindu identity' provided the *raison d'etre* for its protection.

In 1893, the government was sensitized to the strength of the Gaurakshini movement in Bihar and the neighbouring districts. Pamphlets on and appeals for cow-protection were in circulation. Zealous preachers, despatched by the Arya Samaj Leagues in UP and Punjab, lectured in Champaran district. They spoke with passion and fervour. Such was their influence that, in certain villages Muslims were not even allowed to draw water from the wells.[27] These were ominous signs in the wake of large-scale rioting that engulfed Ballia, Ghazipur and Azamgarh and had even spread to distant Bombay, Poona and Yeola in August 1893.[28] A government report had predicted in July 1893:

> I do not feel satisfied that we enjoy immunity from an inroad of riotous Hindus, and if it takes place, there will be terrible bloodshed. The excitement among Hindus here is so great and the League [Cow Preservation] so widespread that the material for an uprising is among us even without external excitement.[29]

The happenings in Shahbad and other districts of Bihar in 1917–18 followed a predictable course. By and large the structure of the riots was the same. The organizers and participants were, as in the past, drawn from the same high-caste Hindus. And the victims in most places were Muslims. In fact, one can draw a striking parallel between the events of 1893 and 1917–18. The following account of the 1893 riots by M.L. Ferrar, commissioner of Gorakhpur division, could well have been written in 1917–18:

> Our rule was practically at an end for some time in certain parts of the district, and the Muhammadans were at the mercy of their enemies, having in most places saved their lives or their property, or both, by being forced to sign a document *[Iqraarnaama]* that they would not sacrifice cows. The Hindus have so far won all along the line, slaying the

[27] W. Hoey to Ferrar, 9 June 1893, UP Government (General Administration Dept), F.No. 730 (B), Box No. 44, 1893, UPSA.

[28] S. Krishnaswamy, '1893: A Year of Unrest in India', *Quarterly Review of Historical Studies*, vol. 4, no. 3, 1966-1967, p. 155.

[29] Hoey to LaTouche, 16 July 1893, op.cit.

Mussalmans, looting them, forcing them to go against their religion, terrifying the lives out of them, and riding roughshod over them in every way.[30]

If this was the price to be paid for cow-protection, it is hard to understand why so many Congress leaders, claiming to be ardent champions of Hindu-Muslim amity, so readily promoted movements connected with it. Tilak made the cow symbol an integral part of the Shivaji festival and assumed a leading role in Poona's Cow-Preservation Society. Others venerated and worshipped the cow and shared a life-long passion for its protection. Gandhi was one of them. He regarded the cow with the same veneration as his mother, declaring that its protection was 'a central fact of Hinduism' and was 'dearer to [him] than anything else'.[31] With the protection of cow, he wrote in *Young India*, 'is bound up not merely the welfare of the cattle of all India and the good name of Hinduism, but, also to a very large extent, the economic welfare of the people'.[32] He presided over a cow-protection conference at Belgaum, attended its meetings in Delhi and Bombay to draft a constitution and worked in close co-operation with Malaviya, Lajpat Rai, Shraddhanand and Moonje.[33] All the time he seemed keen to assure his readers that the work of cow-protection 'does not come to a standstill even for a single moment. I keep all the time thinking of it and also discuss it'.[34] And when Mohamed Ali presented him with a cow to be sent to a *pinjrapole*, the Mahatma was delighted. He wrote:

You are more than a brother to me. I have seen the cow. My bed was lifted to enable me to see her. What love that has prompted the act! May the bond between you twins [Shaukat and Mohamed] and me fructify into an indissoluble bond between Hindus and Mussalmans for the good of

[30] Ferrar to LaTouche, 28 June 1893, ibid.

[31] *Young India*, 29 January 1924, *CWMG*, vol. 24, p. 150, and *Navajivan*, 3 May 1925, vol. 27, p. 18. For arguments in support of cow-protection, see F.No. 12, 1922-23, AICC Papers.

[32] *Young India*, 3 September 1925, *CWMG*, vol. 28, p. 145.

[33] See vol. 25, pp. 512-22. and vol. 26, pp. 35-36 for the draft constitution of the Conference.

[34] *Navajivan*, 1 November 1925, ibid., vol. 28, pp. 404.

our respective faiths, for the good of our country and for the good of humanity. Yes, God is great. He can work wonders.[35]

The Mahatma hoped that as a reciprocal gesture Muslims would voluntarily renounce cow-slaughter during the Khilafat movement. Though firmly opposed to a bargain, he believed that 'the best and the only way to save the cow is to save the Khilafat'.[36] That is why, he said, 'I have [therefore] called Khilafat our Kamadhenu'.[37] In 1925, he recalled:

I gave all the help that I could for the Khilafat, because I wanted to enlist the sympathy in the matter of cow-protection.[38]

Gandhi's expectations were not belied. Muslims of Phulwari Sharif in Bihar renounced eating beef. Abdul Bari assured Gandhi that Muslims in Lucknow would avoid cow-slaughter at *Bakr Id*. The Muslim League passed a cow-protection resolution in December 1919. The Ali Brothers gave up eating beef, and Seth Chotani, president of the Central Khilafat Committee, saved hundreds of cows in Bombay during *Bakr Id*.[39]

But the cow-Khilafat formula did not enthuse everybody. In Gaya, Maulvi Mohammad Sajjad, Naib Amir-i Shariat, refused to follow the Muslim League directive; in fact, Rajendra Prasad and Abul Kalam Azad were deputed by the Congress to prevail upon the Maulvi not to destroy the Hindu-Muslim accord. In August 1921, the Bihar government noticed the tension brewing and was wary of the activities of the militant followers of Maulvi Sajjad, Swami Biswanand and Kripa Baba of Chapra.[40] Yet it was possible then for national leaders to keep the firebrands in

[35] To Mohamed Ali, 8 October 1924, ibid., vol. 25, p. 226.

[36] Speech on Khilafat, 26 January 1921, ibid., vol. 19, p. 283.

[37] U.A. Rao (ed.), *The Way to Communal Harmony*, p. 90.

[38] Speech at the All-India Cow-Protection Conference, Bombay, 28 April 1925, ibid., vol. 26, p. 557.

[39] Mohibbul Hasan, 'Mahatma Gandhi and the Indian Muslims', in S.C. Biswas (ed.), *Gandhi: Theory and Practice, Social Impact and Contemporary Relevance* (Indian Institute of Advanced Study: Shimla, 1969), p. 140. Abdul Bari's position on the subject emerges from his statements and correspondence quoted in Jafri (ed.), *Karawaan-i Gumgushta*, pp. 173-181.

[40] Home Poll. F.No. 18, 1921, NAI; *Hamdam*, 24 August 1920, quoted in ibid., p. 181.

check and to curb their religious zeal in the larger interest of promoting a joint Hindu-Muslim struggle against colonial rule. But there was much less of a chance for such initiatives to succeed in the aftermath of the Khilafat and Non-Co-operation campaigns.[41] The political linkages established by all-India leaders with their constituents in the provinces and localities had snapped and enthusiasm for Hindu-Muslim unity dampened.

Take the case of the Jamiyat al-ulama, a close political ally of the Congress, which commanded considerable influence during the Khilafat agitation and could thus secure strict adherence to its policy on cow-slaughter. But once the influence of the Jamiyat leaders waned, their followers began to take independent positions. In some places the old arrangement continued, but in most areas Muslims began to assert their right to sacrifice cows.[42] In Delhi, they decided to use the Pahari Dhiraj route for taking cows to the slaughter house in violation of a previous agreement.[43] Mohamed Ali commented: 'This was so unlike the spirit of 1920–21 that the contrast was shocking'.[44]

Mohamed Ali explained why the mood had changed. One of the reasons he referred to was the apprehension that, if Muslims accepted the principle of cow-protection, they would then have to give in on other contentious religious issues. In the words of Mohamed Ali: 'Today it was the Pahari Dhiraj; tomorrow it would be something else, and instead of leaving it to us to consider genuine Hindu susceptibilities, the Hindu majority will be more and more aggressive as every day passes in imposing its will upon us and in insisting that Muslims should live on its sufferance in Aryavarta'.[45]

Mohamed Ali also took the opportunity to comment on the

[41] There were, of course, some notable exceptions as in Nagpur where, in October 1924, the citizens heeded to the admonitions of Motilal Nehru and Maulana Azad and resolved their differences amicably. F.No. 50, 1921–25, AICC Papers.

[42] *Akhbaar-i Aam* (Lahore), 21 February 1923, SNNR, Punjab.

[43] *Comrade,* 17 July 1925, and Abdur Rahman to Ansari, 1 July 1925, Hasan (ed.), *Muslims and the Congress,* pp. 13–14.

[44] *Comrade,* 17 July 1925.

[45] Ibid.

petty-mindedness and bigotry of the 'pseudo nationalists'. He added:

> They talk and write as nationalists and run down communals [*sic*]; but only in the use of counters and catchwords of Nationalism are they nationalists for their hearts are narrow and they can conceive of no future for India except to be one of Hindu dominance and the existence of Mussalmans as a minority living on the sufferance of the Hindu majority.... It is my sad conviction that not one of these pseudo-Nationalists would have talked so glibly of Nationalism, majority rule and mixed electorates, if his own community had not been in the safe position of an overwhelming majority. It is they who are the real culprits as narrow communalists, but since the position of their community is safe enough they mouth all the fine phrases of nationalism and parade themselves as nationalists. *The Cow question provides the best topic for the exposure of their pseudo-nationalism, for in the name of nationalism they make demands on their fellow-countrymen so absurd that none has ever heard of them in any other country or nation in the world, and it is time that their nationalism was fully exposed* [emphasis added].[46]

These were harsh sentiments expressed in strong language. But they reflect the social and political perceptions of an influential Muslim and his lack of conviction in the nationalist discourse. Furthermore, Mohamed Ali's remarks reveal the emotional intensity with which the cow question was being debated in the subcontinent.

III

Areas of Hindu-Muslim strife extended far beyond disputations over music before mosque and cow-protection. In a society of unequal opportunities and disparities, economic impulses and motivations raised possibilities of conflict and competition. Sometimes, the tension between the exploiting classes and the exploited took the form of class struggles which were manifested in organized kisan and trade union movements. But more often they tended to acquire a communal colour, with different classes articulating their interests through religious symbols and

[46] Ibid.

idioms.[47] Recent works of K.N. Panikkar on Malabar, of Tanika Sarkar and Tajul Islam Hashmi on Bengal and of Chitra Joshi on the Kanpur labour force illustrate how agrarian conflicts and working-class movements had a marked tendency to correspond to the contours of a communal fracas.[48] Let us first take a cursory look at the roots of agrarian conflicts in Bengal.

Without elaborating on the structure of Bengal agrarian society and the subtle differentiation in the Muslim peasantry, aspects covered by a number of distinguished scholars, one can state the obvious fact that the peasantry in Bengal, largely Muslim, was subservient to groups or classes who happened to be predominantly Hindus: To the Hindus belonged the land and the capital. Magistrates and judges to whom the peasants submitted their cases, police officers who investigated them and lawyers who represented them in law courts were all Hindus. Mymensingh's district magistrate found 'universal complaints among the poorer Muslims of oppression and intimidation by pleaders, mukhtars, backed by the authority of the zamindar's *amala*.[49] Circumstances such as these proved conducive for communal antipathies to take roots in the countryside.

Agrarian discontent was the chief cause of rioting in Mymensingh, for in no other district was the domination of the landlord over the tenant so blatant.[50] The Tenancy Act of 1885 was a dead-letter, while the excesses of landlords, such as enhanced rents, unauthorized cesses and tampering with occupancy rights, were

[47] See, for example, S.B. Chaudhuri, *Civil Disturbances in India,* pp. 75–77; K.K. Sengupta, 'The Agrarian League of Pabna, 1873', *Indian Economic and Social History Review,* vol. 7, 1970, pp. 253–268.

[48] Tanika Sarkar, *Bengal 1928–1934: The Politics of Protest* (Delhi, 1987), p. 106, and *Communal and Pan-Islamic Trends in Colonial India,* pp. 302–319.

[49] Report by R. Nathan, Home Poll. A, F.No. 57–63, December 1907, NAI. Mymensingh was the largest district in the Bengal Presidency in terms of area and population. Nearly three quarters of its population (4,526,422, in 1911) were Muslims. F.A. Sachse, *Bengal District Gazetteer: Mymensingh* (Calcutta, 1917).

[50] Sugata Bose, 'The Roots of Communal Violence in Bengal: A Study of the Kishoreganj Riots, 1930', *Modern Asian Studies,* vol. 16, no. 3, 1982; Sumit Sarkar, *Swadeshi Movement,* pp. 444–449.

facts to be reckoned with. An added irritant was the *Ishwar Britti*. Muslims resented paying this subscription for the upkeep of Hindu idols. In 1907, therefore, rioting at Bakshiganj and Dewanganj began by an attack on the idol erected with the *Ishwar Britti*. This was the pattern in many places—the Kishoreganj subdivision, Pabna, Madaripur and Barisal.[51] 'Discontent always prevails', noted a peasant leader, amongst those who are exploited and the discontent finds vent in class struggles'.[52]

The root cause of the Moplah 'uprisings' in Malabar was economic. Descendants of Arab traders and of converts to Islam, the predominant Muslim peasantry had a long-standing grudge against the Namboodri landlords and Nayar moneylenders. Reduced to insecure tenancy, vulnerable to rack-renting and eviction at the hands of landlords who were sustained by British Indian courts, the Moplahs responded with a series of attacks on the landed castes which 'represented a continuation of the Mapilla challenge to the economic and social power of the upper castes'. These attacks were carried out as ritual acts in which the Moplahs sought martyrdom. Stephen Dale emphasizes that they were not just religious expressions of socio-economic grievances but on occasions the expression of religious drive alone. MacGregor, district collector of Malabar in the 1880s, placed the emphasis elsewhere, arguing that the 'outrages' had an agrarian basis and that 'fanaticism is merely the instrument through which the terrorism of the landed classes is aimed at'.[53] While arriving at similar conclusions in 1881, the Logan Commission proposed changes, which were never ever put into practice, in Malabar's land tenure to mitigate the long-standing plight of the Moplahs. As late as 1900, the region continued to suffer under an oppressive system of subinfeudation. South Malabar, in particular, earned the 'unenviable reputation of being the most rack-rented country on the face of this earth'.[54]

[51] Report by Nathan, op.cit.

[52] *Ganavani,* 28 April 1927, SNNR, Bengal; *Mussalman,* 2 August 1927.

[53] E. Thurston, *Castes and Tribes of Southern India* (Madras, 1909), vol. 4, p. 478.

[54] Quoted in Robert L. Hardgrave Jr., 'The Mapilla Rebellion, 1921:

IV

Sometimes agrarian discontent, as in eastern Bengal and Malabar, found expression in or derived sustenance from the forces of revivalism or fundamentalism, as it is called in recent decades.

There is no standard definition of what constitutes revivalism or fundamentalism. Yet, one can generally comment on its central role which is to modify or transform social, religious and cultural experiences in accordance with 'basic' and 'fundamental' religious tenets. In the second-half of the nineteenth century, stress was laid on the need to reform Indian Islam by purging it of Hindu customs and practices. Restoring the puritanical spirit of early Islam, i.e., the days of the Prophet and the four Khalifas, was thus the cry of the movements conducted in different regions by Shah Abdul Aziz and Haji Shariat Allah. With their grassroots connections and ashraf-jotedar patronage, they were instrumental in raising the levels of religious consciousness outside the well-established composite framework of religious discourse. Islamization, as Asim Roy has so ably demonstrated, became a major component of peasant consciousness.[55] This was equally true of the Meos in Mewat and the Malkanas in Agra district.

In the second-half of the twentieth century, a number of theological seminaries were established with a specific purpose—to reorganize the traditional system of education in order to meet the challenge of the West and of Hindu resurgence, such as the Arya Samaj in Punjab, to raise the levels of Islamic consciousness and to *redefine* the relationship of the Muslim community with others.[56] Their network was extensive and their ideological

---

Peasant Revolt in Malabar', *Modern Asian Studies,* vol. 2, 1, February 1977, p. 65.

[55] S. Abul Hasan Ali Nadwi, *Life and Mission of Maulana Mohammad Ilyas* (Lucknow, 2nd edn., 1983), chapters two and three.

[56] Among the principal movements which aimed either to defend the faith or to renew the pristine purity of Islam were the Ahmadiya movement in Punjab, founded by Mirza Ghulam Ahmad (1883–1908). Its aim was to revitalize the Islamic tradition and counter the polemical writings of Christian missionaries against Islam. The Ahmadiyas were also involved in a bitter and acrimonious debate with some Arya Samaj leaders. See S. Lavan, *The Ahmadiyah Movement: A History and Perspective* (Delhi, 1975).

cohesion was, as and when in evidence, impressive. Of course, the most important of these organizations were the reputed Firangi Mahal in Lucknow, the Dar al-ulum at Deoband and the Nadwat al-ulama in Lucknow. Besides, there was the Madrasa-i Aliya in Kanpur, the Anjuman-i Taleem, [57] the Anjuman-i Ittehad wa Taraqqi,[58] the Anjuman-i Islamia and the Anjuman-i Himayat-i Islam in Lahore,[59] and a chain of institutions run by the Barelwis. Their interests covered education, proselytization and countering the ideological assault of Christian missionaries and Arya Samaj propagandists.[60] But even in the pursuit of such diverse concerns, they altered, in varying degrees, the tenor of discourse, sharpened religious cleavages and stimulated among their followers the feeling of being separate and distinct from others. Islam became a tool for political manipulation, a kind of bogeyman conjured up by turns against the Hindus and Indian nationalism, just as it could be used for the goals of political and social conservatism. All sorts of popularizers of Islam never ceased to emphasize its collective mobilizing powers under the well-worn heading of *umma*.

Hindu revivalism expressed itself in several different ways,

[57] It was founded by Mohammad Shafi and Nawab Fateh Ali Khan Qizilbash in 1910. *Tribune,* 6 May 1911.

[58] Ibid., 30 April 1911.

[59] This was founded at Lahore in 1885. Its aim was to disseminate western learning along with religious education and to improve the 'social, moral and intellectual condition of the Muslims'. By 1905, the Anjuman had established a number of schools in different parts of the Punjab, including one in Lahore which had 1,582 students on the rolls. Its income also increased from Rs 758 in 1885 to Rs 1,10,546 in 1905. In 1910, a Provincial Muslim Educational Conference was organized under the auspices of the Anjuman and was attended by many leading Muslim politicians, including Fazli Husain, Ibid, 10 July 1906, 1 April 1910.

[60] The activities of some Arya Samaj leaders contributed greatly to the growth of communal tension in Punjab. In the 1880s, Pandit Lekh Ram (1858–1897), a devoted follower of Dayanand Saraswati (1824–1883), used his paper, *Arya Gazette,* as a vehicle for venting his wrath against Islam, particularly the Ahmadiyas. He was also the chief spokesman on the issues of cow-protection and the promotion of Hindi in government departments. See Lavan, *Ahmadiyah Movement,* pp. 76–82; Jones, *Arya Samaj,* pp. 149–51.

though its main contours were defined by the cow-protection agitation, the crusade for Hindi, and the *sangathan* of a caste-ridden society. From mid-1884 onwards, the Arya Samaj, the chief vehicle of social and religious transformation in Punjab,[61] sponsored and gradually came to perform ceremonies of readmission to Hinduism. Although individual reconversions had little impact on the general standing of Hindus in relation to other communities, they possessed great symbolic value. They offered hope and signified a new world in which Hindus could fight to maintain themselves and their religion.[62] Har Dayal, an exiled revolutionary, believed that India's future rested on Hindu *sangathan,* Hindu Raj and *shuddhi.* The *shuddhi* of the Muslims and Christians was required 'just as one removes foreign matter from the eye'.[63] He was reiterating the proclaimed ideals of All-India Shuddhi Sabha, established in 1909 by the Arya Samaj in Punjab.

Both Hindu and Muslim revivalist movements initially emerged as a reaction to Christian missionaries and the western system of education. Both assumed the infallibility of their religious beliefs and pinned their hopes in the revival of the idyllic past, when Islam or Hinduism flourished in its pure and pristine form. 'Islam', wrote the *Mohammadi* of Calcutta, 'will again raise its head, and, by dispelling the abhorrent darkness of trinity, scepticism and idolatry she will again illumine the whole world with her radiance'.[64] The Tabligh al-Jamaat had the same message. Its leader, Mohammad Ilyas, exhorted his followers to eschew politics altogether, concentrate on prayers (*ibaadat*), and on the dissemination of the message of Islam with the same spirit that characterized the activities of the Companions of the Prophet Mohammad.[65]

[61] There is considerable historical literature on the Arya Samaj. For example, Jones, *Arya Dharm;* J.T.F. Jordens, *Dayananda Saraswati: His Life and Ideas* (Delhi, 1978) and his biography of *Swami Shraddhananda: His Life and Causes* (Delhi, 1981). And the essays of Arvind Sharma and Kenneth Jones in Robert D. Baird (ed.), *Religion in Modern India* (Delhi, 2nd revised edn. 1989).

[62] Quoted in Emily Brown, *Har Dayal* (Tueson, 1975), pp. 233–34.

[63] See Jones, *Arya Dharm,* p. 231.

[64] *Mohammadi,* 11 February 1927, SNNR, Bengal.

[65] Nadwi, *Life and Mission of Maulana Mohammad Ilyas,* p.89.

Religion was not the only source of revivalism. In a society where the appropriation of separate symbols became a common feature, there was a tendency to elevate, through a conscious, selective process, *some* historical figures on a higher pedestal and to magnify the achievements of *certain* dynasties. There was thus a marked tendency to dwell on the glories of 'Muslim rule' and to harp on the contribution of medieval rulers. The *Hanafi* of Calcutta urged its readers to celebrate the conquests of Mohammad bin Qasim and Bakhtiyar Khalji 'to bring to mind the brilliant achievements attained by our forefathers'.[66]

Hindu revivalists, on the other hand, sought legitimacy by contrasting the oppressive character of medieval rule with the assimilative capacity of the Hindus, their record of tolerance and their rich religious and cultural heritage. Seeing no virtue in any of the medieval sultans, they idolized Prithvi Raj Chauhan, Rana Pratap and Shivaji, who was used by Tilak as a symbol for stimulating resurgent Maratha nationalism for resisting Muslim aggression.[67] In this way, a handful of petty, feudal chiefs with territorial ambitions were appropriated as symbols of both revivalism and nationalism.

The dominant images of the Muslim presence in major literary works of the nineteenth and twentieth centuries are concerned with the degradation of Hindus under 'Muslim rule'. The noted Hindi poet, Bharatendu Harishchandra (1850–1885), hailed the

[66] *Hanafi*, 21 February 1927 and *Dainik Soltan*, 21 February 1927, SNNR, Bengal.

[67] This view was encouraged by the writings of some British historians in the nineteenth and the first quarter of the twentieth centuries. Their aim was to emphasize that the British did more 'for the substantial benefit of the people than the 'despotic', 'intolerant' and 'cruel' medieval Sultans. Henry Elliot, one of the leading British historians of the medieval period, referred to 'the few glimpses we have, even among this single volume, of Hindus slain for disputing with Muhammadans, of general prohibitions against processions, worship and ablution, of other intolerant measures, of idols mutilated, of temples razed, of forcible conversions and marriages ...' His purpose, as he confessed frankly, was to make 'our native subjects more sensitive of the immense advantages' of British rule. See R. Thapar, H. Mukhia, B. Chandra, *Communalism and the Writing of Indian History* (Delhi, 1969).

supplanting of 'Muslim rule' by the British as the termination of centuries of oppression. He referred to the 'wounds in the heart' that were kept green by the sight of the mosque that stood besides the sacred temple of Vishwanath in Varanasi. In another poem, written in 1878, he talked of the Muslims who had taken away the religion, wealth and women of the Hindus.[68] Similar images figure in the works of Marathi writers like Gopal Hari Deshmukh (1823–1892), better known as Lokahitawadi, and Gopal Ganesh Agarkar (1856–1895). In the writings of Tilak there is use of the same images related to 'Muslim' domination as were common in the earlier periods. He, too, referred to the destruction of the Somnath temple by Mahmud of Ghazna, Timur's carnage, Aurangzeb's aggression in Maharashtra, and Ahmad Shah Abdali's raids.[69]

In nineteenth-century Bengali literature the Muslims were referred to under the contemptuous epithet of Yavana. The writings of Bankim Chandra Chatterji, 'positively and fiercely anti-Muslim', and of Romesh Chandra Dutt glorified 'Hindu' rebellion against the medieval Sultans and showed the Muslims in a correspondingly poor light.[70] The *Hanafi* made the point that writers like Bankim caricatured Muslims and depicted them as defilers of Hindu temples and destroyers of Hinduism. In this way, the paper added, the mind of the Hindus was being systematically 'vitiated' against the Muslims.[71]

Nirad C. Chaudhuri, who shares the Bengali bhadralok antipathy towards Islam and its followers,[72] pointed out that

[68] Sudhir Chandra, 'Communal Consciousness in Late 19th Century Hindi Literature', Hasan (ed.), *Communal and Pan-Islamic Trends*, pp. 180–195.

[69] B.G. Gokhale, 'Hindu Responses to the Muslim Presence in Maharashtra', Yohananan Friedman (ed.), *Islam in Asia: South Asia* (Jerusalem, 1984), vol. 1, pp. 162–65.

[70] The comment on Bankim is that of Nirad Chaudhuri, *The Autobiography of an Unknown Indian*, p. 226. And for an analysis of R.C. Dutt's writings, see Sudhir Chandra, 'The Lengthening Shadow: Secular and Communal Consciousness', in Bidyut Chakrabarty (ed.), *Secularism and Indian Polity* (Delhi, 1990).

[71] 12 December 1927, SNNR, Bengal.

[72] Notice Nirad Chaudhuri's observation that while living in Calcutta he

Bengali thinkers and reformers of modern India—from Ram Mohun Roy to Rabindranath Tagore—based their life-work on the formula of a synthesis, by which they understood a synthesis of Hindu and European currents. 'Islamic trends and consciousness did not touch even the arc of their consciousness'. Thus the new Indian culture of the nineteenth century

> built a perimeter of its own and put specifically Muslim influences and aspirations beyond the pale. In relation to it the Muslims stood outside as an external proletariat, and if the Muslims wanted to come into its world they could come only after giving up all their Islamic values and traditions.[73]

Again,

> nothing was more natural for us than to feel about the Muslims in the way we did. Even before we could read we had been told that the Muslims had once ruled and oppressed us, that they had spread their religion in India with the Koran in one hand and the sword in another, that the Muslim rulers had abducted our women, destroyed our temples, polluted our sacred places. As we grow older we read about the wars of the Rajputs, the Marathas, and the Sikhs against the Muslims, and of the intolerance and oppressions of Aurangzeb.[74]

Such sentiments were nurtured more easily in urban areas, which were the foci of revivalist activities. Towards the end of the nineteenth century, in particular, the growth of revivalism, both in its overt and latent forms, took place in cities and towns where cow-protection societies, Hindi Pracharini Sabhas, *tab-*

---

had 'an arrogant contempt for the Muslims and a deep-seated hostility towards them'. From the end of 1906–7, 'we became conscious of a new kind of hatred for the Muslims'. *The Autobiography*, pp. 227-28. In his latest book, too, the author writes in a similar strain. To quote his own words, he was 'strongly anti-Muslim in 1920' and was 'repelled' by the 'idea of living under Muslim social and cultural domination'. In his opinion, Indian Muslims constituted a society of their own with a distinctive culture and could not be absorbed in a unified Indian nation. For this reason, 'no historical argument was too false or too foolish to be trotted out by the Hindus to contest the demand of the Indian Muslims to have their own way of life'. *Thy Hand Great Anarch!*, pp. 38, 330.

[73] *The Autobiography*, pp. 227–28

[74] Ibid., p. 226.

ligh and *tanzim* anjumans and *shuddhi* and *sangathan* groups received material support from their rich patrons. It is, therefore, not surprising that communal riots in the mid-twenties took place with much greater intensity in urban rather than in rural areas.[75] The most serious outburst in UP occurred in Agra, Shahjahanpur and Saharanpur in 1923; at Allahabad and Lucknow in 1926; and at Bareilly, Kanpur and Dehradun in 1927. Calcutta had the largest share of riots in Bengal, while Multan, Lahore and Amritsar figured as rioting centres in Punjab. Western India was relatively quiet, except for some outbursts in Bombay, Pune and Sholapur. Hindu-Muslim relations in South India were generally cordial. The massive rioting in Malabar was more of an exception than a rule. So were the incidents of rioting in Madras city, Vellore and Bangalore.

It would thus seem that Hindu-Muslim riots in the twenties occurred mainly in the Indo-Gangetic belt. There were several reasons why this was so. First, the growth of newspapers in this region[76] and improved systems of travel and communication

[75] There appears to be a consensus on this point in the case of Bengal. It has been recently suggested that apart from localized violence in rural areas during the Swadeshi days, Hindu-Muslim rioting had been an urban phenomenon. Sugata Bose, 'The Roots of Communal Violence in Rural Bengal', op.cit., p.464.

[76] Both British-owned and Indian newspapers played a key part in keeping communal issues alive. The nationalist newspapers were no exception, for they, too, pandered to religious passions and prejudices, jumped on to the communal bandwagon and legitimized Hindu militancy or Muslim communalism. Yet they appeared in the garb of nationalism, justifying their position in terms which carried some measure of credibility. They could thus lend support to the Congress as well as the Hindu Mahasabha. Thus the *Amrita Bazar Patrika* made the distinction between the Congress as a political party with an all-India perspective and concerns, and the Hindu Mahasabha imbued with the mission to revitalize Hinduism and to turn it into 'a new living force, both defensive and even militant if necessary'. *Amrita Bazar Patrika*, 15, 17, 18, 19 August 1923 and editorial comments, 8 and 15 September 1923. Moonje's suggestion of organizing the lathi-wielding Hindus was endorsed by the paper, because 'the Hindus find themselves weak and emasculated, unable to defend their hearth and home, the sanctity of their temples and the honour of their women'. 4 January 1923 and 1 May 1927. Similar views were expressed in the columns of *Tribune*, 11 January

enabled men of religion and politics of all shades to reach out to a wider audience and influence their thinking and modes of expression. Secondly, the eruption of violence in certain areas was linked with two inter-related processes—the communalization of Indian politics, an aspect covered in the previous chapter of this book, and the levels of sectarian feelings generated by powerful currents of religious revivalism. It is noticeable that communal squabbles and controversies figured mostly in Bengal and in the heartland of Aryavarta which were also the strongholds of the Arya Samaj, cow-protection societies, *tabligh* and *tanzim* societies and *shuddhi* and *sangathan* sabhas.

The organizers of *tabligh* and *tanzim* groups defined their identity in explicitly religious terms and asserted their Muslimness through a neatly organized ideological campaign. They heightened the sense of community solidarity and religiosity by exhorting their followers to imbibe the letter and spirit of the Quran, follow the standards of an ideal life set by the Prophet and his Companions *(Ashaab)* and work towards the realization of an Islamic ideal. 'The real ailment of the Muslims', stated Maulana Mohammad Ilyas (1885–1944), chief architect of the *tabligh* movement, 'is that their hearts are devoid of religious consciousness and no eagerness is found in them for seeking the knowledge of Faith. If religious inclination and appreciation of the importance of the Faith is produced in their hearts, Islamism will be revived in them in no time'.[77] This was the inspiration behind the *tabligh* venture.

Tabligh groups had surfaced earlier. The Ahmadiyas, headquartered in Punjab, despatched preachers to thwart the aggressive designs of the Arya Samaj.[78] Murray T. Titus referred to the Jamiyat-i Tabligh al-Islam, with headquarters in Ambala, as a 'strong, growing organization of India-wide character', with

---

1923 and *Leader*, 2 January 1923. For role of the press in fanning the fires of communal animus, see Home Poll. and K.W. F.No. 236, 1926, NAI.

[77] S. Abul Hasan Ali Nadwi, *Life and Mission of Maulana Mohammad Ilyas*. Translated from Urdu by Asif Kidwai (Lucknow, 1983), p. 163.

[78] 'Note on the Tabligh Movement', p. 18, Home Poll. F.No. 6/IX, 1924, NAI.

provincial and district branches.[79] According to the claims of its founder, Syed Ghulam Bhik Nairang, 370 volunteers conducted extensive tours from 1923 to 1928, sponsored 16,000 meetings and converted or 'readmitted' 25,000 people to the Islamic fold.[80]

The Barelwis, with their large following among skilled workers and entrepreneurial groups, also took to *tabligh.* They worked amongst the Malkana Rajputs of Agra district who were converted and reconverted to Islam in rapid succession.[81] The Mazahir-i Ulum in Saharanpur, which in size and influence was second only to Deoband in the subcontinent, was not lacking in proselytical spirit.[82] In April 1923, a local Tabligh al-Islam was established at Aligarh.[83] And in Delhi, the sufi-politician, Hasan Nizami, produced pamphlets on *tabligh* and sought public subscriptions

[79] Murray T. Titus, *Indian Islam* (Delhi, 1979: reprint), p. 201.

[80] Besides, a newspaper, *Tabligh,* was started which came out until the end of 1925 and was resumed as a monthly journal in 1927. *Jamiyat-i Markaziya Tabligh-al Islam Ambala shehar ki satra saala khidmaat ka khulaasa.* (Organization of Tabligh, Ambala: Resume of its activities during the first seventeen years) (Ambala, 1940).

[81] In 1926 when the *shuddhi* and *tabligh* movements were at their height it was common for the Malkanas to be converted and reconverted to Hinduism in rapid succession. It was said that many of them made quite a lot of money out of their conversion and reconversion. *Census of India,* 1931, UP of Agra and Oudh (Allahabad, 1931), p. 499. It was amongst this group that the Barelwis carried out their missionary activity. At the All-India Sunni Conference at Moradabad on 17–19 March 1925, Syed Jamaat Ali Shah detailed some of the work done by the Barelwis and claimed much success for the Anjuman-i Khuddam Al-Sufia and the Ahl-i Sunnat al-Jamaat in establishing madrasas and mosques. While launching a blistering attack on the Ahmadiyas and the Deobandis, i.e., the 'Wahabis', and ruling out the possibility of uniting with them, the Shah called for religious reforms [*deeni islaah*], adherence [*taqlid*] to the fundamentals of Islam and rejection of un-Islamic practices [*rusoomat-i biddat*]. *Filbadiya Khutba-i Sadaarat* (Extempore Presidential Address) (Lahore, n.d.), pp. 15–16, 43–66.

[82] Metcalf, *Islamic Revival,* pp. 132–33.

[83] Its chief organizer was Kunwar Abdul Wahab Khan, who was himself a Muslim Rajput. He was associated with the Jamiyat-i Tabligh of Ambala. Home Poll. F.No. 6/ix, 1924.

for his project of translating the Quran in the Nagri script so as to make it accessible to the common people.[84]

Close to Hasan Nizami's headquarters and Nizamuddin Auliya's *dargah* in Nizamuddin east is the historic Banglewali masjid where Maulana Mohammad Ismail, a descendant of Shah Waliullah, had done the spadework for his son, Mohammad Ilyas, to launch an ideological assault in the region of Mewat in south-west Delhi, now in the state of Haryana. The area was inhabited by the Meos who, even after conversion, adhered to many of their 'Hindu' beliefs and retained their social customs. Some had purely Hindu names or tagged on *Khan* to a Hindu name. They celebrated Diwali, Dussehra and Janmashtami, the birthday of Krishna, and worshipped the *salar*, or banner, of one Salar Masud Ghazi, believed to be one of the generals of Sultan Mahmud of Ghazna. The Meos, like the Hindus, did not marry within the *gotra* and their daughters were not entitled to inherit.[85]

As a representative of the great Waliullahi tradition, Mohammad Ilyas was repelled by the distortions that had crept into the belief structures of the Meos. He launched a crusade against the 'unislamic' practices and sought to draw the Meos into the Islamic fold. He worked amongst the masses after his return to India in September 1925 and was the first Muslim reformer to conceive of an elaborate mass contact programme to spread the meaning of Quran and highlight the virtues of *salaat* (prayer). He established educational centres, founded charitable institutions, and, above all, organized *Jamaats* (groups). Its disciplined members, trained and tutored under a common roof, were fired with religious fervour and a missionary zeal. They travelled far and wide 'acquiring and imparting [of] Islamic knowledge, inviting the attention of the people towards Islamic practices, spreading the message of Allah, hymning his glory and sanctity and offering

[84] For example, *Tabligh Ishtihaaron ka Majmua* [Pamphlets on *Tabligh*] (Delhi, 1925); *Juma wa Idain ke Urdu Khutba at* [Urdu Sermons delivered at Friday prayers and on Id] (Delhi, 1926); *Dalail-i Islam* (Delhi, 1927).

[85] Mujeeb, *Indian Muslims*, pp. 10–11.

prayers and supplication at every step'.[86] The following description is useful :

> Anyone who saw the *Tabligh* parties of Mewat, travelling on foot, with blankets thrown on their shoulders, the *Siparaas* tucked under the arms and parched grain or bread tied in a corner of the mantle, their tongues engaged in *Zikr,* eyes showing the signs of nightly vigil and the mark of *Sajda* on the foreheads would have been reminded of the martyred Companions of the Bir Maona who were killed while going on the mission of teaching the Quran and imparting the knowledge of the commandments of the Shariat on the orders of the Holy Prophet.[87]

These men, formally constituted into the Tabligh al-Jamaat, were eulogized for their piety, simplicity, dedication and missionary spirit. Their impact was considerable, for they revived the faith by introducing the 'real' or 'true' spirit of Islam and translated into reality the Islamic ideal of Muslim brotherhood. Syed Abul Hasan Ali of Nadwat al-ulama reflects on the changes that took place in Mewat. 'Within a few years', he observes, 'the whole region emerged from darkness into light'. According to him,

> the gains of irreligiousness began to appear in Mewat which would not have, otherwise, been possible even after long years of struggle. Thousands of mosques were built where not one was to be seen for miles, and innumerable maktabs and Arabic madrasahs were established... A dislike for Hinduized garments was created and people began to dress themselves according to the specifications of the Shariat. Bracelets got removed from the arms and rings from the ears of men. Beards were grown freely and without compulsion. Polytheistic ceremonies that had become a part of marriage began to be discarded... Religious indifference and innovations and lewd and profane habits and customs started to wither away in the new climate of faith and piety.[88]

The *tanzim* societies, also started in the mid-twenties, could

[86] See Nadwi, op.cit., chapter four, and Maulana Wahiduddin Khan, *Tablighi Tehrik* (Delhi, 1985); C.W. Troll, 'Five Letters of Maulana Ilyas', in Troll (ed.), *Islam in India: Studies and Commentaries* (Delhi, 1985), vol. 2, pp. 138–150 for biographical details and the ideology behind *Tabligh.* Troll's account, however, is entirely based on Nadwi's work.

[87] Nadwi, op.cit., pp. 39–40.

[88] Ibid, p. 40.

not stake any such claims. Its founder was not a traditional *alim* but the Cambridge-educated graduate, Saifuddin Kitchlew, who rose to fame during the Rowlatt Satyagraha and was the principal mobilizer of the Khilafat cause in Punjab. Following his differences with the Congress and his rift with a section of the Khilafat leadership, Kitchlew outlined his *tanzim* scheme at the Belgaum Khilafat Conference in December 1924 and at a Muslim meeting in Amritsar in July 1925. He proposed the formation of Muslim *jathas* [volunteer corps], establishment of primary schools in mosques, Muslim banks, co-operative societies and technical institutes and the proper utilization of the incomes from *auqaf* for the educational and economic progress of the Muslim community.[89] He started a newspaper called *Tanzim*, formed the Jamiyat-i Tanzim and secured the support of a mixed group of journalists, publicists and a few *ulama*. They included Malik Barkat Ali of Lahore, Jalib Dehlawi, editor of the Lucknow paper *Hamdam*, Choudhry Afzal Haq, leader of the Ahrars, Maulana Mazharuddin, editor of the Delhi paper, *Al-Amaan*, Zafar Ali Khan, editor of *Zamindar*, Maulana Abdul Majid of Budaun, Raja Ghazanfar Ali Khan and Mohammad Shafi.[90]

Though launched amid much fanfare, Saifuddin Kitchlew's various projects failed to take off. The *ulama* were the first to raise the banner of revolt. They had weakened the *tabligh* movement through their constant ideological bickerings and were now set to undermine Kitchlew's grandiose plans. The Faridkot-born leader was an 'outsider' and his reformist aspirations could not be legitimized by men of religion, i.e., the *ulama*. More importantly, his scheme to control mosques and *auqafs* posed a serious threat to their own authority, an encroachment on their own sphere of influence. Many Barelwi *ulama* were closely tied to Punjab's *pirs* and to shrine-based structures of

[89] Toufique Kitchlew, *Saifuddin Kitchlew: Hero of Jallianwala Bagh* (National Book Trust: Delhi, 1987) pp. 51–52. Some of Kitchlew's ideas, such as the setting up of co-operative societies, stores and mortgage banks, were incorporated in a resolution adopted by the Muslim League in December 1925. Pirzada (ed.), *Foundations of Pakistan*, vol.2, pp. 73–74.

[90] *Jamiyat-i Markazia Tanzim ka Dastur al-Amal* [Constitution of the Organization for Tanzim] (Amritsar, 1925), pp. 15–16.

mediation. To organize a scheme like Kitchlew's, a network of local organization independent of the structures of imperial influence, proved extremely difficult.[91] The Muslim League president lamented in 1926:

It is a pity that the *Tanzim* has not made the progress that was expected of it, because people are not sufficiently trained to appreciate quiet and solid work and because Dr Kitchlew has been practically single-handed in his efforts. And many of those who were enthusiastic about him when he was advocating the process of revolution left his side when he began to press evolution.[91a]

The protagonists of *shuddhi* and *sangathan* conducted a more effective and ideologically cohesive campaign. Founded by Pandit Bhoj Dutt Sharma in 1907, *shuddhi* sabhas functioned under the aegis of several socio-religious organizations in northern India and could thus count on the existing networks to reach out to a wider audience. Their initial success was facilitated by the Kshatriya Upakarini Sabha, the movement for interclan unity among the Rajputs, and the association of Rampal Singh and Raja Durga Narayan Singh of Tirwa.[92] In 1907, the Rajputs in Agra division flocked to the *shuddhi* sabhas and the Arya Samaj in an attempt to reconvert the Muslim Rajputs.[93] In the wake of the Moplah riots, they gained more recruits. Chief among them was Shraddhanand, who was mainly responsibile for reconverting

[91] Gilmartin, *Empire and Islam*, p. 82; Page, *Prelude to Partition*, pp. 101–104; Thursby, *Hindu-Muslim Relations*. pp. 153–54, 171. Following was the government's assessment:

The organization...as the word Tanzim signifies, is full of potentialities, but it is still in its infancy and unless some new pretext is found to excite public feeling against the Government, it is not likely to be a source of danger to the Government at the present time. If perfected, it is capable of being directed against both the Government as well as the Hindus, as it may suit the needs of the organizer.
Home Poll. F. No. 6/ix, 1925, NAI.

[91a] Pirzada (ed.), *Foundations of Pakistan*, vol. 2, p. 91.

[92] R. Gordon, 'The Hindu Mahasabha and the Indian National Congress 1915 to 1926', *Modern Asian Studies*, vol. 9, 2, April 1975, p. 172.

[93] The society claimed to have converted 1,052 Muslim Rajputs from 1907 to 1910. Lajpat Rai, *History of the Arya Samaj*, p. 121.

many of the Malkana Rajputs and for bringing in eighty-four 'non-Hindu villages' into the Hindu fold.[94] When the *shuddhi* campaign was officially included in the programme of the All-India Hindu Mahasabha in August 1923, it had the unqualified backing of leading Congress stalwarts, such as Malaviya, Lajpat Rai and Moonje.[95]

Moonje was described by the *Mahratta* as a 'staunch Hindu, committed to restoring Hinduism in its proper place'.[96] As Tilak's lieutenant in the Central Provinces, he popularized Ganapati and Shivaji festivals and organized the first Kirtan Conference. As a leading swarajist in the Central Provinces, he spearheaded the *sangathan* movement—the panacea for the ills of the Hindus and the perfect answer to ward off Muslim 'aggression' in Malabar, Kohat and Multan.[97] 'I am glad to tell you', he informed one of his friends, 'that I have been able to organize the Hindus of Nagpur for self-defence. It was a sight for Gods to see when well-built Hindus about 5,000 strong with big lathis in their hands paraded the streets of Nagpur.... I am sure you will be delighted to hear of the Hindu sangathan of Nagpur which is of a purely defensive character'.[98]

Moonje's basic concern was to revive martial traditions so that Hindus could confront a 'bully and savagely aggressive' Muslim community on equal terms. He told a group of Maharashtrians that young Maratha men must always remember

> their national and historical peculiarity which consisted in fighting the Muslims to success. I cannot contemplate a situation with equanimity where along with others even the Maratha youngmen are broken down to submission by Muslims. Therefore I said taste should be cultivated in young men of Maharashtra for wrestling and lathi plays so that they may as readily come out in streets with lathis in hand as Muslim goondas.[99]

[94] *Forward*, 6 January 1927.

[95] For the views of Lajpat Rai, see *Tribune*, 13 December 1924.

[96] Quoted in R.I. Cashman, *The Myth of the Lokamanya: Tilak and Mass Politics in Maharashtra* (California University Press, 1975), p. 189.

[97] 18 December 1923, Moonje Dossier (19), Moonje Papers, National Library, Calcutta.

[98] Ibid.

[99] 20 April 1926, Diary (1).

The Nagpur-based eye surgeon had a two-fold mission: to liberate the country from British rule and to bring some sense into the 'rowdy' and aggressive Muslims. In this respect, the fight for swaraj 'was merely a continuation of the struggle initiated by Prithviraj Chauhan when the Hindu Raj, culture and religion was first assailed under the Mughal impact'.[100] It was no good harping on non-violence as a political creed, for Gandhi's philosophy of Ahimsa had caused 'irreparable' harm to the Hindus alone. Moonje declared:

> In one word I have been saying to Gandhi's followers that I consider my mission in life now to do everything possible so that the teachings of love and Ahimsa, of which we have been saturated since Buddha's and Jaina's time, may not take root at least in Maharashtra... I believe [Gandhi's] philosophy will lead to destruction and extermination of the Hindus from the face of world.[101]

To convince Hindus of the validity of his position and beliefs, Moonje reached out to many sections of society. He appealed to the Raja of Darbhanga and the landlords in the region to recruit their tenantry from the 'martial races'—the Gurkhas, Rajputs and Marathas.[102] He approached and secured the patronage of wealthy Bhatias and other Hindu merchants in Bombay.[103] Such veteran politicians like Khaparde, Kelkar and Jayakar were already playing to his tune in the region. The Amils of Sind, anxious to thwart the Muslim League demand to separate Sind from Bombay Presidency, hitched their fortunes with the Moonje bandwagon. Moonje also secured a footing in Bengal, where he was anxious to 'rouse the latent Hindu mentality'.[104] He even established contact with Rabindranath Tagore, who, according to Moonje's version, approved of his ideas and his rabidly communal Patna speech. The poet is reported to have told Moonje that 'all those bitterness between the Hindus and Muslims is the result of the bungling of Gandhi and [that] he had warned him in time'. Moonje asked Tagore to issue a message to

[100] 3 May 1926, ibid.
[101] 13 July 1926, ibid.
[102] 18 July 1926, ibid.
[103] To Jayakar, 2 June 1925, Jayakar Papers (405).
[104] 17 February 1927, Diary (2).

the Hindus on the occasion of the Shivaji festival. 'It may, I said, inspire the young men of Bengal to come out to carry on the mission of the Hindu Sabha in Bengal. He replied in a way which appeared to be hopeful'.[105]

Such antagonism towards the Muslims, though not generally shared by his swarajist colleagues, was indicative of an ideological strand in the nationalist movement which could be curbed through a sustained ideological campaign and not by setting up peace committees and drawing up paper pacts. The Congress leadership, in general, settled for a soft option by accommodating the various cross-currents even if they undermined its principles and avowed goals. This is further evident from the way in which some of the key Congress figures were allowed to occupy prominent positions in the Hindu Mahasabha and disseminate its pronounced anti-Muslim ideology.

Founded in 1915 to safeguard the 'separate and distinct interests of the Hindu community', the Mahasabha lent a common platform to orthodox groups, patronized by rich bankers, landowners and professional men. The executive committee of the UP Hindu Sabha contained twelve lawyers, three zamindars who were also lawyers, and six commercial and landed magnates. They belonged to the large trading centres, with extensive linkages in local bodies and provincial organizations.[106] In Bihar,

[105] 28 April 1927, Diary (1). Tagore did not require much persuasion, for he had already expressed himself in favour of unity among Hindus 'to counteract the mentality which engenderd fanatical outrages [such as Shraddhanand's murder] and riots'. *Forward*, 29 December 1927.

[106] While the All-India Hindu Mahasabha was founded in April 1915, provincial Hindu Sabhas were already active in Punjab and Bihar since 1907, and at UP since 1914. CP and Berar, Bombay and Bengal had their branches in 1923–24 and Sind in 1926. It is significant, however, that outside UP, Punjab and Central Provinces, the Mahasabha had limited support. It was strongest in the Central Provinces, where as an immigrant community the Brahmins in 1924 and 1925 rallied round it in preference to the Congress as a means of counteracting the non-Brahman movement which was wresting control of local bodies. See Home Poll. F. Nos. 25 and 112, 1924, 1925, NAI. The history of the Sabhas and their activities are covered in: Kenneth W. Jones, 'Politicized Hinduism: The Ideology and Program of the Hindu Mahasabha', Baird (ed.), *Religion in Modern India*, pp. 239–74; and for

the Hindu Sabha was founded by the Maharaja of Darbhanga in 1907 and popularized by two leading lawyers—Parmeshwar and Sachidanand Sinha.[107] In Punjab, the Sabha comprised of, among others, the Lahore bankers and traders, journalists like Gulshan Rai, landowners like Raja Narendranath, and all-India politicians like Lajpat Rai.

The spate of protest meetings against the Lucknow Pact gave impetus to the Hindu Mahasabha. Its prestige was further enhanced soon after the Non-Co-operation movement came to a halt. Spirits were high at the Hindu Mahasabha conference in December 1922, which was held in the Congress pandal at Gaya. A 'Hindu Relief Committee' and the Hindu Raksha Mandal were launched.[108] In August 1923 the Mahasabha listed the *shuddhi* campaign on its agenda. This lent a more specifically religious emphasis to its platform. From now on *shuddhi* was to be conducted by the Mahasabha as well as the All-India Shuddhi Sabha, attached to the Arya Samaj.

The man who occupied a pivotal position in reviving the Mahasabha and in pushing through the *shuddhi* resolution was Madan Mohan Malaviya. His position was of truly special importance, for he had been a key figure in Congress politics since 1886 and exercized a profound influence on Hindu revivalism in UP. His achievements were impressive. He founded one of India's most well-known English dailies—the *Leader*—and also a Hindi newspaper—*Abhyudaya*. He conceived and carried out, with remarkable tenacity and devotion, the project of a Hindu university at Banaras. He was a protagonist of Hindi and the protection of the cow. As the chief ideologue of

background information, see Walder K. Andersen and Shridhar D. Damle, *The Brotherhood in Saffron: The Rashtriya Swayamsevak Sangh and Hindu Revivalism* (Delhi, 1987).

[107] J.S. Jha, 'An Unpublished Correspondence relating to the Bihar Hindu Sabha', *Journal of the Bihar Research Society*, January-December 1968, pp. 339–44.

[108] Among the members were Malaviya, Raja Rampal Singh, Lala Hansraj, Shraddhanand, Khaparde, C. Vijayaraghavachariar, former Congress president, S. Satyamurti, Kelkar, Moonje, Jamnalal Bajaj and K. Natrajan, editor of *Indian Social Reformer*. See Gordon, 'The Hindu Mahasabha', pp. 168–69.

Hindu resurgence and revivalism and as patron of the Prayag Hindu Samaj, the Sanatan Dharm Mahasammelan and the UP Hindu Sabha, Malaviya developed wide-ranging linkages with rulers of princely states, prosperous landowners, commercial magnates and professional men. It was on the strength of their support that he built his political base. He proved that there was no contemporary politician in Allahabad who could match his enthusiasm for the causes associated with Hinduism, his astuteness and his immense organizing capacity. He was a master tactician, adept in the art of political temporizing.

In his address to the Hindu Sabha meet in Gaya, Malaviya dwelt on his community's 'disintegration' and the need to arrest the process through the Hindu Mahasabha.[109] At his behest, *shuddhi*, too, became an integral component of the Mahasabha programme. In December 1925, he urged his audience at Kanpur to establish local branches of the Hindu Sabhas and *akharas* in every village, and thus bring about complete *sangathan*.[110] Following the Mahasabha's decision to contest the provincial elections in November 1926, he used communal slogans against his arch swarajist rivals, especially Motilal Nehru, and incited communal unrest, particularly in Allahabad.[111] 'The real reason', noted a government report, 'why Hindu-Muslim relations are worse in Allahabad is because of Malaviya family and their followers, who constitute the Hindu Sabha. This body with its doctrine of *sangathan* has aroused an aggressive spirit, which has spread into the small towns and villages'.[112] This was not all. A

[110] He stated in his presidential address at the Mahasabha session in Varanasi: 'Friendship could exist only between equals. If the Hindus made themselves strong and the rowdy section among the Muslims could not rob or dishonour Hindus, Hindu-Muslim unity would be established on a stable basis'. *Leader,* 22 August 1923.

[111] 'Note on the Activities of Malaviya', Home Poll. F.No. 187, 1926, NAI. See, Pandey, *The Ascendancy of the Congress,* 119–20, and Page, *Prelude to Partition,* pp. 127–28.

[112] Ibid. And 'Note by Alexander Muddiman', 21 September, F.No. 368, 1925, NAI, for the role of Malaviya's family.

correspondent from Bijnor reported that Malaviya and Bhai Parmanand were busy trying to 'create and fan the communal fire among the electorate'.[113]

Motilal's endeavours to keep the Swaraj party firm against the communal blitzkrieg were thwarted; such was the communal hatred aroused that he considered retiring from public life. During the election campaign he was berated for his anti-Hindu views and pro-Muslim proclivities. Word was spread that he was in league with the Muslims to legalize cow-slaughter.[114]

The election results in UP marked the triumph of the communal forces, headed by Malaviya and financed by G.D. Birla.[115] The swarajists, despite having made concessions to communal sentiments, fought on a non-communal plank but were reduced in size—from 31 in 1923 to 16 members in 1926. The erosion of their base among Muslims was substantial.[116] Not only was their enthusiasm for the Swaraj party dwindling but they were slowly but steadily drifting towards organized communalist formations.

V

British officials, in general, attributed Hindu-Muslim animus to the reforms of 1919. The growing antipathy, observed the governor of Bengal, 'was one of the fruits of the Reforms'.[117] This view is echoed, though with sophistication and scholarly rigour, in the writings of Francis Robinson, G.R. Thursby, David Page and

[113] F.No. 21 (part 2), 1926, AICC Papers, NMML.

[114] Motilal Nehru to Jawaharlal, 2 December 1926, *A Bunch of Old Letters* (Delhi, 1958), pp. 51–52.

[115] In the elections Swami Shraddhanand openly canvassed for Birla, 'one of those very few persons who were eager to do as much as they could for every good cause and in the interest of Hindus particularly'. Shraddhanand, quoted in Jordens, *Swami Shraddhananda*, p. 166. Motilal referred to the 'Malaviya-Lala gang' which was being aided by Birla's money to capture the Congress.

[116] See Page, op.cit., pp. 136–38.

[117] Lytton, *Pundits and Elephants*, pp. 165–66; J. Coatman, *India in 1926–27* (Calcutta, 1928), p. 19; R. Coupland, *The Indian Problem, 1833–1935* (Oxford, 1942).

Ian Talbot.[118] Page was among the first historians to detail the profoundly divisive effects of the Montagu-Chelmsford Reforms. Communal antagonism, he argued, became a 'permanent feature' of provincial politics, political interests began to be consolidated around communal issues, and 'Muslim attitudes' were formed towards the emergence of provincial autonomy and towards the eventual withdrawal of imperial control.[119]

The nationalists analyzed communalism in terms of either the 'one mighty economic force' which divided people 'horizontally into two homogeneous parts' or as a fall-out of government policy which stoked the fires of communal unrest through a collusion with feudal, semi-feudal and reactionary elements.[120] They were able to show how 'British governments in the past and the present have based their policy on creating divisions in our ranks',[121] nursed sectional groups and their leaders, and rewarded them with seats in legislatures, high-sounding titles and honours. Communalism was an acceptable corrective to nationalist zeal provided it did not lead to a community's alienation from government or to political chaos from which the opponents of the raj might benefit.[122]

[118] Thursby, *Hindu-Muslim Relations,* pp. 134–35; Page, op.cit., 260. Talbot is of the view that British officials were 'anxious to limit communal violence rather than to risk encouraging it by dividing and ruling'. *Punjab and the Raj,* p. 4. Francis Robinson maintains that while British policy *played* the main part in establishing a separate Muslim identity in Indian politics and contributed to the development of Muslim separatism, it was not *intended* to do so. The fact was that the British feared the Muslims and sought to pacify them through special concessions. These were aimed not at setting Muslims against Hindus, but at reconciling them to British rule. Robinson concludes: 'There was no deliberate attempt to foster communal hostility; indeed the aim was to avoid it'. *Separatism Among Muslims,* pp. 131–32, 348–49.

[119] Page, op.cit., p. 259.

[120] This was M.N. Roy's classic formulation. Among other writers who endorsed this view were: K.B. Krishna, *The Problem of Minorities or Communal Representation in India* (London, 1939), and Asoka Mehta and Achyut Patwardhan, *The Communal Triangle in India* (Allahabad, 1942).

[121] Jawaharlal Nehru's speech at the Brussells Congress, 10 February 1927, *Selected Works of Jawaharlal Nehru,* vol. 2, p. 275.

[122] Page, op.cit., p. 91.

It is evident from the large mass of archival material that the raj was unabashedly partisan in pitting one community against the other to serve its imperial interests.[123] When repressive measures failed, as in the early 1920s, hopes were pinned 'upon the eternity of the communal situation'. Clandestine means were employed to organize Muslim opposition. This policy was pursued during the civil disobedience movement. Muslims were told to conduct local campaigns, itinerant preachers were financed by the UP government, and Shaukat Ali was pressed into service to revive the *tanzim* movement.[124] 'We have even gone so far', wrote Hailey, 'as to pay from Secret Service Funds the travelling expenses of some...preachers. It is our intention to watch [the] progress [of *tanzim*], and so long as its activity is directed mainly towards countering civil disobedience, to continue to give it moral support'.[125]

In Bengal, the divide and rule policy was put into operation to break the stranglehold of the swarajists and to draw a wedge amongst its supporters. An attempt to sow the seeds of dissension was first made in March 1924, when a Muslim councillor from Malda sought to corner Das by insisting on the implementation of certain provisions of the Bengal pact. Das was able to foil the move. Then, when the demand for ministerial salaries was rejected, Lytton and his aides made much of the fact that the two ministers—Fazlul Haq and A.K. Ghuznavi—were Muslims. The vote of the official and non-official blocs in the council was thrown in to prop up the shaky ministries, who were built up as an effective political counterforce.[126]

The situation in Punjab was different. The presence of well-entrenched landed and commercial classes and their anxiety to be accommodated in the constitutional structures imposed constraints on the administration's options in augmenting its support base. It was easy to play up one sectional group against

[123] For Bengal, see Broomfield, *Elite Conflict*, p. 272; Rajat Ray, *Social Conflict and Political Unrest*, pp. 354–56; Tanika Sarkar, *Bengal*, p. 105.

[124] Hailey to Irwin, 9 June 1930, F. No. 18 (B), Hailey Papers.

[125] Hailey to J. Crerar. Home Member, 25 September 1930, F.No. 19 (B), Hailey Papers.

[126] Broomfield, op.cit., pp. 252–62; Rajat Ray, op. cit., pp. 352–55.

the other and to take advantage of the controversies which beleagured Fazli Husain's ministry. But this strategy could only be partially successful in Punjab, where the lines of cleavages were not always defined in purely communal terms. So, besides inducting communally-oriented groups into positions of power, Edward Maclagan and his successor, Malcolm Hailey, relied heavily upon the 'agriculturists' and their chosen leaders—Fazli Husain, Chhotu Ram and Lal Chand—against the urban-based trading and commercial classes.

Hailey did not undervalue Muslim support but warned against making wholesale concessions in their favour. When it became clear that the swarajists were losing ground and that the body politic was being divided along communal lines, he started wooing the urban Hindus with political concessions to hold 'the balance between the parties'.[127] 'To have carried on with the old arrangement', he observed, 'would have meant that the Hindu party as such was to be permanently excluded; it would have driven them back on opposition and ultimately to swaraj'.[128] This rethinking on Hailey's part adversely affected the fortunes of the Unionists, especially its Muslim constituents. The Registration of Moneylenders Bill was vetoed and the passage of the Land Revenue [Amendment] Bill was obstructed. Fazli Husain's wings were also clipped. While he was relegated to the reserved half of the government, his arch-critic Manohar Lal occupied the ministerial berth. In this way, Hailey divided ministerial offices among the communities and thereby divided the legislative council into communal blocs.[129]

The ministerial reshuffle achieved its immediate goal of encouraging the urban Hindus to turn more whole-heartedly to government and curbing the political ambitions of Fazli Husain and his allies. Hailey commented on its outcome in more general terms and indicated the drift of his policies. 'In the political world', he informed the viceroy,

[127] See Page, op.cit., p. 91.

[128] Hailey to Alexander Muddiman, January 1927, F. No. 10 (A), Hailey Papers.

[129] Azim Husain, *Fazli Husain*, p. 161.

the balance between Muhammadans on the one hand and Sikhs and Hindus on the other created a situation which, if on occasions led to communal troubles embarrassing the government, on the other placed government in a strong situation as holding the balance between the parties. As a consequence, the politically-minded Hindus found themselves unable to maintain a consistent opposition to government and, at all events, during the last three years came definitely to the view that they would have to depend on government if they were to maintain their position vis-a-vis the Muslims.[130]

Hailey was an old hand. He played his cards well. Yet, he was obliged in the last resort to throw his weight behind the Muslim bloc. And when he moved from Lahore to Lucknow, he soon turned into a spokesman of 'Muslim interests'.[131] He advised the viceroy on Muslim representation at the Round Table Conference, sought explicit assurances on the preservation of 'Muslim rights' and insisted on an official pronouncement on the communal question. He believed, as did many of his British contemporaries, that if the decision was 'moderately satisfactory to Muslims', it would be possible to keep the 'great mass of moderate Muslims on our side, and there would be far less tendency on their part to drift into opposition to Government'.[132] Any amount of sophisticated jugglery could not obscure the sinister design behind Hailey's advocacy.

[130] Hailey to Irwin, 16 October 1928, F.No. 14 (A), Hailey Papers.
[131] Page, op.cit., 92–93.
[132] Hailey to viceroy, 7 April 1932, F.No. 23 (B), Hailey Papers.

Chapter Nine

Illusions of Insecurity: The Nehru Report

Some of the issues which polarized political opinion in India came to the fore in 1928 when the All-Parties Conference, stung by Birkenhead's challenge, met to draw up a constitution—one that would represent a consensus as well as reflect the fears and aspirations of variegated groups and parties. Was India to adopt a unitary or a federal model? What will be the position of minorities in either system? Would they be entitled to 'safeguards', such as separate electorates and community-wise representation? If so, were seats to be distributed according to the Lucknow Pact or the newly-formulated Delhi Proposals of March 1927?[1]

The Nehru Committee Report—the swan song of the Congress—faced some of these issues and suggested ways of giving the 'finishing kick to communalism'. But its recommendations, as was predicted, evoked angry protests, generated heated debates, and created fissures in the Congress. This chapter seeks to understand why this was so and suggests new ways of looking at the communal controversies that raged during the years 1927 to 1929. In doing so, the first step is to take note of the Delhi Proposals, which haunted the leading lights at All-Parties meetings.

[1] *Hindustan Times* [20 May 1928] summed up the problems: 'When one thinks of the numerous differences, political as well as communal, that separate the various parties in the country, one is almost overwhelmed with a feeling of despair. Dominion Status or independence, music before mosques, cow-slaughter, separation of Sind, joint electorates or separate electorates, reform for the Frontier Province, representation of minorities in the legislature and services, are all baffling problems, and have, each one of them, proved a stumbling block in the way of the success of past conferences'.

II

Thirty prominent Muslims congregated in Delhi on a common platform to surrender their long-cherished preference for separate electorates. But their offer was conditional. They insisted on the acceptance of four proposals—Muslim representation in the Bengal and Punjab legislative councils in proportion to their population; one-third of reserved Muslim seats in the central legislature; creation of Sind as an independent province; and introduction of reforms in the North-West Frontier Province. 'It is for the other party', stated Mohammad Yaqub, a participant at the Delhi meet, 'to clasp the hand of friendship which the Muslims have extended'.[2]

Predictably, there was reluctance in certain quarters to 'clasp the hand of friendship'. The Provincial Congress Committees in Maharashtra and Berar shared this reluctance.[3] So did Congressmen loyal to the Hindu Mahasabha. Backed by the 'nationalist' press, they denounced the Delhi offer at the AICC meeting on 5 May. But the views of the Nehrus, Srinivasa Iyengar and the Congress Muslims prevailed. Jayakar was won over. Lajpat Rai and Malaviya were silenced for the time being by Motilal Nehru. With Gandhi's backing, he secured the AICC's acquiescence of the Delhi Proposals.[4] 'The Congress', wrote an indignant newspaper editor, 'has become a handmaid of Motilal Nehru and the sole function of the AICC is to register his decrees. It was therefore a foregone conclusion that his views in the matter would prevail'.[5]

Spirited opposition to the Delhi Proposals and to their endorsement by the Congress coincided, much to everybody's relief, with a momentous development—the appointment of an all-British Statutory Commission on 8 November 1927.

[2] To M.C. Chagla, 20 March 1927, M.C. Chagla Papers, NMML.

[3] *Leader*, 9 and 10 April 1927; *Mahratta*, 10 April 1927.

[4] See Mushirul Hasan, 'The Communal Divide: A Study of the Delhi Proposals', in Hasan (ed.), *Communal and Pan-Islamic Trends*, pp. 289–91.

[5] *Surya*, 4 June 1927, SNNR, UP; Moonje to M.R. Jayakar, 10 June 1927, M.R. Jayakar Papers; *Basumati*, 9 May 1927; *Hitavada*, 10 June 1927; SNNR, Bengal.

Archbold, who had served under Minto and was the prime organizer of the 1906 Simla Deputation, had warned Birkenkead only two days earlier that 'there will be no end of a row in India'.[6] He was right, because the composition of the Simon Commission—'an awful political blunder'[7]—was widely denounced in India. It could not have been otherwise. 'Jallianwala Bagh was a physical butchery, the Simon Commission is a butchery of our souls', declared an indignant Jinnah.[8] Sapru, the Liberal leader, was enraged. The Simon Commission, he said, 'must start its work with the very serious handicap that it will not carry with it Indian confidence and support'.[9] Declared Ansari, the Congress president: 'We can have no part or lot in a Commission which has been appointed in direct defiance of the declared will of the people', a line that brought an approving roar from the public in the Congress pandal.[10] The Madras Congress, therefore, voted to boycott the Commission, proclaimed independence as its goal and resolved to draft India's future constitution. The All-India Khilafat Conference, the Jamiyat al-ulama and the Muslim League took their cue from the Congress and adopted the same course of action.

Birkenhead's challenge could be met only if the various political combinations put their heads together to sustain the boycott of the Simon Commission.[11] As Congress president, Ansari gave the lead, appealing for unity and the sinking of differences.[12]

[6] 6 November 1927, L/PO/6/32, IOLR.

[7] Archbold to Hailey, 29 January 1930, ibid.

[8] Quoted in Wolpert, *Jinnah of Pakistan,* p. 91.

[9] *Pioneer Mail,* 24 June 1927, L/PO/100 (iii), IOLR. In his note, John Simon noticed that even the 'Responsivists' went helter skelter into the swarajist camp. 'It is the adherence of these moderate politicians to the policy of boycott which has been the unexpected and disturbing element in the Indian parliamentary situation'. Baldwin Papers, vol. 102, University Library, Cambridge.

[10] Hasan, *A Nationalist Conscience,* pp. 164–65.

[11] 1 December 1927, Hasan (ed.), *Muslims and the Congress,* p. 24.

[12] Notice the comment: 'Now that the talk of boycotting the Simon Commission is swaying the public mind, it is high time for the advanced Hindus to come to an understanding with the Muslims'. *Soltan,* SNNR, Bengal.

The response was impressive. Some leading Khilafatists, estranged from the Congress for one reason or the other, buried their differences and responded to Ansari's pleadings.[13] Jinnah, too, was moved. 'For [to] me, this offer is more valuable than any concession which the British government can make. Let us then grasp the hand of fellowship. This is indeed a bright day; and for achieving this unity, thanks are due to Lord Birkenhead'.[14]

Jinnah had spoken too soon, for bitter feuds and seemingly endless wranglings marred the All-Parties Conference in February 1928. After ten days of it, the strain was so great for Jawaharlal Nehru that he 'fled to avoid riot and insurrection'.[15] When he returned to the conference table, he was 'thoroughly fed up' by 'extremists' on either side—Jinnah, Mohamed Ali and Hasrat Mohani on one side and Lajpat Rai, Moonje and Jairamdas Daulatram, on the other.[16] The deadlock was over the future of Sind.[17] This was expected, for the Hindu Mahasabha's position was well publicized on the eve of the conference. Their intransigence over reservation of Muslim seats in the Punjab and Bengal councils was also known. What irked Jinnah and his group was that Motilal, having pushed through the Delhi Proposal at the AICC meeting, was now soft-pedalling on reservation of seats for Muslims in Bengal and Punjab. Incensed by Motilal's *volte face,* the Muslim League stayed away from the rest of the deliberations.[18] The

[13] Hasan, *A Nationalist Conscience,* pp. 162–64.

[14] Jinnah took the initiative to convene an all-parties conference so as to evolve 'a policy of common and concerted action' to meet the challenge posed by the Statutory Commission. He stressed that 'the principle and the policy underlying the exclusion of Indians from the Commission are proved to be more objectionable than ever'. To Mohamed Ali, 30 November 1927, Mohamed Ali Papers, Jamia Millia Islamia, reproduced in Hasan, *Mohamed Ali: Ideology and Politics,* p. 157.

[15] To Gandhi, 23 February 1928, *Selected Works of Jawaharlal Nehru (SWJN),* vol. 3, p. 36.

[16] To Syed Mahmud, 17 March 1928, ibid., p. 37.

[17] See Hasan, 'The Communal Divide', op. cit., pp. 282–86.

[18] Rejecting the invitation to attend the conference, Mohammad Yaqub stated: 'The strength of opposition on the part of these (Hindu Mahasabha) cannot be overlooked and it seems nearly impossible to obtain support of majority organizations to a reasonable plan providing safeguards for all interests'. *Hindustan Times,* 16 May 1928.

Mahasabha went a step further: its Jabalpur meeting in April rejected the Delhi Proposals. There was, thus, not even a remote chance of a reconciliation. The younger Nehru told the Congress Working Committee:

> It is too much to be hoped that these conflicting viewpoints will be able to accommodate themselves and will agree to a common formula. We are therefore to prepare ourselves for this conflict and to decide on our course of action.[19]

So they did. After the failure of the February and May meetings, the Nehrus, backed by Ansari, Sapru, Annie Besant and Iyengar, garnered their forces to overcome opposition. Some sort of consensus was pushed through—one that was 'neither complete nor of the genuine type but something we can stand for both in All-Parties Conference and the country at large'.[19a] A committee was put together to draw up India's future constitution.[20]

III

The deliberations and decisions of the committee bore the stamp of two of its members—Motilal and Sapru. The Mahatma paid his compliments to Motilal, 'without whose effort there would have been no Committee, there would have been no unanimity, and there would have been no report.'[20a] Irwin, the viceroy, referred to the report as the 'Nehru-Sapru constitution'.[21]

Motilal Nehru and Tej Bahadur Sapru had much in common. Both were lawyers of distinction in Allahabad. Both were Kashmiri Pandits, having grown up in an 'Indo-Persian cultural atmosphere' which was the legacy of the Mughal court in north

[19] 3 May 1928, *SWJN*, vol. 3, p. 38.

[19a] Motilal Nehru to Gandhi, 11 June 1928, F.No G/1, Motilal Nehru Papers, NMML. All future references, unless otherwise stated, are drawn from the same file.

[20] Of the ten members of the committee, Jayakar conveyed his inability to serve on it, N.M. Joshi did not show up at a single meeting, while Ali Imam and G.R. Pradhan attended just a few meetings. Motilal to Gandhi, 27 June 1928, Motilal Nehru Papers.

[20a] *CWMG*, vol. 21, p. 212; Bose, *Collected Works*, p. 165.

[21] Irwin to Birkenhead, 6 September 1928, Irwin Papers, MSS. EUR. C 152/4, IOLR.

India. They were proficient in Persian and Urdu and enjoyed reading and reciting the poetry of Shaikh Sadi, Hafiz Shirazi, Maulana Jalaluddin Rum, Mir Taqi Mir and Ghalib. Motilal's first teacher was Kazi Sadruddin, an oriental scholar attached to the princely court of Khetri. 'In the days of my boyhood', recalled Motilal, 'my earliest impressions were received at the feet of Muslim professors and teachers and the more than half a century that has since elapsed has not in the least blunted the effect which those first impressions produced upon my young mind'.[22] Sapru had a similar background. He was unmoved by the language controversy and remained a consistent protagonist of Urdu, the language which symbolized the composite and syncretic culture of north India.[23] The *Kashmiri Darpan,* published from 1903 to 1906, was an Urdu monthly. 'Let not the language in which Atash, Insha, Wazir...wrote', he stated, 'be despised; let it not persish or even languish....Cultivate the language and develop it'.[24]

In public affairs, Motilal and Sapru evinced a breadth of vision and freedom from a sectarian approach. Secular and broad-minded in their outlook and approach, they wanted to separate religion from politics. Both were uncomfortable with Gandhi's emphasis on religion and spirituality and only reluctantly did Motilal endorse his support to the Khilafat cause. Religion, according to the elder Nehru, signified bigotry, intolerance and narrow-mindedness. Its association with politics, he observed at the Calcutta Congress in 1928, 'has been to the good of neither. Religion has been degraded and politics has sunk into the mire. Complete divorce of one from the other is the only remedy'.[25] This was the thinking which went into the making of the Nehru report.

[22] *Legislative Assembly Debates*, February 1924, vol. 4, 14, p. 784.

[23] Sapru stated: 'I believe the growth of Urdu in the seventeenth and eighteenth century was a natural sequence of comingling of the Hindus and Muslims in north India. It toned down differences and enabled the Hindus to understand the Muslims and the Muslims to understand the Hindus'. Quoted in Sender, *The Kashmiri Pandits*, p. 252. And Sapru's speeches on Urdu in *Hamaari Qaumi Zabaan* (Delhi, 1941).

[24] K.N. Raina (ed.), *Welding the Nation: Academic Addresses and Selected Writings* (Bombay, 1974), p. 13.

[25] *Congress Presidential Addresses, 1911-1934* (New Series), p. 864.

The communal phenomena was an anathema to these stalwarts of Allahabad, a threat to their vision of a secular society. Yet, they recognized the need for an equitable settlement of inter-communal claims. Such was the political climate created by the raj that it was no longer possible to ignore the demands of minorities—the Muslims and the Sikhs in Punjab. Even though Motilal was not directly involved in the negotiations which led to the Lucknow Pact, there is evidence to suggest that the wider agreement between Hindus and Muslims, 'of which the Lucknow Pact was a part,....[was] hammered out at a meeting' in Anand Bhawan in Allahabad.[26]

Motilal and Sapru pronounced separate electorates as a pernicious principle in public life. But there was no doing away with it. Motilal stated in the UP legislative council:

> Over a question like this my motto is peace at any price....Whatever my personal views on the merits of the question may be, there is no doubt that, practically speaking, we cannot be preaching those principles, keep off the actual separate representation of Muhammadans for any length of time. It must come. It has come already in the elections to the Councils and it must go on and filter down to....the lowest rungs of the ladder of public life.'[27]

Sapru also recognized separate electorates as a 'necessary evil'. Participating in the debate on the UP Municipalities Bill, he said:

> Unfortunately we do not live in a world of perfection, every day of our life we realize the imperfections of our surroundings and we realize that compromise is of the very essence of politics...Having regard to the circumstances which exist at present, the only solution lies in providing separate representation to the Muslim community. Separate representation ...is a necessary evil in our present social and political condition.[28]

These were not popular views; in fact, Motilal and Sapru were

[26] B.R. Nanda, *Gokhale, Gandhi and the Nehrus: Studies in Indian Nationalism* (London, 1974), p. 126.

[27] *Proceedings of the United Provinces Legislative Council, 1916. The United Provinces Municipalities Bill, 1915* (henceforth *Proceedings*), p. 227.

[28] Ibid., p. 218

castigated then and later as *Addhu* [half] Mussalmans and accused of 'selling out' Hindu interests. Sapru came to be distrusted by his own Liberal colleagues, including C.Y.. Chintamani and Srinivasa Sastri.[29] 'I have never been looked upon as a good Hindu in any sense of the term', Sapru lamented in August 1932.[30] Motilal was denounced by the 'Malaviya-Lala gang' for his pro-Muslim proclivities. The communalists, aided by Birla money, ganged up against him in the 1926 election campaign.[31] They included Shraddhanand, the high priest of the *shuddhi* movement, who canvassed for men like Birla, 'one of those very few persons who were eager to do as much as they could for every good cause and in the interest of Hindus particularly'.[32] With such forces arrayed against him, Motilal fretted and fumed, and felt that his voice 'will be a cry in the wilderness'. Not quite so. The All-Parties Conference gave him opportunity to have his say.

IV

The Nehru Committee Report, published on 15 August 1928, covered a variety of constitutional issues—an exercise never ever attempted by any representative body in India. A case was made out for dominion status,[33] much to the annoyance of

[29] V.S. Srinivasan to D.V. Gundappa, 15 December 1930, in Jagadisan (ed.), *Letters of Srinivasa Sastri*, p. 203.

[30] Sapru to E. Thompson, 22 August 1932, Sapru Papers, vol. 37, p. 113, National Library, Calcutta.

[31] This was the year, i.e., July 1926, when Motilal and Sapru took the lead in forming the 'Indian National Union', which aimed at creating a 'national consciousness and a national atmosphere in which religious and communal conflicts will be relegated to a subordinate plane'. Other members of the Union were Abul Kalam Azad, Srinivasa Sastri, Hakim Ajmal Khan, Sarojini Naidu and the Raja of Mahmudabad. *Indian Quarterly Register* (henceforth *IQR*), 1926, vol. 2, pp. 90–95.

[32] See f.n. 115, chapter 8 above.

[33] There was an obvious difference in the nationalist and colonial perceptions of dominion status. In an interesting note in the Baldwin Papers it was stated: 'When an Englishman speaks of Dominion Status, he means a constitutional state enjoyed within the Empire by a political entity over which the His Majesty's Government retains no right of supervisory

Jawaharlal Nehru and Bose.[34] Three chapters tried to come to grips with Hindu-Muslim discord. The final recommendations, which bore the impress of considerable labour and thought, dwelt on reservation of seats, form of electorate, and the future status of Sind and the North-West Frontier Province. Also incorporated was a Declaration of Rights guaranteeing religious liberty and cultural autonomy. This was done to 'prevent the harassment and exploitation of any individual and group by another'.[35]

The Committee agreed to Sind's separation from Bombay and its elevation, in company with the North-West Frontier Province, to the status of an independent province. M.S. Aney and Mangal Singh acquiesced grudgingly.[36] But they had the satisfaction of securing a major gain—the rejection of the demand, incorporated in the Delhi Proposals, for reservations in Bengal and Punjab.[37]

---

interference'. Indians, however, were not so much concerned with the *achieved constitutional state* as they were with the 'indeafeasible assurance of such achievement. They were keen to fashion a constitution which would contain within itself the seed of full Dominion Status, growing naturally to its full development in accordance with the particular circumstances of India'. Thus, 'what is to the Englishmen an accomplished process, is to the Indian rather a declaration of right, from which future and complete enjoyment of Dominion privilege will spring'. Baldwin Papers, vol. 103.

[34] Sarvepalli Gopal, *Jawaharlal Nehru: A Biography* (Delhi, 1975), vol. 2, p. 121; Bose, *Collected Works*, p. 169.

[35] *All-Parties Conference 1928: Report of the Committee Appointed by the Conference to determine the Principles of the Constitution for India* (henceforth *All-Parties Conference)* (Allahabad, 1928), p. 29.

[36] Motilal to Gandhi, 27 June 1928, Motilal Nehru Papers.

[37] Jawaharlal Nehru was one of the signatories to the AICC resolution against reservation of seats. See *SWJN*, vol. 3, p. 52. Shuaib Qureshi, however, argued that the Muslim population in Bengal and Punjab should be reflected in the legislatures. In his minute of dissent, he referred to the Congress resolutions passed at Bombay and Madras in May and December 1927 and asked: 'Is it open to Congress to denounce an agreement while the other party to it, the League, stands by it and specially when it has driven one section of it out of its fold on that particular issue? I maintain that it is too late in the day for political explorers to equip expeditions to pick holes in the agreement'. See Page, *Prelude to Partition*, pp. 171–172, and Motilal to members of the All-Parties Conference Committee, 20 July 1927, Hasan

A laboured exercise by Jawaharlal and Bose convinced the authors of the report that Muslims in those provinces did not require any 'adventitious aid' or 'artificial protection'.[38] Such was their distribution of population [Table 9:1] that they were sure of securing effective representation in councils and local bodies.[39] Election results of the Bengal district board were marshalled to lend weight to the argument [Table 9:2].

Muslim candidates did well in elections, even though the electorate was mixed and electoral rolls were based on property or tax-paying qualifications. They won all the seats in Mymensingh[40] and Chittagong districts and fifteen of the sixteen seats in Jessore.[41] Elsewhere, they often managed to bag seats in excess to their population. So, the fear, based on the superior economic and educational standards of the Hindus, was largely imaginary. 'We have seen', observed the report, 'that this superiority has not helped the Hindus of Bengal at the District Board elections and we are sure that the result of Council elections will be even more strikingly in favour of Muslims', especially if they forged electoral alliances with the Congress and with regional parties.[42]

Punjab was no different. Here, as in Bengal, adult suffrage would have a levelling effect and the minorities in both the provinces would cease to have an advantage in voting registers.[43]

The Nehru report identified three natural belts or areas in Punjab: the predominantly Muslim area, the neutral area but

(ed.), *Muslims and the Congress*, pp. 58–62. The circular reflects the serious differences over the principle of reserving seats for the 'majorities' and 'minorities'.

[38] Jawaharlal to Syed Mahmud, 30 June 1928, *SWJN*, p. 51. Bose claimed that 'the greatest achievement of the Nehru Committee was the settlement of the question of Hindu-Muslim-Sikh representation in the Legislatures under the proposed Constitution'. *Collected Works*, p. 167.

[39] Sharif al Mujahid has argued that the conclusions drawn from the aggregate figures are misleading. 'Jinnah and the Congress Party', in D.A. Low (ed.), *The Indian National Congress: Centenary Hindsights* (Delhi, 1988), pp. 221–222.

[40] Bose to Motilal, 12 July 1928, F.No. 2, AICC Papers.

[41] *All-Parties Conference*, p. 47.

[42] Ibid., p. 48.

[43] For a different view, see Mujahid, op. cit., p. 222.

TABLE 9:1

Hindu and Muslim populations in Bengal, 1931

District		Population	Hindu	Per cent.	Muslim	Per cent.
Burdwan	...	15,75,699	12,38,872	78%	2,92,471	19%
Birbhum	...	9,47,554	6,36,425	67%	2,52,908	27%
Bankura	...	11,11,721	10,11,654	91%	51,012	5%
Midnapur	...	27,99,093	24,92,989	89%	2,12,473	8%
Hooghly	...	11,14,255	9,24,061	83%	1,80,217	16%
Howrah	...	10,98,874	8,60,448	78%	2,33,608	21%
24-Parganas	...	27,13,874	17,42,387	65%	9,13,233	34%
Calcutta	...	11,96,734	8,22,293	69%	3,11,155	26%
Nadia	...	15,29,632	5,74,046	38%	9,44,915	62%
Murshidabad	...	13,70,677	5,89,551	43%	7,61,582	56%
Jessore	...	16,71,164	6,34,230	38%	10,35,371	62%
Khulna	...	16,26,148	8,16,620	50%	8,04,909	50%
Rajshahi	...	14,29,018	3,26,018	23%	10,83,105	76%
Dinajpur	...	17,55,432	7,93,832	45%	8,86,723	51%
Jalpaiguri	...	9,83,357	6,64,015	68%	2,35,951	24%
Darjeeling	...	3,19,635	2,36,913	74%	8,391	3%
Rangpur	...	25,94,785	7,46,546	28%	18,36,840	71%
Bogra	...	10,86,419	1,77,629	17%	9,05,638	83%
Pabna	...	14,45,654	3,32,367	23%	11,11,712	77%
Malda	...	10,53,766	4,44,406	43%	5,71,943	54%
Dacca	...	34,32,577	11,24,893	33%	22,93,396	67%
Mymensingh	...	51,30,262	11,74,328	23%	39,27,552	77%
Faridpur	...	23,62,215	8,47,064	36%	15,07,157	64%
Bakarganj	...	29,39,050	8,12,585	27%	21,05,184	72%
Tippera	...	31,09,735	7,50,724	24%	23,56,609	76%
Noakhali	...	17,06,719	3,66,391	22%	13,39,055	78%
Chittagong	...	17,97,038	3,92,352	22%	13,26,208	74%
DIVISIONS						
Burdwan	...	86,47,189	71,64,741	83%	12,22,779	14%
Presidency	...	1,01,08,229	51,79,117	51%	47,71,165	47%
Rajshahi	...	1,06,68,066	29,27,896	27%	57,60,580	54%
Dacca	...	1,38,64,104	39,58,870	21%	98,33,289	71%
Chittagong	...	68,26,414	15,46,243	23%	50,30,088	74%

• Excluding Cooch Bihar State, Chittagong H.T. and Tripura State.

Source: Issued by R.G. Ghose, 148, Manicktolla Street, Calcutta.

TABLE 9:2

Statement about elected members of the District Boards in Bengal, 1927-8

Districts	Total no. of seats	No. of Hindu members	No. of Muslim members
24 Parganas	20	16(64.2)	4(34.6)
Bogra	15	4(16.6)	11(82.5)
Bakarganj	20	5(28.7)	15(70.6)
Midnapur	22	1(88.2)	1(6.8)
Rajshahi	18	7(21.3)	11(76.6)
Rangpur	18	7(31.5)	11(68.1)
Khulna	16	11(50.0)	5(49.8)
Hooghly	20	17(81.9)	3(16.0)
Mymensingh	22	Nil(24.3)	22(74.9)
Pabna	16	3(24.1)	13(75.8)
Noakhali	16	6(22.3)	10(77.6)
Jalpaiguri	16	14(50.0)	2(24.8)
Tippera	19	13(25.8)	6(74.1)
Nadia	20	15(39.1)	5(60.2)
Burdwan	16	14(78.0)	2(18.5)
Murshidabad	15	7(45.1)	8(53.6)
Faridpur	20	8(36.3)	12(63.5)
Malda	15	8(40.6)	7(51.6)
Howrah	12	10(79.3)	2(20.3)
Birbhum	16	15(68.1)	1(25.1)
Bankura	10	9(86.3)	1(4.6)
Jessore	16	1(38.2)	15(61.7)
Dacca	22	16(34.2)	6(65.4)
Chittagong	20	Nil(22.6)	20(72.8)
Dinajpur	18	4(44.1)	14(49.1)

N.B. The figures given in brackets are ratios to the total population.
Source: *All-Parties Conference*, appendix c, pp. 154-5.

with a Muslim majority, and the Hindu-Sikh area. In the north and north-west, no other community could encroach on the 'Muslim reserve'.[44] In the 'Hindu-Sikh area' in the south the two communities were evenly matched.[45] Between these two zones there was a third area where Muslims were predominant, such as Lahore and Gurdaspur districts, though not so in the north and north-west. The inference drawn was that while Muslims would capture 47.3 per cent of the legislative council seats from the 'overwhelmingly Muslim zone', the Hindus and Sikhs would jointly capture nearly 30 per cent. The remaining seats lay in either a predominantly Muslim area or in zones where Muslims were numerically strong. 'Allowing for every contingency', ran the report, 'we cannot conceive of Muslims not capturing enough seats in this area to give them a clear majority in the provincial legislature.[46]

All this made some sense. At least, Muslim groups in Bengal and Punjab thought so. By September 1928, 'barring a few die-hards of the Shafi school, the great bulk of the Mussalmans' had given their nod to the Nehru report.[47] Ansari, whose role in the All-Parties Conference was generously commended by Gandhi and others, was jubilant. The Punjab Khilafatists, led by Saifuddin Kitchlew and Zafar Ali Khan[48] and supported by Sardar Habibullah Khan, deputy-president of the council, and Mohammad Alam Khan,[49] leader of the Nationalist Party, 'have almost overwhelmed the forces of reaction'.[50] The picture was

[44] The districts included in the overwhelmingly Muslim zone were: Gujrat (86.2%), Shahpur (82.8%), Jhelum (99.7%), Rawalpindi (82.6%), Attock (90.9%), Miawali (86.3%), Montgomery (71.8%), Lyallpur (60.8%), Jhang (83.3%), Multan (82.6%), Muzaffargarh (86.8%), Dera Ghazi Khan (88.3%), Sialkot (61.9%), Gujranwala (71.9%) and Sheikpura (63.3%). Figures given in brackets are ratios to the total population.

[45] This zone included the districts of Hissar, Rohtak, Gurgaon, Karnal, Ambala, Shimla, Kangra, Hoshiarpur and Ludhiana.

[46] *All-Parties Conference*, pp. 44–5.

[47] Motilal to Annie Besant, 30 September 1928, *Bunch of Old Letters*, p. 65.

[48] He introduced the resolution in support of the Nehru report at the Delhi Provincial Conference in October 1928. *IQR*, 1928, vol. 2, p. 437.

[49] *Tribune*, 21 and 28 August 1928.

[50] Ansari to Motilal, 19 September 1928, F. No. 105, supplementary, AICC Papers.

no different in Bengal, where Azad was deputed to canvas support for the report. The Bengal Provincial League and the Khilafat Committee were satisfied, particularly after their bitter experience with the Lucknow Pact which had disregarded the interests of their constituents with contempt.[51] So was Abdur Rahim, once a vocal advocate of separate electorates. Rejection of the report, he said, would be a 'political blunder'.[52]

Motilal's spirits were bolstered notwithstanding the powerful dissent, led by his own son, over dominion status. With Bengal and Punjab in his pocket he had no fear from other quarters, who were to be 'easily settled by throwing a few crumbs here and there'. This was sheer arrogance. More was to follow. The UP Muslims need to be told, he wrote to Gandhi who had kept aloof from the All-Parties Conference and had refrained from expressing his views on the Nehru report, that their co-religionists in Bengal and Punjab 'do not need the other provinces to champion their cause'.[53] The storm in UP was brewing when Motilal wrote these lines.

The anger in UP was because the Nehru report postulated the ideal of dominion status. Hasrat Mohani did not approve of it.[54] A unitary central government was also an anathema, because the Muslim League demand was for a decentralized federal government in which residuary powers would be vested in the component provinces.[55] What irked political activists most was that the Nehru report proposed the abolition of separate electorates, discarded weightages and did not agree to reserving one-third of the seats in the legislature for Muslims. Shuaib

[51] *Mussalman*, 2 October 1928; *Khadem*, 22 August 1928; *Mohammadi*, 23 August 1928; *Soltan*, 7 September 1928; SNNR, Bengal.

[52] *IQR*, 1928, vol.2, p. 148. In the resolution moved in the Bengal legislative council, Rahim dropped both communal electorates and reservation of seats and voted against Fazlul Haq's amendment for separate electorates. Motilal to Jinnah, 2 August 1928, Pirzada (ed.), *The Collected Works of Quaid–e–Azam Mohammad Ali Jinnah*, vol. 3, p. 302.

[53] 24 November 1928, Motilal Nehru Papers.

[54] Hasrat had stated his position in 1924 when he announced that the 'real Muslim feeling is for independence'. *Hindustan Times*, 14 November 1924.

[55] *IQR*, vol. 2, p. 404; *Haqiqat, Sada-i Muslim, Mansur, Mashriq, Aligarh Mail*, for the week ending 8 and 15 September, 1928, SNNR, UP.

Qureshi protested but was silenced. The principle of weightage, so argued his detractors, had no place in joint or mixed electorates. The report observed:

> It is of course not physically impossible to reserve a larger proportion of seats for Muslim minorities than their population would justify, but, apart from the obvious injustice of such a course not only to the majorities but to the minorities as well, it will in our opinion be harmful to the development of Muslims themselves on national lines. We have allowed them their full share on the population basis by reservation and anything over and above that share they must win by their own effort. We do not propose to impose any restrictions on their right to contest a larger number of seats than those reserved for them.[56]

Mohamed Ali was not convinced and declared angrily:

> You make compromises in your constitution, with false doctrines, immoral conceptions and wrong ideas, but you make no compromises with our communalists—with separate electorates and reserve seats. Twenty-five per cent is our proportion of the population and yet you will not give us 33 per cent in the Assembly. You are a Jew, a bania.[57]

Equally powerful was his indictment of joint electorates. He and others assumed that non-Muslim voters in most constituencies would hardly ever vote for Muslim candidates. Such was the mutual antipathy that separate electorates had become vital to 'our political existence as our experience... has convinced us that Muslims will disappear from all legislative bodies unless separate electorates is guaranteed to us'.[58]

Equally emphatic was the plea for weightage, which was justified in terms of the 'historical and political importance' of the UP Muslims and was accepted by the Lucknow Pact.[59] Without weightage, Hindus would establish a 'legalized tyranny of

[56] *All-Parties Conference*, p. 52.

[57] Speech at the All-India Khilafat Conference, Calcutta, 25 December 1928, *IQR*, vol. 2, p. 403.

[58] 'Memorandum submitted by the Muslims of the United Provinces', *Indian Statutory Commission: Selection from Memoranda and Oral Evidence by Non-Officials* (henceforth *ISC*), vol. 6, part 1, p. 338.

[59] *Representation of the Muslims of the UP to the Indian Statutory Commission* (Allahabad, 1928), p. 172. Also, H.A. Haroon, *The Constitution of the Future Commonwealth and the Rights of the Muslim Minority: A Representation* (Karachi, 1928).

numbers' and usher in a 'Brahmin or Kayasth domination'.[60] This was an exaggerated fear and did not quite reflect the objective position of certain segments of Muslim society in UP.

Those Muslims who chose to be in government employment had little cause to complain, for they invariably held on to their position because the government secured, either by a rule or by convention, a proportion of Muslims. This was fixed at 30 per cent. For instance, one-third of the vacancies filled by competitive examinations in the Civil Service [Executive] were reserved for Muslims. Similarly, under the rules regulating appointments to the Police Service, the Governor-in-Council was empowered to announce, with a view to preventing the preponderance of any community, vacancies reserved for particular communities. This power was often used to favour Muslims. The bias in their favour extended to the Subordinate Revenue Service: it was laid down that not less than two Muslims would be appointed for every five Hindus. In the Subordinate Educational Service, on the other hand, 30 per cent of the appointments were, by convention, reserved for Muslims.[61] The result of this preference is reflected in Table 9:3, which sets out the proportion of Hindus and Muslims in some services.

TABLE 9.3

Proportion of Hindus and Muslims Appointed to certain Services, 1918-23

Name of Service	Hindus	Muslims
Listed Posts of Collectors	—	1
Deputy Collectors	75	55
Tahsildars	87	87
Naib-tahsildars	104	73
Inspectors of Police	25	32
Sub-Inspectors of Police	333	238
Registrars of Cooperatives	37	23

Source: *Proceedings of the UP Legislative Council, February and March 1923*, vols. 12 and 14, p. 30 and p. 420.

[60] Mohamed Ali, quoted in R.A. Jafri (ed.), *Nigarishaat-i Mohamed Ali* (Hyderabad, 1944), vol. 2, p. 23; 'Representation of the Muslims', p. 149; *Moslem Outlook*, 19 August 1928.

[61] Note by T. Sloan; 10 December 1928, *ISC*, vol. 6, part 1, pp. 346–47.

Figures on representation to elected local bodies tell the same story. In 1925-26, one-fourth of the 1,408 elected district board members were Muslims.[62] In March 1928, 66 out of 240 members of Notified Area Committees[63] were Muslims.[64] So were 391 out of 935 members of municipal boards. Likewise, 30 per cent of those who served on the legislative council were Muslims. This was in addition to those nominated by the government. The Nehru Committee was right in arguing that Muslims stood to gain under its proposed arrangement, because in several urban towns they were in a majority while in others they were a strong and influential minority.[65] But several Muslim groups in UP pointed out that, as a minority in every district, they would not have a chance of winning a 'fair proportion' of seats with joint electorates. Even if the electoral unit was smaller than the district, they would still not fare any better, because in districts where Muslims were most numerous, such as Budaun and Moradabad, their proportion in rural areas was so low that they had no chance of gaining seats in a system of straight voting with mixed electorates.[66]

Government servants and landowners had their own reasons to join the anti-Nehru report bandwagon. Having gained their position in the councils either through nomination or through separate electorates, their strategy was to work in close co-operation

[62] *Report*, UP., vol. 2, p. 231.

[63] The Municipalities Act of 1900 for the first time recognized non-municipal urban areas as distinct units of local self-government. They were designated 'notified areas' and their status was, with many important reservations, modelled on that of municipalities. The question whether a town would be set up as a notified area was decided on a combination of factors—population, industrial development, importance for commerce, or as junctions for railways or roads. By 1928, UP had 54 notified areas, and each notified area committee consisted of four elected and one nominated member. Ibid., p. 224.

[64] Brass, *Religion and Politics*, p. 172.

[65] Muslims were in a majority in fourteen municipalities, including Deoband, Najibabad, Bijnor, Chandpur, Saharanpur, Moradabad, Budaun, Sambhal and Amroha. The large towns in which they formed nearly 50 per cent of the population were Meerut, Aligarh, Bareilly and Lucknow. For district-wise distribution of Muslim population, see Robinson, *Separatism*, pp. 12–13.

[66] For details, see *Report*, UP, vol. 3, pp. 6–7.

with the government and press for the retention of separate electorates. When a Muslim Conference agreed to forego separate electorates in March 1927, these legislators were the first to protest. Joint electorates, they said in one voice, were detrimental to the 'political advancement of the Muslim community'.[67] This was another way of saying that their own prospect of getting elected was endangered. There was another danger. Adult suffrage, in effect, meant the disappearance of reserved seats and the enfranchisement of over fifteen million voters, mainly tenants. The landlords, therefore, faced the prospect of being ousted from general constituencies as well. Hailey informed John Simon:

> Curiously enough, the Nehru Committee's Report is likely to work in our favour for the landowners are not unnaturally perturbed at the prospect of adult suffrage and the abolition of reserve seats they now hold.[68]

In November 1928, these concerns were voiced in a memorandum submitted to the Statutory Commission by Nawab Jamshed Ali Khan, president, Muzaffarnagar Zamindar Association, Munshi Ihtisham Ali, president, UP Muslim League, and the Raja of Jahangirabad, an affluent landlord of Barabanki.[69] They claimed to speak on behalf of the 'Muslims of the United Provinces', though they were primarily concerned to defend their own class interests. That is why they opposed all forms of self-governing schemes and were aggrieved that the Nehru report proposed the abolition of the nominated elements and of special constituencies. They appealed to their British patrons to incorporate separate electorates and weightage in their recommendations and added a few more demands to appear more representative. These were: effective Muslim representation on all autonomous institutions created by legislatures, safeguards for Urdu and for the exercise of religious rights, and an adequate share in services.

The All-Parties Muslim Conference was more emphatic in its

[67] *Leader*, 29, 30 March and 11 May 1927, and *Searchlight*, 3, 8 April, 1927.
[68] Hailey to Simon, 28 August 1928, F. No. 13–B, Hailey Papers.
[69] *ISC*, vol. 6, part 1, pp. 338–39.

preference for a federal system, with complete autonomy and residuary powers in the constituent provinces. In fact, the Conference served as a platform through which organized Muslim political opinion was expressed in the early nineteen-thirties.

The Ali Brothers were not just the principal spokesmen of the Muslim Conference but were most vocal in the cacophony of protest orchestrated against the Nehru report.[70] They were angry that the Congress, having accepted the Delhi offer, now advanced certain propositions which would make their community subservient everywhere. Its leaders, complained the Ali Brothers, buckled under pressure from the Hindu Mahasabha. Wrote Shaukat Ali:

> I know the present Hindu mentality well. They do not want our friendship; they want our allegiance and God-willing, they will never get that. For any honourable peace and pact we are always ready but not for the slavery of the Hindus; just as we do want to remain slaves of the English....It is no good to exasperate us. Our record is there now, and the future will show how we serve Islam and the motherland.[71]

The impetuous Shaukat was forthright in his condemnation of Ansari, indicting him for his 'blind adherence to Motilal Nehru and other Hindus' and accusing him of 'betraying' his community. He charged:

> Non-co-operation was ruined by these people, chances for Hindu-Muslim friendship have been throttled.. ., Swaraj Party dismembered and now you see what is being done to kill the Congress, which has ceased to be National now. It has become an adjunct of the Hindu Mahasabha and will soon be a seeker of favours at the door of the English.[72]

Again,

> It is you [Ansari] who has changed while the Central Khilafat Committee and I stand where we were, not in a spirit of obstinacy but because we consider that Motilal and his Committee have intentionally or uninten-

[70] I have discussed their angry response to the Nehru report in *Mohamed Ali: Ideology and Politics*, pp. 94–101, and *A Nationalist Conscience*, pp. 170-74.

[71] To Ansari, 19 May 1929, Hasan (ed.), *Muslims and the Congress*, p. 70.

[72] Ibid.

tionally treated the Muslim point of view with undeserved contempt.... It is so easy to play the generous liberal-minded patriot at the expense of one's own people. For the time being it pays and gains the applause and I congratulate Azad on the part he played in the affair.[73]

These words were matched by an aggressive campaign, launched by the Ali Brothers in the company of Haji Abdullah Haroon of Sind and Maulvi Shafi Daudi of Bihar. But their efforts were rewarded in Bombay alone. Bihar, Bengal and Punjab did not waver in their commitment to the Nehru report. In UP, too, the Muslim League was divided. This became evident when the Raja of Mahmudabad, an enthusiastic supporter of the Nehru report, trounced Mohamed Ali, the hero of the Khilafat days, in the contest for the League presidency. Mohamed Ali's unexpected defeat may well be interpreted as a verdict against his political stance.

It was hard to swallow this bitter pill. So, towards the end of December 1928, the Ali Brothers made a desperate bid to turn the table on their opponents. In co-operation with Shafi Daudi, they disrupted meetings of the All-India Khilafat Committee and the Central Khilafat Committee and adopted dilatory tactics. They were noisy and abrasive, with the senior Ali— Shaukat— hurling abuses at his detractors. Amid the pandemonium, a group of Khilafatists, led by Tasadduq Ahmad Khan Sherwani, Mohammad Alam and Maulvi Mujibur Rahman, resigned from the executive committee. Over forty signatories condemned the 'methods of obstruction and procrastination adopted by the representatives of the other party'. They met separately to endorse the Nehru report and boycotted the Khilafat Conference which met under Mohamed Ali's presidentship.[74]

The Khilafat Conference turned out to be a tame affair. The Ali Brothers were humbled. The splintered factions they had united were in complete disarray after the Calcutta meeting. They sought refuge in the All-Parties Muslim Conference, a command performance initiated by the redoubtable Aga Khan.

[73] 6 September, F. No. 105, AICC Papers.

[74] *IQR*, 1928, vol. 2, pp. 405–7.

It was now Ansari's turn to fire his guns at Shaukat Ali. Chiding him for his conduct in Calcutta, he said:

> After seeing how partisan spirit had utterly blinded you and how under its influence you had acted unfairly, unjustly, and in a manner I could never have dreamt you capable of acting, my faith in your righteousness and fair play completely broke down.... I had been a loyal co-worker of yours for the last 18 years, who had idolized you, worshipped the very ground on which you trod, [and] had given you such friendship, love and loyalty.... But when I saw the clay feet of my idol I felt as if the world had turned topsy-turvy and that I could never, in future, trust any one whoever it might be....

Ansari added that his political convictions were at variance with the Ali Brothers and that he could not 'be the same with you [Shaukat] as I have been before'. He was sad that the life-long bond of friendship had to be severed. 'At our age', he wrote, 'new friendship and new attachments are difficult.... Life in future would be the less fuller, the less richer for want of such friends as you and I have been'. But, then, 'I bow to the inexorable march of events and have fortified myself against whatever the future may have in store, and have prepared myself to go on working in the service of my faith and my country, in the best manner that I can do'.[75]

The Ansari-Shaukat differences could not be resolved through the mediation of friends. This was no less true of the gulf that separated Mohamed Ali and Gandhi, the two men who symbolized Hindu-Muslim friendship during the Khilafat and Non-Co-operation movements. Gandhi admitted that the Ali Brothers had 'a fairly heavy list of complaints' against him and that he could not make an 'impression on them as they distrusted the role of my associates'.[76] One of them was that the Mahatma 'had defeated all Muslim attempts for a compromise' and was 'giving free reins to the communalism of the majority'.[77]

There was thus no basis for a reconciliation. The Mahatma was

[75] To Shaukat Ali, 14 May 1929, Hasan (ed.), *Muslims and the Congress*, pp. 64-66.

[76] To Motilal Nehru, 12 August 1928, Motilal Nehru Papers.

[77] Mohamed Ali's statement, quoted in Hasan, *Mohamed Ali: Ideology and Politics*, p. 101.

no longer interested in an amicable settlement of the 'Muslim claims', while the Congress was seen as a mere tool in the hands of the Hindu Mahasabha. So, the brothers—Shaukat and Mohamed—appealed to the British for the redressal of their grievances, something they had not done before in the course of their public life. Mohamed Ali rushed to London to attend the Round Table Conference before lampooning Gandhi for his ill-timed civil disobedience movement. Instead of civil disobedience, he advised his co-religionists to press their demand for freedom in London. But he soon realized the futility of his own advice, for neither the Indian delegates at the Round Table Conference could agree on a unified set of demands nor was the British government inclined to come to terms with nationalist aspirations in India. In fact, Mohamed Ali knew, much before he left the Indian shores for what turned out to be his final journey, that his mission was condemned as traitorous by those very people with whom he had worked in the past. And in London, the Maulana felt that his 'real place was in the fight in India, not in the futile conference chamber in London'.[78] In Oxford, where he had once studied Modern History, he addressed the students in their tail coats, talked cricket and made them laugh. But he made

> little or no impression and quite failed to put across the case for the Muslims to a youthful but intelligent audience who were to provide a fair number of the nations' political leaders in later years.[79]

Shaukat Ali was also a spent force, isolated from the mainstream of nationalist politics and spurrned by a section of his own community for his proximity with British officials. His pension— Rs 150 per month—was restored from 1 October 1930, 'that date being fixed as the time when he went to the Round Table Conference and may be regarded as having publicly abandoned his previous subversive activities'.[80] The viceroy found this 'difficult and shifty customer' in 'the most amazing frame of

[78] Nehru, *An Autobiography*, p. 120.

[79] Box No. 2, Benthall Papers, Centre for South Asian Studies, Cambridge.

[80] Haig to Hailey, 20 December 1933, F. No. 27/A, Hailey Papers.

mind',[81] an impression confirmed later when Shaukat told Hailey in December 1933 that he would not accept any settlement with the Congress which did not 'embrace peace with the Government'. At the same time, he insisted on being rewarded for his loyalty and betrayed considerable pique at the neglect by the government of 'one who has smashed Gandhi'.[82]

Shaukat Ali was taken to task by the Congress Muslims for his views on dominion status, his stance on the Ahrar agitation in Kashmir,[83] and his pro-British pronouncements at the Round Table Conference. The *Medina* of Bijnor was unsparing in its criticizm.[84] The *Hamdam* of Lucknow was aghast at his London speech which reflected his 'slave mentality'.[85] In its editorial on 6 February 1932, the paper observed:

> He who was yesterday trying to dig the foundations of Englishmen in India is today their best friend and is trying his utmost to injure the national movement.... When a man who has always subsisted on public subscriptions is invited to lunch by Viceroys and Governors, it is not strange that he should abandon his past beliefs and rub his forehead on the threshold of Government.[86]

This was an uncharitable comment from a colleague who had for years worked in close co-operation with the Ali Brothers. Shaukat Ali knew it. He had no defence to offer except to argue that he was still devoted to the 'Muslim cause', which the Nehru Committee had summarily dismissed. Around the same time, another prominent leader—Mohammad Ali Jinnah—was echoing the same sentiment, the same sense of disillusionment with the Congress strategy of dealing with the communal problem.

[81] Irwin to Samuel Hoare, 15 February 1932, MSS. EUR. E. 240, F. No. 5, Samuel Hoare Papers, IOLR.

[82] Hailey to Haig, 15 December 1933, F. No. 27/A, Hailey Papers.

[83] *Medina*, for the week ending 12 March 1932, SNNR, UP.

[84] Ibid., for the week ending 17 October 1931.

[85] *Hamdam* (Lucknow), for the week ending 7 November 1931.

[86] Ibid. Shaukat Ali visited Mysore in July 1931 and expressed preference for dominion status within the British Empire. In another speech he stated that there could be no peace for India except within the British Empire. L/P and S/, F. No. 13, IOLR. Compare this with Shaukat Ali's views on dominion status quoted in *Hamdard*, 23 August 1928.

Jinnah's views were, of course, of much greater consequence in determining the future course of India's history. It need not have been so had the fateful meeting of the All-Parties National Convention in December 1928 been more sober and sympathetic in meeting his viewpoint.

IV

M.A. JINNAH: 'Are you an Indian first, or a Muslim'?
THE RAJA OF MAHMUDABAD: I happened to say that I was a Muslim first and an Indian afterwards. So he didn't agree with me'.
JINNAH: 'No, you are an Indian first'.
THE RAJA OF MAHMUDABAD: 'And he said it with such violence in his voice that tears rolled down my cheek'.[87]

Sarojini Naidu's ambassador of Hindu-Muslim unity lived up to his reputation for several decades. He radicalized the Muslim League in 1913, presided over the affairs of the Bombay Home Rule League, and brought the Congress and the League closer to each other. He was, as is well known, the architect of the Lucknow Pact and a consistent protagonist of Hindu-Muslim unity. What attracted the young M.C. Chagla to Jinnah was 'his sterling nationalism and patriotism'. As a brilliant lawyer and a fearless critic of the government, he sustained his reputation all over the country. Such was the goodwill he enjoyed in his own city that the people built a Hall, which they named after him.[88]

Though marginalized in the early 1920s and rebuffed by the Gandhian leadership, Jinnah was unrepentant in his indifference to the pan-Islamic euphoria and irreconciled to the mixing up of religion with politics. His nationalistic credentials were, as always, impeccable. Though distanced from the common people, he made his presence felt in the Central Assembly as leader of the Independent Party.[89] He was *en rapport* with the swarajists, particularly its leader Motilal Nehru. He opposed the

[87] Typescript of a B.B.C. (British Broadcasting Corporation) interview with Jeremy Bennet. The Raja of Mahmudabad was eleven years old and addressed Jinnah then and later as 'uncle'.

[88] Chagla, *Roses in December*, p. 78.

[89] For Jinnah's role in the Assembly, see Wolpert, *Jinnah of Pakistan*, pp. 80-83, and Mujahid, op. cit., pp. 217–19.

formation of a 'Muslim Party', refused to sign the 'Majority Report' of the Reforms Enquiry Committee, blessed the Indian National Union, floated by Motilal and Azad,[90] and stayed away from the unhappy communal wranglings. The Delhi offer of March 1927 was his brainchild. This was the first time that Muslims had agreed to have joint electorates, and, in the judgement of some, 'the chance of a lifetime, a rare unexpected opportunity for a new start on a real national political life'.[91]

Though never ever tied to the Congress, Jinnah's political concerns were no different from many of its leaders. The cause of India's freedom and of communal amity were close to his heart—a passion he shared in equal measure with Azad, Ajmal Khan and Ansari. No wonder, his leaving India in May 1928 caused anxiety in Congress circles.[92] Jinnah's absence from the country, Motilal told Purshotamdas Thakurdas, 'is most disappointing. I can think of no other responsible Muslim to take his place'.[93] Ansari was equally upset, because Jinnah was, in his judgement, 'the only man to deliver the goods on behalf of the Muslim League'.[94] So, when Jinnah returned to India in October, Motilal was delighted. He confided in Thakurdas again:

> So much depends on Jinnah that I have a mind to go to Bombay to receive him. If I have the necessary funds within the next few days I hope to create a strong opinion amongst the Mussalmans to greet Jinnah on his arrival. Therefore please lose no time to raise as much money as you can for this great enterprise.[95]

Jinnah did not disappoint. He was unhappy that the Nehru Committee repudiated two of his favourite schemes—the Lucknow Pact and the Delhi Proposals. But he was neither bitter nor indignant. Though troubled by Ruttie's serious illness and by

[90] Chagla, op. cit., p. 91.

[91] Ibid., p. 93.

[92] There was talk of postponing the All-Parties Conference until Jinnah's return from Europe but Jawaharlal Nehru was not agreeable to the suggestion. See Page, *Prelude to Partition*, pp. 166–67.

[93] Motilal to Purshotamdas, 28 April 1928, F. No. 40, Thakurdas Papers.

[94] Ansari to Jawaharlal Nehru, 29 March 1928, F. No. G 60, AICC Papers.

[95] 28 April 1928, Thakurdas Papers.

the anti-Nehru report crusade in UP, Jinnah kept his cool and, as always, appeared unruffled. With meticulous care, he took charge of the Muslim League and negotiated with Motilal and other Congress leaders with his usual skill and aplomb. The one time disciple of Dadabhai Naoroji faced the Congress-dominated All-Parties National Convention in a spirit of compromise. Little did he anticipate the belligerent mood of those who had turned up in full strength at Calcutta in the festive Christmas week.

Jinnah proposed three amendments to the Nehru report: first, that one-third of the central legislature should consist of Muslims; secondly, in the event of adult suffrage not coming into effect, the Bengali and Punjabi Muslims should have reserved seats for ten years; and finally, residuary powers must vest in the provinces. He pleaded for statesmanship and cited constitutional precedents from other countries where, he said, political adjustments were made not on a population basis but on principles of equity. 'We are here, as I understand, for the purpose of entering into a solemn contract.... What we want is that Hindus and Muslims should march together until our object is attained'. He emphasized the need for mutual adjustments and co-operation not as a 'naughty' or 'spoilt' child but as the country's well-wisher. In a speech reminiscent of his earlier pronouncements, Jinnah said:

> We are all sons of this land. We have to live together and whatever our differences may be, let us at any rate not create more bad blood. If we cannot agree, let us at any rate agree to differ, but let us part as friends. Believe me there is no progress of India until the Mussalmans and Hindus are united, and let no logic, philosophy or squabble stand in the way of coming to a compromise and nothing will make me more happy than to see a Hindu-Muslim union.[96]

The last line may have been borrowed from his own evidence before the Parliamentary Select Committee in 1919. When asked whether he wished to see complete elimination of political distinctions between Muslims and Hindus, his answer was: 'Yes, nothing will please me more when that day comes'.

The Hindu Mahasabha and Sikh delegates were in no mood to listen to Jinnah at the Convention. They refused to accept 33 per cent Muslim representation at the Centre. The Liberals, along

[96] Quoted in Wolpert, op. cit., p. 101.

with the Hindu communalists, stood firmly against vesting residuary powers in the provinces. Jayakar warned the delegates that, having once restrained his supporters from rebelling against the Nehru report, it would be impossible for him to persuade them to accept further concessions. They listened to his admonition rather than take note of Jinnah's pleading. Jinnah was mocked, rebuffed and rejected by a hostile gathering. He was never ever going to return to such an unfriendly assembly.

Soon after the December Convention, Jinnah found himself in the company of the Aga Khan, Mohammad Shafi, Ibrahim Rahimtoola, Maulvi Shafi Daudi, Haji Abdullah Haroon, Shaukat Ali and other politically reactionary leaders from UP, Bengal and Punjab. He had no ideological affinity with them, no common ground on which to build the edifice of national unity and integration. Yet, he was there because neither the Congress nor the Calcutta Convention paid heed to his warnings.

Those who listened to him at the Muslim conference saw merit in the amendments which, on the one hand, encapsulated the long-standing demands of their organization and, on the other, reconciled their conflicting regional claims. In this way, delegates from UP were satisfied.[97] So were representatives from Bengal and Punjab, who were told that reservations were absolutely essential, because the voting strength of the Muslims was far below their population.[98] They were won over by Jinnah's insistence that, in the event of adult suffrage not being introduced, the Convention should reserve seats for Muslim majorities in accordance with their population. Jinnah had, at last, vindicated his claim that the amendments embodied the 'united will of the

[97] 'The heavens would not have fallen if a few amendments that were proposed had been generously accepted and the sad chapter of communal bickering and disharmony closed. The short-sightedness of Hindu politicians on this occasion could not be surpassed', declared Khaliquzzaman from the vantage point of Pakistan. *Pathway to Pakistan,* p. 98. Chagla's statement quoted in Uma Kaura, *Muslims and Indian Nationalism: The Emergence of the demand for India's Partition* (Delhi, 1977), p. 40.

[98] Notice the version of Mohammad Azizul Haque, one of the Muslim League delegates who participated in the All-Parties National Convention. Quoted in Sayeed, *Pakistan: The Formative Phase,* pp. 70–71.

Muslim community'. So what if the Convention questioned his credentials? After all, Muslim leaders in different provinces, having ignored Jinnah for nearly a decade, were now trickling into his camp to lend legitimacy and stature to his leadership. In this way, 'failure' at the Convention brought unexpected rewards to Jinnah, unforeseen by his band of admirers less than a decade ago when he refused to be swept by the pan-Islamic tide and chose, instead, to pursue his concerns in an unobtrusive manner.

In 1929-30, Jinnah was estranged from the Congress but the rejection of his stand at the Calcutta Convention did not mark the 'parting of ways'. He was in a defiant mood; yet, he was not averse to sorting out his differences with the Congress leadership. He parleyed with his *bete noire*, Gandhi, conducted talks with Malaviya and backed various initiatives to resolve the communal deadlock.[99] His stand was unambiguous. The Hindu-Muslim question must be tackled as a 'national problem' and not just as a 'communal dispute'. 'Unless the majority community and the leaders grasp that elementary principle and deal with it in that spirit', he told Chagla who had parted company with his political mentor over the 'Fourteen Points', 'it will not be possible to get the minority community into line with any national progamme'.[100] This is what he said to Sapru as well. Ignoring Sapru's indiscretion and outburst at the Convention, Jinnah wrote to the Liberal leader in a conciliatory mood:

> I have always counted upon your support and I know that if we could sit together the settlement can be arrived at in ten minutes, because I know that you look upon this question as a Nationalist and an Indian and, believe me, so do I. It is the duty of every Nationalist who wants self-government for India to take with him seventy millions of Mussalmans and other communities, and any reasonable concessions, though not logical, that can secure the whole-hearted support and co-operation of such a large body of people in our country is. . . essential.

[99] The viceroy, too, found evidence to indicate that Jinnah was keen on a rapprochement. The only hurdle was the Hindu Mahasabha, which 'seems to be stiffening in its attitude towards Muslim claims'. Irwin to Peel, 21 March 1929, L/PO/F.No. 6/42, IOLR.

[100] Chagla, op. cit., p. 97.

> After all, are the proposals of the Mussalmans so very radical? Even the fifteen points,...if accepted, I cannot see how they can seriously prejudice the Hindu interest in the future constitution...

Jinnah concluded with the comment that the settlement of the Hindu-Muslim question was a national problem and had to be dealt with accordingly.

> I have no hesitation in saying that it is obvious for every nationalist to do his utmost to find a solution without which there is no hope for any real advancement on the part of India towards Dominion Status, responsible government or self-government, or by whatever name you may describe the goal for which we have been working.[101]

Jinnah wrote this lengthy letter from his home. The address—Mount Pleasant Road, Malabar Hill, Bombay. It was despatched on 14 December. The year was 1929, nearly a year after he is supposed to have told one of his friends of his irrevocable break with the nationalist forces. The 'parting of ways' had yet to take place.

V

Some important points stand out in the discussion on the Nehru report. The first relates to the view, advanced by I.H. Qureshi, Aziz Ahmad, Khalid bin Sayeed, K.K. Aziz and other historians of Pakistan, that the Muslim community's rejection of the report was 'swift, unmistakable and unqualified'.[102] Such an interpretation stands refuted, for it has been shown that leaders from Bengal and Punjab saw the Nehru proposals in a favourable light and that they went over to the Muslim Conference only after the National Convention. Political opinion was divided in UP, with the Congress Muslims, led by Ansari, Azad and the Raja of Mahmudabad, being vocal supporters of the Nehru report.

The second issue concerns the approach of the Nehru Committee to the communal issue. The underlying strain of its argument was that abolishing separate electorates and communal representation was a panacea of all ills and their disappearance would, in

[101] 5 December 1928, vol. 31, pp. 389–90, Sapru Papers.
[102] Aziz, *Britain and Muslim India*, p. 92.

particular, encourage people to think in terms of larger political and economic problems. 'We shall then find Hindus and Muslims and Sikhs in one party acting together and opposing another party which also consists of Hindus and Muslims'.[103] This prophecy stemmed from Jawaharlal Nehru's simplistic analysis of communalism and his view that 'we must...begin to think of and act on common economic issues. If we do so, the myth of communalism will automatically disappear. Conflict there may be, but it will be between different classes and not different religions'.[104] Nothing of the sort happened.

The development of parties on non-communal lines did not take place because the Congress strategy of mass mobilization was flawed from the outset. Instead of emphasizing the commonality of Hindu-Muslim interests, the Congress sought a following sometimes by exploiting religious issues and more often by concluding pacts for immediate political gains. Believing, as Jawaharlal did, that communalism was not 'such a power as it is made out to be',[105] it was considered both convenient and expedient to mollify the 'educated classes in search of office and employment'. This was attempted in the Lucknow compact [1916], the Ansari-Lajpat Rai proposals [1923][106] and the much-maligned Bengal Pact.

The ostensible logic behind these formal proposals was that Muslims—always treated as a monolith entity in Congress literature —required some measure of safeguards because their interests were somehow different from others. This was, quite evidently, a questionable assumption. The concern for securing 'safeguards' was restricted to professional Muslims, government servants and the landowning class. Outside these circles, there

[103] *All-Parties Conference*, p. 49.

[104] Presidential Address at Punjab Political Conference, Amritsar, 11 April 1928, *SWJN*, vol. 3, pp. 225–26. Or, his view that 'representation by economic units will not only ensure real and effective legislatures representing the life of the country or every interest therein, but will also automatically do away with the problem of communal representation'. Statement at All-Parties Conference, 8 March 1928, *SWJN*, vol. 3, p. 37.

[105] Address at the Punjab Political Conference, op. cit.

[106] I have discussed the Ansari-Lajpat Pact or the Indian National Pact in *A Nationalist Conscience*, pp. 116–18.

was no all-India consciousness of a unified Muslim community, with the same set of demands and concerns. There was none. What was, after all, common between western-educated professional Muslims and their less privileged brethren in the countryside? How could they agree to press a common cause and unite on the same platform? They did not until the early nineteen-forties.[107]

In its anxiety to keep divisive forces in check and maintain togetherness in the face of the communal onslaught, the Congress perpetuated the communal categories created by the raj and fostered, despite protestations to the contrary, a climate and an ethos in which the rank and file of the party thought and acted as 'Muslims', 'Hindus' and 'Sikhs'. At the same time, by legitimizing the status of sectarian leaders, the Congress willy-nilly encouraged alignments which did not cut across caste, community and regional barriers. Having done so, it was futile to expect those Muslims who had extracted major concessions under the Act of 1919, to be easily swayed by the sanctimonious arguments of the Nehru Committee. They were not. The organizers of the Muslim Conference spurned Congress overtures for reconciliation and appealed to their overlords in Delhi and London to save them from the unhappy prospect of 'Hindu domination'.

Jawaharlal Nehru argued in February 1928 that communalism had 'feet of clay', that it was a 'myth with no connection with reality' and that it would not 'endure'.[108] He was mistaken in his beliefs. On other occasions, he and his father took serious note of heightened communal consciousness in the country, hardening of attitudes, and the tendency to judge most contemporary issues from a community-oriented standpoint. This was reflected in the painful discourse at the Congress-sponsored confabulations in 1927 and 1928. Both father and son found the atmosphere nauseating. They were no less alarmed by the steadily increasing influence of communal forces in Congress. Motilal had a taste of

[107] Notice the comment of the governor of Bengal. He was exasperated by the fact that Muslims were 'so hopelessly divided amongst themselves...(that) there seems no possibility of getting them together as a party....' Stanley Jackson to Irwin, 19 April 1929, F. No. 23, Irwin Papers.

[108] Presidential Address at the Punjab Conference, op. cit.

it during the 1926 election and, again, at the National Convention.[109]

There can be little doubt that the Hindu Mahasabha, in alliance with a motley of Sikh factions, jeopardized the prospect of a Congress-League reunion. Lajpat Rai's speech delivered from a Hindu Mahasabha platform was widely circulated at the Convention as his last will and testament.[110] He had earlier warned Gandhi and Motilal neither to negotiate with Jinnah nor to soften their stand on communal representation.[111] Moonje, Malaviya, Kelkar and Jayakar said the same. 'You should tell Mahatmaji,' Moonje wrote to Malaviya, 'that if he were to yield on these points [Jinnah's amendments], you would be painfully obliged to lead the opposition on behalf of the Hindus even against him, Jinnah and Motilal combined'.[112] Muslims must know, Moonje told the Mahatma, 'that no compromise is possible for the purpose of tampering nationalism with communalism.'[113] They met in August 1929, soon after the Gandhi-Jinnah talks. The following is the recorded conversation of their meeting:

MOONJE: What do you advise us to do Mahatmaji in regard to the negotiations you have opened with Jinnah for the amendment of the Nehru report [and] in acceptance of the 14 points of Jinnah?

GANDHI: You are not well informed. I did not open negotiations with Jinnah. [Sarojini] Naidu pressed me to meet Jinnah and you do not mean to say that I should not have gone to see Jinnah when he had expressed a desire that I should see him.

MOONJE: [By travelling from Sabarmati to Bombay in weak health] you have thus endowed him [Jinnah] with an amount of

[109] Motilal wrote: 'The silly resolution which the Hindu Sabha passed at Surat just before the Calcutta Convention was in a great measure responsible for the deadlock that ensued'. To Gandhi, 14 September 1929, Motilal Papers.

[110] Ibid.

[111] To Motilal, n.d., F. No. 108, supplementary, AICC Papers. A letter signed by Kelkar, Jayakar, Moonje and K.M. Munshi warned Gandhi that 'if any terms are settled by you without consulting the leaders of Hindu opinion in the country, it will not be acceptable to the Hindu community'. F. No. 437, Jayakar Papers.

[112] To Malaviya, 31 July 1928, ibid.

[113] To Gandhi, 5 August 1929, ibid.

importance and greatness which proves most embarrassing to or rather as an obstacle in the way of the Hindus to bring around the Muslims to an understanding with the Hindus....

GANDHI: .....I simply heard Jinnah fully and came away expressing no opinion of my own. I do not represent anybody and do not want to say anything on behalf of anybody.[114]

The Mahatma was not obliged to offer an explanation. He also had no reason to sound defensive. But, then, such was the hegemonic influence of the Hindu Mahasabha in the late nineteen-twenties that even the secular-oriented Congress leadership often succumbed to its ideological pressures.[115] Notice, for example, how the Malaviya-Lajpat Rai combination used a communal platform as a means of rallying public support from 1922 onwards and made concessions to communal feelings which were already running high. Yet, they and their allies adorned the Swarajist benches and occupied important positions in the Congress heirarchy. Malaviya represented the Mahasabha point of view at the 1931 Round Table Conference and was immediately rewarded with a presidential chair at the 1932 Congress. In this way, the most communally-minded leader could assume the nationalist garb and freely sail between the Mahasabha and the Congress.[116] No attempt was ever made to curb this trend.

[114] Diary, 22 August 1929, Moonje Papers.

[115] In July 1926, Sri Prakasa, a swarajist candidate for the Banaras-Gorakhpur Assembly seat, urged Motilal Nehru not to put forward Sapru's suggestion [that the constituencies in which riots occurred should be disfranchised. Motilal agreed and went further in suggesting (a) that recipients of honours belonging to riot-ridden districts would have their names removed, and (b) exclusion from public service of anybody belonging to the area] regarding the Hindu-Muslim *entente* 'as a plank of our platform. It is too dreadful'. F. No. 1? 1, AICC Papers.

[116] Jawaharlal Nehru, *Recent Essays and Writings* (Allahabad, 1934), and *An Autobiography*, p. 136. During the debate on the extension of reforms to the Frontier Province, Syed Murtaza, a swarajist from Madras, observed that the most communally-minded Hindu can pose as a nationalist and pretend that he asks for the abolition of communal representation and of separate electorates only because their existence is incompatible with nationalism'. *The Frontier Question in the Assembly* (Delhi, 1926), pp. 26–27.

The Congress Muslims were the first to criticize their party for its failure to curb the influence of the Mahasabha and to come to terms with Jinnah and his group. Azad, Khaliquzzaman and Chagla, enthusiastic supporters of the Nehru report, expressed their indignation.[117] So did Ansari who, in his correspondence with Gandhi and Motilal, voiced his anguish over the Congress response to the Delhi Proposals and the developments thereafter. He observed with uncharacteristic candidness:

> I have not the slightest doubt that if we had stuck to [the Delhi proposals] we would have gradually overcome the opposition of the Hindu Mahasabha and Hindu-Muslim unity would have been an accomplished fact by now. But, we wanted to be just and fair and in our effort to do justice and bring greater harmony and unity in the shape of the Nehru Constitution, I am afraid we lost at Lucknow what we had gained at Madras.

Ansari then commented on how at the Calcutta Convention, 'it was the Hindu Mahasabha which completely did the work of destruction, and how Jayakar, Malaviya, Moonje and 'Hindu Mahasabha friends destroyed all chances of understanding'. He added:

> After that the communalist Muslims got the chance and the Muslim attitude hardened as shown by the absurd resolutions passed at the All-Parties Conference at Delhi and subsequently the Fourteen Points of Mr. Jinnah.[118]

[117] The reactions of the Congress Muslims is examined in: *A Nationalist Conscience*, chapter eight.

[118] Ansari to Gandhi, 13 February 1930, Hasan (ed.), *Muslims and the Congress*, pp. 95–96. This letter along with the replies of Gandhi (from Sabarmati), Motilal and Jawaharlal reached the viceroy through the Nawab of Bhopal who, in turn, had received the correspondence from Ansari. Irwin's comment was: 'The general impression of the three replies to Ansari seems that the writers felt they had to do something, had burnt their boats and hoped, without being sanguine, for the best'. Irwin to Wedgwood Benn, 27 February 1930, L/PO/6/16, IOLR.

Chapter Ten

Reflections

Who killed India? Was it the work of an insane individual, a stab in the back as in a communal riot; or a diabolical conspiracy of a gang? Was it a case of slow poisoning? Or, as it might be, was it a mere cunning master plan, in which the victim himself was hypnotically induced to commit suicide....

That an imperialist power planned the dismemberment of our country is not surprising. The wonder, and the tragedy is that India should have been killed by the children of India....

Khwaja Ahmad Abbas, 'The Last Page', 1947*

This study has tried to argue that, notwithstanding common religious experiences and shared symbols, the followers of Islam in India did not constitute a monolith entity. The diversity of responses to the early Congress movement and the mixed reactions to the Lucknow Pact and the Nehru report illustrate both the range and depth of intra-community and intra-regional divisions that set Muslims apart and laid to rest the notion of a unified community. In 1918, India's secretary of state was met by a cascade of not one, but forty-four deputations from Muslim groups and organizations. Each one of them played a separate tune. And each one of them made the patently hollow claim of representing its community. Likewise, the Simon Commission was innundated with numerous representations and petitions from several quarters. Their demands were not always the same. At the Round Table Conferences in London, too, 'Muslim' delegates, reflecting different shades of opinion and interests,

* K.A. Abbas, *I am not an Island: An Experiment in Autobiography* Delhi, 1977), pp.280.

staked certain claims which were at variance and in conflict with each other.

The Muslim League's success in the 1940s does not alter the basic thrust of our argument. Nor does it vindicate or legitimize the ideological underpinnings of Jinnah's two-nation theory, for the birth of Pakistan in August 1947 was neither imminent nor historically inevitable. It was more of an aberration, a historical accident, caused by a complex configuration of forces at a particular juncture. Indian nationalists of all shades, including the socialists and communists, failed to grasp this reality. As a result, they bowed to the mounting pressure of the Muslim League and, though for different reasons, acquiesced in India's partition.

Nobody can deny that the Muslim League enjoyed considerable popular support. Yet, the birth of Pakistan symbolized, more than anything else, Jinnah's personal triumph, his answer to the obdurate Congress leadership which had persistenly refused to treat him on equal terms. It also reflected the effectiveness of his political strategy which was coolly worked out with active government support. Most British officials in India were at first averse to dealing with Jinnah.[1] But they could not forever rebuff his

[1] Some official and 'non-official' impressions at the Round Table Conference are illustrative. Malcolm Hailey thought that in the plenary session Jinnah was always 'the perfect bounder and as slippery as the eels which his forefathers purveyed in the Bombay market'. The secretary of state recalled in 1934: 'Of all the Indians I have met I think I have disliked Jinnah the most. Throughout the Round Table Conference discussions he invariably behaved like a snake, and no one seemed to trust him'. Benthall found Jinnah's speech 'clever' and 'offensive' and found him 'thoroughly disloyal and purely out for his own ends'. Hailev to Irwin, 14 November 1920, F.No. 34, Hailey Papers; Hoare to viceroy, 5 April 1934, F.No. 4 Hoare Papers; 9 January 1931, Diaries, Box 12, Benthall Papers. The Raja of Mahmudabad recalled a luncheon meeting at the governor's house in 1936, the year he joined the Muslim League. The host asked him if he knew that the estate was a gift from the British sovereign, 'adding after I had nodded in assent, that I held it at his pleasure'. The governor then asked the Raja to dissociate himself from one whom he called 'the arch enemy of the British Raj'. 'After a few minutes of conversation I realized that this 'arch enemy' was none other than M.A. Jinnah. On my asking what I was expected to do, he ordered that I should join the National Agriculturist party and made it clear that the British government had no intention of letting the activities of

initiatives. The future Quaid demanded a price for supporting the war efforts; the government grudgingly agreed to his terms. In his interview with Jinnah on 27 June 1940, the viceroy, Linlithgow, 'gave proof of our determination to have full regard to Muslim opinion and to the legitimate rights of so large a minority of the people of India'. He made clear to Whitehall that, in order to enlist Jinnah's support 'at this stage', it was 'essential that any declaration that might be made should not preclude a fair and unprejudiced hearing for the Muslim League's proposal for the creation of two India's'.[2]

In the behind-the-scenes negotiations that took place then and later, there was no attempt to ascertain the views or the wishes of the people, both Hindus and Muslims. The predictable collapse of the interim ministry and the fire of violence in Bihar and Bengal, which nobody tried to extinguish, offered an opportunity and an excuse to the Congress and League leaders to hammer out the modalities of transferring power to two separate nations. Mountbatten, the impetuous representative of the Crown, was anxious to hasten the process and preside over the liquidation of an Empire which had already lost its *raison d'etre.* Asking the people to sit in judgement on an issue that had already been settled was an act of deception, a monumental fraud. Those privileged to vote in the 1946 elections, under a restricted franchise, did so in an atmosphere vitiated by communalism. The die was cast and they could not, even if they wanted to, reverse a process that was well underway.

Jinnah and his party continue and that I would have to watch my steps in future'. Raja of Mahmudabad, 'Some Memories', C.H. Philips and D.A. Wainright (eds.), *The Partition of India: Policies and Perspectives, 1935-1947* (London, 1970), p. 384.

[2] L/PJ/8/507. This was a reiteration of the viceroy's earlier position, when he told the secretary of state that while there was 'danger' in 'leaning too heavily on the Muslim Community or attaching undue weight to the more exaggerated claims, it would be as foolish to underrate the importance of their support to us'. He added: 'It would be short-sighted and unfair to all not to give the fullest consideration to its [Muslim community's] legitimate claims'. Linlithgow to secretary of state, 28 November 1939, L/PO/258 (iii), IOLR. For a perceptive and sensitive description and analysis of Jinnah's political role and his relationship with the government, see Ayesha Jalal, *The Sole Spokesman: Jinnah, the Muslim League and the Demand for Pakistan* (Cambridge, 1985).

II

Those who lived through the nineteen-twenties could have hardly predicted the collapse of the imperial edifice in their lifetime. Likewise, they could have barely visualized that Hindu-Muslim strife would, in the end, culminate in the vivisection of the country. The period covered in this book cannot therefore be treated, except with the benefit of hindsight, as the 'Prelude to Partition'.

There can be no doubt that Hindu-Muslim cleavages widened in the aftermath of the Khilafat and Non-Co-operation agitations. The Khilafat movement itself was bogged down in religious issues instead of concentrating on the consolidation and integration of anti-colonial forces. In consequence, a popular political movement, a gift of history, was a great opportunity absurdly wasted. The Congress, caught up in its factional struggles and hemmed in by diverse ideological positions, was unable to steer its ship through the rough currents of communalism. Gandhi, who had once piloted a remarkable Hindu-Muslim alliance, developed cold feet in dealing with the communal monster and thereby lost much of the political initiative he commanded from the days of the Rowlatt Satyagraha. His political heir, Jawaharlal Nehru, understood communalism in very different terms. He was no doubt troubled by the country being 'caught in a whirlpool of mutual hatred', but like the Mahatma he could find no way out of the 'impenetrable darkness'. His remedy was to 'scotch our so-called religion and secularize our own intelligenstia'.[3] He cited the example of Europe which had got rid of religion by mass education and argued that religion would not be able to stand the test of large-scale education. This process, he stated, 'is bound to be repeated in India'.[4] Noble thought, yes, but quite out of tune with the realities of Indian social and political life.

[3] To Syed Mahmud, 25 May 1926, *SWJN*, vol. 2, p. 235.

[4] To Syed Mahmud, 14 July 1927, ibid., p. 329. Or, his view expressed in January 1940. 'If we have adult franchise, it is just possible that we might get over this separatist tendency as the masses will think more along economic lines. That is why adult franchise is essential and that is why Jinnah is opposing a Constituent Assembly generally and adult franchise specially ....'. To S. Satyamurti, 23 January 1940, Satyamurti Papers, NMML.

The nationalistic discourse on communalism was, in general, flawed by such formulations.

At the same time, there was one aspect of the Gandhi-Nehru discourse which is beyond reproach. This is related to their view, which was sadly not aired as frequently as it should have been, that communal rivalries alone should not be projected as *the* Indian reality but that notice should be taken of large areas of mutual co-operation and tangible expressions of inter-communal understanding. After all, the governor of Bengal, where Hindu-Muslim conflicts were almost endemic, commented on how the 'rank and file' of the communities co-operated with each other in all 'daily business of life', and that it was 'only at rare intervals, when religious feelings became inflamed, that they treat each other as enemies and clashes occur'.[5] O.M. Martin, who served in the province from 1915 to 1926, observed the same. Hindu-Muslim unity, he added, was not a temporary occurrence but an old and cherished tradition'.[6]

Most people, Hindus and Muslims alike, clung to their inherited ideas, traditions and customs. This was so in the case of, for example, the Meos, the Malkana Rajputs, the Khojas, Bohras and Memons in western India, and the Moplahs in Malabar. Given their long, uninterrupted history of social mingling and cultural fusion, it is hard to think of a different scenario. Similar trends, syncretic and composite, were at work elsewhere. Islam in Punjab provided a 'repertoire' of concepts and styles in authority which had served to encompass potentially competing values, including the values of tribal kinship, within a common Islamic idiom.[7] Islam in Bengal took many forms and assimilated values and symbols not always in conformity with Quranic ideals and precepts. Cultural idioms of Islam underwent a rapid transformation, giving birth to a set of popular beliefs and practices which, in essence, represented the popular culture of rural Bengal rooted in the pre-Islamic past.[8]

[5] Lytton, *Pundits and Elephants*, p. 172.

[6] 'Memoirs of O.M. Martin' [Typescript], Centre for South Asian Studies, Cambridge.

[7] David Gilmartin, 'Customary Law and *Shariat* in Punjab', in Ewing (ed.), *Shariat and Ambiguity*, p. 44.

[8] Rafiuddin Ahmad, 'Conflict and Contradictions in Bengali Islam: Problems of Change and Adjustment', in ibid., p. 115.

In most parts of the country and in most periods of Indian history, Hindus and Muslims identified themselves with certain common cultural and religious symbols. It was thus common for Hindus to observe Muharram with solemnity[9] and to gather around shrines of the sufis and other venerated holy men and seek their intercession to avert calamities, cure diseases, procure children for the childless, or even improve the circumstances of the dead. Frederick Graham Cracknell, magistrate and collector of Etawah and Kanpur, reported that the *mela* commemorating Badiuddin or Shah Madaar, who settled in Makanpur in Bilhaur tahsil in the fifteenth century, was attended by 50,000 people, mostly Hindus. In 1931, Hindus and Muslims flocked to the shrine in equal numbers despite a Hindu-Muslim clash in the area.[10]

The extent to which narrow religious barriers were transcended and strict codes of behaviour transgressed is evident from Bahraich in eastern UP, where the outbreak of cholera in 1930 prompted Muslims to join the Hindus in great force to worship the goddess Bhawani to induce her to remove the pestilence.[11] In the Bengal countryside, pre-Islamic ceremonies relating to birth, marriage and death continued to be observed. As a concession to the 'reformist' movements, the 'outer labels' were discarded to make the rituals and practices look 'Islamic'.[12] The *Census* report of 1921 summed up the situation as:

There are...communities among the Muslim population, chiefly among converts from Hinduism, whose religious ritual and exercises

[9] *Census of India*, 1931, UP of Agra and Oudh, vol. 1, appendix e, p. 515.

[10] Cracknell Papers, Centre for South Asian Studies, Cambridge. Or, the later day experience of Mohammad Mujeeb of the Jamia Millia Islamia, Delhi: 'I remember that shortly after the orgy of violence in Bihar I visited the grave of a sufi on the banks of the Ganges. The Muslims living in the *dargah* had fled and the place looked desolate. But soon a group of Hindu women appeared. They performed circumambulations and prostrations, as if nothing had happened that affected their sentiments of veneration for the tomb of a Muslim saint'. M. Mujeeb, 'The Partition of India in Retrospect', Philips and Wainright (eds.), *The Partition of India*, p. 407.

[11] *Census of India*, 1931, p. 515.

[12] Rafiuddin Ahmad, op. cit., p. 134.

have a very strong tinge of Hinduism and who retain caste and observe Hindu festivals and ceremonies along with those of their own religion.... The rigidity of intolerance of view, which is a marked feature of the religion of Islam in its purer form, does not extend to the masses, who are quite willing to recognize and assist the efforts of their neighbours to keep on peaceful terms with the unknown powers.[13]

It is not intended to portray an idyllic picture as such but to highlight a certain facet of communal relations which tends to be overlooked in the face of stark and irrefutable evidence on Hindu-Muslim antagonism. Harping on conflicts alone and turning a blind eye to instances of Hindu-Muslim co-operation and fraternization has not just distorted our perspective but has strained India's fragile social fabric. To discover elements of communal tensions, even if one is thrown back into India's pre-colonial past, is a legitimate historical exercise in so far as it does not offer a one-sided view.

III

An important conclusion that flows from this study is that political developments until the early 1930s were not necessarily leading towards a communal impasse. In reaching this conclusion, I have neither ignored the powerful communal currents sweeping across the country nor minimized the importance of the heated debates at the Round Table Conferences and in the wake of the Communal Award.[14] What is being suggested is that the India of the early 1930s, despite its contradictions and fractious polity, can hardly be characterized as a communally polarized society. I have shown elsewhere the presence of Muslims in the Congress,[15] their joining the ranks of satyagrahis during the civil disobedience campaign [Table10:1], their identification with

[13] *Census of India,* 1921, vol. 1, p. 115.

[14] I have discussed these controversies in *A Nationalist Conscience,* chapter nine. See Bidyut Chakrabarty, 'The Communal Award of 1932 and its Implications in Bengal', *Modern Asian Studies,* vol. 23, 3, 1989.

[15] 'Congress Muslims and Indian Nationalism: Dilemma and Decline', in Jim Masselos (ed.), *Struggling and Ruling : Indian National Congress 1885-1985* (Delhi, 1987).

progressive and radical literary and political movements,[16] and their responding to the Muslim Mass Contact Campaign, launched by Jawaharlal Nehru in 1937.[17]

But this was not all. One of the unstated facts of twentieth century Indian history is that, until the mid-thirties, there was no worthwhile organization which could legitimately claim to represent the large Muslim constituency. The Muslim League, in political wilderness during the Khilafat movement, was needlessly treated by the Congress as its political adversary. It was, as one contemporary stated, a 'souless' body, devoid of any programme.[18] Its ranks were in disarray, with splits taking place one after the other. In 1927, the League's membership plummeted to 1,330.[19] Provincial branches fared no better. The Bombay branch could boast of only 71 members in 1928.[20] They included men like Syed Abdullah Brelvi, Abbas Tyabji and M.C. Chagla whose heart was with the Congress rather than the League.

Such was the apathy that the 1929 session was adjourned for lack of a quorum. The adjourned meeting, held four months

[16] Ralph Russell, 'Leadership in the All-India Progressive Writers Movement, 1935-1947', in Pandey (ed.), *Leadership in South Asia,* and my 'Nationalist and Separatist Trends in Aligarh, 1920-1947', Gupta (ed.), *Myth and Reality*. In 1932, a group of young men—Sajjad Zaheer, Ahmed Ali, Rashid Jahan and Mahmuduzzafar—produced a collection of short stories, *Angare,* which was symptomatic of the radical political trends amongst some Muslims. The stories were 'a declaration of war by the youth of the middle class' against the prevailing social norms, political values, and religious institutions. Sajjad Zaheer, son of Wazir Hasan, and his group were the forerunners of the All-India Progressive Writer's Association, which met for the first time in Lucknow on 9-10 April 1936, coinciding with the Congress meeting in that city at the same time. This summary is based on Carlo Coppola, 'The Angare Group: The Enfants Terribles of Urdu Literature', *Annual of Urdu Studies*, vol. 1. 1981.

[17] Mushirul Hasan, 'The Muslim Mass Contacts Campaign: Analysis of a Strategy of Political Mobilization', in Richard Sisson and Stanley Wolpert (eds.), *Congress and Indian Nationalism: The Pre-Independence Phase* (Berkeley, 1988).

[18] *Jiddat* (Lucknow), for the week ending 9 December 1933, SNNR, UP. And the editorial comments of *Mussalman*, 3 July 1930.

[19] Chagla Papers, NMML.

[20] Sayeed, *Pakistan: The Formative Phase*, p. 176.

later in Delhi, ended in a fiasco.[21] When Iqbal presented his address at Allahabad in 1930 demanding the establishment of a Muslim state in north-western India, the meeting did not have its quorum of 75 members.[22] Even after the annual subscription was reduced from Rs 6 to Re 1, the organizers of the 1933 session in Delhi had a busy time filling up the empty hall with students of the Anglo-Arabic College.[23] A split at this juncture was the last straw, with Mian Abdul Aziz of Peshawar and Haji Hidayat Husain of Kanpur heading rival factions.[24] 'A little oversight or a little expression of inactivity', warned one of League's office-bearers, 'means life-long suffering and probably bondage'.[25]

The leadership, which had lost much of its political initiative to the All-Parties Muslim Conference,[26] was divided, disorganized and lacking in imagination. Jinnah was nursing his political wounds at his home in Hampstead. Liaquat Ali Khan, who is credited with having persuaded Jinnah to return to India, was himself angling for a High Commissionership in London.[27] The Aga Khan, exhausted after his hectic lobbying at the Round Table Conferences, was left with no political options. He was attracted to the idea of acquiring a sort of Vatican in the territory of a protected ruler either in India or in the Persian Gulf.[28] In 1934, the year of Jinnah's return to India, Hailey commented:

[21] *Mussalman,* 3 July 1930.

[22] Mukhtar Zaman, 'Duaazda Manzil se Manzil-i Pakistan', *Nuqqush* [Iqbal Number], September 1977, p. 501. Notice the comments of Sayeed, pp. 176-77 and Khaliquzzaman, *Pathway to Pakistan,* pp. 108-9. For a recent analysis of 'Muslim Politics' during this period, see Mukul Kesavan, '1937 as a landmark in the course of communal politics in the UP', Occasional Papers on History and Society, second series, no. xi, NMML.

[23] *Sarfaraz* (Lucknow), for the week ending 9 December 1933, SNNR, UP.

[24] Wolpert, *Jinnah of Pakistan,* pp. 134-35.

[25] *Annual Report of the All-India Muslim League for the Years 1932 [up to 15 November]* (Delhi, n.d.), p. 2.

[26] This was admitted by Mohammad Yaqub. He stated that the Muslim Conference 'has devided [*sic*] our energies and caused a great deat of harm to the All-India Muslim League'. *Annual Report of the All-India Muslim League for the Year 1931* (Delhi, n.d.), p. 4.

[27] Liaquat Ali Khan to Willingdon, 14 September 1934, F.No. 4. Hoare Papers.

[28] Hoare to Willingdon, 8 March 1935, Hoare Papers.

TABLE 10:1

List of Convicted and Imprisoned in District Jail, Fyzabad.

		Place of Birth	Occupation	Period of Conviction	Duration
1	·Maulana Ziman Khan	Gonda	Teacher	Not Known	Not Known
2	Niyaz Ahmad	Etah	"	"	"
3	Shaikh Mohammad Fakhir	Allahabad	Sufi pir	Six months	from 27 September 1930
4	Maulana Mohammad Miyan	Muzaffarnagar	Teacher, Arabic madrasa	One year	" 9 October 1930
5	Maulana Rashid Husain	Deoband	Teacher	"	"
6	Manzar Ali Sokhta	Allahabad	Lawyer	One Month	" November 1930
7	Maulana Murtaza Husain	Barabanki	Not Known	Six Months	" 17 September 1930
8	Sadiq Ali	Allahabad	Student	"	" 6 November 1930
9	Maulana Ghulam Husain	Fyzabad	Lawyer	"	" 15 May 1930
10	Maulana Manzoor Ali	Allahabad	Lawyer	Three Months	" 14 August 1930
11	Abdul Hakeem	Lucknow	Lawyer	Six Months	" 3 August 1930
12	Idris Khan Lodi, (President, Badaun district Congress Committee)	Budaun	Lawyer	Six Months	" 20 November 1930
13	Maulana Manzoor Nabi	Saharanpur	Lawyer	One year	Not known
14	Maulana Ahamad Zamman Khan	Gonda	Lawyer	Not known	"

•This list is merely illustrative. Details from other jail records may help to give a more rounded picture.

Source: *Aseeran-i Watan* (Lucknow, 1931), Part 1, pp. 65-86, PIB 6/18, IOLR.

> It is a fatality of the Muslims at present that they have too many third class leaders. A community only shows real solidarity when it is in serious danger, and the fact that the Muslims have gained a great deal of their demands by the Communal Award removes some of that sense of danger and prevents reunion under a strong leadership.[29]

If the League did not represent the Muslims, who did? Nobody. The Muslim Conference, cobbled together by the Khilafatists or the Leaguers, was a splintered structure. It petered out after a brief and lazy existence. The All-India Nationalist Muslim Party, founded in July 1929 by Ansari and other Congress Muslims, also collapsed within a few years.[30] The only organization to have survived and kept up its elan as a national entity was the Jamiyat al-ulama-i Hindi. There were, then, the Khudai Khidmatgars in the North-West Frontier Province, the Ahrars in Punjab and Kashmir, the All-India Momin Conference in eastern UP and Bihar, and the Khaksars in upper India.[31] Although their area of operation was limited, these groups were led by charismatic figures who were able to introduce a level of ideological cohesion among their followers. More importantly, they had a much greater degree of affinity with the Congress whose policies and programmes they endorsed.

It is thus clear that until the mid-thirties there existed neither a sharp communal political polarization between Hindus and Muslims nor any significant solidarity in the Muslim 'community'. Communal and divisive forces were strong, but not strong enough to destroy the social fabric of Indian society. It was still possible, despite the dismal prophecy of contemporary analysts, to curb communal instincts and to integrate estranged groups and factions into a broadbased nationalist alliance.[32] Jinnah had

[29] Hailey to the Nawab of Chhatari, 15 February 1934, F.No 27-A, Hailey Papers.

[30] Hasan, *A Nationalist Conscience*, pp. 202-210

[31] Praveen Saberwal, 'The Role of the Nationalist Muslims in Indian Politics, '1923-1947' (Unpublished Ph.D. thesis, Jamia Millia Islamia, 1990: forthcoming)

[32] Notice the comment of *Mussalman* which was echoed in different ways by the Muslim intelligentsia in the twentieth century. 'We believe', wrote the Calcutta paper, 'that Hindus and Muslims must unite, that they will

pleaded for such an approach at the All Parties National Convention in December 1928, and, again, during his talks with Rajendra Prasad in 1935.[33] But the Congress could not break the Hindu Mahasabha stranglehold and found itself trapped in the cross-fire between communalists of all shades. It considered the Muslim League as its political adversary, though certain elements within its own ranks, backed by the Hindu Mahasabha and Rashtriya Swayamsevak Sangh (RSS), were, in fact, out to wreck all prospects of a Hindu-Muslim rapprochement.

The Congress had repeatedly sworn by the principles of national integration and secularism. But when the occasion came to oppose partition and stand by proclaimed ideals and goals, its top leadership readily accepted the partition plan. Only one man, who was unfairly and unjustly condemned and ridiculed by Muslim League leaders, was irreconciled to his party's decision and stayed aloof from the festivities that accompanied independence. He was Mohandas Karamchand Gandhi. The dawn of freedom had arrived, but at what cost. Partition symbolized his personal tragedy, the defeat and negation of all that he had stood for, just as it reflected the failure of the Congress to keep the country united. He trudged on and on in riot-ravaged Bihar and Bengal to provide the healing touch. Here was the Mahatma in body and spirit.

---

contribute their diverse culture, tradition and history in order to build up a new wondrous type of nationality—a nationality not simple and unitary, but strange, complex and multi-fold, like a jewel with many facets each iridescent with the gleam of latent fire'. *Mussalman*, 29 January 1926.

[33] Hasan, *A Nationalist Conscience*, pp. 238-39.

Biographical Notes

ALI, AMEER [1849–1928]: played an important part in two Muslim political organizations that began in Bengal, the Central National Mohammedan Association, founded in 1876, and the Muslim League. From 1908 to 1913, he and the Aga Khan were instrumental in setting up and running a London branch of the Muslim League. He resigned in 1913 because the League, in his view, had been taken over by 'extremists'. During the visit of Mohamed Ali and Wazir Hasan to London, Ameer Ali sought the permission of the Lord Chancellor to attend the proposed controversial dinner. He was advised not to attend.

ALI, ASAF [1888–1953]: educated at St. Stephen's College, Delhi; called to the Bar in London, 1912; returned to India at the outbreak of War and joined the Home Rule League; participated in Khilafat activities and gave up his practice during Non-Co-operation movement; general secretary, Indian National Congress, 1927, and working committee member, 1930; member, legislative assembly, 1934–46; arrested in August 1942, and released in May 1945; minister of transport and railways in interim government, formed in August 1946.

ALI, MOHAMED [1878–1931]: educated at M.A.O. College, Aligarh, and Lincoln College, Oxford, from 1898 to 1902. On his return, joined the Rampur education department and the Baroda service. Launched the *Comrade* on 11 January 1911, which was hailed as the 'new star in the firmament of Indian journalism'. From 1911 to May 1915, he was active in the Kanpur mosque agitation, the pan-Islamic movement and the Aligarh Muslim university movement; interned with Shaukat Ali, May 1915 to December 1919; led a Khilafat deputation to Europe, January-September, 1920; imprisoned, 1921–23; president, Indian National Congress, 1923; joined campaign against the Nehru Report, 1928; urged Muslims to remain aloof from civil disobedience movement; attended Round Table Conference, 1930–31.

ALI, SHAUKAT [1873–1938]: born into a family associated with the court of Rampur. His father died while he was seven years old. His mother, Begum Abadi Bano, later known as 'Bi Amma', sent Shaukat to Aligarh college in 1888; sub-deputy opium agent till 1912; organized Muslim university fund collections; founded with Abdul Bari and M.H. Kidwai the Anjuman-i Khuddam-i Kaaba, 1913; interned with his younger brother, Mohamed Ali, May 1915 to December 1919; secretary, Central Khilafat Committee till interned with his brother in September 1921; president, Khilafat Conference at Kakinada, 1923; became estranged from Congress after 1923 and campaigned against the Nehru Report; one of the organizers of the All-India Muslim Conference, 1929–31; attended the Round Table Conference, 1931; member, legislative assembly, 1935. Halide Edib described him as 'a very big man in every sense...He has a flowing beard, a shock of picturesque grey hair, and eyes which twinkle like those of a mischievous boy. His dress is suggestive of the vagueness of his politics. He wears a long shirt over tight Indian trousers and leggings; and a loose Arab *Mashlak* (mantle) with a Turkish *Kalpak* (fur cap) in the fashion of about sixteen years ago. His attire is reminiscent of a combination of Indian, Muslim, Arab and Turk; in a word, it is a reflection of Pan-Islamism...In carricatures he is represented as a big baby to whom the King gives a pretty doll so as to keep him quiet'.

ANSARI, MUKHTAR AHMAD [1880–1936]: educated at Queen's College, Banaras, Muir Central College, Allahabad, Nizam College, Hyderabad; went to England in 1901 where he was the first Indian house surgeon in the Charing Cross Hospital, London; began practice at Delhi in 1910; led the Indian Medical Mission to Turkey, 1912–13, for which he received a special award from the Ottoman consul-general. According to Meston, 'in Moslem circles he [Ansari] commands considerable respect.... His work in the Medical Mission during the last Turkish War is a matter of pride to them...'; founded the Home Rule League at Delhi, 1917, and was elected its president; chairman, reception committee, Muslim League, Delhi, 1918; played a leading part in the Khilafat movement; president, Muslim League, Nagpur, 1920, and All-India Khilafat Conference, Gaya, 1922; member, Congress Civil Disobedience Enquiry Committee, 1922, and opposed Council entry till mid-1923; chairman, reception committee, Special Congress, Delhi, September, 1923; drafted a National Pact with Lajpat Rai for improving Hindu-Muslim relations, 1923; president, Congress, 1927; founder of the All-India Muslim Nationalist Party, July 1929;

opposed Gandhi's civil disobedience movement in 1930, but said or did nothing against the Congress policy 'because of my loyalty and my deep attachment to the Congress and to those who have got its reins in their hands'; president, Congress Parliamentary Board, 1934.

AZAD, ABUL KALAM [1888–1958]: son of Maulana Khairuddin Ahmad (d. 1909), who worked in Calcutta under the patronage of a wealthy Surati merchant, Haji Zachariah; travelled to Egypt and Turkey where Azad came into contact with Iranian revolutionaries and the Young Turks. Azad was associated with several journals and magazines. He wrote for the *Ahsan al-Akhbaar*, a Calcutta journal, and started a literary journal, *Lisan al-Sidq*, in 1904. On Shibli's suggestion, he edited the *Al-Nadwa* and then joined the *Vakil* of Amritsar, an Urdu newspaper. On 12 July 1912, Azad launched *Al-Hilal* under the patronage and financial support of Haji Nur Mohammad, son of a wealthy merchant who had brought Azad's father, Maulana Khairuddin Ahmad, to Calcutta. For the next four years, through *Al-Hilal* and *Al-Balagh*, Azad expressed his ideas on religious reforms, education and politics. In July 1914, he started a society known as the Jamiyat-i Hizbullah. Its object, according to the *Al-Hilal* of 8 July 1914, was 'to send preachers to stay in cities, towns and villages where the religious condition of Muslims may be deplorable; where superstition and intrigues are prevalent and where brotherhood and sympathy for the misfortunes of Islam and zeal for communal work are forgotten.' But the 'Party of God' remained restricted in size and gained nothing like the publicity enjoyed by the Anjuman-i Khuddam-i Kaaba. In August 1915, Azad launched the Dar al-Irshaad (College of Divinity) with practically the same objects as those of the Jamiyat-i Hizbullah. But this organization also failed to secure any widespread support. By this time the career of *Al-Hilal* had ended (in November 1914), when its security deposit was forfeited by the Bengal government. In November 1915, Azad launched the *Al-Balagh*, but that too was closed in March 1916. Soon afterwards he was interned in Ranchi in Bihar, where he remained until January 1920.

BANERJEA, SURENDRANATH [1848–1925]: educated at Doveton College, Calcutta; founder, Indian Association, 1876; proprietor, *Bengalee*, 1878; editor, 1877; member Bengal legislative council, 1893–1901; president, Indian National Congress, 1895, 1902; played a leading part in the agitation against the partition of Bengal in 1905 and the swadeshi and boycott movements which followed; left Congress in 1918 following differences over the Montagu-Chelmsford Reforms; minister in Bengal government, 1921–23; defeated in the elections to the Bengal legislative council, 1923.

BARI, ABDUL [1876–1926]: *alim* of Firangi Mahal, Lucknow, and *pir* of the Ali Brothers, M.M. Chotani, and of the wife and sister of Abdul Majid Khwaja; one of the founders of the Anjuman-i Khuddam-i Kaaba; took a leading part in the Kanpur mosque agitation and the Khilafat movement; president, Jamiyat al ulama-i Hind, December 1919; after 1923, he was estranged from the Congress and complained that 'those who pretended to be our friends at one time and made a catspaw of the *ulama* now seem anxious to get rid of them'.

BILGRAMI, SYED HOSAIN [1844–1926]: was first private secretary to Salar Jung and then to the Nizam himself; director of Public Instruction Hyderabad State, 1887–1902, and member of the universities in commission; member of the secretary of state's council 1907–1909; elected trustee of Aligarh College in 1886. His brother Syed Ali Bilgrami (1851–1911) was author of several important works and held high positions in the Nizam's service; his half-brother, Major Syed Hasan (d. 1915) was secretary of the Muslim League, 1908–10.

BUTLER, SPENCER HARCOURT [1869–1938]: was deputy-commissioner, Lucknow, 1906–7; secretary to the foreign department, 1908–10; council of the governor general, 1910–15; lieutenant-governor, 1918–20, and governor of UP, 1920–23. He was a supporter of the Muslim university movement and considered it politically expedient for government to lead the educational movement and encourage denominational universities, which would provide religious instruction and inevitably tend to keep 'alive the Hindu-Muslim feelings'. Later, when the Foundation Committee rejected the government's terms for the university in July 1913, Butler tried to persuade the Raja of Mahmudabad to avoid political agitation on the question and urged the Aga Khan to exert his influence in restraining his co-religionists from political agitation. On the other hand, he was disappointed with the decision of the India Council. 'It makes one wonder', he wrote to Lovat Fraser, 'for the future of the Empire when an arrangement of this kind, worked out by the Government of India in communication with the Muslim leaders, is upset by men of the calibre of Morison and LaTouche'. Butler's assessment of some Muslim leaders was: 'Aga Khan is clever but a weather cock. Mahmudabad is weak as water; so is Rampur and unreliable to boot. The Nawab of Dacca hates Aligarh and all its works as much as he hates the Aga Khan... Wazir Hasan is a born intriguer and a mischievous fellow. He is a Shia and plays on Mahmudabad's religious weakness'.

CHAGLA, MOHAMED CURRIM [b. 1900]: educated at St. Xavier's High School and College, Bombay, and Lincoln College, Oxford; president of the Oxford Indian Majlis, 1922; professor of constitutional law, Government Law College, Bombay, 1927–30; wrote articles and addressed public meetings in favour of the Nehru Report, August-December 1928; secretary of the Bombay Muslim League, but resigned over the Nehru Report controversy; vice-chancellor of Bombay University, 1946–47; judge of the Bombay High Court 1941–47.

CHELMSFORD, 3rd Baron & 1st Viscount [1868–1933]: called to the Bar, 1893; governor of Queensland, 1905–09; governor of New South Wales, 1909–13; viceroy of India, 1916–21; first lord of admiralty, 1924.

CHINTAMANI, CHIRRAVOORI YAJNESWARA [1880–1941]: editor of *Leader* (Allahabad), 1909–23 and 1926–1941; member, UP legislative council, 1916–23; general secretary, National Liberal Federation of India, 1918–20 and 1923–29; Minister of education and industries, UP, 1921–23; member, UP legislative council, 1927–36.

DAS, CHITTA RANJAN [1870–1925]: son of a reputed solicitor of the Calcutta High Court; joined legal profession after his return to India in 1894; came into prominence as counsel for defence in the trial of Aurobindo Ghose; joined the Congress in 1906; came to the forefront of national politics in 1917 when invited to preside over the Bengal provincial conference; member, non-official Jallianwala Bagh enquiry committee; allied with Gandhi, 1920, and became leader of Non-Co-operation in Bengal; president, Indian National Congress, 1922; organized the Swaraj Party with Motilal Nehru and succeeded in having his policy of Council entry accepted by the

Congress; elected to the Bengal legislative council, 1923; mayor, Calcutta corporation, 1924–25; chief architect of the 'Bengal Pact'.

FAZLI HUSAIN [1877–1936]: educated at Government College, Lahore, and Christ College, Cambridge; began practice in Sialkot, 1901–08 and later in Punjab High Court, Lahore, 1905–20; elected to the Punjab legislative council, 1920; appointed minister of education in 1921; returned unopposed to Punjab legislative council, 1923; re-appointed minister of education, 1924; appointed revenue member in 1926.

HARDINGE, BARON, Hardinge of Penshurst [1858–1944]: was viceroy of India 1910–16, and witness to many important developments among Muslims. The annulment of Bengal's partition, the rejection of the Muslim university scheme and the Kanpur mosque affair all happened during his viceroyalty. He was on the best of terms with Ajmal Khan, Ansari and Mohamed Ali and extended support to the Indian Medical Mission to Constantinople. But relations turned sour around 1913. The viceroy urged the secretary of state not to encourage the 'self-imposed mission' of Mohamed Ali and Wazir Hasan to London. He described the former as a 'mischievous agitator' and the latter as a 'man of no importance'.

'HALI', ALTAF HUSAIN [1837–1914]: author of *Hayaat-i-Javed,* a biography of Syed Ahmad Khan, and of a famous epic poem—*Mussadas,* a comment on the history of Islam, highlighting Muslim achievements in conquest, literature and sciences and contrasting it with the decay and backwardness in his times. The *Mussadas* is often characterized as 'the Bible of the new movement', because its contribution in creating a widespread awakening among Muslims was 'next only to that of the Aligarh college and the Muslim Educational Conference'.

HAQ, FAZLUL [1873–1962]: educated in Calcutta University; joined government service as a deputy-registrar, 1906; resigned and joined the Bar in 1912; entered Bengal legislative council, 1913; secretary, Bengal Presidency Muslim League, 1913–16, and from 1916–21 president of the All-India Muslim League; took a leading part in Congress-League negotiations, 1916; joint-secretary, Congress, 1917; secretary, Congress, 1918–19; resigned from the Congress after acceptance of non-co-operation resolution; minister of education in Bengal government, 1924; represented Muslims at the Round Table Conferences, 1930-32; founded the Krishak Praja Party in 1927; mayor of Calcutta, 1935–36; chief minister of Bengal, 1 April 1937–38 to March 1943.

HAQ, MAZHARUL [1866–1930]: educated in Patna and in England; called to the Bar, 1891; attended the Muslim Convention at Dacca in 1906 and was one of the founders of the All-India Muslim League; president, All-India Muslim League, Bombay, 1915; instrumental in bringing about accord at Lucknow in December 1916; supported Gandhi in Champaran, 1917; became a non-co-operator at Gandhi's call in 1920; launched the *Motherland*, an English weekly on 30 September 1921; opposed Council entry; elected first Indian chairman of the Saran district board, 1924–27; defeated in the election to the Bihar legislative council in 1926; retired from public life after 1927.

HASAN, MAHMUD [1851–1920]: graduated from Deoband in 1873 and joined the staff there; principal of the Dar al-ulum, 1890; launched an anti-British campaign in favour of Turkey, 1911; moved to the Hejaz with his associates to avoid arrest, 1915; arrested by the British in 1916, and was interned at Malta, 1917-20; returned to India in June 1920 and joined the Khilafat movement.

HASAN, WAZIR [1874–1947]: educated at Muir Central College, Allahabad; began legal practice in Jaunpur, moving later to Pratapgarh and then to Lucknow; one of the founder members of the All-India Muslim League and its assistant secretary, 1910–12, and secretary, 1912–19; member, AICC, 1919; dominated Muslim League politics, 1913–16, when he played an important role in Congress-League rapprochment; member, UP legislative council, 1916–19; resigned from the Muslim League in 1919; appointed second judicial commissioner, 1921; one of the Puisne Judges of the chief court after its inauguration in 1925; received knighthood in 1934.

HUSAIN, RAJA GHULAM [1882–1917]: commenced public career as the associate of Mohamed Ali and sub-editor of *Comrade*. His was a 'sobering influence on the brave enthusiast of the Muslim cause, Mohamed Ali, whose generous impulses proved more profitable when allied with the 'sweetness and light' of his admirable colleague'. [*New Era,* 1 Sept 1917]. After *Comrade* ceased publication Ghulam Husain joined the *Indian Daily Telegraph* before launching the *New Era* on 7 April 1917. He was a supporter of the Sultania College scheme, launched in May 1917 by Syed Husain Bilgrami, Abdur Rahim of Bengal, Ajmal Khan, Ali Imam and the Nawab of Bhopal. The scheme aimed to bring the best educational facilities within the reach of middle class Muslims, and to offer 'adequate outlet to the suppressed spirit of devotion and service'. This, according to the *New Era* [5 May 1917], would 'rescue modern education among Muslims from the taint of commercialism and lift it to a high plain of duty and patriotic endeavour'. When the University Foundation Committee [8 April 1917] resolved to accept the university on the lines of the Banaras Hindu University, the *New Era* [14 April 1917] described it as a 'surrender' and explained it in terms of 'expediency, partisan differences, threats of revolt, vague fears of possible injury to Muslim educational interests, a growing sense of futility of all further efforts, intellectual fogginess....'

IQBAL, MOHAMMAD [1876–1938]: educated at the Scotch Mission College, Sialkot, Government College, Lahore, Cambridge and Munich; returned from Europe in July 1908; associated with the Anjuman-i Himayat-i Islam of Lahore and with Punjab Muslim League; secretary of the Punjab Khilafat Committee in 1919; resigned from both the Muslim League and the Khilafat Committee after the non-co-operation resolution was passed in September 1920; attended the Calcutta Unity Conference, October 1927; one of the few Muslims in Punjab who opposed the Nehru Report; presided over the annual session of the All-India Muslim League in 1930 and called for the establishment of an autonomous state in the north-west of British India. Iqbal's fame rests on his collection of Urdu and Persian poems and his lectures on the reconstruction of the religious thought of Islam. He is regarded as one of the greatest Urdu poets of the twentieth century.

JAYAKAR, MUKUND RAMRAO [1873–1959]: educated at Elphinstone School and St. Xavier's College, Bombay; called to the Bar in London in 1905; practised as a barrister in Bombay High Court; member, Bombay legislative council, 1923, and was leader of the Swaraj Party in the council, 1923–25; member, legislative assembly, 1926–30, and deputy leader of the Nationalist Party;

attended Round Table Conference in London and was member of the Federal Structure Committee; closely associated with the All-India Hindu Mahasabha and the *sangathan* movement.

KHALIQUZZAMAN, CHOUDHRY [1889–1973]: educated at M.A.O. College, Aligarh, 1907–16; joined Congress in 1916 acting as a member of the reception committee; took a leading part in the Home Rule movement, 1917–18; elected president of the Lucknow Congress Committee in March 1920; gave up practice during the Non-Co-operation movement; joined the swarajists, January 1923; chairman, Lucknow municipal board, 1923; a leading Muslim politician in the 1930s and 1940s; after Independence, governor of East Pakistan.

KHAN, AGA [1875–1958]: assumed spiritual headship of the Ismailis in August 1885; member of the imperial legislative council, 1902–4; led the Simla Deputation to Minto, 1906; president, All-India Muslim League, 1907–13; resigned because he found it impossible to lead the Muslims 'for my advise will be loyalty of the kind that means trust and confidence and that trust and confidence the Muslims are not now giving to government; president of the All-Parties Muslim Conference at Delhi, December 1928; chairman of the British Indian delegation to the Round Table Conference 1930, 1931; led the Indian delegation to the League of Nations, 1932, 1934–47; president of the League of Nations, 1937.

KHAN, HAKIM AJMAL [1863–1927]: family came from Kashgar, Turkestan and held important positions under the Mughal emperor, Babur; produced a long line of physicians of which the most famous was Hakim Sharif Khan, Ajmal's grandfather; educated in the Islamic branches of learning and learnt medicine from his father, Haji Mahmud Khan and his brother; founder member of the All-India Muslim League; board of management of the Nadwat al-ulama; chairman, reception committee, All-India Muslim League, 1910; trustee of Aligarh college; visited Europe 1911; became involved in active politics on his return; president, Muslim League, 1919; took part in the Khilafat agitation and was the first to renounce his title in April 1920; chancellor, Jamia Millia Islamia, November 1920; president, Indian National Congress and All-India Khilafat Conference, Ahmedabad, December 1921; member, Congress civil disobedience enquiry committee and voted in favour of Council entry; joined the swarajists, January 1923; retired from politics in 1925 because of ill-health. He was described by C.F. Andrews as 'quiet, humble, modest, with all the dignity of a man of character, learning and religious sincerity. ...' As a 'moderate' leader, he had little in common with Mohamed Ali and his colleagues, though their differences never came to the fore except during the Khilafat movement when they disagreed over the conduct of the agitation. In the estimate of Hardinge, Ajmal was 'much respected generally throughout India, and as far as I know absolutely loyal in every way. I used to see him a good deal at Delhi and often talked to him of Muslim affairs, especially in connection with the war'.

KHWAJA, ABDUL MAJID [1885–1962]: educated at M.A.O. College, Aligarh, and Christ College, Cambridge; on his return to India set up practice first at Aligarh and then at Patna; elected trustee of Aligarh, 1912; succeeded Shaukat Ali as secretary of the Aligarh Old Boys' Association, 1915; organized the Home Rule League at Aligarh; gave up practice during the Non-Co-operation movement; principal, Jamia Millia Islamia, 1922; secretary, Congress working committee, 1923; chairman, Aligarh municipal board, 1923; member of the Muslim Nationalist Party, founded by Ansari and Azad.

KIDWAI, MUSHIR HUSAIN [b. 1878]: belonged to a petty zamindar family of Gadia in Barabanki district; one of the founders of the Anjuman-i Khuddam-i Kaaba; president, Oudh Khilafat Conference, May 1920; joined the swarajists, 1923; president of the socialist group of legislative assembly members formed in March 1924.

KHAN, ZAFAR ALI [1873–1956]: educated at M.A.O. College, Aligarh, from where he graduated in 1895; joined the service of the Nizam of Hyderabad; took over as editor of the *Zamindar*, formerly edited by his father, Sirajuddin Ahmad; visited Turkey in 1912 to deliver the purse collected by the Indian Muslims through the Indian Crescent Mission; one of the leading figures in the Khilafat movement, and went to England, Paris and the Middle East as member of the Khilafat delegation, 1925; joined the Ahrar Party in 1929; member, Punjab legislative council, 1937–46.

KIFAYATULLAH [1875–1952]: prominent *alim* of the Ahl-i Hadith school and head of the Aminiya Madrasa, Delhi; first president of the Jamiyat al-ulama, 1919; took leading part in the Khilafat movement and went to prison.

KITCHLEW, SAIFUDDIN [1884–1963]: educated in India, England and Germany; started legal practice at Rawalpindi in 1913; moved to Amritsar in 1915, where he took prominent part in the Rowlatt Satyagraha; sentenced to life imprisonment but was released under amnesty December 1919; took a leading part in the Khilafat movement and gave up practice in 1920; member, Non-Co-operation Committee of the Central Khilafat Committee, 1920–21; interned for supporting the Karachi resolutions; conducted the *tanzim* campaign during 1924–27.

MADANI, HUSAIN AHMAD [1879–1957]: educated at Deoband, 1892–99; joined its teaching staff on graduation and was principal of the Dar al-ulum from 1926 to 1957; joined Mahmud Hasan in his pan-Islamic schemes, 1915–16; arrested along with his leader and three other associates, 1916; interned at Malta by the British, 1917–20; joined the Khilafat movement and interned for supporting the Karachi resolutions, 1921–23.

MALAVIYA, MADAN MOHAN [1861–1946]: educated in Hindi and Sanskrit at the Dharmjyan Updeshak Pathsala, the English district school and Muir Central College, Allahabad; edited the *Hindustan*, 1887–89; *Indian Union*, 1889–92; *Abhyudaya*, 1907–09; member, UP legislative council, 1902–12; president, Indian National Congress, 1909 and 1918; member, imperial legislative council, 1910–19; founded Banaras Hindu university, 1916; president, All-India Hindu Mahasabha, 1923–25.

MESTON, JAMES SCORGIE [1865–1943]: educated at Aberdeen Grammar School, Aberdeen University, Balliol College, Oxford; entered ICS, 1885; assistant magistrate and collector of Saharanpur, Basti, Moradabad, Pratapgarh, 1885–89; served as assistant commissioner and as settlement officer before becoming third secretary to UP government, 1899–1903; secretary to the government of India, finance department, 1906–12; lieutenant-governor, UP, 1912–18.

MOHAMMAD ALI MOHAMMAD, Raja of Mahmudabad [1889–1931]: descendant of Qazi Nasrullah, a Siddiqi Sheikh of Baghdad, who came to India in the thirteenth century; Mahmudabad's ancestors settlled at Mahmudabad in the sixteenth century and greatly increased their estate in the eighteenth century; member, UP legislative council, 1908–9; governor-general's council, 1907–20; played a leading role in the Kanpur mosque agitation and the Muslim University movement; supported the Home Rule movement 'with a clique of noisy and aggressive Muslims of the young party, who make the Raja's house their headquarters and live and agitate at his expense'; president, All-India Muslim League, 1915–19; Home Member, UP government, 1920–25; president, British Indian Association, 1817–21, 1930–31; vice-chancellor, Aligharh Muslim univeristy 1920–23; encouraged boycott of Simon Commission, 1927; supported the Nehru Report, 1928; president, Muslim League, 1928.

MOHANI, HASRAT [1877–1951]: leading journalist, poet, and politician; founded the *Urdu-i Moalla* in 1903 which was published intermittently until the 1930s; attended the Surat Congress in 1907 and joined the 'extremist' group of Tilak; was in the forefront of the Kanpur mosque affair, the 'Silk Letter Conspiracy', and the Khilafat Conference at Delhi, November 1919; demanded complete independence for India at the Khilafat Conference and the Congress at Ahmedabad, December 1921; president, All-India Muslim League at Ahmedabad, 1921; imprisoned in 1922; joined Shaukat Ali in the campaign against the Nehru Report.

MOHSINUL MULK, NAWAB MEHDI ALI HASAN [1837–1907]: settled in Aligarh in 1893; secretary, Aligarh College, 1898–1907; main organizer of the Urdu Defence Association in 1900 in response to MacDonnell's Hindi resolution; but was forced to retrace his steps by the lieutenant-governor; played a leading role in organizing the Muslim memorial, deputation and League of 1906 and, in the words of Khaliquzzaman, 'the greatest boon that [he] conferred on his people was the securing of separate electorates'.

MONTAGU, EDWIN SAMUEL [1879–1924]: educated at Clifton, City of London School and Trinity College, Cambridge; Liberal M.P., 1906–22; parliamentary under-secretary of state for India, 1910–14; secretary of state for India, 1917–22.

MOONJE, BALKRISHNA SHEORAM [1872–1948]: educated in Hislop College, Nagpur, and Grant Medical College, Bombay, 1894–98; started practice as an eye specialist in Nagpur, 1901; attended Congress session in 1904, and helped organize the Central Provinces' Conference in 1905; joined 'extremists' after the Surat split in 1907; took part in the Home Rule League; member, swaraj party, and responsive co-operation party and the Hindu Mahasabha; president, All-India Hindu Mahasabha, Patna, 16 April 1927; founder of *sangathan* and was accused by Muslims of fomenting communal trouble throughout India; closely associated with the *shuddhi* movement; bitterly opposed to the Delhi proposals and to any negotiations with Jinnah after the All-Parties National Convention.

NOON, FIROZ KHAN [b. 1893]: belonged to one of the important landowning families of Punjab; graduated from Oxford in 1917; member, Punjab legislative council, 1920; minister for local self-government, 1927–31, and later minister for education, 1931–36; high commissioner for India in Great Britain, 1936–41; labour member, viceroy's executive council, July 1942-September 1945.

PHULWARI, SHAH MOHAMMAD SULAIMAN [1859–1935]: leading Qadiriya *pir* and pan-Islamist *alim* from Phulwari and a close associate of Abdul Bari; educated at Firangi Mahal, Lucknow, and the Hejaz (1885–86); took a leading part in the Khilafat and Non-Co-operation movements.

NADVI, SYED SULAIMAN [1884–1953]: educated at Phulwari Sharif, Madrasa Imdadiyya, Darbhanga, and Nadwat al-ulama, Lucknow; edited *Al-Nadwa*, 1912; one of the founders of *Dar al-Musannifin*, Azamgarh, 1914; member, Khilafat delegation to Europe, 1920, and of delegation to the Hejaz 1924–25.

NARENDRANATH, (Raja) [1864–1945]: educated in Calcutta and Lahore; appointed assistant commissioner of Gurdaspur in 1887, deputy commissioner of Montgomery in 1895, and promoted to officiate as commissioner for the Lahore division in 1911; represented the landholder's constituency in the Punjab legislative council, 1921–37; president, All-India Hindu Mahasabha Conference, 1927, and for many years president of the Punjab provincial

Hindu Sabha; attended the Round Table Conference, 1930–31. After 1931, he emerged as a champion of the interests of Hindu commercial and professional classes. 'I for one', he wrote in June 1926, 'cannot whole-heartedly join any political party unless that party undertakes to protect the just and legitimate rights of the Hindus of the Punjab'.

RAHIM, ABDUR [1867–1947]: called to the Bar [Middle Temple], 1890; practised as Advocate at the Calcutta magistracy, 1900–03; member, royal commission on public services, 1913–15; officiated as chief justice, Madras, July-October 1916 and July-October 1919; member, executive council of the governor of Bengal, 1920–25; elected to central legislative assembly in 1931 and was its president, from 1935 to 1945.

RAI, LALA LAJPAT [1865–1928]: educated at the Lahore College, 1890; passed the Law examination in 1886; practised first at Hissar and later at Lahore; joined Congress in 1888; seconded a resolution on the boycott of British cloth at the Congress in 1905; deported to Burma in 1907; went to England in 1908 and delivered lectures on Indian political situation; established the Indian Home Rule League in the United States on 15 October 1916; arrested in 1921 while presiding over the Punjab provincial political conference; president of the Special Congress session, Calcutta, September 1920, and opposed Gandhi's non-co-operation resolution; supported non-co-operation at Nagpur; joined swaraj party; founded an Urdu daily, *Bande Matram* and an English weekly, *The People;* president of the Agra provincial Hindu conference, Etawah, 27 October 1928, where he supported the Nehru Report; closely associated with the Hindu Sabha, the *shuddhi* and *sangathan* movements.

RAM, CHHOTU [1881–1945]: born in a poor Jat family; served as private secretary to Raja Rampal Singh of Kalakankar; president, district Congress committee, Rohtak, 1917–20; editor of the *Jat Gazette*; resigned from Congress over non-co-operation; one of the founders of the Unionist Party and its leader in the Punjab legislative council, 1926–36; minister in the Punjab government, 1924–45.

READING, RUFUS DANIEL ISAACS, 1st Marquess of [1860–1935]: educated at University College, London, and Brussels and Hanover; M.P., 1904–13; solicitor-general, 1910; attorney-general, 1910–13; lord chief justice of England, 1913–21; viceroy of India, 1921–26.

SAPRU, TEJ BAHADUR [1875–1949]: advocate, Allahabad High Court, 1896–1926; member, UP legislative council, 1913–16; member, imperial legislative council, 1916–20; member, AICC, 1906–1917; president, UP Liberal League, 1918–20; member, Reforms Enquiry Committee, 1924; played a leading role in the making of the Nehru Report, 1928; delegate to the Round Table Conferences, 1930–32. 'It has been a very hum–drum sort of life' Sapru said on his 70th birthday, 'punctuated in private spheres by occasional moments of happiness and more by sorrow than anything else. In public life there has been nothing remarkable except that I have represented a school of thought which is on the wane'.

SHERWANI, TASSADUQ AHMAD KHAN [d. 1935]: member of the Bilona branch of the Sherwani Pathan family; one brother, Nisar Ahmad Khan, became a superintendent of post offices, resigning his post in the Non-Co-operation movement, and another, Fida Ahmad Khan, managed a sugar factory in Etah; educated in Aligarh and at Cambridge where he was a contemporary of Jawaharlal Nehru; a close friend of Ansari and Mohamed Ali and followed them in the Aligarh Muslim University movement and the Home Rule League. 'He had a genial personality', wrote Khaliquzzaman, 'and was loved and respected by his friends and foes alike'.

SEN GUPTA, JATINDRA MOHAN [1885–1933]: associated with political movements in Bengal since 1919; vice-president, Bengal provincial Congress committee; member, Congress working committee, 1922; elected mayor of Calcutta corporation for the first time in 1925 after the death of C.R. Das. At the same time, he was elected president of the Bengal Congress committee and also the leader of the Congress party in the legislative council.

SHAFI, MOHAMMAD [1869–1932]: president, All-India Muslim League, 1913; president, All-India Muslim Educational Conference, 1916; member, provincial and imperial legislative councils, 1909–19; education member, government of India, 1919–22; law member, government of India, 1922–24; led the campaign in Punjab against the boycott of Simon Commission.

SHRADDHANAND [1856–1926]: educated at Queen's College, Banaras, and University College, Lahore; started legal practice in 1885; took an active interest in the Arya Samaj and emerged leader of its Gurukul section in 1893; founded the Gurukul at Hardwar in 1902; organized the Rowlatt Satyagraha in Delhi and was invited by the Muslims to address them in Juma Masjid, Delhi; chairman of the reception committee of Congress, Amritsar, December 1919; launched the *shuddhi* movement towards the end of 1922 and reconverted many Malkana Rajputs to Hinduism; killed by a Muslim fanatic, Abdur Rashid.

SMITH, JAMES ROBERT DUNLOP. held several important positions in Punjab before joining Minto as his private secretary. He was the key figure in the negotiations surrounding the Simla deputation and provided Minto with the notes from which he began to draft his reply. He knew many Muslims, including Mohamed Ali, exchanged letters on a wide range of issues. He also tried to secure a government appointment for Mohamed Ali.

SUBHANI, AZAD [b. 1873]: rose to prominence during the pan-Islamic agitations of 1913–14; leading local agitator during the Kanpur mosque agitation; joined the Anjuman-i Khuddam-i Kaaba; president, All-India Khilafat Conference, September 1920; introduced resolution demanding complete independence at the Muslim League session in January 1922. After the Khilafat movement, he became associated with the labour movement in Kanpur.

SUHRAWARDY, HUSAIN SHAHEED [1893–1963]: son of Zahid Suhrawardy, judge of the Calcutta High Court; educated at St. Xavier's College, Calcutta, and Oxford university; member, Bengal legislative council, 1921, and was deputy mayor of Calcutta for three successive years; minister, Bengal government, 1927-43, chief minister 1946.

TYABJI, BADRUDDIN [1844–1906]: educated in England; called to the Bar [Middle Temple], 1867; leading Bombay barrister; member, Bombay legislative council; founder member, Bombay Presidency Association, 1885; president of the Indian National Congress 1887; Judge of the Bombay High Court.

TILAK, BAL GANGADHAR [1856–1920]: born in an orthodox Chitpavan Brahmin family of petty landowners; studied Sanskrit, Law and Mathematics in Poona; one of the founders of the Deccan Education Society and the Fergusson college in 1885; imprisoned for 'sedition' on 14 September 1897, and in July 1908; released on

17 June 1914; launched the Home Rule agitation 1916, and rejoined the Congress; played a leading part in the Congress-Muslim League negotiations, and supported the Lucknow Pact. 'There is a feeling among the Hindus', he said, 'that too much has been given to the Muslims. As a Hindu I have no objection to making this concession.... We cannot rise from our present intolerable condition without the aid of the Muslims. So in order to gain the desired end there is no objection to give a percentage, a greater percentage, to the Muslims.'

VIQARUL MULK, NAWAB MUSHTAQ HUSAIN [1841–1917]: put forward the scheme for the formation of a Muslim political association; member, Simla Deputation, and chairman, League's foundation session at Dacca; secretary, Aligarh College, 1907-1913. He was spokesman for those who opposed an increase in British authority at Aligarh and came into conflict with Archbold, Morison's successor. In 1909, Hewett was forced to intervene amid widespread criticizm. Hewett was compelled to retreat and Archbold resigned. Viqarul Mulk was also unhappy with the government proposal for a Muslim university and, at the Foundation Committee's meeting on 26 December 1912, joined Mohamed Ali and Azad in denouncing the leadership of the movement.

Bibliography

PRIVATE PAPERS

Aligarh Muslim University Archives, Aligarh [AMUA]
- Syed Ahmad Khan Papers
- Papers relating to the Non-Co-operation movement at the M.A.O. College, Aligarh

India Office Library and Records, London [IOLR]
- Beck Papers
- Chelmsford Papers
- Dunlop Smith Papers
- Hailey Papers
- Harcourt Butler Papers
- Hardinge Papers
- Irwin Papers
- Lytton Papers
- Meston Papers
- Montagu Papers
- Reading Papers
- Ronaldshay Papers

National Archives of India, New Delhi [NAI]
- Jayakar Papers
- Tyabji Papers

National Library, Calcutta
- Moonje Papers
- Sapru Papers

Nehru Memorial Museum and Library [NMML]
- All-India Congress Committee Papers
- Chagla Papers
- Chhatari Papers
- Chintamani Papers
- Daryabadi Papers
- Khwaja Papers

Motilal Nehru Papers
Satyamurti Papers
Thakurdas Papers

University Library, Cambridge
Baldwin Papers
Crewe Papers
Hardinge Papers

Jamia Millia Islamia, New Delhi [JMI]
Mohamed Ali Papers

Centre for South Asian Studies, Cambridge
Allanson Papers
Benthall Papers
Curry Papers
Hume Papers
Martin Papers
Tegart Papers

GOVERNMENT RECORDS

National Archives of India, New Delhi [NAI]

Records of the Home Department of the Government of India, filed as Home Political. Home Political files are divided into A, B and D (Deposit) categories.

The Uttar Pradesh State Archives, Lucknow [UPSA]
Records of the UP government in the General Administration, Education and Police Departments.

OFFICIAL PUBLICATIONS

Census of India, 1921, vol. xv. *Punjab and Delhi,* part I. (Lahore, 1923).
Census of India, 1921, vol. xvi. *United Provinces of Agra and Oudh,* part I. (Allahabad, 1923).
Census of India, 1921, vol. xv. *Punjab and Delhi,* part II. (Lahore, 1923).
Census of India, 1921, vol. v. *Bengal,* part I. (Calcutta, 1923).
Census of India, 1921, vol. v. *Bengal,* part II. (Calcutta, 1923).
Census of India, 1931, vol. v. *Bengal,* part II. (Calcutta, 1933).
District Gazetteer of the United Provinces of Agra and Oudh, Aligarh, vol. vi.
District Gazetteer of the United Provinces of Agra and Oudh, Agra, vol. xiii.

District Gazetteer of the United Provinces of Agra and Outh, Bareilly, vol. xiii.

District Gazetteer of the United Provinces of Agra and Oudh, Lucknow, vol. xxxvii.

District Gazetteer of the Bengal Presidency, Mymensingh, (Calcutta, 1917).

Government of India, *India in 1917-18* to *India in 1927-28,* reports prepared annually for presentation to Parliament.

Nathan, R. *Progress of Education in India 1887-88 to 1891-92. Fourth Quinquennial Review* (Calcutta, 1893).

Proceedings of the United Provinces Legislative Council, 1916 (Allahabad, 1917)

Proceedings of the United Provinces Legislative Council, 1923 (Allahabad, 1924)

Punjab Administration Report, 1922-23 (Lahore, 1924)

Punjab Administration Report, 1924-25 (Lahore, 1926)

Punjab Legislative Council Debates, 1923-26

Report of the Working of the System of Government, United Provinces of Agra and Oudh, in three vols. (Allahabad, 1928)

Report on the Working of Municipalities in the Punjab (Lahore, 1924)

Report on the Working of Municipal Politics in the Punjab, 1922-23 (Lahore, 1924)

Report on the Administration of Bengal, 1889-90 (Calcutta, 1890)

Report on the Administration of Bengal, 1918-19 (Calcutta, 1921)

Report on the Administration of Bengal, 1920-21 (Calcutta, 1923)

Report on the Administration of Bengal, 1921-23 (Calcutta, 1923)

Report of the Municipality of the Suburbs of Calcutta, 1875-76 (Calcutta, 1876)

Resolution Reviewing the Reports of the Working of Municipalities in East Bengal and Assam, 1906-7 (Shillong, 1908)

Resolution Reviewing the Reports on the Working of Municipalities in Bengal, 1920-21 (Calcutta, 1922)

Resolution Reviewing the Reports on the Working of Municipalities in Bengal, 1925-26 (Calcutta, 1927)

Resolution Reviewing the Reports on the Working of Districts Boards in Bengal, 1923-24 (Calcutta, 1925)

PARLIAMENTARY PAPERS

Year	Command Number	Short Title
1888	5327	*Report of the Public Service Commission,* 1886-7, with appendices (Calcutta, 1888).
1914	8382	*Royal Commission on the Public Services in India.* vol. I, Report.
1914	7293	*Royal Commission on the Public Services in India.* vols. II to XI, Appendices to the Reports.
1918	9109	*Report on Indian Constitutional Reforms.*
1918	9178	*Addresses Presented to His Excellency the Viceroy and the Right Honourable the Secretary of State for India.*
1925	2361	*Views of Local Governments on the Working of Reforms, 1923.*
1925	2362	*Views of Local Governments on the Working of Reforms, 1924.*
1930	3568	*Report of the Indian Statutory Commission,* vol. I, *Survey.*
1930	3569	*Report of the Indian Statutory Commission,* vol. II, *Recommendations.*

NEWSPAPERS AND JOURNALS

Aligarh Institute Gazette (Aligarh)
Amrita Bazar Patrika (Calcutta)
Asr-i Jadeed (Meerut)
Bombay Chronicle (Bombay)
Comrade (Calcutta, Delhi)
Forward (Calcutta)
Inqilaab (Lahore) [1937–39]
Kayastha Samachar (Allahabad)
Leader (Allahabad)
Mahratta (Poona)
Mussalman (Calcutta)
Moslem Chronicle (Calcutta)
Moslem Outlook (Calcutta)
Searchlight (Patna)
Tribune (Lahore)

and

Reports on or Selections from Native Newspapers [SNNR] from Punjab, UP, and Bengal, [NAI] and [IOLR].

PUBLISHED BOOKS AND UNPUBLISHED THESES

Abbas, K.A. *I am not an Island: An Experiment in Autobiography* (Delhi, 1977)

Adhikari, G. (ed.), *Documents of the History of the Communist Party of India*, vol. III–B (Delhi, 1979)

Ahmad, A. *Islamic Modernism in India and Pakistan 1857–1946* (London, 1967)

————*Studies in Islamic Culture in the Indian Environment* (Oxford, 1964)

————*An Intellectual History of Islam* (Edinburgh, 1969)

Ahmad, I. (ed.), *Caste and Social Stratification Among the Muslims* (Delhi, 1973).

Ahmad, Q. and Jha, J.A. *Mazharul Haque* (Delhi, 1976)

Ahmad, R. *Bengal Muslims 1871–1906: A Quest for Identity* (Delhi, 1981)

Ali, I. *The Punjab Under Imperialism, 1885–1947* (Princeton University Press. 1988)

Ali, H M. *Observations on the Mussulmans of India* (London, 1917 edn.)

Ali, Mohamed. *My Life a Fragment: An Autobiographical Sketch of Maulana Mohamed Ali* (Lahore, 1966 edn.)

Ali, Salim. *The Fall of A Sparrow* (Delhi, 1985)

All-Parties Conference, 1928: Report of the Committee appointed by the Conference to determine the principles of the Constitution for India (Allahabad, 1928)

Andrews, C.F. *Zakaullah of Delhi* (Cambridge, n.d.)

Ansari, K.H. 'The Emergence of Muslim Socialists and their Ideas in India between 1917 and 1947' (Unpublished Ph.D. thesis, University of London, 1985)

Arthur, T.C. *Reminiscences of an Indian Police Official* (London, 1894)

Ashraf, M. *Muslim Attitudes towards British Rule and Western Culture in India* (Delhi, 1982)

Aziz, K.K. *Britain and Muslim India* (London, 1968)

Baird, R.D. (ed.), *Religion in Modern India* (Delhi, 2nd rev. edn., 1989)

Banerjea, S. *Speeches and Writings of Surendranath Banerjea* (Madras, 1912)

———— *A Nation in Making* (Calcutta: reprint, 1963)
Baljon, J.M.S. *Reforms and Religious Ideas of Sir Sayyid Ahmad Khan* (Leiden, 1949)
Bayly, C.A. *The Local Roots of Indian Politics—Allahabad 1880–1920* (Oxford, 1975)
———— *Rulers and Townsmen and Bazaars: North Indian Society in the Age of British Expansion 1770–1870* (Cambridge, 1983)
Blunt, W.S. *India Under Ripon: A Private Diary* (London, 1909)
Bose, S.K. (ed.), *Subhash Chandra Bose Netaji: Collected Works,* vol. 1, (Calcutta, 1981)
Brass, P. *Language, Religion and Politics in North India* (Cambridge, 1974)
Broomfield, J.H. *Elite Conflict in a Plural Society: Twentieth Century Bengal* (University of California Press, 1968)
Brown, E. *Har Dayal: Hindu Revolutionary and Rationalist* (Tueson, 1975)
Brown, J.M. *Gandhi's Rise to Power: Indian Politics 1915–1922* (Cambridge, 1972)
Bukhsh, K. *Studies: Indian and Islamic* (London, 1927)
Burke, E. and Lapidus, I.M. (eds.), *Islam Politics and Social Movements* (University of California Press, 1988)
Case, M.H. 'The Aligarh Era: Muslim Politics in North India 1860–1910' (Unpublished Ph.D. thesis, Chicago, 1970)
Cashman, R.I. *The Myth of the Lokamanya: Tilak and Mass Politics in Maharashtra* (University of California Press, 1975)
Chagla, M.C. *Roses in December: An Autobiography* (Bombay, 1977)
Chandra, B. *Communalism in Modern India* (Delhi, 1984)
———— *et al. India's Struggle for Independence* (Delhi, 1987)
Chaudhuri, N.C. *The Autobiography of an Unknown Indian* (London, 1951)
———— *Thy Hand Great Anarch! India 1921-52* (London, 1987)
Choudhry, P. *Punjab Politics: The Role of Sir Chhotu Ram* (Delhi, 1984)
Cole, J.R.I. *Roots of North Indian Shiism in Iran and Iraq: Religion and State in Awadh 1722-1859* (Delhi, 1989)
Cotton, H. *India and Home Memoirs* (London, 1911)
Coupland, R. *The Indian Problem, 1833-1935* (New York, 1944)
Cragg, K. *Counsels in Contemporary Islam* (Edinburgh, 1963)
Dale, S.F. *The Islamic Society on the South Asian Frontier: The Mapillas of Malabar, 1498-1922* (London, 1980)
Datta, V.N. *Maulana Azad* (Delhi, 1990)

——— and Cleghorn, B.E. (eds.) *A Nationalist Muslim and Indian Politics* (Delhi, 1974)

Douglas, I.H. *Abul Kalam Azad: An Intellectual and Religious Biography,* eds. Gail Minault and C.W. Troll (Delhi, 1988)

Dutt, R.P. *India Today* (Bombay, 1949 edn.)

Dwarkadas, K. *India's Fight For Freedom* (Bombay, 1966)

Eveling, H. (ed.), *The Development of Indonesian Society* (Queensland, 1979)

Ewing, K.P. (ed.). *Shariat and Ambiguity in South Asian Islam* (Delhi, 1988)

Farquhar, J.N. *Modern Religious Movements in India* (Delhi, 1967 edn.)

Faruqi, Z.H. *The Deoband School and the Demand for Pakistan* (Delhi, 1967)

Gallagher, J. Johnson, G. and Seal, A. (eds.), *Locality, Province and Nation: Essays on Indian Politics 1870–1940* (Cambridge, 1973)

Gandhi, M.K. *The Collected Works of Mahatma Gandhi* (Delhi, in process of publication)

——— *An Autobiography or the Story of My Experiments with Truth* (Ahmedabad: reprint, 1958)

Gandhi, Rajmohan. *Understanding the Muslim Mind* (Delhi, 1987)

Gellner, E. (ed.), *Islamic Dilemmas: Reformers, Nationalists and Industrialization* (Berlin, 1985)

Gordon, L.A. *Bengal: The Nationalist Movement 1876–1940* (New York, 1974)

Gilmartin, D. *Empire and Islam: Punjab and the Making of Pakistan* (London, 1988)

Gopal, S. (ed.), *British Policy in India 1858–1905* (Cambridge, 1965)

——— *Jawaharlal Nehru—A Biography, 1889–1947,* vol. 1, (Delhi, 1975)

——— (ed.), *Selected Works of Jawaharlal Nehru* (Delhi, in process of publication)

Gupta, A.K. (ed.), *Myth and Reality: The Struggle for Freedom in India 1945–47* (Delhi, 1987)

Hamid, A. *Muslim Separatism in India: A Brief Survey 1858–1947* (Lahore, 1971)

Hardy, P. *The Muslims of British India* (Cambridge, 1972)

——— *Partners in Freedom—and True Muslims: The Political Thought of some Muslim Scholars in British India* (Lund: Studentlitteratur, 1971)

Hasan, Khalid, 'Saadat Hasan Manto: Not of Blessed Memory', *Annual of Urdu Studies,* vol. 4. 1984
Hasan, Khalid. *Scoreboard* (Lahore, 1984)
Hasan, Mushirul. *Nationalism and Communal Politics in India, 1916–1928* (Delhi, 1979)
———— *Mohamed Ali: Ideology and Politics* (Delhi, 1981)
————*A Nationalist Conscience: M.A. Ansari, the Congress and the Raj* (Delhi, 1987)
———— (ed.) *Communal and Pan-Islamic Trends in Colonial India* (Delhi: 2nd rev. edn. 1985)
———— (ed.) *Muslims and the Congress: Select Correspondence of Dr. M.A. Ansari 1912–1935* (Delhi, 1979)
———— (ed.) *Mohamed in Indian Politics: Select Writings* (Delhi: in three volumes)
Hasan, Z. *Dominance and Mobilization: Rural Politics in Uttar Pradesh, 1930–1980* (Delhi, 1989)
Hashmi, T.I. 'Peasants and Politics in East Bengal, 1920–1947' (Unpublished Ph.D. thesis, University of Western Australia, 1986)
Hayat, A. *Mussalmans of Bengal* (Calcutta, 1966)
Hill, J.L. 'Congress and Representative Institutions in the United Provinces 1886–1901' (Unpublished Ph.D. thesis, Duke University, 1966)
Holderness, T.W. *Peoples and Problems of India* (London, 1911)
Holt, P. M. *et al. The Cambridge History of Islam: The Central Islamic Lands,* vol. 1 (Cambridge, 1970)
Hourani, A. *Arabic Thought in the Liberal Age, 1798–1939* (Oxford, 1970)
Hunter, W.W. *Indian Mussalman: Are They Bound in Conscience to Rebel against the Queen* (Calcutta, 1945 edn.)
Husain, A. *Fazli Husain: A Political Biography* (Bombay, 1936)
Ikram, S.M. *History of Muslim Civilization in India and Pakistan* (Lahore, 1961)
———— *Modern Muslim India and the Birth of Pakistan* (London, 1965)
Iqbal, A. *Life and Times of Maulana Mohamed Ali* (Delhi: reprint, 1978)
———— (ed.*, Selected Speeches and Writings of Maulana Mohamed Ali* (Lahore, 1944)
Iqbal, M. *Reconstruction of Religious Thought in Islam* (London, 1934)
Jagadisan, M.R. (ed.), *Letters of Srinivasa Sastri* (Asia Publishing House, 1963 edn.)
Jalal, A. *The Sole Spokesman: Jinnah, The Muslim League and the Demand for Pakistan* (Cambridge, 1985)

Jones, K.W. *Arya Dharm: Hindu Consciousness in 19th–Century Punjab* (University of California Press, 1976)

Jones, R.L. *A Fatal Friendship: The Nawabs, the British and the City of Lucknow* (Delhi, 1985)

Jordens, J.T.F. *Dayananda Saraswati: His Life and Ideas* (Delhi, 1978)

——— *Swami Shraddhananda: His Life and Causes* (Delhi, 1981)

Joshi, V.C. (ed.), *Lala Lajpat Rai: Writings and Speeches*, vol. 1, (Delhi, 1966)

Kahin, G.M. *Nationalism and Revolution in Indonesia* (Cornell, 1952)

Kapur, Rajiv. *Sikh Separatism: The Politics of Faith* (London, 1986)

Karim, A. *Letters on Hindu-Muslim Pact* (Calcutta, 1924)

Kaura, U. *Muslims and Indian Nationalism: The Emergence of the Demand for India's Partition 1928–1940* (Delhi, 1977)

Keddie, N.R. *Sayyid Jamal-ad Din "al-Afghani": A Political Biography* (University of California Press, 1972)

——— *Islamic Response to Imperialism: Political and Religious Writings of Sayyid Jamal ad-Din "al-Afghani"* (University of California Press, 1968)

Kedourie, E. *Afghani and Abduh: An Essay on Religious Unbelief and Political Activism in Modern Islam* (London, 1966)

Khaliquzzaman, C. *Pathway to Pakistan* (Lahore, 1961)

Kidwai, M.H. *Pan-Islamism and Bolshevism* (London, 1937)

Kiernan, V.G. trans, *Poems from Iqbal* (London, 1955 edn.)

——— trans. *Poems by Faiz* (London, 1971)

Kitchlew, T. *Saifuddin Kitchlew: Hero of Jallianwala Bagh* (Delhi, 1987)

Kumar, R. *Essays in the Social History of Modern India* (Delhi, 1983)

——— *The Making of a Nation: Essays in Indian History and Politics* (Delhi, 1989)

——— (ed.), *Essays on Gandhian Politics: The Rowlatt Satyagraha of 1919* (London, 1971)

Latif, S.A. *The Influence of English Literature on Urdu Literature* (London, 1925)

Lavan, S. *The Ahmadiyah Movement: A History and Perspective* (Delhi, 1974)

Lawrence, second Marquess of Zetland. *Essayez* (London, 1956)

Lelyveld, D. *Aligarh's First Generation: Muslim Solidarity in British India* (Princeton University Press, 1978)

Low, D.A. (ed.), *Soundings in Modern South Asian History* (University of California Press, 1968)

——— (ed.), *The Indian National Congress: Centenary Hindsights* (Delhi, 1988)

Lytton, Earl of. *Pundits and Elephants. Being the experience of five*

years as Governor of an Indian Province (London, 1942)
Malik, H. *Sir Sayyid Ahmad Khan and Muslim Modernization in India and Pakistan* (New York, 1980)
———— (ed.), *Iqbal: Poet-Philosopher of Pakistan* (New York, 1971)
McLane, J.R. *Indian Nationalism and the Early Congress* (Princeton University Press, 1987)
Mcpherson, K. *The Muslim Microcosm: Calcutta, 1918 to 1935* (Heidelberg, 1974)
Mehrotra, S.R. *The Emergence of the Indian National Congress* (Delhi, 1971)
Mehta, A. and Patwardhan, A. *The Communal Triangle in India* (Allahabad, 1942)
Menon, M.U. 'Partition Literature: A Study of Intizar Husain', *MAS*, vol. 14, no. 3, 1980
Metcalf, B.D. *Islamic Revival in British India: Deoband, 1860–1900* (Princeton University Press, 1982)
———— (ed.), *Moral Conduct and Authority: The Place of Adab in Islam* (California University Press, 1984)
Metcalf, T.R. *Land, Landlords and the Raj: Northern India in the Nineteenth Century* (California University Press, 1979)
Minault, G. *The Khilafat Movement: Religious Symbolism and Political Mobilization in India* (Columbia University Press, 1982)
Mitra, H.N. (ed.), *Indian Annual Register* (later *Indian Quarterly Register*) (Calcutta, 1919 onwards)
Moore, R.J. *The Crisis of Indian Unity 1917–1940* (Delhi, 1974)
Muhammad, S. (ed.), *The Aligarh Movement: Basic Documents 1864–1898* (Meerut, 1978)
———— *Sir Syed Ahmad Khan: A Political Biography* (Meerut, 1969)
Mujeeb, M. *The Indian Muslims* (London, 1967)
Nadwi, A.H.A. *Life and Mission of Maulana Mohammad Ilyas* (Lucknow, 1983)
———— *Muslims in India* (Lucknow, 1980)
Nagar, P. *Lala Lajpat Rai: The Man and his Ideas* (Delhi, 1977)
Nanda, B.R. *Gandhi, Pan-Islamism, Imperialism and Nationalism* (Delhi, 1989)
Nehru, J. *A Bunch of Old Letters* (Bombay, 2nd edn. 1966)
———— *An Autobiography* (London, 1936)
Niemeijer, A.C. *The Khilafat Movement in India, 1919–1924* (The Hague, 1972)
Nizami, K.A. *Religion and Politics in India during the Thirteenth Century* (Bombay, 1961)

Noer, D. *The Modernist Muslim Movement in Indonesia 1900–1942* (Oxford, 1973)
Noman, M. *Rise and Growth of the Muslim League* (Allahabad, 1942)
Noorani, A.G. *Badruddin Tyabji* (Delhi, 1969)
Oldenburg, V.T. *The Making of Colonial Lucknow, 1856–1877* (Princeton University Press, 1984)
Page, D. *Prelude to Partition: The Indian Muslims and the Imperial System of Control, 1920–1932* (Delhi, 1982)
Pande, B.N. (ed.), *A Centenary History of the Indian National Congress*, in three volumes (Delhi, 1985)
Pandey, G. *The Ascendancy of the Congress in Uttar Pradesh 1926–1934 A Study in Imperfect Mobilization* (Delhi, 1985)
Panikkar, K.N. *Against Lord and State: Religion and Peasant Uprisings in Malabar 1836–1921* (Delhi, 1989)
Philips, C.H. (ed.), *The Evolution of India and Pakistan 1859–1947: Select Documents* (London, 1962)
Pirzada, S. (ed.), *The Collected Works of Quaid-e-Azam Mohammed Ali Jinnah*, vol. 1 (Karachi, 1984)
—————— (ed.), *Foundations of Pakistan: All India Muslim League Documents 1906–1947*, in two volumes (Karachi, 1970)
Prasad, R. *India Divided* (Bombay, 1946)
—————— *An Autobiography* (Asia Publishing House, 1957)
Qadiri, K.H. *Hasrat Mohani* (Delhi, 1985)
Qureshi, I.H. *The Muslim Community of the Indo-Pakistan Subcontinent 610–1947* (The Hague, 1962)
—————— *Ulema in Politics: A Study Relating to the Political Activities of the Ulema in the South-Asian Subcontinent from 1556 to 1947* (Karachi, 1974)
Rab, A.S.M. *A.K. Fazlul Haq: Life and Achievements* (Lahore, n.d.)
Rahman, F. *Islam* (London, 1966)
Rai, Lajpat. *A History of the Arya Samaj* (Bombay, 1967)
Raina, K.M. *Welding the Nation: Academic Addresses and Selected Writings* (Bombay, 1974)
Ray, R.K. *Social Conflict and Political Unrest in Bengal 1875–1927* (Delhi, 1984)
Ray, S. (ed.), *Selected Works of M.N. Roy*, in two vols. (Delhi, 1988)
Reading, Rufus Isaccs. *First Marquess of Reading, by his son, 1914–1935* (London, 1945)
Reeves, P.D. 'The Landlords' response to Political Change in the United Provinces of Agra and Oudh, India, 1921–1937' (Unpublished Ph.D. thesis, Australia National University, 1963)
Rizvi, S.A.A. *Shah Abdul Aziz: Puritanism, Sectarian Polemics, and*

Jihad (Canberra, 1982)

———— *Shah Wali Allah and His Times* (Canberra, 1980)

Rizvi, S.M. *History of the Dar al-Ulum Deoband,* in two volumes (Deoband, n.d.)

Robinson, F. *Separatism Among Indian Muslims: The Politics of United Provinces' Muslims, 1860–1923* (Cambridge, 1975)

Ronaldshay, Earl of. *India: A Bird's-Eye View* (London, 1924)

Roy, A. *The Islamic Syncretistic Tradition in Bengal* (Princeton University Press, 1983)

Russell, R. *Ghalib: The Poet and His Age* (London, 1977)

Saberwal, S. *India: The Roots of Crisis* (Delhi, 1986)

Shaikh, Farzana. *Community and Consensus in Islam: Muslim Representation in Colonial India* (Cambridge, 1989)

Sharar, A.H. *Lucknow: The Last Phase of an Oriental Culture.* Translated and edited by E.S. Harcourt and Fakhir Hussain (London, 1975)

Sarkar, S. *The Swadeshi Movement in Bengal, 1903–1908* (Delhi, 1973)

———— *Modern India, 1885–1947* (Delhi, 1983)

Sarkar, T. *Bengal, 1928–1934: The Politics of Protest* (Delhi, 1987)

Sayeed, K.B. *Pakistan: The Formative Phase 1857–1948* (Karachi, 1968 edn.)

Schimmel. A. *Gabriel's Wing: A Study into the Religious Ideas of Sir Muhammad Iqbal* (Leiden, 1963)

Seal, A. *The Emergence of Indian Nationalism: Competition and Collaboration in the Later Nineteenth Century* (Cambridge, 1968)

Sender, H. *The Kashmiri Pandits: A Study of Cultural Choice in India* (Delhi, 1988)

Sisson, R. and Wolpert, S. (ed.), *Congress and Indian Nationalism: The Pre-Independence Phase* (University of California Press, 1988)

Smith, D.E. (ed.), *Religion and Political Modernization* (Yale University Press, 1974)

Smith, W.C. *Modern Islam in India* (Lahore, 1947)

Stokes, E.T. *Peasants and the Raj: Studies in Agrarian Society and Peasant Rebellion in Colonial India* (Cambridge, 1978)

Stratchey, J. *India* (London, 1888)

Talbot, I. *Punjab and the Raj, 1849–1947* (Delhi, 1988)

Tendulkar, D.G. *Mahatma: Life of Mohandas Karamchand Gandhi,* vol. 1, (Delhi, reprint, 1969)

Thursby, G.R. *Hindu-Muslim Relations in British India* (Leiden, 1975)

Tinker, H. *The Foundations of Local Self-Government in India, Pakistan and Burma* (London, 1968)

Titus, M.T. *Indian Islam: The Religious Quest of India* (Delhi, 1979 edn.)

Troll, C.W. *Sayyid Ahmad Khan: A Reinterpretation of Muslim Theology* (Delhi, 1978)

——— (ed.), *Islam in India: Studies and Commentaries*, vol. 1 (Delhi, 1982)

Tyabji, B. *Memoirs of an Egoist* (Delhi, 1988)

Washbrook, D. *The Emergence of Provincial Politics. The Madras Presidency, 1870–1920* (Cambridge, 1976)

Wasti, S.R. *Lord Minto and the Indian Nationalist Movement 1905 to 1910* (Oxford, 1964)

Wolpert, S. *Tilak and Gokhale: Revolution and Reform in the Making of Modern India* (University of California Press, 1962)

——— *Jinnah of Pakistan* (New York, 1984)

——— *Morley and India, 1906–1910* (University of California Press, 1967)

Zaidi, A.M. (ed.), *The Muslim School of Congress* (Delhi, 1987)

——— (ed.), *The Evolution of Muslim Political Thought in India*, vol. 4 (Delhi, 1980)

Ziring, L. *Pakistan: The Enigma of Political Development* (Dawson: Westview, 1980)

ARTICLES

Amin, Shahid. 'Gandhi as Mahatma; Gorakhpur District, Eastern UP, 1921–2', in Ranajit Guha (ed.), *Subaltern Studies III: Writings on South Asian History and Society* (Delhi, 1984)

Barrier, N.G. 'The Arya Samaj and Congress Politics in the Punjab, 1848–1908', *Journal of Asian Studies*, 27 May 1967

Bayly, C.A. 'The Pre-History of 'Communalism'? Religious Conflict in India 1700–1860', *Modern Asian Studies (MAS,)* 19, 2, 1985

——— 'Patrons and Politics in Northern India', *MAS*, 7, 3, 1973

Bose, S. 'The Roots of 'Communal' Violence in Rural Bengal: A study of the Kishoreganj Riots, 1930', *MAS*, 16, 3, 1982

Brass, P. 'Elite Groups, Symbol Manipulation, and Ethnic Identity among the Muslims of South Asia', in David Taylor and Malcolm Yapp (eds.), *Political Identity in South Asia* (London, 1979)

Brennan, L. 'The Illusions of Security: The Background to Muslim Separatism in the United Provinces', *MAS*, 18, 2, 1984

Broomfield, J.H. 'Four Lives: History as Biography', *South Asia*, August 1971

Chandra, S. 'Communal Consciousness in Late 19th Century Hindi Literature', in Mushirul Hasan (ed.), *Communal and Pan-Islamic Trends in Colonial India* (Delhi, 1985)

——— 'The Lengthening Shadow: Secular and Communal Consciousness', in Bidyut Chakrabarti (ed.), *Secularism and Indian Polity* (Delhi, 1990)

Chatterjee, P. 'Agrarian Relations and Communalism in Bengal, 1926–1935', in Ranajit Guha (ed.), *Subaltern Studies I: Writings on South Asian History and Society* (Delhi, 1982)

Cleghorn, B. 'Religion and Politics: The Leadership of the All-India Hindu Mahasabha, Punjab and Maharashtra, 1920–1939', in B.N. Pandey (ed.), *Leadership in South Asia* (Delhi, 1977)

Cotton, H. 'India Old and New', *Asiatic Review*, July 1914

——— 'India Now and After', *Contemporary Review*, February 1915

Gilbert, I.A. 'Autonomy and Consensus under the Raj: Presidency (Calcutta), Muir (Allahabad); M.A.O. (Aligarh)', in S.H. Rudolph and I.I. Rudolph (eds.), *Education and Politics in India: Studies in Organization, Society and Polity* (Delhi, 1972)

Gordon, R.A. 'The Hindu Mahasabha and the Indian National Congress 1915–1926', *MAS*, 9,2, 1975

——— 'Non-Cooperation and Council Entry 1919–1920', *MAS*, 7, 3, July 1973

Gupta, K.K.S. 'The Agrarian League of Pabna, 1873', *The Indian Economic and Social History Review*, 7, 1970

Hardgrave R.L. Jr. 'The Mapilla Rebellion, 1921: Peasant Revolt in Malabar,' *MAS*, 2, 1, 1977

Hasan, M. 'Mahatma Gandhi and the Indian Muslims', S.C. Biswas (ed.), *Gandhi Theory and Practice: Social Impact and Contemporary Relevance* (Shimla, 1969)

Hasan, Mushirul. 'The Communal Divide: A Study of the Delhi Proposals', in *Communal and Pan-Islamic Trends*

——— 'Nationalist and Separatist Trends in Aligarh, 1920–1947', in A.K. Gupta (ed.), *Myth and Reality: The Struggle for Freedom in India 1945–47* (Delhi, 1987)

——— 'Communal and Revivalist Trends in Congress', in *Communal and Pan-Islamic Trends*

——— 'Sectarianism in Indian Islam: The Shia-Sunni Divide in the United Provinces', *The Indian Economic and Social History Review*, 27, 2, 1990

——— 'Congress Muslims: Dilemma and Decline, 1928–1934', in Jim Masselos (ed.), *Struggling and Ruling: Indian National Congress 1885-1947* (Delhi, 1986)

———— 'The Muslim Mass Contacts Campaign: Analysis of a Strategy of Political Mobilization', in Richard Sisson and Stanley Wolpert (eds.) *Congress and Indian Nationalism: The Pre-Independence Phase* (University of California Press, 1988)

Jalal, A. and Seal, A. 'Alternative to Partition: Muslim Politics Between the Wars', *MAS*, 15, 3, 1981

Krishna, G. 'The Development of the Indian National Congress as a Mass Organization 1918–1923', *Journal of Asian Studies*, 25, 3, May 1966

Masselos, J. 'Change and Custom in the Format of the Bombay Muharram during the Nineteenth and Twentieth Centuries', *South Asia*, December 1982

Mujahid, Sharif Al. 'Jinnah and the Congress Party', in D.A. Low (ed.), *The Indian National Congress: Centenary Hindsights* (Delhi, 1988)

Owen, H.F. 'Negotiating the Lucknow Pact', *Journal of Asian Studies*, 31, 3, May 1972

Pandey, G. 'Rallying Round the Cow: Sectarian Strife in the Bhojpur Region c. 1888–1917,' in Ranajit Guha (ed.), *Subaltern Studies II: Writings on South Asian History and Society* (Delhi, 1983)

Qureshi, M.N. 'The Ulama of British India and the Hijrat', *MAS*, 13, i, 1979

Ray, R.K. 'Revolutionaries, Pan-Islamists and Bolsheviks: Maulana Abul Kalam Azad and the Political Underworld in Calcutta, 1905–1925', in *Communal and Pan-Islamic Trends*

———— 'Masses in Politics: The Non-Cooperation Movement in Bengal 1920–23', *The Indian Economic and Social History Review*, 11, December 1974

Roff, W.R. 'South-East Asian Islam in the Nineteenth Century', in P.M. Holt, Ann K.S. Lambton, Bernard Lewis (eds.), *Cambridge History of Islam*, vol. 2 (Cambridge, 1970)

Robinson, F. 'Islam and Muslim Separatism', in David Taylor and Malcolm Yapp (eds.), *Political Identity in South Asia* (London, 1979). Revised version in *Communal and Pan-Islamic Trends*

———— 'Islam and Muslim Society in South Asia', *Contributions to Indian Sociology*, 17, 2, 1983

———— 'Problems in the History of the Firangi Mahall: Family of Learned and Holy Men', in *Oxford University Papers on India*, vol 2 (Delhi, 1987)

———— 'Municipal Government and Muslim Separatism in the United Provinces 1883–1916', *MAS*, 7, 3, 1973

Sarkar, Tanika. 'Communal Riots in Bengal', in *Communal and Pan-Islamic Trends*

Stewart, C.C. 'Islam', in A.D. Roberts (ed.), *The Cambridge History of Africa* (Cambridge, 1986)

URDU BOOKS, ARTICLES AND PROSCRIBED LITERATURE [PP: IOLR]

Afghani, A. *Syed Jamaluddin Afghani* (Amritsar, 1940)
Ahmad, B. *Tark-i Mavalaat* (Deoband, 1920), PP. 53–54.
Ahmad, C.H. *Tehrik-i Pakistan aur Nationalist Ulama* (Lahore, 1966)
Ahmad, K. *Tazkirat-al ulama* (Calcutta, 1934)
Ahmad, M. *Dard-i Khilafat* (Aligarh, n.d.), PP. 142
Adalat Gaushala Parastaan (Jabalpur, 1922)
Al Akhaam al-Quraniya Mavalaat al-Burtaniya (Delhi, 1920)
Bulbulaan-i Hurriyat ke Taraane (Jaunpur, 1920), PP. 47
Butalawi, A.H. *Iqbal ke Aakhri do Saal* (Karachi, 1961)
Daryabadi, A.M. *Mohamed Ali: Diary ke Chand Auraaq* (Hyderabad, 1943)
Fazl-al Khitaab (Delhi. n.d.)
Fiil Badiya Khutba-i Sadarat (Lahore, n.d.)
Ghaffar, A. *Aasaar-i Jamaluddin* (Delhi, 1940)
——— *Hayaat-i Ajmal* (Aligarh, 1950)
Hasan, Maḥmud. *Tark-i Mavalaat* (Bijnor, 1919)
Inayatullah, M.M. *Masla-i Taleem aur Tark-i Mavalaat* (Aligarh, 1920)
Ikram, S.M. *Mauj-i Kausar* (Lahore, 1970)
——— *Ruud-i Kausar* (Karachi, 1958)
Ismail, S.M. (ed.), *Makaatib-i Hali* (Karachi, 1950)
Islam, M. *Taraana-i Khilafat* (Deoband, 1914), PP. 43
Jafri, R.A. *Auraaq-i Gumgushta* (Lahore, 1968)
Jamiyat-i Markazia Tanzim Ka Mujawaza Dastur-al'Amal (Amritsar, 1925)
Kashmiri, S. 'Zafar Ali Khan', *Nuqqush (Shakhsiaat Number)*, January 1955.
Khan, R.A. and Manzar, M. *Deoband aur Bareilly ikhtilaaf par nazaa aur faislakun Munaazara* (Sambhal, 1966)
Madani, H.A. *Naqsh-i Hayaat: Khudnawisht Sawanah* (Karachi, 1979 edn.)
Maqalaat-i Hali, vol. 1, (Delhi, 1934)
Mirza, J. *Hayaat-i Amir Shariat* (Lahore, 1970)
Miyan, M. *Ulama-i Haq aur unke Mujahidaana Kaarname* (Delhi, 1946)
Mohammad, M.W. *Islam ki Faryaad*, PP. 44 (Delhi, 1971)
Naqvi, M. A. *Wahiduddin Salim: Hayaat aur Adabi Khidmaat* (Aligarh, 1969).

Nomani, Shibli. *Makaatib-i Shibli* (Azamgarh, 1928)
——— *Maqalaat-i Shibli* (Azamgarh, 1938)
——— *Safarnama-i Rum wa Misr-o-Shaam* (Azamgarh, 1921)
Qadiri, B.A. *Ahl-i Hadith aur Angrez* (Karachi, 1967)
Qasuri, M.S. *Akaabir Tehrik-i Pakistan* (Lahore, 1979 edn.)
Rahman, M.A. *Maimaaraan-i Pakistan* (Lahore, 1976 edn.)
Razi, Maulana. *Mutahidda Qaumiyat aur Islam* (Lahore, 1967 edn.)
Rozeena, P. *Jamiyat al-ulama-i Hind: Dastaaveez Markazi Ijlaas, 1919–1945,* in two volumes (Islamabad, 1980)
Rudaad-i Nadwat al-ulama, 22–24 April 1984, vol. 1 (Kanpur, n.d.)
Shah, S.G. *Khoon-i Khirman aur sada-i intiqaam,* PP. 8.
Shahjahanpuri, A.S. *Allama Iqbal aur Maulana Mohamed Ali* (Karachi, 1984)
Siddiqi, A.H. *Congress i ulama ki siyasi karwaten* (Delhi, n.d.)
Usmani, S.A. *Tark-i Mavalaat par zabardast taqreer* (Delhi, 1339 A.H.)

Index